trust *in* cyberspace

Fred B. Schneider, Editor

Committee on Information Systems Trustworthiness

Computer Science and Telecommunications Board
Commission on Physical Sciences, Mathematics, and Applications
National Research Council

NATIONAL ACADEMY PRESS
Washington, D.C. 1999

NOTICE: The project that is the subject of this report was approved by the Governing Board of the National Research Council, whose members are drawn from the councils of the National Academy of Sciences, the National Academy of Engineering, and the Institute of Medicine. The members of the committee responsible for the report were chosen for their special competences and with regard for appropriate balance.

Support for this project was provided by the Defense Advanced Research Projects Agency and the National Security Agency. Any opinions, findings, conclusions, or recommendations expressed in this material are those of the authors and do not necessarily reflect the views of the sponsors.

Library of Congress Cataloging-in-Publication Data

Trust in cyberspace / Fred B. Schneider, editor; Committee on
Information Systems Trustworthiness, Computer Science and
Telecommunications Board, Commission on Physical Sciences,
Mathematics, and Applications, National Research Council.
     p. cm.
   Includes bibliographical references and index.
   ISBN 0-309-06558-5 (casebound)
   1. Computer networks—Security measures. 2.
Telecommunication—Government policy—United States. 3. Internet
(Computer network)—Security measures. I. Schneider, Fred B. II.
National Research Council (U.S.). Committee on Information Systems
Trustworthiness.
   TK5105.59 .T78 1999
   384.3—ddc21
                       98-58061

Additional copies of this report are available from:
National Academy Press
2101 Constitution Avenue, N.W.
Box 285
Washington, DC 20055
800/624-6242
202/334-3313 (in the Washington metropolitan area)

Printed in the United States of America

The National Academy of Sciences is a private, nonprofit, self-perpetuating society of distinguished scholars engaged in scientific and engineering research, dedicated to the furtherance of science and technology and to their use for the general welfare. Upon the authority of the charter granted to it by the Congress in 1863, the Academy has a mandate that requires it to advise the federal government on scientific and technical matters. Dr. Bruce Alberts is president of the National Academy of Sciences.

The National Academy of Engineering was established in 1964, under the charter of the National Academy of Sciences, as a parallel organization of outstanding engineers. It is autonomous in its administration and in the selection of its members, sharing with the National Academy of Sciences the responsibility for advising the federal government. The National Academy of Engineering also sponsors engineering programs aimed at meeting national needs, encourages education and research, and recognizes the superior achievements of engineers. Dr. William A. Wulf is president of the National Academy of Engineering.

The Institute of Medicine was established in 1970 by the National Academy of Sciences to secure the services of eminent members of appropriate professions in the examination of policy matters pertaining to the health of the public. The Institute acts under the responsibility given to the National Academy of Sciences by its congressional charter to be an adviser to the federal government and, upon its own initiative, to identify issues of medical care, research, and education. Dr. Kenneth I. Shine is president of the Institute of Medicine.

The National Research Council was organized by the National Academy of Sciences in 1916 to associate the broad community of science and technology with the Academy's purposes of furthering knowledge and advising the federal government. Functioning in accordance with general policies determined by the Academy, the Council has become the principal operating agency of both the National Academy of Sciences and the National Academy of Engineering in providing services to the government, the public, and the scientific and engineering communities. The Council is administered jointly by both Academies and the Institute of Medicine. Dr. Bruce Alberts and Dr. William A. Wulf are chairman and vice chairman, respectively, of the National Research Council.

Preface

Experts have known for some time that networked information systems are not trustworthy and that the technology needed to make them trustworthy has not, by and large, been at hand. Our nation is nevertheless becoming dependent on such systems for operating its critical infrastructures (e.g., transportation, communication, finance, and energy distribution). Over the past 2 years, the implications of this dependence—vulnerability to attack and susceptibility to disaster—have become a part of the national agenda. Concerns first voiced from within the defense establishment (under the rubric of "information warfare") led the executive branch to create the President's Commission on Critical Infrastructure Protection and, later, the Critical Infrastructure Assurance Office. The popular press embraced the issues, carrying them to a public already sensitized by direct and collateral experience with the failings of computing systems and networks. A subject once discussed only in the technical literature is now appearing regularly on the front pages of newspapers and being debated in the Congress. The present study, initiated at the request of the Defense Advanced Research Projects Agency (DARPA) and the National Security Agency (NSA) some 2 years ago, today informs a discussion of national significance. In particular, this study moves the focus of the discussion forward from matters of policy and procedure and from vulnerabilities and their consequences toward questions about the richer set of options that only new science and technology can provide.

The study committee was convened by the Computer Science and Telecommunications Board (CSTB) of the National Research Council

(NRC) to assess the nature of information systems trustworthiness and the prospects for technology that will increase trustworthiness. The committee was asked to examine, discuss, and report on interrelated issues associated with the research, development, and commercialization of technologies for trustworthy systems and to use its assessment to develop recommendations for research to enhance information systems trustworthiness (see Box P.1). This volume contains the results of that study: a detailed research agenda that examines the many dimensions of trustworthiness (e.g., correctness, security, reliability, safety, survivability), the state of the practice, and the available technology and science base. Since economic and political context is critical to the successful development and deployment of new technologies, that too is discussed.

The alert reader will have noted that the volume's title, *Trust in Cyberspace*, admits two interpretations. This ambiguity was intentional. Parse "trust" as a noun (as in "confidence" or "reliance") and the title succinctly describes the contents of the volume—technologies that help make networked information systems more trustworthy. Parse "trust" as a verb (as in "to believe") and the title is an invitation to contemplate a future where networked information systems have become a safe place for conducting parts of our daily lives.[1] Whether "trust" is being parsed as a noun or the verb, more research is key for trust in cyberspace.

COMMITTEE COMPOSITION AND PROCESS

The study committee included experts from industry and academia whose expertise spanned computer and communications security, software engineering, fault-tolerance, systems design and implementation, and networking (see Appendix A). The committee did its work through its own expert deliberations and by soliciting input and discussion from key officials in its sponsoring agencies, other government officials, academic experts, and representatives of a wide range of developers and users of information systems in industry (see Appendix B). The committee did not make use of classified information, believing that detailed knowledge of threats was not important to the task at hand.

The committee first met in June 1996 and eight times subsequently. Three workshops were held to obtain input from a broad range of experts in systems security, software, and networking drawn primarily from industry (see Appendixes C and D). Since information about the NSA R2

---

[1]One reviewer, contemplating the present, suggested that a question mark be placed at the end of the title to raise questions about the trustworthiness of cyberspace today. And this is a question that the report does raise.

BOX P.1
Synopsis of Statement of Task

• Propose a research agenda that identifies ideas for relevant long-term research and the promotion of fundamental or revolutionary (as opposed to incremental) advances to foster increased trustworthiness of networked information systems. Perspectives on where and what kinds of research are needed should be sought from across the relevant technical and business communities.

• Assess, in part by undertaking dialogue within relevant segments of the technical and business communities, and make recommendations on how to further the development and deployment of trustworthy networked information systems, subsystems, and components.

• Assess and make recommendations concerning the effectiveness and directions of the existing research programs in DARPA and NSA R2 as they affect the development of trustworthy networked information systems.

• Examine the state of the market for security products and capabilities and the extent and emphases of private-sector research activities with an eye toward illuminating where federal R&D efforts can best be targeted.

• Assess and develop recommendations for technology policy options to improve the commercial security product base (availability, quality, and affordability), expand awareness in industry of the security problem and of available technology and tools for enhancing protections, and foster technology transfer.

---

research program is less widely available than for relevant programs at DARPA and other federal agencies, the entire committee visited NSA for a more in-depth examination of R2's research program; subsequent meetings between NSA R2 personnel and a subset of the committee provided still further input to the study. Staff tracked the progress of relevant activities in the legislative and executive branches in government, including the President's Commission on Critical Infrastructure Protection, the Critical Information Assurance Office, and congressional hearings. Staff also sought input from other governmental and quasi-governmental organizations with relevant emphases. Additional inputs included perspectives from professional conferences, the technical literature, and government reports gleaned by committee members and staff.

In April 1997, the committee released an interim report that outlined key concepts and known technologies. That report, subject to the NRC review process, generated a number of comments that helped to guide the committee in its later work.

ACKNOWLEDGMENTS

The committee is grateful to the many thoughtful reviewers of its interim and final reports, and it appreciates the efforts of the review coordinator. The committee would like to acknowledge Thomas A. Berson (Anagram Laboratories), Dan Boneh (Stanford University), Eric A. Brewer (University of California, Berkeley), Dorothy Denning (Georgetown University), Bruce Fette (Motorola), John D. Gannon (University of Maryland), Li Gong (JavaSoft Inc., Sun Microsystems Inc.), Russ Housley (SPYRUS), John C. Klensin (MCI Communications Corporation), Jimmy Kuo (McAfee Associates Inc.), Steven B. Lipner (Mitretek Systems), Keith Marzullo (University of California, San Diego), Alan J. McLaughlin (Massachusetts Institute of Technology), Robert Morris, Sr. (National Security Agency [retired]), Peter G. Neumann (SRI International), Jimmy Omura (Cylink Corporation), Stewart Personick (Drexel University), Roy Radner (New York University), Morteza Rahimi (Northwestern University), Jeffrey I. Schiller (Massachusetts Institute of Technology), Michael St. Johns (@Home Network), Joseph Sventek (Hewlett-Packard Laboratories), J. Marty Tenenbaum (CNgroup Inc.), Abel Weinrib (Intel Corporation), Jeannette M. Wing (Carnegie Mellon University), and Mary Ellen Zurko (Iris Associates Inc.).

The committee appreciates the support of its sponsoring agencies and especially the numerous inputs and responses to requests for information provided by Howard Frank, now at the University of Maryland, Teresa Lunt, now at SRI International, Robert Meushaw at NSA, and John Davis at NSA and the Critical Infrastructure Assurance Office. The support of K. David Nokes at Sandia National Laboratories was extremely helpful in facilitating this study and the preparation of this report.

In addition, the committee would like to thank Jeffrey Schiller for his valuable perspective on Internet standards setting. The committee would also like to thank individuals who contributed their expertise to the committee's deliberations: Robert H. Anderson (RAND Corporation), Ken Birman (Cornell University), Chip Boylan (Hilb, Rogal, and Hamilton Company), Robert L. Constable (Cornell University), Dale Drew (MCI Security Services), Bill Flanagan (Perot Systems Corporation), Fred Howard (Bell Atlantic Voice Operations), Keith Marzullo (University of California, San Diego), J S. Moore (University of Texas, Austin), Peter G. Neumann (SRI International), John Pescatore (Trusted Information Systems), John Rushby (SRI International), Sami Saydjari (Defense Advanced Research Projects Agency), Dan Shoemaker (Bell Atlantic Data Operations), Steve Sigmond (Wessels Arnold Investment Banking), Gadi Singer (Intel Corporation), Steve Smaha (Haystack Inc.), Kevin Sullivan (University of Virginia), L. Nick Trefethen (Oxford University), and Werner Vogels (Cornell University). The committee would also like to thank the participants at the workshops for their valuable insights.

Several members of the Computer Science and Telecommunications Board provided valuable guidance to the committee and were instrumental in the response-to-review process. For these contributions, the committee would like to thank David D. Clark, Jim Gray, and Butler Lampson. The committee also acknowledges the helpful feedback from CSTB members Donald Norman and Ed Lazowska.

Special thanks are owed Steve Crocker for his seminal role in launching this study and in helping to shape the committee. The committee—and the chairman especially—benefited from Steve's involvement.

Finally, the committee would like to acknowledge all the hard work by the staff of the National Research Council. Marjory Blumenthal's contributions to the content and conduct of this study were pivotal. Not only was Marjory instrumental in moving the committee from its initial discussions through the production of an interim report and then to a first draft of this report, but her insights into the nontechnical dimensions of trustworthiness were also critical for Chapter 6. This committee was truly fortunate to have the benefit of Marjory's insights, and this chairman was thankful to have such a master in the business as a teacher and advisor. Alan Inouye joined the project midstream. To him fell the enormous task of assembling this final report. Alan did a remarkable job, remaining unfailingly upbeat despite the long hours required and the frustrations that accompanied working to a deadline. First Leslie Wade and later Lisa Shum supported the logistics for the committee's meetings, drafts, and reviews in a careful yet cheery fashion. As a research associate, Mark Balkovich enthusiastically embraced a variety of research and fact-finding assignments. Thanks to Jane Bortnick Griffith for her support as the interim director of CSTB who inherited this challenging project midstream and did the right thing. Herb Lin was available when we needed him despite his numerous other commitments. The contributions of Laura Ost (editor-consultant) and Patricia Spellman (copy editor) are gratefully acknowledged. Rita Gaskins, David Padgham, and Cris Banks also assisted in completing the report.

Fred B. Schneider, *Chair*
Committee on Information Systems Trustworthiness

Contents

trust in
cyberspace

This is the tale of the infosys folk:
Multics to UNIX to DOS.
We once had protection that wasn't a joke
Multics to UNIX to DOS.
Now hackers and crackers and similar nerds
Pass viruses, horses, and horrible words
Through access controls that are for the birds.
Multics to UNIX to DOS.

—With apologies to Franklin P. Adams

Executive Summary

The nation's security and economy rely on infrastructures for communication, finance, energy distribution, and transportation—all increasingly dependent on networked information systems. When these networked information systems perform badly or do not work at all, they put life, liberty, and property at risk. Interrupting service can threaten lives and property; destroying information or changing it improperly can disrupt the work of governments and corporations; and disclosing secrets can embarrass people or hurt organizations. The widespread interconnection of networked information systems allows outages and disruptions to spread from one system to others; it enables attacks to be waged anonymously and from a safe distance; and it compounds the difficulty of understanding and controlling these systems. With an expanding fraction of users and operators who are technologically unsophisticated, greater numbers can cause or fall victim to problems. Some see this as justification for alarm; others dismiss such fears as alarmist. Most agree that the trends warrant study and better understanding.

Recent efforts, such as those by the President's Commission on Critical Infrastructure Protection, have been successful in raising public awareness and advocating action. However, taking action is constrained by limited knowledge and technologies for ensuring that networked information systems perform properly. Research is needed, and this report gives, in its body, a detailed agenda for that research. Specifically, the report addresses how the trustworthiness of networked information systems can be enhanced by improving computing and communications tech-

1

nology. The intent is to create more choices for consumers and vendors and, therefore, for the government. The report also surveys technical and market trends, to better inform public policy about where progress is likely and where incentives could help. And the report discusses a larger nontechnical context—public policy, procedural aspects of how networked information systems are used, how people behave—because that context affects the viability of technical solutions as well as actual risks and losses.

TRUSTWORTHY NETWORKED INFORMATION SYSTEMS— BENEFITS, COSTS, AND CONTEXT

Networked information systems (NISs) integrate computing systems, communication systems, people (both as users and operators), procedures, and more. Interfaces to other systems and control algorithms are their defining elements; communication and interaction are the currency of their operation. Increasingly, the information exchanged between NISs includes software (and, therefore, instructions to the systems themselves), often without users knowing what software has entered their systems, let alone what it can do or has done.

Trustworthiness of an NIS asserts that the system does what is required—despite environmental disruption, human user and operator errors, and attacks by hostile parties—and that it does not do other things. Design and implementation errors must be avoided, eliminated, or somehow tolerated. Addressing only some aspects of the problem is not sufficient. Moreover, achieving trustworthiness requires more than just assembling components that are themselves trustworthy.

Laudable as a goal, ab initio building of trustworthiness into an NIS has proved to be impractical. It is neither technically nor economically feasible for designers and builders to manage the complexity of such large artifacts or to anticipate all of the problems that an NIS will confront over its lifetime. Experts now recognize steps that can be taken to enhance trustworthiness after a system has been deployed. It is no accident that the market for virus detectors and firewalls is thriving. Virus detectors identify and eradicate attacks embedded in exchanged files, and firewalls hinder attacks by filtering messages between a trusted enclave of networked computers and its environment (from which attacks might originate). Both of these mechanisms work in specific contexts and address problems contemplated by their designers; but both are imperfect, with user expectations often exceeding what is prudent.

The costs of NIS trustworthiness are borne by a system's producers and consumers and sometimes by the public at large. The benefits are also distributed, but often differently from the costs. The market has responded best in dimensions, such as reliability, that are easy for consumers (and producers) to evaluate, as compared with other dimensions, such as security, which addresses exposures that are difficult to quantify or even fully articulate. Few have an incentive to worry about security problems since such problems rarely prevent work from getting done, and publicizing them sometimes even tarnishes the reputation of the institution involved (as in the case of banks).

Market conditions today strongly favor the use of commercial off-the-shelf (COTS) components over custom-built solutions, in part because COTS technology is relatively inexpensive to acquire. The COTS market's earliest entrants can gain a substantial advantage, so COTS producers are less inclined to include trustworthiness functionality, which they believe can cause delay. COTS producers are also reluctant to include in their products mechanisms to support trustworthiness (and especially security) that can make systems harder to configure or use. While today's market for system trustworthiness is bigger than that of a decade ago, the market remains small, reflecting current circumstances and perceptions: to date, publicized trustworthiness breaches have not been catastrophic, and consumers have been able to cope with or recover from the incidents. Thus, existing trustworthiness solutions—though needed—are not being widely deployed because often they cannot be justified.

Today's climate of deregulation will further increase NIS vulnerability in several ways. The most obvious is the new cost pressures on what had been regulated monopolies in the electric power and telecommunications industries. One easy way to cut costs is to reduce reserve capacity and eliminate rarely needed emergency systems; a related way is to reduce diversity (a potential contributor to trustworthiness) in the technology or facilities used. Producers in these sectors are now competing on the basis of features, too. New features invariably lead to more complex systems, which are liable to behave in unexpected and undesirable ways. Finally, deregulation leads to new interconnections, as some services are more cost-effectively imported from other providers into what once were monolithic systems. Apart from the obvious dangers of the increased complexity, the interconnections themselves create new weak points and interdependencies. Problems could grow beyond the annoyance level that characterizes infrastructure outages today, and the possibility of catastrophic incidents is growing.

The role of government in protecting the public welfare implies an interest in promoting the trustworthiness of NISs. Contemporary examinations of issues, ranging from information warfare to critical infrastructure, have advanced hypotheses and assumptions about specific, substantial, and proactive roles for government. But their rationales are incomplete. Part of the problem stems from the difficulty of describing the appropriate scope for government action when the government's own NISs are creatures of private-sector components and services. The rise of electronic commerce and, more generally, growing publication and sharing of all kinds of content through NISs are generating a variety of different models for the role of government and the balance of public and private action. In all of these contexts, debates about cryptography policy and the alleged inhibition of the development and deployment of technology (encryption and authentication) that can advance many aspects of trustworthiness make discussion of government roles particularly sensitive and controversial. The necessary public debates have only just begun, and they are complicated by the underlying activity to redefine concepts of national and economic security.

Technology offers the opportunities and imposes the limits facing all sectors. Research and development changes technological options and the cost of various alternatives. It can provide new tools for individuals and organizations and better inform private and public choices and strategies. Once those tools have been developed, demands for trustworthiness could be more readily met. Due to the customary rapid rate of upgrade and replacement for computing hardware and software (at least for systems based on COTS products), upgrades embodying enhanced trustworthiness could occur over years rather than decades (impeded mostly by needs for backward compatibility). Moreover, the predominance of COTS software allows investments in COTS software that enhance trustworthiness to have broad impact, and current events, such as concern about the "year 2000" and the European Union monetary conversion, are causing older software systems to be replaced with new COTS software. Finally, communications infrastructures are likely to undergo radical changes in the coming years: additional players in the market, such as cable and satellite-based services, will not only lead to new pricing structures, but will also likely force the introduction of new communications system architectures and services. Taken together, these trends imply that now is the time to take steps to develop and deploy better technology.

AN AGENDA FOR RESEARCH

The goal of further research would be to provide a science base and engineering expertise for building trustworthy NISs. Commercial and industrial software producers have been unwilling to pay for this research, doing the research will take time, and the construction of trustworthy NISs presupposes appropriate technology for which this research is still needed. Therefore, the central recommendations of this study concern an agenda for research (outlined below). The recommendations are aimed at federal funders of relevant research—in particular, the Defense Advanced Research Projects Agency (DARPA) and the National Security Agency (NSA). But the research agenda should also be of interest to policymakers who, in formulating legislation and initiating other actions, will profit from knowing which technical problems do have solutions, which will have solutions if research is supported, and which cannot have solutions. Those who manage NISs can profit from the agenda in much the same way as policymakers. Product developers can benefit from the predictions of market needs and promising directions for addressing those needs.

Research to Identify and Understand NIS Vulnerabilities

Because a typical NIS is large and complex, few people are likely to have analyzed one, much less had an opportunity to study several. The result is a remarkably poor understanding today of design and engineering practices that foster NIS trustworthiness. Careful study of deployed NISs is needed to inform NIS builders of problems that they are likely to encounter, leading to more-intelligent choices about what to build and how to build it. The President's Commission on Critical Infrastructure Protection and other federal government groups have successfully begun this process by putting NIS trustworthiness on the national policy agenda. The next step is to provide specific technical guidance for NIS designers, implementers, and managers. A study of existing NISs can help determine what problems dominate NIS architecture and software development, the interaction of different aspects of trustworthiness in design and implementation or use, and how to quantify the actual benefits of using proposed methods and techniques.

The public telephone network (PTN) and the Internet, both familiar NISs, figure prominently in this report. Both illustrate the scope and nature of the technical problems that will confront developers and operators of future NISs, and the high cost of building a global communications infrastructure from the ground up implies that one or both of these two networks will furnish communications services for most other NISs. The trustworthiness and vulnerabilities of the PTN and the Internet are thus likely to have far-reaching implications. But PTN trustworthiness, for example, would seem to be eroding as the PTN becomes increasingly dependent on complex software and databases for establishing calls and for providing new or improved services to customers. Protective measures need to be developed and implemented. Some Internet vulnerabilities are being eliminated by deploying improved protocols, but the Internet's weak quality-of-service guarantees, along with other routing-protocol inadequacies and dependence on a centralized naming-service architecture, remain sources of vulnerability for it; additional research will be needed to significantly improve the Internet's trustworthiness.

Operational errors today represent a major source of outages for both the PTN and the Internet. Today's methods and tools for facilitating an operator's understanding and control of an NIS of this scale and complexity are inadequate. Research and development are needed to produce conceptual models (and ultimately methods of control) that can allow human operators to grasp the state of an NIS and initiate actions that will have predictable, desired consequences.

Research in Avoiding Design and Implementation Errors

The challenges of software engineering, formidable for so many years, become especially urgent when designing and implementing an NIS. And new problems arise in connection with all facets of the system development process. System-level trustworthiness requirements must be transformed from informal notions into precise requirements that can be imposed on individual components, something that all too often is beyond the current state of the art. When an NIS is being built, subsystems spanning distributed networks must be integrated and tested despite their limited visibility and limited control over their operation. Yet the trend has been for researchers to turn their attention away from such integration and testing questions—a trend that needs to be reversed by researchers and by those who fund research. Even modest advances in testing methods can have a significant impact, because testing so dominates system development costs. Techniques for composing subsystems in ways that contribute directly to trustworthiness are also badly needed.

Whereas a large software system, such as an NIS, cannot be developed defect free, it is possible to improve the trustworthiness of such a system by anticipating and targeting vulnerabilities. But to determine, analyze, and—most importantly—prioritize these vulnerabilities requires a good understanding of how subsystems interact with each other and with the other elements of the larger system. Obtaining such an understanding is not possible without further research.

NISs today and well into the foreseeable future are likely to include large numbers of COTS components. The relationship between the use of COTS components and NIS trustworthiness is unclear—does the increased use of COTS components enhance or detract from trustworthiness? How can the trustworthiness of a COTS component be improved by its developers and (when needed) by its users? Moreover, more so than most other software systems, NISs are developed and deployed incrementally, significantly evolving in functionality and structure over a system's lifetime. Yet little is known about architectures that can support such growth and about development processes that facilitate it; additional research is required.

There are accepted processes for component design and implementation, although the novel characteristics of NISs raise questions about the utility of these processes. Modern programming languages include features that promote trustworthiness, such as compile-time checks and support for modularity and component integration, and the potential exists for further gains from research. The performance needs of NISs can be inconsistent with modular design, though, and this limits the applicability of many extant software development processes and tools.

Formal methods should be regarded as an important piece of technology for eliminating design errors in hardware and software; increased support for both fundamental research and demonstration exercises is warranted. Formal methods are particularly well suited for identifying errors that only become apparent in scenarios not likely to be tested or testable. Therefore, formal methods could be viewed as a technology that is complementary to testing. Research directed at the improved integration of testing and formal methods is likely to have payoffs for increasing assurance in trustworthy NISs.

New Approaches to Computer and Communications Security

Much security research during the past two decades has been based on models that focus on protecting information from unauthorized access by specifying which users should have access to data or other system resources. These models oversimplify: they do not completely account for malicious or erroneous software, they largely ignore denial-of-service attacks, and they are unable to represent defensive measures, such as virus scan software or firewalls—mechanisms that, in theory, should not work or be needed but do, in practice, hinder attacks. The practical impacts of this "absolute security" paradigm have been largely disappointing. A new approach to security is needed, especially for environments (like NISs) where foreign and mobile code and COTS software cannot be ignored. The committee recommends that rather than being based on "absolute security," future security research be based on techniques for identifying vulnerabilities and making design changes to reposition those vulnerabilities in light of anticipated threats. By repositioning vulnerabilities, the likelihood and consequences of attacks can be reduced.

Effective cryptographic authentication is essential for NIS security. But obstacles exist to more widespread deployment of key-management technology, and there has been little experience with public-key infrastructures—especially large-scale ones. Issues related to the timely notification of revocation, recovery from the compromise of certification authority private keys, and name-space management all require further attention. Most applications that make use of certificates have poor certificate-management interfaces for users and for system administrators. Research is also needed to support new cryptographic authentication protocols (e.g., for practical multicast communication authentication) and to support faster encryption and authentication/integrity algorithms to keep pace with rapidly increasing communication speeds. The use of hardware tokens holds promise for implementing authentication, although using personal identification numbers constitutes a vulnerability (which might be somewhat mitigated through the use of biometrics).

Because NISs are distributed systems, network access control mechanisms, such as virtual private networks (VPNs) and firewalls, can play a central role in NIS security. VPN technology, although promising, is not being used today in larger-scale settings because of the proprietary protocols and simplistic key-management schemes found in products. Further work is needed before wholesale and flexible VPN deployments will become realistic. Firewalls, despite their limitations, will persist into the foreseeable future as a key defense mechanism. And as support for VPNs is added, firewall enhancements will have to be developed for supporting sophisticated security management protocols, negotiation of traffic security policies across administratively independent domains, and management tools. The development of increasingly sophisticated network-wide applications will create a need for application-layer firewalls and a better understanding of how to define and enforce useful traffic policies at this level.

Operating system support for fine-grained access control would facilitate construction of systems that obey the principle of least privilege, which holds that users be accorded the minimum access that is needed to accomplish a task. This, in turn, would be an effective defense against a variety of attacks that might be delivered using foreign code or hidden in application programs. Enforcement of application-specific security policies is likely to be a responsibility shared between the application program and the operating system. Research is needed to determine how to partition this responsibility and which mechanisms are best implemented at what level. Attractive opportunities exist for programming language research to play a role in enforcing such security policies.

Finally, defending against denial-of-service attacks can be critical for the security of an NIS, since availability is often an important system property. This dimension of security has received relatively little attention up to now, and research is urgently needed to identify ways to defend against such attacks.

Research in Building Trustworthy Systems from Untrustworthy Components

Even when it is possible to build them, highly trustworthy components are costly. Therefore, the goal of creating trustworthy NISs from untrustworthy components is attractive, and research should be undertaken that will enable the trustworthiness of components to be amplified by the architecture and by the methods used to integrate components.

Replication and diversity can be employed to build systems that amplify the trustworthiness of their components, and there are successful commercial products (e.g., hardware fault-tolerant computers) in the marketplace that do exactly this. However, the potential and limits of the approach are not understood. For example, research is needed to determine the ways in which diversity can be added to a set of software replicas, thereby improving their trustworthiness.

Trustworthiness functionality could be positioned at different places within an NIS. Little is known about the advantages and disadvantages of the various possible positionings and system architectures, and an analysis of existing NISs should prove instructive along these lines. One architecture that has been suggested is based on the idea of a broadly useful core minimum functionality—a minimum essential information infrastructure (MEII). But building an MEII would be a misguided initiative, because it presumes that such a "core minimum functionality" could be identified, and that is unlikely to be the case.

Monitoring and detection can be employed to build systems that enhance the trustworthiness of their components. But limitations intrinsic in system monitoring and in technology to recognize incidents such as attacks and failures impose fundamental limits on the use of monitoring and detection for implementing trustworthiness. In particular, the limits and coverage of the various approaches to intruder and anomaly detection are necessarily imperfect; additional study is needed to determine their practicality.

A number of other promising research areas merit investigation. For example, systems could be designed to respond to an attack or failure by reducing their functionality in a controlled, graceful manner. And a variety of research directions involving new types of algorithms—self-stabilization, emergent behavior, biological metaphors—may be useful in designing systems that are trustworthy. These new research directions are speculative. Thus, they are plausible topics for longer-range research that should be pursued.

IMPLEMENTING THE RESEARCH AGENDA

Research in NIS trustworthiness is supported by the U.S. government, primarily through DARPA and NSA, but also through other Department of Defense and civilian agencies. Much of DARPA and NSA funding goes to industry research, in part because of the nature of the work (i.e., fostering the evaluation and deployment of research ideas) and, in part, because the academic personnel base is relatively limited in areas relating to security. There is also industry-funded research and development work in NIS trustworthiness; that work understandably tends to have more direct relevance to existing or projected markets (it emphasizes development relative to research). A firm calibration of federal funding for trustworthiness research is difficult, both because of conventional problems in understanding how different projects are accounted for and because this is an area where some relevant work is classified. In addition, the nature of relevant research often implies a necessary systems-development component, and that can inflate associated spending levels.

DARPA's Information Technology Office provides most of the government's external research funding for NIS trustworthiness. Increasingly, DOD is turning to COTS products, which means that DARPA can justifiably be concerned with a much broader region of the present-day computing landscape. But DARPA-funded researchers are being subjected to pressure to produce short-term research results and rapid transitions to industry—so much so that the pursuit of high-risk theoretical and experimental investigations is seemingly discouraged. This influences what research topics get explored. Many of the research problems outlined above are deep and difficult, and expecting short-term payoff can only divert effort from the most critical areas. In addition, DARPA has deemphasized its funding of certain security-oriented topics (e.g., containment, defending against denial-of-service attacks, and the design of cryptographic infrastructures), which has caused researcher effort and interest to shift away from these key problems. Therefore, DARPA needs to increase its focus on information security and NIS trustworthiness research, especially with regard to long-term research efforts. DARPA's mechanisms for communicating and interacting with the research community are generally effective.

NSA funds information security research through R2 and other of its organizational units. The present study deals exclusively with R2. In contrast to DARPA, NSA R2 consumes a large portion of its budget internally, including significant expenditures on nonresearch activities. NSA's two missions—protecting U.S. sensitive information and acquiring foreign intelligence information—can confound its interactions with others in the promotion of trustworthiness. Its defensive mission makes knowing how to protect systems paramount; its offensive need to exploit system vulnerabilities can inhibit its sharing of knowledge. This tension is not new. What is relevant for future effort is the lingering distrust for the agency in the academic research community and some quarters of industry, which has had a negative impact on R2's efforts at outreach. The rise of NISs creates new needs for expertise in computer systems that NSA is challenged to develop internally and procure externally. R2's difficulty in recruiting and retaining highly qualified technical research staff is a reason for "outsourcing" research, when highly skilled research staff are available elsewhere. R2's effectiveness depends on better leveraging of talent both outside and inside the organization.

The committee believes that increased funding is warranted for both information security research in particular and NIS trustworthiness research in general. The appropriate level of increased funding should be based on a realistic assessment of the size and availability of the current population of researchers in relevant disciplines and projections of how this population of researchers may be increased in the coming years.

TRUST IN CYBERSPACE?

Cyberspace is no longer science fiction. Today, networked information systems transport millions of people there to accomplish routine as well as critical tasks. And the current trajectory is clear: increased dependence on networked information systems. Unless these systems are made trustworthy, such dependence may well lead to disruption and disaster. The aphorism "Where there's a will, there's a way" provides a succinct way to summarize the situation. The "way," which today is missing, will require basic components, engineering expertise, and an expanded science base necessary for implementing trustworthy networked information systems. This study articulates a research agenda so that there will be a way when there is a will.

1

Introduction

The security of our nation, the viability of our economy, and the health and well-being of our citizens rely today on infrastructures for communication, finance, energy distribution, and transportation. All of these infrastructures depend increasingly on networked information systems. That dependence, with its new levels and kinds of vulnerabilities, is attracting growing attention from government and industry. Within the last 2 years, the Office of Science and Technology Policy in the White House, the President's National Security Telecommunications Advisory Committee, the President's Commission on Critical Infrastructure Protection, the Defense Science Board, and the General Accounting Office have each issued reports on the vulnerabilities of networked information systems.[1] Congressional hearings,[2] articles in the popular press, and concern

---

[1]See *Cybernation: The American Infrastructure in the Information Age: A Technical Primer on Risks and Reliability* (Executive Office of the President, 1997), *Reports from the Eight NSTAC Subcommittee Investigations* (NSTAC, 1997), *Critical Foundations: Protecting America's Infrastructures* (PCCIP, 1997), *Report of the Defense Science Board Task Force on Information Warfare Defense (IW-D)* (Defense Science Board, 1996), and *Information Security—Computer Attacks at Department of Defense Pose Increasing Risks: A Report to Congressional Requesters* (U.S. GAO, 1996).

[2]Such as testimony titled "Weak Computer Security in Government: Is the Public at Risk?" presented before the Senate Governmental Affairs Committee on May 19, 1998, and testimony titled "Future Threats to the Department of Defense Information Systems: Y2K & Frequency Spectrum Reallocation," presented before the Senate Armed Services Committee on June 4, 1998.

about the impending year 2000 problem have further heightened public awareness. Most recently, Presidential Decision Directive 63[3] has called for a national effort to assure the security of our increasingly vulnerable critical infrastructures.

Although proposals for action are being advanced, their procedural emphasis reflects the limitations of available knowledge and technologies for tackling the problem. These limitations constrain effective decision making in an area that is clearly vital to all sectors of society. Creating a broader range of choices and more robust tools for building trustworthy networked information systems is essential. To accomplish this, new research is required. And since research takes time to bear fruit, the nation's dependence on networked information systems will greatly exceed their trustworthiness unless this research is initiated soon.

Articulating an agenda for that research is the primary goal of this study; that detailed agenda and its rationale constitute the core of this report.

TRUSTWORTHY NETWORKED INFORMATION SYSTEMS

Networked information systems (NISs) integrate computing systems, communications systems, and people (both as users and operators). The defining elements are interfaces to other systems along with algorithms to coordinate those systems. Economics dictates the use of commercial off-the-shelf (COTS) components wherever possible, which means that developers of an NIS have neither control over nor detailed information about many system components. The use of system components whose functionality can be changed remotely and while the system is running is increasing. Users and designers of an NIS built from such extensible system components thus cannot know with any certainty what software has entered system components or what actions those components might take. (Appendix E contains a detailed discussion of likely developments in software for those readers unfamiliar with current trends.)

A trustworthy NIS does what people expect it to do—and not something else—despite environmental disruption, human user and operator errors, and attacks[4] by hostile parties. Design and implementation errors must be avoided, eliminated, or somehow tolerated. It is not sufficient to

---

[3]Available online at <http://www.ciao.gov>.

[4]In the computer security literature, "vulnerability," "attack," and "threat" are technical terms. A vulnerability is an error or weakness in the design, implementation, or operation of a system. An attack is a means of exploiting some vulnerability in a system. A threat is an adversary that is motivated and capable of exploiting a vulnerability.

address only some of these dimensions, nor is it sufficient simply to assemble components that are themselves trustworthy. Trustworthiness is holistic and multidimensional.

Trustworthy NISs are challenging systems to build, operate, and maintain. There is the intrinsic difficulty of understanding what can and cannot happen within any complex system and what can be done to control the behavior of such a system. With the environment only partially specified, one can never know what kinds of attacks will be launched or what manifestations failures may take. Modeling and planning for the behavior of a sentient adversary are especially hard.

The trustworthiness of an NIS encompasses correctness, reliability, security (conventionally including secrecy, confidentiality, integrity, and availability), privacy, safety, and survivability (see Appendix K for definitions of these terms). These dimensions are not independent, and care must be taken so that one is not obtained at the expense of another. For example, protection of confidentiality or integrity by denying all access trades one aspect of security—availability—for others. As another example, replication of components enhances reliability but may increase exposure to attack owing to the larger number of sites and the vulnerabilities implicit in the protocols to coordinate them. Integrating the diverse dimensions of trustworthiness and understanding how they interact are central challenges in building a trustworthy NIS.

Various isolated dimensions of trustworthiness have become defining themes within professional communities and government programs:

- Correctness stipulates that proper outputs are produced by the system for each input.
- Availability focuses on ensuring that a system continues to operate in the face of certain anticipated events (failures) whose occurrences are uncorrelated.
- Security is concerned with ensuring that a system resists potentially correlated events (attacks) that can compromise the secrecy, integrity, or availability of data and services.

While individual dimensions of trustworthiness are certainly important, building a trustworthy system requires more. Consequently, a new term—"trustworthiness"—and not some extant technical term (with its accompanying intellectual baggage of priorities) was selected for use in this report. Of ultimate concern is how people perceive and engage a system. People place some level of trust in any system, although they may neither think about that trust explicitly nor gauge the amount realistically. Their trust is based on an aggregation of dimensions, not on a few narrowly defined or isolated technical properties. The term "trustworthiness" herein denotes this aggregation.

To be labeled as trustworthy, a system not only must behave as expected but also must reinforce the belief that it will continue to produce expected behavior and will not be susceptible to subversion. The question of how to achieve assurance has been the target of several research programs sponsored by the Department of Defense and others. Yet currently practiced and proposed approaches for establishing assurance are still imperfect and/or impractical. Testing can demonstrate only that a flaw exists, not that all flaws have been found; deductive and analytical methods are practical only for certain small systems or specific properties.[5] Moreover, all existing assurance methods are predicated on an unrealistic assumption—that system designers and implementers know what it means for a system to be "correct" before and during development.[6] The study committee believes that progress in assurance for the foreseeable future will most likely come from figuring out (1) how to combine multiple approaches and (2) how best to leverage add-on technologies and other approaches to enhance existing imperfect systems. Improved assurance, without any pretense of establishing a certain or a quantifiable level of assurance, should be the aim.

WHAT ERODES TRUST

The extent to which an NIS comes to be regarded as trustworthy is influenced, in large part, by people's experiences in using that system. However, generalizations from individual personal experience can be misleading. The collection of incidents in Neumann (1995) and its associated online database suggests something about the lay of the land, although many kinds of attacks are not chronicled there (for various reasons). Other compilations of information on the trustworthiness of specific infrastructures can be found at the CERT/CC Web site[7] and other sources. But absent scientific studies that measure dominant detractors of NIS trustworthiness, it is hard to know what vulnerabilities are the most significant or how resources might best be allocated in order to enhance a system's trustworthiness. Rigorous empirical studies of system outages and their causes are a necessary ingredient of any research agenda in-

---

[5]See Chapter 3 for a more detailed discussion.

[6]Requirements invariably change through the development process, and the definition of system correctness changes accordingly.

[7]The Computer Emergency Response Team (CERT)/Coordination Center (CC) is an element of the Networked Systems Survivability Program in the Software Engineering Institute at Carnegie Mellon University. See <http://www.cert.org>.

tended to further NIS trustworthiness. Empirical studies of normal system operations are also important, because having baseline data can be helpful for detecting failures and attacks by monitoring usage (Ware, 1998).

But perceptions of trustworthiness are just that and, therefore, can be shaped by the popular press and information from organizations that have particular advocacy agendas. A predominant cause of NIS outages might not be a good topic for newspaper stories, although anecdotes of attacks perpetrated by hackers seem to be.[8]

Trust in an NIS is not unduly eroded when catastrophic natural phenomena in a region, such as earthquakes or storms, disrupt the operation of NISs only in that region. But when environmental disruption has disproportionate consequences, trust is eroded. Regional and long-distance telephone outages caused by a backhoe accidentally severing a fiber-optic cable (Neumann, 1995) and a power outage disrupting Internet access in the Silicon Valley area as a result of rodents chewing cable insulation (Neumann, 1996) are just two illustrations. The good news is that the frequency and scope of accidental man-made and natural disruptions are not likely to change in the foreseeable future. Building a trustworthy NIS for tomorrow that can tolerate today's levels of such disruptions should suffice.

Errors made in the operation of a system also can lead to systemwide disruption. NISs are complex, and human operators err: an operator installing a corrupted top-level domain name server database at Network Solutions effectively wiped out access to roughly a million sites on the Internet in July 1997 (Wayner, 1997); an employee's uploading of an incorrect set of translations into a Signaling System 7 processor led to a 90-minute network outage for AT&T toll-free telephone service in September 1997 (Perillo, 1997). Automating the human operator's job is not necessarily a solution, for it simply exchanges one vulnerability (human operator error) for another (design and implementation errors in the control automation).

Controlling a complex system is difficult, even under the best of circumstances. Whether or not human operators are involved, the geographic scope and the speed at which an NIS operates mean that assembling a current and consistent view of the system is not possible. The control theory that characterizes the operation of such systems (if known at all) is likely to be fraught with instabilities and to be highly nonlinear. When operators are part of the picture, details of the system's operating

---

[8]The classification and restricted distribution of many government studies about vulnerability and the frequency of hostile attacks, rather than informing the public about real risks, serve mostly to encourage speculation.

status must be distilled into a form that can be understood by humans. Moreover, there is the difficulty of designing an operator interface that facilitates human intervention and control.

The challenge of implementing software that satisfies its specification is well known, and failing to meet that challenge invariably compromises system trustworthiness. NIS software is no exception. An oft-cited example is the January 1990 9-hour-long outage (blocking an estimated 5 million calls) that AT&T experienced due to a programming error in software for its electronic switching systems (Neumann, 1995). More recently, software flaws caused an April 1998 outage in the AT&T frame-relay network (a nationwide high-speed data network used by business) (Mills, 1998), and in February 1998 the operation of the New York Mercantile Exchange and telephone service in several major East Coast cities were interrupted by a software failure in Illuminet, a private carrier (Kalish, 1998).

The challenges of developing software can also be responsible for project delays and cost overruns. Problems associated with software thus can undermine confidence and trust in a system long before the system has been deployed. NIS software is especially difficult to write, because it typically integrates geographically separated system components that execute concurrently, have idiosyncratic interfaces, and are sensitive to execution timings.

Finally, there are the effects of hostile attacks on NIS trustworthiness and on perceptions of NIS trustworthiness. Evidence abounds that the Internet and the public telephone networks not only are vulnerable to attacks but also are being penetrated with some frequency. In addition, hackers seeking the challenge and insiders seeking personal gain or revenge have been successful in attacking business and critical infrastructure computing systems. Accounts of successful attacks on computer systems at military sites are perhaps the most disturbing, since tighter security might be expected there; Box 1.1 contains just a few examples of recent attacks on both critical and noncritical DOD computers. The Defense Information Systems Agency (DISA) estimates that DOD may have experienced as many as 250,000 attacks on its computer systems in a recent year and that the number of such attacks may be doubling[9] each year (U.S. GAO, 1996). The exact number of attacks is not known because DISA's own penetration attempts on these systems indicate that only about 1 in 150 attacks is actually detected and reported (U.S. GAO, 1996).

---

[9]Specifically, defense installations reported 53 attacks in 1992, 115 in 1993, 255 in 1994, and 559 in 1995.

BOX 1.1
Sampler of Department of Defense Computer Penetrations

• Rome Laboratories discovered that more than 150 Internet intrusions were made into 30 computer systems on its network between March 23 and April 16, 1994. The attacks, which used Trojan horses and network "sniffers," had been launched by a 16-year-old British hacker and an unknown accomplice from commercial Internet providers. The attackers took control of laboratory support systems and stole tactical and artificial intelligence research data (U.S. GAO, 1996).

• The U.S. Naval Academy computer system was successfully penetrated in December 1994. Sniffer programs were installed on servers, the system's name and address were changed (making the system inaccessible to authorized users), files were deleted, password files were compromised, and more than 12,000 passwords were changed (U.S. GAO, 1996).

• In March 1997, a computing system at Anderson Air Force Base in Guam was penetrated by a 15-year-old working from Croatia and using programs freely available on the Internet (Associated Press, 1997).

• During the Gulf War, e-mail and information about troop movements and missile capabilities were stolen from Department of Defense (DOD) computers by hackers based in Eindhoven, The Netherlands. The information was then offered for sale to the Iraqis, who rejected the offer, thinking it a hoax (Schultz, 1997).

• As part of a June 1997 exercise ("Eligible Receiver"), an NSA hacker team demonstrated how to break into DOD computers and the U.S. electric power grid system. They simulated a series of rolling power outages and 911 emergency telephone overloads in Washington, D.C., and other cities. They also succeeded in showing how to break into unclassified systems at four regional military commands and the National Military Command Center in Washington, D.C. And they showed how to gain supervisory-level access to 36 networks, enabling e-mail and telephone service disruptions (Gertz, 1998; Myers, 1998).

• In October 1997, the U.S. State Department shut down portions of one of its international computer systems after the General Accounting Office discovered evidence of an intruder in computers at two overseas posts. The affected computer system links computers in Washington, D.C., with 250 U.S. embassies and consulates (Zuckerman, 1996).

Similarly troubling statistics about private-sector computer break-ins have been reported (Hardy, 1996; Power, 1996; War Room Research LLC, 1996).

Attacks specifically directed at NISs running critical infrastructures are not frequent at present, but they do occur. According to FBI Director Louis Freeh speaking at the March 1997 Computer Crime Conference in New York City, a Swedish hacker shut down a 911 emergency call system in Florida for an hour (Milton, 1997). And in March of 1997, a series of commands sent from a hacker's personal computer disabled vital services to the Federal Aviation Administration control tower at the Worcester, Massachusetts, airport (*Boston Globe*, 1998).

To a first approximation "everything" is becoming interconnected. The June 1997 Pentagon cyber-war game "Eligible Receiver" (Gertz, 1998; Myers, 1998) demonstrated that computers controlling electric power distribution are, in fact, accessible from the Internet. It is doubtless only a matter of time before the control network for the public telephone network is discovered to be similarly connected—having just one computer connected (directly or indirectly) to both networks suffices. Thus, the Internet will ultimately give ever larger numbers and increasingly sophisticated attackers access to the computer systems that control critical infrastructures. The study committee therefore concluded that resisting attack is a dimension of trustworthiness that, although not a significant source of disruption today, has the potential to become a significant cause of outages in the future.

Interconnection within and between critical infrastructures further amplifies the consequences of disruptions, making the trustworthiness of one system conditional on that of another. The lesson of the Northeast power blackout in the late 1960s was that disruptions can propagate through a system with catastrophic consequences. Three decades later, in July 1998, a tree shorting a powerline running to a power plant in Idaho brought about cascading outages that ultimately took down all three of the main California–Oregon transmission trunks and interrupted service for 2 million customers (Sweet and Geppert, 1997). Was the lesson learned?

The interdependence of critical infrastructures also enables disruption to propagate. An accidental fiber cut in January 1991 (Neumann, 1995) blocked 60 percent of the long-distance calls into and out of New York City but also disabled air traffic control functions in New York, Washington, D.C., and Boston (because voice and data links to air traffic control centers use telephone circuits) and disrupted the operation of the New York Mercantile Exchange and several commodity exchanges (because buy and sell orders, as well as pricing information, are communicated using those circuits). The impact of such a disruption could easily extend to national defense functions.[10] Furthermore, a climate of deregulation is promoting cost control and product enhancements in electric power distribution, telecommunications (Board on Telecommunications and Computer Applications, 1989), and other critical infrastructures—

---

[10]In March 1997, DISA disclosed that a contract had been awarded to Sprint for a global telecommunications network designed primarily to carry signal intelligence data to Fort Meade (Brewin, 1997). According to the Defense Science Board (1996), the U.S. government procures more than 95 percent of its domestic telecommunications network services from U.S. commercial carriers.

actions that increase vulnerability to disruption by diminishing the cushions of reserve capacity and increasing the complexity of these systems.

THIS STUDY IN CONTEXT

Network security, information warfare, and critical-infrastructure protection have already been the subject of other national studies. The most visible of these studies—summarized in Appendix F—have focused on the expected shape and consequences of widespread networking, defending against information warfare and other cyber-threats, the coordination of federal and private-sector players in such a defense, and national policies affecting the availability of certain technological building blocks (e.g., cryptography). The absence of needed technology has been noted, and aggressive programs of research to fill broadly characterized gaps are invariably recommended.

A Computer Science and Telecommunications Board study almost a decade ago anticipated the role networked computers would play in our society along with the problems that they could create (CSTB, 1991). Its opening paragraph summarized the situation—then and today—with remarkable clarity:

> We are at risk. Increasingly, America depends on computers. They control power delivery, communications, aviation, and financial services. They are used to store vital information, from medical records to business plans to criminal records. Although we trust them, they are vulnerable—to the effects of poor design and insufficient quality control, to accident, and perhaps most alarmingly, to deliberate attack. The modern thief can steal more with a computer than with a gun. Tomorrow's terrorist may be able to do more damage with a keyboard than with a bomb.

More recently, in October 1997, the President's Commission on Critical Infrastructure Protection released a report (PCCIP, 1997) that discusses the vulnerability of U.S. infrastructures to physical as well as cyber-threats. Based substantially on the commission's recommendations and findings, Presidential Decision Directive 63 (White House National Security Council, 1998) outlines a procedure and administrative structure for developing a national infrastructure protection plan. The directive orders immediate federal government action, with the goal that, within 5 years, our nation's critical infrastructures will be protected from intentional acts that would diminish the functioning of government, public services, the orderly functioning of the economy, and the delivery of essential telecommunications, energy, financial, and transportation services. Among the directive's general principles and guidelines is a request that research for protecting critical infrastructures be undertaken.

The present study offers a detailed agenda for that research. It is an agenda that was developed by analyzing current approaches to trustworthiness and by identifying science and technology that currently do not, but could, play a significant role. The agenda thus fills the gap left by predecessor studies, with their focus on infrastructure vulnerabilities and the wider consequences. Articulating a research agenda is a necessary first step in obtaining better methods of infrastructure protection.

The research agenda should be of interest to researchers, who will ultimately execute the agenda, and to funders of research, who will want to give priority to research problems that are urgent and approaches that are promising. The research agenda should also be of interest to policymakers who, in formulating legislation and initiating other actions, will profit from knowing which technical problems do have solutions, which will have solutions if research is supported, and which cannot have solutions. NIS operators can profit from the agenda in much the same way as policymakers will. And product developers should be interested in the research agenda for its predictions of market needs and promising directions to address those needs.

SCOPE OF THIS STUDY

The premise of this report is that a "trust gap" is emerging between the expectations of the public (along with parts of government) and the capabilities of NISs. The report is organized around an agenda and call for research aimed at improving the trustworthiness of NISs and thereby narrowing this gap. To develop this agenda, the study committee surveyed the state of the art, current practice, and trends with respect to computer networking and software. The committee also studied connections between these technical topics and current economic and political forces; those investigations, too, are summarized in the report.

Some of the research problems in the proposed agenda are new. Others are not new but warrant revisiting in light of special requirements and circumstances that NIS developers and operators face. The networked environment imposes novel constraints, enables new types of solutions, and changes engineering trade-offs. Characteristic elements of NISs (COTS software, extensible components, and evolution by accretion) affect software development practices. And the need to simultaneously support all of the dimensions of trustworthiness invites reconsidering known approaches for individual dimensions of trustworthiness with an eye toward possible interactions.

The Internet and public telephone network figured prominently in the study committee's thinking, and that emphasis is reflected in Chapter 2 of this report. The attention is justified on two grounds. First, the

Internet and public telephone network are themselves large and complex NISs. Studying extant NISs is an obvious way to understand the technical problems that will be faced by developers and operators of future NISs. Second, the high cost of building a global communications infrastructure from the ground up implies that one or both of these two networks is likely to furnish communications services for most other NISs.[11] With such a pivotal role, the trustworthiness and vulnerabilities of these communications fabrics need to be understood.

Commercial software packages and systems—and not systems custom-built from scratch—are also a central subject of this report, as is most evident in Chapter 3 on software development. This focus is sensible given the clear trend in government and military procurement to adapt and depend on commodities and services intended for the mass market.[12] Research that ignores COTS software could have little impact on trustworthiness for tomorrow's NISs.[13] In the past, computer science research programs serving military needs could safely ignore commercial software products and practices; that course now invites irrelevance.

Chapter 4 concerns security. The extensive treatment of this single dimension of trustworthiness merits comment, especially given the relative infrequency with which attacks today are responsible for NIS outages. A research agenda must anticipate tomorrow's needs. Hostile attacks are the fastest-growing source of NIS disturbances. Indications are that this trend will continue[14] and that, because they can be coordinated, attacks are potentially the most destabilizing form of trustworthiness breach. Furthermore, the study committee found that past approaches to security (i.e., the

---

[11]For example, during the Persian Gulf conflict, the Internet was used to disseminate intelligence and counterintelligence information. Moreover, defense experts believe that public messages originating within regions of conflict will, in the future, provide warnings of significant political and military developments earlier than normal intelligence gathering. These experts also envision the Internet as a back-up communications medium if other conventional channels are disrupted during conflicts (U.S. GAO, 1996).

[12]According to the *Report of the Defense Science Board Task Force on Information Warfare Defense (IW-D)* (Defense Science Board, 1996), COTS systems constitute over 90 percent of the information systems procured by DOD. Moreover, the widespread use of COTS systems in military systems for the coming century is urged in National Defense Panel (1997).

[13]Research that takes into account COTS commodities and services is likely to be applicable to the development of custom-designed systems as well. Methods suitable for systems built from scratch, however, may not apply in the presence of the added constraints that COTS purchases impose.

[14]The present study was conducted without access to classified material. Unclassified studies, such as U.S. General Accounting Office (1996), point to the growing incentive to attack infrastructure and defense computing systems, as these systems become more critical, and to the expanding base of potential attackers that is accompanying the growth of the Internet.

"Orange Book" [U.S. DOD, 1985] and its brethren) are less and less relevant to building a trustworthy NIS: inappropriate disclosure of information is only one of many security policies of concern, and custom construction and/or complete analysis of an entire NIS or even significant parts of an NIS is impractical. The typically complex trust relationships that exist among the parts of an NIS add further complication.

The "holy grail" for developers of trustworthy systems is technology to build trustworthy systems from untrustworthy components. The subject of Chapter 5, this piece of the research agenda is the most ambitious. What is being sought can be achieved today for single dimensions of trustworthiness, lending some credibility to the vision being articulated. For example, highly reliable computing systems are routinely constructed from unreliable components (by using replication). As another example, firewalls enable networks of insecure processors to be protected from certain forms of attack. And new algorithmic paradigms and system architectures could result in the emergence of desirable system behavior from seemingly random behaviors of system components. Without further research, though, it is impossible to know whether approaches like these will actually bear fruit for NIS trustworthiness. Fleshing out highly speculative research directions with details is impossible without actually doing some of the research, so the discussions in Chapter 5 are necessarily brief.

The viability of technological innovations is invariably determined by the economic and political context, the subject of Chapter 6. The economics of building, selling, and operating trustworthy systems is discussed, because economics determines the extent to which technologies for trustworthiness can be embraced by system developers and operators, and it determines whether users can justify investments in supporting trustworthiness. The dynamics of the COTS marketplace and an implied limited diversity have become important for trustworthiness so they, too, are discussed. Risk avoidance is but a single point in a spectrum of risk management strategies; for NISs (because of their size and complexity) it is most likely an unrealistic one. Thus, alternatives to risk avoidance are presented in the hope of broadening the perspectives of NIS designers and operators. Finally, since there is more to getting research done than articulating an agenda, the chapter reviews the workings of DARPA and NSA (likely candidates to administer this agenda), U.S. cryptography policy, and the general climate in government regarding regulation and trustworthiness.

REFERENCES

Associated Press. 1997. "Fifteen Year Old Hacker Discusses How He Accessed U.S. Military Files," Associated Press, March 1.

Board on Telecommunications and Computer Applications, National Research Council. 1989. *Growing Vulnerability of the Public Switched Networks: Implications for National Security Emergency Preparedness.* Washington, DC: National Academy Press.

Boston Globe. 1998. "Youth Faces Computer Crime Charges: U.S. Attorney Says Federal Case Is First Involving a Juvenile," *Boston Globe,* March 18. Available online at <http://www.boston.com>.

Brewin, Bob. 1997. "DISA Discloses Secret NSA Pact with Sprint," *Federal Computer Week,* March 10. Available online at <http://www.fcw.com/pubs/fcw/1997/0310/disansa.htm>.

Computer Science and Telecommunications Board (CSTB), National Research Council. 1991. *Computers at Risk: Safe Computing in the Information Age.* Washington, DC: National Academy Press.

Defense Science Board. 1996. *Report of the Defense Science Board Task Force on Information Warfare Defense (IW-D).* Washington, DC: Office of the Under Secretary of Defense for Acquisition and Technology, November 21.

Executive Office of the President, Office of Science and Technology Policy. 1997. *Cybernation: The American Infrastructure in the Information Age: A Technical Primer on Risks and Reliability.* Washington, DC: Executive Office of the President.

Gertz, Bill. 1998. "'Infowar' Game Shut Down U.S. Power Grid, Disabled Pacific Command," *Washington Times,* April 16, p. A1.

Hardy, Quentin. 1996. "Many Big Firms Hurt by Break-ins," *Wall Street Journal,* November 21, p. B4.

Kalish, David E. 1998. "Phone Outage Hits East Coast," Associated Press, February 25. Available online at <http://wire.ap.org>.

Mills, Mike. 1998. "AT&T High Speed Network Fails Red Cross, Banks Scramble to Adjust," *Washington Post,* April 14, p. C1.

Milton, Pat. 1997. "FBI Director Calls for Effort to Fight Growing Danger of Computer Crime," Associated Press, March 4.

Myers, Laura. 1998. "Pentagon Has Computers Hacked," Associated Press, April 16.

National Defense Panel. 1997. *Transforming Defense: National Security in the 21st Century.* Arlington, VA: National Defense Panel, December.

National Security Telecommunications Advisory Committee (NSTAC). 1997. *Reports from the Eight NSTAC Subcommittee Investigations.* Tysons Corner, VA: NSTAC, December 10-11. Available online at <http://www.ncs.gov/nstac/NSTACReports.html>.

Neumann, Peter G. 1995. *Computer Related Risks.* New York: ACM Press.

Neumann, Peter G. 1996. "Rats Take Down Stanford Power and Silicon Valley Internet Service," *RISKS Digest,* Vol. 18, Issue 52, October 12. Available online at <http://catless.ncl.ac.uk/Risks/18.52.html#subj1>.

Perillo, Robert J. 1997. "AT&T Database Glitch Caused '800' Phone Outage," *Telecom Digest,* Vol. 17, Issue 253, September 18. Available online at <http://massis.lcs.mit.edu/telecom-archives/archives/back issues/1997.volume.17/vol17.iss251-300>.

Power, Richard G. 1996. Testimony of Richard G. Power, Computer Security Institute, before the Permanent Subcommittee on Investigations, Committee on Government Affairs, U.S. Senate, Washington, DC, June 5.

President's Commission on Critical Infrastructure Protection (PCCIP). 1997. *Critical Foundations: Protecting America's Infrastructures.* Washington, DC: PCCIP, October.

Schultz, Gene. 1997. "Crackers Obtained Gulf War Military Secrets," *RISKS Digest,* Vol. 18, Issue 96, March 31. Available online at <http://catless.ncl.ac.uk/Risks/18.96.html#subj6>.

Sweet, William, and Linda Geppert, eds. 1997. "Main Event: Power Outages Flag Technology Overload, Rule-making Gaps," *IEEE Spectrum, 1997 Technology Analysis and Forecast.*

U.S. Department of Defense (DOD). 1985. *Trusted Computer System Evaluation Criteria,* Department of Defense 5200.28-STD, the "Orange Book." Ft. Meade, MD: National Computer Security Center, December.

U.S. General Accounting Office (GAO). 1996. *Information Security—Computer Attacks at Department of Defense Pose Increasing Risks: A Report to Congressional Requesters.* Washington, DC: U.S. GAO, May.

War Room Research LLC. 1996. *1996 Information Systems Security Survey.* Baltimore, MD: War Room Research LLC, November 21.

Ware, Willis H. 1998. *The Cyber-posture of the National Information Infrastructure.* Washington, DC: RAND Critical Technologies Institute. Available online at <http://www.rand.org/publications/MR/MR976/mr976.html>.

Wayner, Peter. 1997. "Human Error Cripples the Internet," *New York Times,* July 17. Available online at <http://www.nytimes.com/library/cyber/week/071797dns.html>.

White House National Security Council. 1998. *White Paper: The Clinton Administration's Policy on Critical Infrastructure Protection: Presidential Decision Directive 63.* Washington, DC: The White House, May 22.

Zuckerman, M.J. 1996. "Post-Cold War Hysteria or a National Threat," *USA Today,* June 5, p. 1A.

2

Public Telephone Network and Internet Trustworthiness

The public telephone network (PTN) and the Internet are both large NISs. Studying their trustworthiness thus gives insight into the technical problems associated with supporting trustworthiness in an NIS. Identifying the vulnerabilities in these networks is also valuable—any NIS is likely to employ one or both of these networks for its communication and could inherit those vulnerabilities.

In some ways, the Internet and PTN are very similar. No single entity owns, manages, or can even have a complete picture of either.

- The PTN in the United States comprises five distinct regional Bell operating companies and a large number of independent local telephone companies, all interconnected by long-distance providers.[1]
- The U.S. portion of the Internet consists of a few major Internet service providers (ISPs) along with a much larger number of local or regional network providers, sometimes referred to as downstream service providers (DSPs). The ISPs are interconnected, either by direct links or by using network access points distributed around the country.
- Both networks involve large numbers of subsystems operated by different organizations. The number and intricate nature of the interfaces that exist at the boundaries of these subsystems are one source of complexity for these networks. The increasing popularity of advanced services is a second source.

---

[1]Additional consolidation among the regional operating companies remains a real possibility; at the same time, pressure for competition in the local telephone market will probably increase the number of major players.

The vulnerabilities of the PTN and Internet are exacerbated by the dependence of each network on the other. Much of the Internet uses leased telephone lines as its physical transport medium. Conversely, telephone companies rely on networked computers to manage their own facilities, increasingly employing Internet technology, although not necessarily the Internet itself. Thus, vulnerabilities in the PTN can affect the Internet, and vulnerabilities in Internet technology can affect the telephone network.

This chapter, a study of vulnerabilities in the PTN and the Internet, has three parts. The first discusses the design and operation of both networks. The second examines environmental disruption, operational errors, hardware and software design and implementation errors, and malicious attacks as they apply to the networks. Finally, the chapter concludes by analyzing two emerging issues: Internet telephony and the expanding use of the Internet by business.

NETWORK DESIGN

The Public Telephone Network

Network Services and Design

The PTN has evolved considerably over the past decades. It is no longer simply a network comprising a set of linked telephone switches, many of which are connected by copper wires to each and every telephone instrument in the country. There are now many telephone companies that provide advanced services, such as toll-free numbers, call forwarding, network-based programmable call distribution, conference calling, and message delivery. The result is a network that is perhaps more flexible and responsive to customer needs but also more complex. The flexibility and complexity are sources of vulnerability.

Some of the advanced services also have intrinsic vulnerabilities. With call forwarding, for example, a caller can unknowingly reach a number different from the one dialed. Consequently, a caller can no longer make assumptions about what number a call will reach, and the recipient no longer knows what number a caller is intending to reach. Havoc could result if an attacker modified the telephone network's database of forwarding destinations.[2] As a second example, with network-

---

[2]In one recent case, a plumber call forwarded his competitor's telephone number to his own, thereby gaining the callers' business without their knowledge of the deception. Call forwarding could also subvert the purpose of dial-back modems used for security. Here, the presumption is that only authorized users have access to certain telephone numbers.

based programmable call distribution, a voice menu greets callers and allows a company to direct its incoming calls according to capabilities in different offices, time zones, and so on. The menus and distribution criteria can be modified directly by the company and uploaded into a telephone network database. But, as with call forwarding, a database that can be modified by telephone network customers constitutes a potential vulnerability.

The telephone network is made up of many different kinds of equipment that can be divided roughly into three major categories: signaling, transmission, and operations. Signaling equipment is used to set up and tear down calls. This category also includes databases and adjunct processors used for number translation and call routing. Transmission equipment carries the actual conversations. Operations equipment, including the operations support system (OSS), is used for provisioning, database updates, maintenance, billing, and the like.

All communication between modern central-office switches takes place over a dedicated data network using protocols, such as Signaling System 7 (SS7), which the switches use to set up calls, establish who pays for the call, return busy signals, and so on. Such out-of-band signaling helps prevent fraud (such as the deceptions of the 1960s and 1970s made possible by the infamous "blue boxes," which sent network control tones over the voice path) and helps conserve resources (i.e., no voice path need ever be allocated if the target number is busy). However, out-of-band signaling does introduce new vulnerabilities.[3] Failure of the signaling path can prevent completion of a call, even if there is an available route for the call itself.

Authentication

Authentication is a key part of any scheme for preventing unauthorized activity. In a network containing programmable elements, authentication is an essential ingredient for protecting those elements from per-

---

When such users try to log in, the site calls them back. But the system has no way of knowing whether the person who answers the callback is really the authorized user, and call forwarding could cause the callback to be redirected.

[3]SS7 messages are carried over a mix of private and public X.25 (data) networks, providing out-of-band signaling. However, such networks, especially public ones, are subject to various forms of attacks. There is even a curious semicircularity here, since the X.25 interswitch trunks usually are provisioned from telephone company long-distance circuits, although not from the switched circuits that SS7 manages. Owing to deregulation designed to foster competition, telephone companies must allow essentially anyone to connect into SS7 networks for a modest fee ($10,000). SS7 is a system that was designed for use by a closed community, and thus embodies minimal security safeguards. It is now employed by a much larger community, which makes the PTN subject to a broad range of "insider" attacks.

forming actions illicitly requested by attackers. Specifically, in the PTN, the OSSs must be able to authenticate requests in order to control changes in the configuration of the elements constituting the network. In addition, authentication is required to support certain advanced services, such as caller ID.[4] To prevent caller ID from subversion, all elements in the path from the caller to the recipient must be authenticated.

The need for authentication by OSSs is growing because interconnections among previously isolated networks has increased the risk of external intrusions. As the PTN's management networks convert to the Transmission Control Protocol/Internet Protocol (TCP/IP) and are connected to other TCP/IP-based networks, ignoring authentication may prove disastrous. Historically, proprietary protocols and dedicated networks were used for the network's management, so knowledge of these was restricted to insiders, and there was little need for authentication or authorization of requests.

The Internet

Network Services and Design

The Internet, a successor to the ARPANET (McQuillan and Walden, 1977), is a worldwide packet-switched computer-communications network. It interconnects two types of processors: hosts and routers. Hosts are the source and destination for all communications; routers[5] forward packets received on one communications line to another and thereby implement a communication. A shared set of protocols and service architecture was designed to provide support for various forms of robust communication (e.g., e-mail, remote terminal access, file transfer, the World Wide Web) despite outages and congestion. Little design effort was devoted to resisting attacks, although subsequent Department of Defense research has done so. And the designers elected to eschew service guarantees in favor of providing service on a "best effort" basis. For example, the Internet Protocol (IP), a datagram service used extensively by the Internet, does not guarantee delivery and can deliver duplicates of messages.[6]

---

[4]Caller ID is an advanced service that identifies the originator of a telephone call to a suitably equipped receiver. As this service becomes more pervasive, it will be used more and more for identification and authentication by systems employing the telephone network for communications. Here, then, is a vulnerability that can propagate from a communications fabric into an NIS that is built on top of that fabric.

[5]Routers sometimes act as hosts for purposes of network management and exchanging routing protocol messages.

[6]ISPs are now beginning to offer quality of service features (e.g., using RSVP), so the best-efforts notion of IP service may change over the next few years.

The Internet's protocols have proven remarkably tolerant to changes in the size of the network and to decades of order of magnitude improvements in communications bandwidth, communications speed, and processor capacity. In electing for "best effort" services, the Internet's designers made it easier for their protocols to tolerate outages of hosts, routers, and communications lines. Selecting the weaker service model also simplified dealing with router memory and processing capacity limitations. The Internet protocols were designed to operate over a range of network technologies being explored by the military in the 1970s from 56-kbps ARPANET trunks to 10-Mbps Ethernets and a mix of satellite and low-speed tactical packet radio networks. Despite two decades of network technology evolution, these protocols perform relatively well in today's Internet, which has a backbone and other communications lines that are far faster.

Routing protocols in the Internet implement network-topology discovery, calculation of shortest routes, and recovery (i.e., alternate route selection) from link and router outages. Initially, all of the Internet's routers were owned and operated by a single entity, making it reasonable to assume that all routers were executing compatible protocols and none would behave maliciously. But as the Internet matured, ownership and control of the routers became disbursed. More robust but less cooperative routing protocols were developed, thereby limiting the Internet's vulnerability to malicious and faulty routers. The Exterior Gateway Protocol (Mills, 1984) was originally employed for communication with routers outside an originating domain; today, the Border Gateway Protocol (BGP) (Rekhter and Li, 1995; Rekhter and Gross, 1995; Traina, 1993, 1995) is used.

A routing protocol must resolve the tension between (1) performance gains possible given information about the far reaches of the network and (2) increased vulnerability that such dependence can bring. By trusting information received from other domains, a router can calculate near-optimal routes, but such routes are useless if based on inaccurate information provided by malicious or malfunctioning routers. Conversely, restricting the information that routers share allows routing tables to be smaller, hence cheaper to compute, but sacrifices control over route quality. Today's Internet routing protocols generally favor cost over route quality, but ISPs override this bias toward minimum hop routes in the context of interdomain routing.[7]

Communication in the Internet depends not only on the calculation of routing tables but also on the operation of the Domain Name Service

---

[7]ISPs use the local policy feature of the Border Gateway Protocol (BGP) to favor routes that might not be selected by BGP on a minimum-hop basis. This is necessary to balance traffic loads and to reduce vulnerability to configuration errors, or malicious attacks, on BGP.

(DNS) (Mockapetris, 1987a,b). The most important function of this service is to map host names, such as <www.nas.edu>, into numeric IP addresses. DNS also maps IP addresses into host names, defines inbound mail gateways, and so on. The name space implemented by DNS is tree structured. The top level has a handful of generic names (.COM, .NET, .GOV, and the like)[8] as well as two-letter names corresponding to International Organization for Standardization (ISO) country codes (.US, .UK, .DE, .RU, and so forth). Definitive information for each level of the tree is maintained by a single master server; additional servers for a domain copy their information from it. Subtrees of the name space can be (and generally are) delegated to other servers. For example, .COM and .NET currently reside by chance on the same server as do the root name servers; .US, though, is delegated. Individual sites or machines may cache recently retrieved DNS records; the intended lifetime of such cache entries is controlled by the source of the cached records.

Network management tasks in the Internet are implemented using the Simple Network Management Protocol (SNMP) (Case et al., 1990). SNMP itself is quite elementary—it merely uses the User Datagrams Protocol (UDP) to read and alter predefined parameters. These parameters, called management information bases (MIBs), are organized in a tree structure with branches representing MIB type, protocol structure, device type, and vendor. The hard task in managing a network is not the mechanics of changing values of parameters; it is knowing what MIB variables to set in order to effect some desired change in network behavior. SNMP provides no assistance here. Most of the deployed implementations of SNMP also lack good security features, so the protocol has been used primarily to retrieve data from MIBs in managed devices, not to make changes to these MIBs. Instead, Telnet, a protocol that can be used with a variety of user authentication technologies, is often used for modification of MIBs. The latest version (3) of SNMP promises to overcome these security limitations.

Perhaps the most visible Internet service is the World Wide Web.[9] The Web is implemented by servers that communicate with Web browsers (clients) using the Hypertext Transfer Protocol (HTTP) (Berners-Lee et al., 1996) to retrieve documents represented in Hypertext Markup Language (HTML) (Berners-Lee and Connolly, 1995). HTML documents con-

---

[8]At this time, there is an active debate over how many new top-level names to add and who should make the decisions. The outcome of this debate may change some of the details presented here; the overall structure, however, is likely to remain the same. Several of the generic top-level domain names are decidedly U.S.-centric. .MIL and .GOV are restricted to U.S. military and government organizations, and most of the entries in the .EDU domain are from the United States.

[9]Indeed, many think that the Web is the Internet.

tain data (text, images, audio, video, and so on), as well as uniform resource locators (URLs) (Berners-Lee et al., 1994) to reference other HTML documents. An HTML document can be a file stored by a Web server or the output from a program, known as a common gateway interface (CGI) script, run by the Web server in response to a client request. CGI scripts, although not necessarily installed or managed by system administrators, are basically network servers accessible to Internet users. Bugs, therefore, can be a source of vulnerability.

HTTP treats each client request as separate and independent. Thus, information about past interactions must be stored and retrieved explicitly by the server in processing each request, usually an unnatural style of programming. The information can be stored by the client, as "cookies" (Kristol and Montulli, 1997) or as hidden fields in URLs and forms, or it can be stored by the server, or it can be stored as part of a secure socket layer[10] (SSL) session index (if the HTTP session is being cryptographically protected). Observe that with the latter two schemes, the server's state becomes visible to the client and the client must implement any security.

HTTP uses TCP and makes large numbers of short-lived TCP connections (even between the same pairs of hosts). TCP, however, was designed to support comparatively long-lived connections. Web browsers thus cannot benefit from TCP's congestion-control algorithms (Stevens, 1997; Jacobson, 1988). That means that the load imposed by the Web on the Internet's routers and communications lines not only is disproportionately high but also reduces network throughput. Although HTTP 1.1 (Fielding et al., 1997) is mitigating this particular problem, it does exemplify a broader concern: Deploying an application that does not match assumptions made by the Internet's designers can have a serious global impact on Internet performance.

For implementing a trustworthy NIS, the Internet's "best effort" service semantics is probably not good enough. Bandwidth, latency, route diversity, and other quality of service (QOS) guarantees are likely to be needed by an NIS. Efforts are under way to correct this Internet deficiency. But accommodating QOS guarantees seems to require revisiting a fundamental architectural tenet of the Internet—that intelligence and state exist only at the network's periphery. The problem is that, without adding state to routers (i.e., the "inside" of the network), the Internet's routers would lack a basis for processing some packets differently from others to enforce differing QOS guarantees.

The most ambitious scheme to provide QOS guarantees in the Internet relies on the new Resource Reservation Protocol (RSVP) (Braden et al., 1997). This protocol transmits bandwidth requests to the routers in a

---

[10]Available on line at <http://home.netscape.com/eng/ssl3/ssl-toc.html>.

communications path on a hop-by-hop basis. The receiver makes a request of an adjacent router; that router, in turn, passes the request to its predecessor, and so on, until the sender is reached. (Special messages convey the proper path information to the receiver, and thence to each router.) The RSVP bandwidth requests feed the Internet's integrated services model (Shenker and Wroclawski, 1997) with parameters that include bandwidth, latency, and maximum packet size. With RSVP, bandwidth reservations in routers are not permanent. They may be relinquished explicitly or, if not periodically refreshed, they expire.

Note that RSVP reservations are not required for packets to flow. The term "soft state" has been coined for such saved information—information whose loss may impair performance but does not disrupt functional correctness (i.e., the Internet's "best effort" semantics). The use of soft state in RSVP means that changes in routings or the reboot of a router cannot cause a communications failure, and packets will continue to flow, albeit without performance guarantees. By periodically refreshing reservations, performance guarantees can be reactivated.

Differentiated service, an alternative to RSVP for providing QOS in the Internet, employs bits in packet headers to indicate classes of service. Each class of service has associated service guarantees. The bits are inspected at network borders, and each network is responsible for taking appropriate measures in order to satisfy the guarantees.

Authentication (and other Security Protocols)

Concern about strong and useable authentication in the Internet is relatively new. The original Internet application protocols used plaintext passwords for authentication, a mechanism that was adequate for casual log-ins but was insufficient for more sophisticated uses of a network, especially in a local area network environment. Rather than build proper cryptographic mechanisms—which were little known in the civilian sector at that time—the developers of the early Internet software for UNIX resorted to network-based authentication for remote log-in and remote shell commands. The servers checked their clients' messages by converting the sender's IP address into a host name. User names in such messages are presumed to be authentic if the message comes from a host whose name is trusted by the server. Senders, however, can circumvent the check by misrepresenting their IP address[11] (something that is more difficult with TCP).

---

[11]A number of different attacks are known. They can be accomplished in a number of ways, such as sequence number guessing (Morris, 1985) or route corruption (Bellovin, 1989). Alternatively, the attacker can target the address-to-name translation mechanism (Bellovin, 1995).

BOX 2.1
Open Systems Interconnection Network Layers

Physical link: Mechanical, electrical, and procedural interfaces to the transmission
                  medium that convert it into a stream that appears to be free of unde-
                  tected errors
Network: Routes from sender to receiver within a single network technology
                  and deals with congestion (X.25, frame relay, and asynchronous
                  transfer mode fall into this layer)
Internetwork: Sometimes combined with the network layer; provides routing and
                  relay functions from the sender to the receiver and deals with con-
                  gestion (Internet Protocol falls into this layer)
Transport: Responsible for end-to-end delivery of data (Transmission Control
                  Protocol and User Datagram Protocol fall into this layer)
Session: Allows multiple transport-layer connections to be managed as a sin-
                  gle unit; not used on the Internet
Presentation: Chooses common representations, typically application dependent,
                  for data; rarely used on the Internet
Application: Deals with application-specific protocols

But cryptographic protocols—a sounder basis for network authentication and security—are now growing in prominence on the Internet.
Link-layer encryption has been in use for many years. (See Box 2.1 for the
names and descriptions of various network layers.) It is especially useful
when just a few links in a network need protection. (In the latter days of
the ARPANET, MILNET trunks outside the continental United States
were protected by link encryptors.) Although link-layer encryption has
the advantage of being completely transparent to all higher-layer devices
and protocols, the scope of its protection is limited. Accordingly, attention is now being focused on network-layer encryption (see Box 2.2).
Network-layer encryption requires no modification to applications, and it
can be configured to protect host-to-host, host-to-network, or network-to-
network traffic. Cost thus can be traded against granularity of protection.

Network-layer encryption is instantiated in the Internet as the IP Security (IPsec) protocol, which is designed to run on the Internet's hosts
and routers, or on hardware outboard to either.[12] The initial deployment
of IPsec has been in network-to-network mode. This mode allows virtual
private networks to be created so that the otherwise insecure Internet can
be incorporated into an existing secure network, such as a corporate net-

---

[12]RFC 2401, *Security Architecture for the Internet Protocol*, and RFC 2411, *IP Security Document Roadmap*, are both forthcoming (<ftp://ftp.isi.edu/in-notes>).

BOX 2.2
A History of Network-level Encryption

Link-level encryption is an old idea. It first emerged in the form of Vernam's online teletype encryptor in 1917 (Kahn, 1976). Various forms were used by assorted combatants during World War II. But link encryption has a number of drawbacks, notably a very limited scope of protection. This is especially problematic for a multinode network like the ARPANET or the Internet, in which every single link must be protected and messages exist in plaintext at every intermediate hop. Encryption at this level is also a rather complex problem if the link level itself is a multiaccess network.

The military used link encryption with ARPANET technology to protect the communications lines connecting interface message processors (IMPs) in several Department of Defense packet networks. The difficulties of scaling this technology economically to some environments led to the development of the private line interface (PLI) encryptor (BBN, 1978), which operated at (for the ARPANET) the network layer. With the advent of the Internet and the presumed imminent arrival of Open Systems Interconnection (OSI) networks, it rapidly became obvious that a more flexible encryption strategy was necessary. The result was Blacker (Weissman, 1992), which sat between a host and an IMP and operated on X.25 packets. Blacker ignored Internet Protocol (IP) addresses (although these had been mapped algorithmically into X.25 addresses by the host); it did, though, look at the security labels in the IP header.

As IMPs fell out of favor as the preferred switches, a new hardware strategy was necessary. Furthermore, the National Security Agency wanted to use public-key technology—a success in the Secure Telephone Unit III (STU III) deployment—for data. Accordingly, the Secure Data Network System (SDNS) project devised a true network-layer encryption standard known as Security Protocol at Level 3 (SP3). SP3 could operate directly over X.25 networks; it also could (and generally did) operate with OSI or IP network layer headers below it. It could handle host-to-host, host-to-network, and network-to-network encryption. Several SP3 devices, such as Caneware and the Network Encryption System (NES), were built and deployed.

This standard achieved a fundamental advance by enabling network managers or designers to trade cost for granularity of protection. The other fundamental advance in SP3 was the separation of the key-management protocol from the actual cryptographic layer. In effect, key management became just another application, tremendously simplifying the entire concept. SP3 served as the model for OSI's Network-Layer Security Protocol (NLSP), but the protocol was complicated by the need to work with both connection-oriented and connectionless network layers, and very few NLSP products were ever deployed.

Both SDNS and OSI also specified transport-level encryption protocols (SP4 and TLSP, respectively). These never caught on, and they appear to be an evolutionary dead end.

SP3 was the inspiration for swIPe (Ioannidis and Blaze, 1993), a simple host-based IP encryptor. This, in turn, gave rise to the Internet Engineering Task Force's working group on IPsec. Although IP Security (IPsec) is, in many ways, very similar to SP3, its overall model is more complete. Much more attention was paid to issues such as firewall integration, selective bypass (one need not encrypt traffic to all destinations), and so on. The initial deployment of IPsec appears to be in network-to-network mode; host-to-network mode, for telecommuters, appears to be following closely behind.

work. The next phase of deployment for IPsec will most likely be the host-to-network mode, with individual hosts being laptops or home machines. That would provide a way for travelers to exploit the global reach of the Internet to access a secure corporate network.

It is unclear when general host-to-host IPsec will be widely deployed. Although transparent to applications, IPsec is not transparent to system administrators—the deployment of host-to-host IPsec requires outboard hardware or modifications to the host's protocol system software. Because of this impediment to deploying IPsec, the biggest use of encryption in the Internet is currently above the transport layer, as SSL embedded into popular Web browsers and servers. SSL, although quite visible to its applications, affects only those applications and not the kernel or the hardware. SSL can be deployed without supervision by a central authority, the approach used for almost all other successful elements of Internet technology.

Higher still in the protocol stack, encryption is found in fairly widespread use for the protection of electronic mail messages. In this manner, an e-mail message is protected during each Simple Mail Transfer Protocol (Postel, 1982), while spooled on intermediate mail relays, while residing in the user's mailbox, while being copied to the recipient's machine, and even in storage thereafter. However, no secure e-mail format has been both standardized by the Internet Engineering Task Force (IETF) and accepted by the community. Two formats that have gained widespread support are S/MIME (Dusse et al., 1998a,b) and PGP (pretty good privacy) (Zimmerman, 1995). Both have been submitted to the IETF for review.

Findings

1. The PTN is becoming more vulnerable as network elements become dependent on complex software, as the reliance on call-translation databases and adjunct processors grows, and as individual telephone companies increasingly share facilities with the Internet.

2. As the PTN is increasingly managed by OSSs that are less proprietary in nature, information about controlling OSSs will become more widespread and OSSs will be vulnerable to larger numbers of attackers.

3. New user services, such as caller ID, are increasingly being used to provide authenticated information to customers of the PTN. However, the underlying telephone network is unable to provide this information with high assurance of authenticity.

4. The Internet is becoming more secure as its protocols are improved and as enhanced security measures are more widely deployed at higher levels of the protocol stack. However, the Internet's hosts remain vulnerable, and the Internet's protocols need further improvement.

5. The operation of the Internet depends critically on routing and name to address translation services. This list of critical services will likely expand to include directory services and public-key certificate servers, thereby adding other critical dependencies.

6. There is a tension between the capabilities and risks of routing protocols. The sharing of routing information facilitates route optimization, but such cooperation also increases the risk that malicious or malfunctioning routers can compromise routing.

NETWORK FAILURES AND FIXES

This section examines some causes for Internet and PTN failures. Protective measures that already exist or might be developed are also discussed. The discussion is structured around the four broad classes of vulnerabilities described in Chapter 1: environmental disruption, operational errors, hardware and software design and implementation errors, and malicious attacks.

Environmental Disruption

In this report, environmental disruption is defined to include natural phenomena, ranging from earthquakes to rodents chewing through cable insulation, as well as accidents caused by human carelessness. Environmental disruptions affect both the PTN and the Internet. However, the effects and, to some extent, the impact of different types of disruption differ across the two networks.

Link Failures

The single biggest cause of PTN outages is damage to buried cables (NRIC, 1997). And the single biggest cause of this damage is construction crews digging without proper clearance from telecommunications companies and other utilities. The phenomenon, jocularly known in the trade as "backhoe fading," is probably not amenable to a technological solution. Indeed, pursuant to the Network Reliability and Interoperability Council (NRIC) recommendation, the Federal Communications Commission (FCC) has requested legislation to address this problem.[13]

The impact of backhoe fading on network availability depends on the redundancy of the network. Calls can be routed around failed links, but only if other links form an equivalent path. Prior to the 1970s, most of the

---

[13]Both the proposed text and the letter to Congress are available online at <http://www.fcc.gov/oet/nric>.

nation's telephone network was run by one company, AT&T. As a regulated monopoly, AT&T was free to build a network with spare capacity and geographically diverse, redundant routings. Multiple telephone companies compete in today's market, and cost pressures make it impractical for these telephone companies to build and maintain such capacious networks. Furthermore, technical innovations, such as fiber optics and wave division multiplexing, enable fewer physical links to carry current levels of traffic. The result is a telephone network in which failure of a single link can have serious repercussions.

One might have expected that having multiple telephone companies would contribute to increased capacity and diversity in the telephone network. It does not. Major telephone companies lease circuits from each other to lower their own costs. This practice means that backup capacity may not be available when needed. To limit outages, telephone companies have turned to newer technologies. Synchronous optical network (SONET) rings, for example, provide redundancy and switch-over at a level below the circuit layer, allowing calls to continue uninterrupted when a fiber is severed. Despite the increased robustness provided by SONET rings, the very high capacity of fiber optic cables results in a greater concentration of bandwidth over fewer paths because of economic considerations. This means that the failure, or sabotage, of a single link will likely disrupt service for many customers.

The Internet, unlike the PTN, was specifically designed to tolerate link outages. When a link outage is detected, the Internet routes packets over alternate paths. In theory, connections should continue uninterrupted. In practice, though, there may not be sufficient capacity to accommodate the additional traffic on alternate paths. The Internet's routing protocols also do not respond immediately to notifications of link outages. Having such a delay prevents routing instabilities and oscillations that would swamp routers and might otherwise arise in response to transient link outages. But these delays also mean that, although packets are not lost when a link fails, packet delivery can be delayed. In addition to the route damping noted here, there is a disturbing trend for ISPs to rely on static configuration of primary and backup routes in BGP border routers. This means that Internet routing is less dynamic than was originally envisioned. The primary motivations for this move away from less-constrained dynamic routing are a desire for increased route stability and reduced vulnerability to attacks or configuration errors by ISPs and DSPs.

Congestion

Congestion occurs when load exceeds capacity. Environmental disruptions cause increased loads in two ways. First, the load may come from outside the network—for example, from people checking by telephone with friends and relatives who live in the area of an earthquake. Second, the load may come from within the network—existing load that is redistributed in order to mask outages caused by the environmental disruption. In both scenarios, network elements saturate, and the consequences are an inability to deliver service, perhaps at a time when it is most needed.

The PTN is able to control congestion better than the Internet is. When a telephone switch or telephone transmission facility reaches saturation, new callers receive "reorder" (i.e., "fast" busy) signals and no further calls are accepted. This forestalls increased load and congestion. PTN operations staff can even block call attempts to a given destination at sources, thereby saving network resources from being wasted on calls that are unlikely to be completed. For example, when an earthquake occurs near San Francisco, the operations staff might decide to block almost all incoming calls to the affected area codes from throughout the entire PTN.

Congestion management in the Internet is problematic, in part, because no capabilities exist for managing traffic associated with specific users, connections, sources, or destinations, and it would be difficult to implement such capabilities. All that a simple router can do[14] is discard packets when its buffers become full. To implement fairness, routers would have to store information about users and connections, something they are not built to do. Retaining such information would require large amounts of storage. Managing this storage would be difficult, because the Internet has no call-teardown messages that are visible to routers. Furthermore, the concept of a "user"—that is, an entity that originates or receives traffic—is not part of the network or transport layers of the Internet protocols.

Choking-back load offered by specific hosts (in analogy with PTN reorder signals) is also not an option for preventing Internet congestion, since an IP-capable host can have connections open to many destinations concurrently. Stopping all flows from the host is clearly inappropriate. More generally, avoiding congestion in the Internet is intrinsically hard because locales of congestion (i.e., routers and links) have no straightforward correspondence to the communications abstractions (i.e., connections) that end points see. This problem is particularly acute for the highly dynamic traffic flows between ISPs. Here, very high speed (e.g.,

---

[14]In fact, routers can transmit an ICMP (Internet Control Message Protocol) Source Quench message to advise a host of congestion, but there has never been a standard, accepted response to receipt of a Source Quench, and many hosts merely ignore such messages. In such circumstances the resources needed to construct and send the Source Quench may be wasted and may compound the problem!

OC-12) circuits are used to carry traffic between millions of destinations over short intervals, and the traffic mix can completely change over a few seconds.

Although congestion in the Internet is nominally an IP-layer phenomena—routers have too many packets for a given link—measures for dealing successfully with congestion have resided in the TCP layer (Jacobson, 1988). Some newer algorithms work at the IP level (Floyd and Jacobson, 1993), but more research is needed, especially for defining and enforcing flexible and varied policies for congestion control. One suggestion involves retaining information about flows from which packets have been repeatedly dropped. Such flows are deemed uncooperative and, as such, are subjected to additional penalties (Floyd and Fall, 1998); cooperating flows respond to indications of congestion by slowing down their transmissions.

More research is also needed to measure and understand current Internet traffic as well as expected future trends in that traffic. Some work has been done (e.g., Thompson et al., 1997), but far too little is known about usage patterns, flow characteristics, and other relevant parameters. Having such information is likely to enable better congestion control methods. However, usage patterns are dictated by the application designs and, as new applications arise and become popular, traffic characteristics change. Today, the use of the Web has changed packet sizes radically compared to a time when file transfer and e-mail were the principal applications. Even within the Web environment, when a very popular Web site arises, news of its location spreads quickly, and traffic flows shift noticeably!

Two further difficulties are associated with managing congestion in networks. First, there appears to be a tension between implementing congestion management and enforcing network security. A congestion control mechanism may need to inspect and even modify traffic being managed, but strong network security mechanisms will prohibit reading and modifying traffic en route. For example, congestion control in the Internet might be improved if IP and TCP headers were inspected and modified, but the use of IPsec will prevent such actions.

A second difficulty arises when a network comprises multiple independent but interconnected providers. In the Internet, no single party is either capable of or responsible for most end-to-end connections, and local optimizations performed by individual providers may lead to poor overall utilization of network resources or suboptimal global behavior. In the PTN, which was designed for a world with comparatively few telephone companies but in which switches can be trusted, competitive pressures are now forcing telephone companies to permit widespread interconnections between switches that may not be trustworthy. This opens telephone networks to both malicious and nonmalicious failures (NRIC, 1997).

Findings

1. Technical and market forces have reduced reserve capacity and the number of geographically diverse, redundant routings in the PTN. Failure of a single link can now have serious repercussions.

2. Current Internet routing algorithms are inadequate. They do not scale well, they require CPU (central processing unit)-intensive calculations, and they cannot implement diverse or flexible policies. Furthermore, little is known about how best to resolve the tension between the stability of routing algorithms and the delay that precedes a routing change in response to an outage.

3. A better understanding is needed of the Internet's current traffic profile and how it will evolve. In addition, fundamental research is needed into mechanisms for supporting congestion management in the Internet, especially congestion management schemes that do not conflict with enforcing network security.

4. Networks formed by interconnecting extant independent subnetworks present unique challenges for controlling congestion (because local provider optimizations may not lead to good overall behavior) and for implementing security (because trust relationships between network components are not homogeneous).

Operational Errors

"To err is human" the saying goes, and human operator errors are indeed responsible for network outages, as well as for unwittingly disabling protection mechanisms that then enable hostile attacks to succeed. Located in a network operations center (see Box 2.3), operators take actions based on their perceptions of what the network is doing and what it will do, but without direct knowledge of either. In these circumstances, the consequences of even the most carefully considered operator actions can be surprising—and devastating.

With regard to the PTN, the Network Reliability and Interoperability Council found that operational errors caused about one in every four telephone switch failures (NRIC, 1996). Mistakes by vendors, mistakes in installation and maintenance, and mistakes by system operators all contributed. For example, in 1997, an employee loading an incorrect set of translations into an SS7 processor led to a 90-minute network outage for toll-free telephone service (Perillo, 1997), and the recent outage of the

---

BOX 2.3
Network Operations Centers

Each public telephone network (PTN) or Internet constituent has some form of network operations center (NOC). For a small downstream service provider (DSP), the NOC may be a portion of a room in a home or office. For a local telephone company, long-distance carrier, or national-level Internet service provider (ISP), an NOC could occupy considerably more space and likely will involve substantial investments in equipment and infrastructure. A large network provider may have multiple, geographically dispersed NOCs in order to share the management load and provide backup.

The purpose of an NOC is to monitor and control the elements of a network: switches, transmission lines, access devices, and so on. Human operators monitor a variety of graphical images of network topology (physical and logical) that show the status of network elements. Ordinary computer monitors often serve as these display devices.[1] A typical display could indicate which switch interfaces or switches appear to be malfunctioning, or which circuits are out of service. Some displays may even indicate which links are approaching saturation.

The displays rarely tell an operator how to solve a problem whose symptoms are being depicted. Human understanding of network operation (with help from automated tools) must be brought to bear. For example, PTN switches are configured with secondary and tertiary routes (selected through the use of offline network analysis tools) that can be used when a primary link fails or becomes saturated. And Internet routers execute algorithms to determine automatically the shortest routes to each destination. But there is also considerable manual configuration of constraints on routing, especially at the interfaces between ISPs.

Most NOC operators are trained to deal with common problems. If the operator does not know how to deal with a problem, then an operations manual usually is

---

AT&T frame relay network (Mills, 1998) was attributed in part to operational procedures.[15]

The Internet has also been a victim of operational errors, although the frequency and specific causes have not been analyzed thoroughly as for the PTN. Examples abound, however. Perhaps the most serious incident occurred in July 1997, when a process intended to generate a major part of the DNS from a database failed. Automated mechanisms alerted operators that something was wrong, but a system administrator overrode the warning, causing the apparent deletion of most machines in that zone. There are also numerous instances of the bogus information stored by misconfigured DNS servers propagating into name server caches and then confusing machines throughout the Internet. Similar problems have occurred with regard to Internet routing as well. For example, in April 1997, a small ISP

---

[15]Two independent software bugs also contributed to this frame relay network outage.

available for consultation. The manual is important because of the complexity of the systems and the difficulty of attracting, training, and retaining highly skilled operators to provide 24-hour, 7-day coverage in the NOC. However, operations manuals usually cover only a predetermined set of problems; combinations of failures can easily lead to symptoms and problems not covered by the manual. For problems not covered, the usual procedure is to contact an expert, who may be on call for such emergencies. In the Internet environment, the expert might be able to access the NOC (e.g., via a dial-up link) to assist in diagnosis and corrective action. (Note, though, that having facilities for remote access introduces new vulnerabilities.)

The set of controls available to NOC operators is network specific. In the PTN, there are controls for rerouting calls through switches and multiplexors, for blocking calls to a particular area code or exchange during natural disasters, and so on. In an ISP, there are controls for changing router tables and multiplexors, among other things. In both the PTN and an ISP, the NOC will have provisions for calling out physical maintenance teams when, for example, a cable breaks or a switching element fails. A telephone company often services its own equipment, but external maintenance must be ordered for the equipment of another provider; external maintenance in the Internet is common because ISPs typically rely on equipment provided by many vendors, including long-distance and local telephone companies. Consolidation in the Internet business may blur these distinctions, as most long-distance telephone companies are also major ISPs.

---

[1]Many NOCs also have one or more televisions, usually tuned to news channels such as CNN, to provide information about events such as natural disasters that may affect network traffic (e.g., earthquakes). Some events can cause disruption of service owing to equipment failures, or may create traffic surges because of breaking news (e.g., announcement of a toll-free number).

---

claimed to be the best route to most of the Internet. Its upstream ISP believed the claim and passed it along. Routing in the Internet was then disrupted for several hours because of the traffic diverted to this small ISP.

Exactly what constitutes an operational error may depend on system capacity. A system operating with limited spare capacity can be especially sensitive to operational missteps. For example, injecting inappropriate, but not technically incorrect, routing information led to a day-long outage of Netcom's (a major ISP) own internal network in June 1996 as the sheer volume of resulting work overloaded the ISP's relatively small routers. And this incident may foreshadow problems to come—many routers in the Internet are operating near or at their memory or CPU capacity. It is unclear how well the essential infrastructure of the Internet could cope with a sudden spike in growth rates.

That operator errors are prevalent should not be a surprise. The PTN and the Internet are both complex systems. Large numbers of separate and controllable elements are involved in each, and the control parameters for these elements can affect network operation in subtle ways. Operator errors can be reduced when a system does the following:

• Presents its operators with a conceptual model that allows those operators to predict the effects of their actions and their inaction (Wickens et al., 1997; Parasuraman and Mouloua, 1996);
• Allows its operators to examine all of the system's abstractions, from the highest to the lowest level, whichever is relevant to the issue at hand.

The entire system must be designed—from the outset—with controllability and understandability as a goal. The reduction of operational errors is more than a matter of building flashy window-based interfaces. The graphics are the easy part. Moreover, with an NIS, there is the added problem of components with different management interfaces provided by multiple vendors. Rarely can the NIS developer change these components or their interfaces, which may make the support of a clean systemwide conceptual model especially difficult.

An obvious approach to reducing operational errors is simply to implement automated support and remove the human from the loop. The route-configuration aids used by PTNs are an example of such automation. More generally, better policy-based routing mechanisms and protocols will likely free human operators from low-level details associated with setting up network routes. In the Internet, ISPs currently have just one policy tool: their BGP configurations (Rekhter and Li, 1995; Rekhter and Gross, 1995; Traina, 1993, 1995). But even though BGP is a powerful hammer, the sorts of routing policies that are usually desired do not much resemble nails. Not surprisingly, getting BGP configurations right has proven to be quite difficult. Indeed, the internal network failure mentioned above was directly attributable to an error in use of the BGP policy control mechanisms.

Finally, operational errors are not only a matter of operators producing the right responses. Maintenance practices—setting up user accounts and access privileges, for example—can neutralize existing security safeguards. And poor maintenance is an oft-cited opening for launching a successful intrusion into a system. The network operations staff at the Massachusetts Institute of Technology, for example, reports that about 6 weeks after running vulnerability-scan software (e.g., COPS) on a public UNIX workstation, the workstation will again become vulnerable to intrusion as a result of misconfiguration. Managers of corporate or university networks often cite similar problems with firewall and router configuration which, if performed improperly, can lead to access control violations or denial of service.

Findings

1. Operational errors are a major source of outages for the PTN and Internet. Some of these errors would be prevented through improved operator training and contingency planning; others require that systems be designed with operator understandability and controllability as an initial design goal.

2. Improved routing management tools are needed for the Internet, because they will free human operators from an activity that is error prone.

3. Research and development is needed to devise conceptual models that will allow human operators to grasp the state of a network and understand the consequences of control that they may exert. Also, research is needed into ways in which the state of a network can be displayed to a human operator.

Software and Hardware Failures

The PTN and Internet both experience outages from errors in design and implementation of the hardware and software they employ. A survey by the NRIC (1996) found that software and hardware failures each accounted for about one-quarter of telephone switch outages. This finding is inconsistent with the commonly held belief that hardware is relatively bug free but software is notoriously buggy. A likely explanation comes from carefully considering the definition of an outage. Within telephone switches, software failures are prone to affect individual telephone calls and, therefore, might not always be counted as causing outages.

Comparable data about actual outages of Internet routers do not seem to be available. One can speculate that routers should be more reliable than telephone switches, because router hardware is generally newer and router software is much simpler. However, against that, one must ask whether routers are engineered and provisioned to the same high standards as telephone switches have been. Moreover, most failures in packet routing are comparatively transient; they are artifacts of the topology changes that routing protocols make to accommodate a failure, rather than being direct consequences of the failure itself.

One thing that is fairly clear is that the Internet's end points, including servers for such functions as the DNS, are its least robust components. These end points are generally ordinary computers running commercial operating systems and are heir to all of their attendant ills. (By contrast, telephony end points either tend to be very simple, as in the case of the ordinary telephone, or are built to telephone industry standards.) Two examples illustrate the fragility of the Internet's end points. First, many problems have been reported with BIND, the most common DNS server used on the Internet (e.g., CERT Advisories CA 98.05, April 1998, and CA 97.22, August 1997[16]); some of these result in corrupted data or in DNS failures. Second, the so-called "ping of death" (CERT Advisory CA-96.26, December 1996) was capable of crashing most of the common end points on the Internet. Fortunately, Cisco routers were not vulnerable; if they had been, the entire infrastructure would have been at risk.

Even without detailed outage data, it can be instructive to compare the PTN and Internet; their designs differ in rather fundamental ways, and these differences affect how software and hardware failures are handled. The PTN is designed to have remarkably few switches, and it depends on them. That constraint makes it necessary to keep all its switches running virtually all the time. Consequently, switch hardware itself is replicated, and the switch software is tasked with detecting hardware and software errors. Upon detecting an error, the software recovers quickly without a serious outage of the switch itself. Individual calls in progress may be sacrificed, though, to restore the health of the switch.

This approach does not work for all hardware and software failures. That was forcefully illustrated by the January 1990 failure of the AT&T long-distance network. That outage was caused by a combination of hardware and software, and the interaction between them:[17]

> The incident began when a piece of trunk equipment failed and notified a switch of the problem. Per its design, the switch took itself offline for a few seconds while it tried to reinitialize the failing equipment; it also notified its neighbors not to route calls to it. When the switch came back on-line, it started processing calls again; neighboring switches were programmed to interpret the receipt of new call setup messages as an indication that the switch had returned to service. Unfortunately, a timing bug in a new version of that process caused those neighboring switches to crash. This crash was detected and (correctly) resulted in a rapid restart—but the failure/restart process triggered the same problem in their neighbors.

The "switches" for the Internet—its routers—are also intended to be reliable, but they are not designed with the same level of redundancy or error detection as PTN switches. Rather, the Internet as a whole recovers and compensates for router (switch) failures. If a router fails, then its neighbors notice the lack of routing update messages and update their

---

[16]CERT advisories are available online at <http://www.cert.org>.
[17]Based on Cooper (1989).

own route tables accordingly. As neighbors notify other neighbors, the failed router is dropped from possible packet routes. In the meantime, retransmissions by end points preserve ongoing conversations by causing packets that might have been lost to reenter the network and traverse these new routes.

Finding

Insufficient data exist about Internet outages and how the Internet's mechanisms are able to deal with them.

Malicious Attacks

Attacks on the PTN and Internet fall into two broad categories, according to the nature of the vulnerability being exploited. First, there are attacks related to authentication. This category includes everything from eavesdroppers' interception of plaintext passwords to designers' misplaced trust in the network to provide authentication. In theory, these attacks can be prevented by proper use of cryptography. The second category of attacks is harder to prevent. This category comprises attacks that exploit bugs in code. Cryptography cannot help here (Blaze, 1996), nor do other simple fixes appear likely. Software correctness (see Chapter 3) is a problem that does not seem amenable to easy solutions. Yet, as long as software does not behave as intended, attackers will have opportunities to subvert systems by exploiting unintended system behavior.

Attacks on the Telephone Network

Most attacks on the PTN perpetrate toll fraud. The cellular telephony industry provides the easiest target, with caller information being broadcast over unencrypted radio channels and thus easily intercepted (CSTB, 1997). But attacks have been launched against wireline telephone service as well. Toll fraud probably cannot be prevented altogether. Fortunately, it does not have to be, because it is easily detected with automated traffic analysis that flags for investigation of abnormal patterns of calls, credit card authorizations, and other activities.

The NRIC (1997) reports that security incidents have not been a major problem in the PTN until recently. However, the council does warn that the threat is growing, for reasons that include interconnections (often indirect) of OSSs to the Internet, an increase in the number and skill level of attackers, and the increasing number of SS7 interconnections to new telephone companies. The report also notes that existing SS7 firewalls are neither adequate nor reliable in the face of the anticipated threat. As

noted earlier, this threat has increased dramatically because of the substantially lower threshold now associated with connection into the SS7
system.

Routing Attacks. To a would-be eavesdropper, the ability to control call
routing can be extremely useful. Installing wiretaps at the end points of
a connection may be straightforward, but such taps are also the easiest to
detect. Interoffice trunks can yield considerably more information to an
eavesdropper and with a smaller risk of detection. To succeed here, the
eavesdropper first must determine which trunks the target's calls will
use, something that is facilitated by viewing or altering the routing tables
used by the switches. Second, the eavesdropper must extract the calls of
interest from all the calls traversing the trunk; access to the signaling
channels can help here.

How easy is it for an eavesdropper to alter routing tables? As it turns
out, apart from the usual sorts of automated algorithms, which calculate
routes based on topology, failed links, or switches, the PTN does have
facilities to exert manual control over routes. These facilities exist to
allow improved utilization of PTN equipment. For example, there is
generally a spike in business calls around 9:00 a.m. on weekdays when
workers arrive in their offices. If telephone switches in, say, New York
are configured to route other East Coast calls through St. Louis or points
further west (where the workday has not yet started), then the 9:00 a.m.
load spike can be attenuated. However, the existence of this interface for
controlling call routing offers a point of entry for the eavesdropper, who
can profit from exploiting that control.

Database Attacks. OSSs and the many databases they manage are employed to translate telephone numbers so that the number dialed by a
subscriber is not necessarily the number that will be reached. If an attacker can compromise these databases, then various forms of abuse and
deception become possible. The simplest such attack exploits network-
based speed dialing, a feature that enables subscribers to enter a one- or
two- digit abbreviation and have calls directed to a predefined destination. If the stored numbers are changed by an attacker, then speed-dialed
calls could be routed to destinations of the attacker's choice. Beyond
harassment, an attacker who can change speed dialing numbers can impersonate a destination or can redial to the intended destination while
staying on the line and eavesdropping. Other advanced telephone services controlled by OSSs and databases include call forwarding, toll-free
numbers, call distribution, conference calling, and message delivery. All
could be affected by OSS and database vulnerabilities. In one successful
attack, the database entry for the telephone number of the probation of-

fice in Del Ray Beach, Florida, was reconfigured. People who called the probation office when the line was busy had their calls forwarded to a telephone sex line in New York (Cooper, 1989).[18]

Because a subscriber's chosen long-distance carrier is stored in a telephone network database, it too is vulnerable to change by attackers. Here the incentive is a financial one—namely, increased market share for a carrier. In a process that has come to be known as "slamming," customers' long-distance carriers are suddenly and unexpectedly changed. This problem has been pervasive enough so that numerous procedural safeguards have been mandated by the FCC and various state regulatory bodies.

Looking to the future, more competition in the local telephone market will lead to the creation of a database that enables the routing of incoming calls to specific local telephone carriers. And, given the likely use of shared facilities in many markets, outgoing local calls will need to be checked to see what carrier is actually handling the call. In addition, growing demand for "local number portability," whereby a customer can retain a telephone number even when switching carriers, implies the existence of one more database (which would be run by a neutral party and consulted by all carriers for routing of local calls). Clearly, a successful attack on any of these databases could disrupt telephone service across a wide area.

In contrast to the Internet, the telephone system does not depend on having an automated process corresponding to the Internet's DNS translation from names to addresses.[19] One does not call directory assistance before making every telephone call, and success in making a call does not depend critically on this service. Thus, in the PTN, an Internet's vulnerability is avoided but at the price of requiring subscribers to dial telephone numbers rather than dialing subscriber names. Furthermore, unlike DNS, the telephone network's directory service is subject to a sanity test by its clients. If a human caller asks directory assistance for a neighbor's number and is given an area code for a town halfway across the country, the caller would probably doubt the accuracy of the number and conclude that the directory assistance service was malfunctioning. Still, tampering with directory assistance can cause telephone calls to be misdirected.

---

[18]There is even a historical precedent for such attacks. The original telephone switch was invented by an undertaker; his competitor's wife was a telephone operator who connected anyone who asked for a funeral home to her own husband's business.

[19]This is not strictly true; calls to certain classes of telephone numbers (e.g., 800, 888, and 900) do result in a directory lookup to translate the called number into a "real" destination telephone number. In these instances, the analogy between the PTN and the Internet is quite close.

Facilities. The nature of the telephone company physical plant leads to another class of vulnerabilities. Many central offices normally are un-staffed and, consequently, they are vulnerable to physical penetration, which may go entirely undetected. Apart from the obvious problems of intruders tampering with equipment, the documentation present in such facilities (including, of course, passwords written on scraps of yellow paper and stuck to terminals) is attractive to "phone phreaks."[20] A simi-lar vulnerability is present in less populated rural areas, which are served by so-called remote modules. These remote modules perform local switching but depend on a central office for some aspects of control. Remote modules are invariably deployed in unstaffed facilities, hence subject to physical penetration.

Findings

1. Attacks on the telephone network have, for the most part, been directed at perpetrating billing fraud. The frequency of attacks is increas-ing, and the potential for more disruptive attacks, with harassment and eavesdropping as goals, is growing.

2. Better protection is needed for the many number translation and other databases used in the PTN.

3. SS7 was designed for a closed community of telephone companies. Deregulation has changed the operational environment and created op-portunities for insider attacks against this system, which is fundamental to the operation of the PTN.

4. Telephone companies need to enhance the firewalls between OSSs and the Internet and safeguard the physical security of their facilities.

Attacks on the Internet

The general accessibility of the Internet makes it a highly visible tar-get and within easy reach of attackers. The widespread availability of documentation and actual implementations for Internet protocols means that devising attacks for this system can be viewed as an intellectual puzzle (where launching the attacks validates the puzzle's solution). In-ternet vulnerabilities are documented extensively on CERT's Web site,[21] and at least one Ph.D. thesis (Howard, 1997) is devoted to the subject.

---

[20]A phone phreak is a telephone network hacker.

[21]The Computer Emergency Response Team (CERT)/Coordination Center is an element of the Networked Systems Survivability Program in the Software Engineering Institute at Carnegie Mellon University. See <http://www.cert.org>.

This subsection concentrates on vulnerabilities in the Internet's infrastructure, since this is what is most relevant to NIS designers. Vulnerabilities in end systems are amply documented elsewhere. See, for example, Garfinkel and Spafford (1996).

Name Server Attacks. The Internet critically depends on the operation of the DNS. Outages or corruption of DNS root servers and other top-level DNS servers—whether owing to failure or successful attacks—can lead to denial of service. Specifically, if a top-level server cannot furnish accurate information about delegations of zones to other servers, then clients making DNS lookup requests are prevented from making progress. The client requests might go unanswered, or the server could reply in a way that causes the client to address requests to DNS server machines that cannot or do not provide the information being sought. Cache contamination is a second way to corrupt the DNS. An attacker who introduces false information into the DNS cache can intercept all traffic to a specific targeted machine (Bellovin, 1989). One highly visible example of this occurred in July 1997, when somebody used this technique to divert requests for a major Web server to his own machines (*Wall Street Journal*, 1997).

In principle, attacks on DNS servers are easily dealt with by extending the DNS protocols. One such set of extensions, Secure DNS, is based on public-key cryptography (Eastlake and Kaufman, 1997) and can be deployed selectively in individual zones.[22] Perhaps because this solution requires the installation of new software on client machines, it has not been widely deployed. No longer merely a question of support software complexity, the Internet has grown sufficiently large so that even simple solutions, such as Secure DNS, are precluded by other operational criteria. A scheme that involved changing only the relatively small number of DNS servers would be quite attractive. But lacking that, techniques must be developed to institute changes in large-scale and heterogeneous networks.

Routing System Attacks. Routing in the Internet is highly decentralized. This avoids the vulnerabilities associated with dependence on a small number of servers that can fail or be compromised. But it leads to other vulnerabilities. With all sites playing some role in routing, there are many more sites whose failure or compromise must be tolerated. The

---

[22]However, configuration management does become much harder when there is partial deployment of Secure DNS.

damage inflicted by any single site must somehow be contained, even though each site necessarily serves as the authoritative source for some aspect of routing. Decentralization is not a panacea for avoiding the vulnerabilities intrinsic in centralized services. Moreover, the trustworthiness of most NISs will, like the Internet, be critically dependent both on services that are more sensibly implemented in a centralized fashion (e.g., DNS) and on services more sensibly implemented in a decentralized way (e.g., routing). Understanding how either type of services can be made trustworthy is thus instructive.

The basis for routing in the Internet is each router periodically informing neighbors about what networks it knows how to reach. This information is direct when a router advertises the addresses of the networks to which it is directly connected. More often, though, the information is indirect, with the router relaying to neighbors what it has learned from others. Unfortunately, recipients of information from a router rarely can verify its accuracy[23] because, by design, a router's knowledge about network topology is minimal. Virtually any router can represent itself as a best path to any destination as a way of intercepting, blocking, or modifying traffic to that destination (Bellovin, 1989).

Most vulnerable are the interconnection points between major ISPs, where there are no grounds at all for rejecting route advertisements. Even an ISP that serves a customer's networks cannot reject an advertisement for a route to those networks via one of its competitors—many larger sites are connected to more than one ISP.[24] Such multihoming becomes a mixed blessing, with the need to check accuracy, which causes traffic addressed from a subscriber net arriving via a different path to be suspect and rejected, being pitted against the increased availability that multihoming promises. Some ISPs are now installing BGP policy entries that define which parts of the Internet's address space neighbors can provide information about (with secondary route choices). However, this approach undermines the Internet's adaptive routing and affects overall survivability.

Somehow, the routing system must be secured against false advertisements. One approach is to authenticate messages a hop at a time. A number of such schemes have been proposed (Badger and Murphy, 1996; Hauser et al., 1997; Sirois and Kent, 1997; Smith et al., 1997), and a major router vendor (Cisco) has selected and deployed one in products. Unfor-

---

[23]In a few cases it actually is possible to reject inaccurate information. For example, an ISP will know what network addresses belong to its clients, and neighbors of such a router generally will believe that and start routing traffic to the ISP.

[24]The percentage of such multihomed sites in the Internet is currently low but appears to be rising, largely as a reliability measure by sites that cannot afford to be offline.

tunately, the hop-at-a-time approach is limited to ensuring that an authorized peer has sent a given message; nothing ensures that the message is accurate. The peer might have received an inaccurate message (from an authorized peer) or might itself be compromised. Thus, some attacks are prevented but others remain viable.

The alternative approach for securing the routing system against false advertisements is, somehow, for routers to employ global information about the Internet's topology. Advertisements that are inconsistent with that information are thus rejected. Schemes have been proposed (e.g., Perlman, 1988), but these do not appear to be practical for the Internet. Perlman's scheme, for example, requires source-controlled routing over the entire path. Routing protocol security is an active research area, and appropriately so.

Routing in the Internet is actually performed at two levels. Inside an autonomous system (AS)—a routing domain under the control of one organization—an interior routing protocol is executed by routers. Attacking these routers can affect large numbers of users, but wiretapping of these systems appears to be rare and therefore of limited concern.[25] Of potentially greater concern are attacks on BGP, the protocol used to distribute routing information among the autonomous ISPs around the world. Because BGP provides the basis for all Internet connectivity, a successful attack can have wide-ranging effects. As above, it is easy to secure BGP against false advertisements on a hop-at-a-time basis and difficult to employ global information about topology. Moreover, even if false advertisements could be discarded, successful attacks against BGP routers or against the workstations used to download configuration information into the BGP routers could still have devastating effects on Internet connectivity.

To secure BGP against a full range of attacks, a combination of security features involving both the routers and a supporting infrastructure

---

[25]Attacks against an interior routing protocol or against an organization's routers can deny or disrupt service to all of the hosts within that AS. If the AS is operated by an ISP, then the affected population can be substantial in size. Countermeasures to protect link state intradomain routing protocols have been developed (Murphy and Hofacker, 1996) but have not been deployed, primarily because of concerns about the computational overhead associated with the signing and verification of routing traffic (specifically, link state advertisements). Countermeasures for use with distance vector algorithms (e.g., DVRP) are even less well developed, although several proposals for such countermeasures have been published recently. Because all of the routers within an AS are under the control of the same administrative entity, and because there is little evidence of active wiretapping of intra-AS links, there may be a perception that the proposed cryptographic countermeasures are too expensive relative to the protection afforded.

needs to be developed and deployed. Each BGP router must be able to verify whether a routing update it receives is authentic and not a replay, or a previous, authentic update, where an authentic routing update is one that no attacker can modify (undetectably) and one for which the source of the update can be verified to be the "owner" of the portion of the IP address space being advertised.[26] Thus, implementing BGP security involves creating an infrastructure that codifies the assignment to organizations (e.g., ISPs, DSPs, subscribers) of AS numbers and portions of IP address space. Because of the BGP routing system's size (approximately 50,000 routes and 4,000 ISPs), deployment of these countermeasures is not a certainty. Moreover, after deployment some residual BGP vulnerabilities will still remain. For example, a router that is authorized to advertise a route to a network may suppress propagation of route withdrawal messages it receives, thus continuing to advertise the route for some time. But this can cause traffic to the network in question to be discarded.

It is worth noting that the routing system of the Internet closely mirrors call routing in the PTN, except that, in the PTN, a separate management and control network carries control functions. Any site on the Internet can participate in the global routing process, whereas subscribers in the PTN do not have direct access to the management and control network. The added vulnerabilities of the Internet derive from this lack of isolation. As network interconnections increase within the PTN, it may become vulnerable to the same sorts of attacks as the Internet is now.

Protocol Design and Implementation Flaws. The design and implementation of many Internet protocols make them vulnerable to a variety of denial-of-service attacks (Schuba et al., 1997). Some attacks exploit buggy code. These are perhaps the easiest to deal with; affected sites need only install newer or patched versions of the affected software. Other attacks exploit artifacts of particular implementations, such as limited storage areas, expensive algorithms, and the like. Again, updated code often can cure such problems.

The more serious class of attacks exploits features of certain protocols. For example, one type of attack exploits both the lack of source address verification and the connectionless nature of UDP to bounce packets between query servers on two target hosts (CERT Advisory CA-96.01). This process can continue almost indefinitely, until a packet happens to be dropped. And, while the process continues, computation and network bandwidth are consumed. The obvious remedy would be for hosts to detect this attack or any such denial-of-service attack, much the same way

---

[26]Because of the route and address aggregation features of BGP, the route verification requirements are even more complex than described here.

virus-screening software detects and removes viruses. But, if it is cheaper for an attacker to send a packet than it is for a target to check it, then denial of service is inevitable from the sheer volume of packets. Even cryptography is not a cure: authenticating a putatively valid packet is much harder (it requires substantial CPU resources) than generating a stream of bytes with a random authentication check value to send the victim.[27]

Findings

1. New countermeasures for name server attacks are needed that work well in large-scale, heterogeneous environments.

2. Cryptography, while not in itself sufficient, is essential to the protection of both the Internet and its end points. Wider deployment of cryptography is needed. Algorithms for authentication only are largely free from export and usage restrictions, yet they can go a long way toward helping.

3. Cryptographic mechanisms to secure the DNS do exist; however, deployment to date has been limited.

4. No effective means exist to secure routing protocols, especially on backbone routers. Research in this area is urgently needed.

5. Attacks that result in denial of service are increasingly common. Wider use of updated software and patches, new product development, and better software engineering are needed to deal with this problem.

EMERGING ISSUES

Internet Telephony

What are the security implications if, as predicted by many pundits, today's traditional telephone network is replaced by an Internet-based transport mechanism? Will telephony become even less secure, owing to all the security problems with the Internet discussed earlier in this chapter? Or will some portion of the Internet used only for telephony be resistant to many of the problems described in the preceding sections?

Recall that many current PTN vulnerabilities are related either to the services being provided or to the physical transport layer. Rehosting the PTN on the Internet will have no effect on these vulnerabilities. Thus, the OSSs and database lookups related to advanced PTN services, with their

---

[27]Encryption is even worse in this regard, as the cost of decryption is often greater than the cost of authentication and because a receiver might have to both decrypt and authenticate a packet to determine if it is valid. The Encapsulating Security Payload (ESP) protocol of IPsec counters this denial-of-service vulnerability by reversing the order in which these operations are applied (i.e., a receiver authenticates ciphertext prior to decrypting it).

associated vulnerabilities, would be unaffected by the move to an Internet-based telephone system. Similarly, if access to the Internet-based telephone system is accomplished by means of twisted pairs (albeit twisted pairs carrying something like integrated services digital network (ISDN) or asymmetric digital subscriber line (ADSL)), then interconnections of some sort will still be needed. These would likely be routers or switches, but such interconnections are at least as programmable and at least as vulnerable.

Call routing in an Internet-based telephone system would be different, but likely no more secure. At the very least, IP routing would be involved. Most probably, a new database would be introduced to map telephone numbers to domain names or IP addresses. Both, of course, raise serious security and reliability concerns.

In at least two respects, both noted earlier in this chapter, an Internet-based telephone system could be significantly more vulnerable to attack than today's PTN. The primary active elements of an Internet-based network—the routers—are, by design, accessible from the network they control, and the network's routing protocols execute in-band with the communications they control. By contrast, virtually the entire PTN is now managed by out-of-band channels. Considerable care will be needed to deliver the security of out-of-band control by using in-band communications. The other obvious weakness of the Internet is its end points, personal computers and servers, because attacks on them can be used to attack the telephone system.

Finding

The PTN is likely to become more vulnerable with the rise of Internet telephony, most notably because Internet-based networks use in-band channels for routing and have end points that are prone to failure. Attention to these issues is needed.

Is the Internet Ready for "Prime Time"?

Whether the Internet is "ready for business" depends on the requirements of the business. There are already numerous examples of businesses using the Internet for advertising, marketing, sales of products and services, coordination with business partners, and various other activities. On the other hand, the Internet is also viewed—and rightly so—as being less reliable and less secure than the PTN. Specifically, the Internet is perceived as more susceptible to interception (i.e., eavesdropping) and has proved to be more susceptible to active attacks (e.g., server flooding,

Web site modification). Consequently, most Internet-savvy business users restrict what they entrust to the Internet.

The Internet is also more prone to outages than the PTN. Thus, it would be unwise for utility companies and other critical infrastructure providers to abandon the PTN and rely on remote access through the Internet for controlling power distribution substations, because individual ISPs are less likely than individual telephone companies to survive local power interruptions.[28]

Few established businesses seem willing to forgo their telephone order centers for Internet-only access, although a small and growing number of newer businesses, such as Virtual Vineyards and Amazon.com, do maintain an Internet-only presence. Abandoning the PTN for the Internet seems unwise for businesses such as brokerage houses or mail-order catalog companies, where continued availability of service is critical. For example, during the stock market frenzy on October 27-28, 1997, customers of Internet-based brokerage systems experienced unusual delays in executing trades. But the magnitude of their delays was relatively small and was commensurate with the delays suffered by telephone-based access and even some of the stock market's back-end systems. Still, it is sobering to contemplate the effect of an Internet-related failure that coincided with a spike in market activity.

Mail-order firms, brokerage houses, and others do make extensive use of the Internet as an avenue of customer access. But it is not the only avenue of access, and neither the customers nor the business have become wholly dependent on it. If, for example, these and similar businesses reduced their other avenues of access (e.g., to save money), then an Internet outage could have a significant impact. Consider a scenario in which banks acquire the capability to download customer money onto smart cards through the Internet. Over time, banks might reduce the number of automatic teller machines available (just as the numbers of physical bank branches and tellers have fallen as automated teller machines have proliferated). A prolonged failure of this Internet cash distribution mechanism could overload the few remaining available machines and tellers.

In theory, the risks associated with using the Internet can be evaluated and factored into a risk management model (see Chapter 6). Most businesses, however, are not fully cognizant of these risks nor of the return on investments in protection. As a result, the level of protection

---

[28]Internet service providers have differing plans for dealing with power system failures, which may make it impossible to access computers and data following such a failure. The failure need not even be widespread. By contrast, telephone networks are under central control, can easily implement backup power systems, and require very little electrical current for an ordinary telephone line.

adopted by many business users of the Internet does not seem commensurate with that afforded their physical assets. For example, it seems as though the quality of burglar alarms and physical access control systems deployed by most businesses is considerably higher than the level of Internet security countermeasures they deploy (see Chapter 4).

Moreover, businesses that make extensive use of Internet technology may do so in a fashion that externalizes the risks associated with such use. If infrastructure suppliers, such as telephone companies and electric and gas utilities, do not take adequate precautions to ensure the availability of their systems in the face of malicious attacks over the Internet, then the public will bear the brunt of the failure. Because many of these businesses operate in what is effectively a monopoly environment, the free-market forces that should eventually correct such cost externalization may not be effective.

Of particular concern is that most of the security countermeasures adopted by businesses connecting to the Internet are designed only to thwart the most common attacks used by hackers. Most hackers, however, are opportunistic and display only a limited repertoire of skills. Protection against that hacker threat is insufficient for warding off more capable, determined threats, such as criminals or terrorists.

And while in one sense the Internet poses no new challenges—a system that can be accessed from outside only through a cryptographically protected channel on the Internet is at least as secure as the same system reached through a conventional leased line—new dangers arise precisely because of pervasive interconnectivity. The capability to interconnect networks gives the Internet much of its power; by the same token, it opens up serious new risks. An attacker who may be deflected by cryptographic protection of the front door can often attack a less protected administrative system and use its connectivity through internal networks to bypass the encryption unit protecting the real target. This often makes a mockery of firewall-based protection.

Findings

1. The Internet is ready for some business use, but it is not at a point where it would be prudent for businesses to abandon the PTN in favor of the Internet. For managing critical infrastructures, the Internet is too susceptible to attacks and outages to be a viable basis for control.

2. Risk management, especially to guard against highly skilled attackers, deserves further attention in the business community.

REFERENCES

Badger, M.R., and S.L. Murphy. 1996. "Digital Signature Protection of the OSPF Routing Protocol," pp. 93-102 in *Proceedings of the Symposium on Network and Distributed System Security*. Los Alamitos, CA: IEEE Computer Society Press.

Bellovin, Steven M. 1989. "Security Problems in the TCP/IP Protocol Suite," *Computer Communications Review*, 19(2):32-48.

Bellovin, Steven M. 1995. "Using the Domain Name System for System Break-ins," pp. 199-208 in *Proceedings of the 5th USENIX UNIX Security Symposium, Salt Lake City, Utah*. Berkeley, CA: USENIX Association.

Berners-Lee, T., and D. Connolly. 1995. *Hypertext Markup Language—2.0*. RFC 1866. November.

Berners-Lee, T., L. Masinter, and M. McCahill. 1994. *Uniform Resource Locators (URL)*. RFC 1738. December.

Berners-Lee, T., R. Fielding, and H. Frystyk. 1996. *Hypertext Transfer Protocol—HTTP 1.0*. RFC 1945. May.

Blaze, Matt. 1996. *Afterword*. 2nd Ed. *Applied Cryptography*, Bruce Schneier, ed. New York: John Wiley & Sons.

Bolt, Beranek, and Newman (BBN). 1978. "Appendix H: Interfacing a Host to a Private Line Interface," *Specification for the Interconnection of a Host and an IMP*. BBN Report 1822. Cambridge, MA: BBN, May.

Braden, R., L. Zhang, S. Berson, S. Herzog, and S. Jamin. 1997. *Resource ReSerVation Protocol (RSVP)—Version 1 Functional Specification*. RFC 2205. September.

Case, J.D., M. Fedor, M.L. Schoffstall, and C. Davin. 1990. *Simple Network Management Protocol (SNMP)*. RFC 1157. May.

Computer Science and Telecommunications Board (CSTB), National Research Council. 1997. *The Evolution of Untethered Communications*. Washington, DC: National Academy Press.

Cooper, Brinton. 1989. "Phone Hacking," *RISKS Digest*, Vol. 8, Issue 79, June 14. Available online at <http://catless.ncl.ac.uk/Risks/8.79.html#subj4>.

Dusse, S., P. Hoffman, and B. Ramsdell. 1998a. *S/MIME Version 2 Certificate Handling*. RFC 2312. March.

Dusse, S., P. Hoffman, B. Ramsdell, L. Lundblade, and L. Repka. 1998b. *S/MIME Version 2 Message Specification*. RFC 2311. March.

Eastlake, D., and C. Kaufman. 1997. *Domain Name System Security Extensions*. RFC 2065. January.

Fielding, R., J. Gettys, J. Mogul, H. Frystyk, and T. Berners-Lee. 1997. *Hypertext Transfer Protocol—HTTP 1.1*. RFC 2068. January.

Floyd, S., and K. Fall. 1998. "Promoting the Use of End-to-End Congestion Control in the Internet," *IEEE/ACM Transactions on Networking*. Available online at <ftp://ftp.ee.lbl.gov/papers/collapse.feb98.ps>.

Floyd, S., and V. Jacobson. 1993. "Random Early Detection Gateways for Congestion Avoidance," *IEEE/ACM Transactions on Networking*, 1(4):397-413.

Garfinkel, S., and E. Spafford. 1996. *Practical UNIX and Internet Security*. Newton, MA: O'Reilly and Associates.

Hauser, R., T. Przygienda, and G. Tsudik. 1997. "Reducing the Cost of Security in Link-State Routing," pp. 93-101 in *Proceedings of the Symposium on Network and Distributed System Security*. Los Alamitos, CA: IEEE Computer Society Press.

Howard, John D. 1997. "An Analysis of Security Incidents on the Internet 1989-1995," Ph.D. thesis, Department of Engineering and Public Policy, Carnegie Mellon University, Pittsburgh, PA.

Ioannidis, John, and Matt Blaze. 1993. "The Architecture and Implementation of Network Layer Security in UNIX," pp. 29-39 in *Security IV, Santa Clara, California*. Berkeley, CA: USENIX Association.

Jacobson, V. 1988. "Congestion Avoidance Control," pp. 314-329 in *SIGCOMM 88, Stanford California*. Los Alamitos, CA: IEEE Computer Society.

Kahn, David. 1976. *The Code Breakers*. 8th Ed. New York: Macmillan.

Kristol, D., and L. Montulli. 1997. *HTTP State Management Mechanism*. RFC 2109. February.

McQuillan, J.M., and D.C. Walden. 1977. "The ARPA Network Design Decisions," *Computer Networks*, August, pp. 243-289.

Mills, D.L. 1984. *Exterior Gateway Protocol Formal Specification*. RFC 904. April.

Mills, Mike. 1998. "AT&T High Speed Network Fails: Red Cross, Banks Scramble to Adjust," *Washington Post*, April 14, p. C1.

Mockapetris, P.V. 1987a. *Domain Names—Concepts and Facilities*. RFC 1034. November.

Mockapetris, P.V. 1987b. *Domain Names—Implementation and Specification*. RFC 1035. November.

Morris, Robert T. 1985. *A Weakness in the 4.2 BSD UNIX TCP/IP Software*. Murray Hill, NJ: AT&T Bell Laboratories, February.

Murphy, Jamie, and Charlie Hofacker. 1996. "Explosive Growth Clogs the Internet's Backbone," *New York Times*, July 3.

Network Reliability and Interoperability Council (NRIC). 1996. *Network Reliability: The Path Forward*. Washington, DC: Federal Communications Commission. Available online at <www.fcc.gov/oet/info/orgs/nrc/>.

Network Reliability and Interoperability Council (NRIC). 1997. *Final Report of the Network Reliability and Interoperability Council*. Washington, DC: Federal Communications Commission, July 15.

Parasuraman, Raja, and Mustapha Mouloua, eds. 1996. *Automation and Human Performance: Theory and Applications*. Mahwah, NJ: Lawrence Erlbaum Associates.

Perillo, Robert J. 1997. "AT&T Database Glitch Caused '800' Phone Outage," *Telecom Digest*, Vol. 17, Issue 253, September 18. Available online at <http://massis.lcs.mit.edu/telecom-archives/archives/back issues/1997.volume.17/vol17.iss251-300>.

Perlman, Radia. 1988. "Network Layer Protocols with Byzantine Robustness," Ph.D. thesis, Computer Science Department, Massachusetts Institute of Technology, Cambridge, MA.

Postel, J. 1982. *Simple Mail Transfer Protocol*. RFC 821. August.

Rekhter, Y., and P. Gross. 1995. *Application of the Border Gateway Protocol in the Internet*. RFC 1772. March.

Rekhter, Y., and T. Li. 1995. *A Border Gateway Protocol 4 (BGP-4)*. RFC 1771. March.

Schuba, Christoph L., Ivan Krsul, Markus G. Kuhn, Eugene H. Spafford, Aurobindo Sundaram, and Diego Zamboni. 1997. "Analysis of a Denial of Service Attack on TCP," pp. 208-233 in *Proceedings of 1997 IEEE Symposium on Security and Privacy*. Los Alamitos, CA: IEEE Computer Society Press.

Shenker, S., and J. Wroclawski. 1997. *General Characterization Parameters for Integrated Service Network Elements*. RFC 2215. September.

Sirois, K.E., and Stephen T. Kent. 1997. "Securing the Nimrod Routing Architecture," pp. 74-84 in *Proceedings of the Annual Internet Society (ISOC) Symposium on Network and Distributed System Security*. Los Alamitos, CA: IEEE Computer Society Press.

Smith, B.R., S. Murthy, and J.J. Garcia-Luna-Aceves. 1997. "Securing Distance-Vector Routing Protocols," pp. 85-92 in *Proceedings of the Annual Internet Society (ISOC) Symposium on Network and Distributed System Security*. Los Alamitos, CA: IEEE Computer Society Press.

Stevens, W. 1997. *TCP Slow Start, Congestion Avoidance, Fast Retransmit, and Fast Recovery Algorithms.* RFC 2001. January.

Thompson, Kevin, George J. Miller, and Rick Wilder. 1997. "Wide-Area Internet Traffic Patterns and Characteristics," *IEEE Network,* 11(6):10-23.

Traina, P. 1993. *Experience with the BGP-4 Protocol.* RFC 1773. March.

Traina, P. 1995. *BGP-4 Protocol Analysis.* RFC 1774. March.

Wall Street Journal. 1997. "An Internet Stunt Causes Trouble for Kashpureff," November 4.

Weissman, Clark. 1992. "Blacker: Security for the DDN: Examples of A1 Security Engineering Trades," pp. 286-292 in *Proceedings of the 1992 IEEE Symposium on Security and Privacy.* Los Alamitos, CA: IEEE Computer Society Press.

Wickens, Christopher D., Anne S. Mavor, and James P. McGee, eds. 1997. *Flight to the Future: Human Factors in Air Traffic Control.* Washington, DC: National Academy Press.

Zimmerman, Philip R. 1995. *The Official PGP User's Guide.* Cambridge, MA: MIT Press.

3

Software for Networked Information Systems

INTRODUCTION

Background

Computing power is becoming simultaneously cheaper and more dispersed. General-purpose computers and access to global information sources are increasingly commonplace on home and office desktops. Perhaps most striking is the exploding popularity of the World Wide Web. A Web browser can interact with any Web site, and Web sites offer a wide variety of information and services. A less visible consequence of cheap, dispersed computing is the ease with which special-purpose networked information systems (NISs) can now be built.

An NIS built to support the activities of a health care provider, such as a medium-sized health maintenance organization (HMO) serving a wide geographic area, is used as an illustration here and throughout this chapter. HMO services might include maintenance of patient records, support for administration of hospitals and clinics, and support for equipment in laboratories. The NIS would, therefore, comprise computer systems in hospital departments (such as radiology, pathology, and pharmacy), in neighborhood clinics, and in centralized data centers. By integrating these individual computer systems into an NIS, the HMO management would expect both to reduce costs and to increase the quality of patient care. For instance, although data and records—such as laboratory test results, x-ray or other images, and treatment logs—previously might have traveled independently, the information now can be transmitted and accessed together.

In building an NIS for an HMO, management is likely to have chosen a "Web-centric" implementation using the popular protocols and facilities of the World Wide Web and the Internet. Such a decision would be sensible for the following reasons:

- The basic elements of the system, such as Web servers and browsers, can now be commercial off-the-shelf (COTS) components and, therefore, are available at low cost.
- A large, growing pool of technical personnel is familiar with the Web-centric approach, so the project will not become dependent on a small number of individuals with detailed knowledge of locally written software.
- The technology holds promise for extensions into consumer telemedicine, whereby patients and health care providers interact by using the same techniques as are commonly used on the rest of the Internet.

Clearly, the HMO's NIS must exhibit trustworthiness: it must engender feelings of confidence and trust in those whose lives it affects. Physicians must be confident that the system will display the medical record of the patient they are seeing when it is needed and will not lose information; patients must be confident that physician-entered prescriptions will be properly transmitted and executed; and all must be confident that the privacy of records will not be compromised. Achieving this trustworthiness, however, is not easy.

NIS trustworthiness mechanisms basically concern events that are not supposed to happen. Nonmalicious users living in a benign and fault-free world would be largely unaffected were such mechanisms removed from a system. But some users may be malicious, and the world is not fault free. Consequently, reliability, availability, security and all other facets of trustworthiness require mechanisms to foster the necessary trust on the part of users and other affected parties. Only with their failure or absence do trustworthiness mechanisms assume importance to a system's users. Users seem unable to evaluate the costs of not having trustworthiness mechanisms except when they experience actual damage from incidents (see Chapter 6 for an extended discussion). So, while market forces can help foster the deployment of trustworthiness mechanisms, these forces are unlikely to do so in advance of directly experienced or highly publicized violations of trustworthiness properties.

Although the construction of trustworthy NISs is today in its infancy, lessons can be learned from experience in building full-authority and other freestanding, high-consequence computing systems for applications such as industrial process control and medical instrumentation. In such systems, one or more computers directly control processes or devices whose malfunction could lead to significant loss of property or life. Even systems in which human intervention is required for initiating potentially dangerous events can become high-consequence systems when human users or operators place too much trust in the information being displayed by the computing system.[1] To be sure, there are differences between NISs and traditional high-consequence computing systems. An intent of this chapter is to identify those differences and to point out lessons from high-consequence systems that can be applied to NISs, as well as unique attributes of NISs that will require new research.

The Role of Software

Software plays a major role in achieving the trustworthiness of an NIS, because it is software that integrates and customizes general-purpose components for some task at hand. In fact, the role of software in an NIS is typically so pervasive that the responsibilities of a software engineer differ little from those of a systems engineer. NIS software developers must therefore possess a systems viewpoint,[2] and systems engineers must be intimately familiar with the strengths (and, more importantly, the limitations) of software technology.

With software playing such a pervasive role, defects can have far-reaching consequences. It is notoriously difficult to write defect-free software, as the list of incidents in, for example, Leveson (1987) or Neumann (1995) confirms. Beyond the intrinsic difficulty of writing defect-free software, there are constraints that result from the nature of NISs. These constraints derive from schedule and budget; they mean that a software developer has only limited freedom in selecting the elements of the software system and in choosing a development process:

• An NIS is likely to employ commercial operating systems, purchased "middleware," and other applications, as well as special-purpose code developed specifically for the NIS. The total source code size for the system could range from tens to hundreds of millions of lines. In this setting, it is infeasible to start from scratch in order to support trustworthiness.

---

[1]This is a particularly dangerous state of affairs, since designers may assume that system operation is being monitored, when in fact it is not (Leveson, 1995).

[2]Once succinctly stated as, "You are not in this alone." That is, that you need to consider not only the narrow functioning of your component but also how it interacts with other components, users, and the physical world in achieving system-level goals. Another aspect of the "systems viewpoint" is a healthy respect for the potential of unexpected side effects.

• Future NISs will, of necessity, evolve from the current ones. There is no alternative, given the size of the systems, their complexity, and the need to include existing services in new systems. Techniques for supporting trustworthiness must take this diversity of origin into account. It cannot be assumed that NISs will be conceived and developed without any reuse of existing artifacts. Moreover, components reused in NISs include legacy components that were not designed with such reuse in mind; they tend to be large systems or subsystems having nonstandard and often inconvenient interfaces. In the HMO example, clinical laboratories and pharmacies are likely to have freestanding computerized information systems that exemplify such legacy systems.

• Commercial off-the-shelf software components must be used to control development cost, development time, and project risk. A commercial operating system with a variety of features can be purchased for a few hundred dollars, so development of specialized operating systems is uneconomical in almost all circumstances. But the implication is that achieving and assessing the trustworthiness of a networked information system necessarily occur in an environment including COTS software components (operating systems, database systems, networks, compilers, and other system tools) with only limited access to internals or control over their design.

• Finally, the design of NIS software is likely to be dictated—at least, in part—by outside influences such as regulations, standards, organizational structure, and organizational culture. These outside influences can lead to system architectures that aggravate the problems of providing trustworthiness. For example, in a medical information system, good security practices require that publicly accessible terminals be logged off from the system after relatively short periods of inactivity so that an unauthorized individual who happens upon an unattended terminal cannot use it. But in emergency rooms, expecting a practitioner to log in periodically is inconsistent with the urgency of emergency care that should be supported by an NIS in this setting.

Fortunately, success in building an NIS does not depend on writing software that is completely free of defects. Systems can be designed so that only certain core functionality must be defect free; defects in other parts of the system, although perhaps annoying, become tolerable because their impact is limited by the defect-free core functionality. It now is feasible to contemplate a system having millions of lines of source code and embracing COTS and legacy components, since only a fraction of the code has to be defect free. Of course, that approach to design does depend on being able to determine or control how the effects of defects propagate. Various approaches to software design can be seen as providing artillery for attacking the problem, but none has proved a panacea. There is still no substitute for talented and experienced designers.

Development of a Networked Information System

The development of an NIS proceeds in phases that are similar to the phases of development for other computerized information systems:

- Decide on the structure or architecture of the system.
- Build and acquire components.
- Integrate the components into a working and trustworthy whole.

The level of detail at which the development team works forms a V-shaped curve. Effort starts at the higher, systems level, then dips down into details as individual software components are implemented and tested, and finally returns to the system level as the system is integrated into a cohesive whole.

Of the three phases, the last is the most problematic. Development teams often find themselves in the integration phase with components that work separately but not together. Theoretically, an NIS can grow by accretion, with service nodes and client nodes being added at will. The problem is that (as illustrated by the Internet) it is difficult to ensure that the system as a whole will exhibit desired global properties and, in particular, trustworthiness properties. On the one hand, achieving a level of connectivity and other basic services is relatively easy. These are the services that general-purpose components, such as routers, servers, and browsers, are designed to provide. And even though loads on networks and demands on servers are hard to predict, adverse outcomes are readily overcome by the addition or upgrade of general-purpose components. On the other hand, the consequences of failures or security breaches propagating through the system are hard to predict, to prevent, and to analyze when they do occur. Thus, basic services are relatively simple to provide, whereas global and specialized services and properties—especially those supporting trustworthiness—are difficult to provide.

SYSTEM PLANNING, REQUIREMENTS, AND TOP-LEVEL DESIGN

Planning and Program Management

A common first step in any development project is to produce a planning and a requirements document. The planning document contains information about budget and schedules. Cost estimation and scheduling are hard to do accurately, so producing a planning document is not a straightforward exercise. Just how much time a large project will require, how many staff members it will need (and when), and how much it will cost cannot today be estimated with precision. The techniques that exist, such as the constructive cost model (COCOMO) (Boehm, 1981), are only as good as the data given them and the suitability of their models for a given project. Estimation is further complicated if novel designs and the implementation of novel features are attempted, practices common in software development and especially common in leading-edge applications such as an NIS.

Although every attempt might be made to employ standard components (e.g., operating system, network, Web browsers, database management systems, and user-interface generators) in building an NIS, the ways in which the components are used are likely to be sufficiently novel that generalizing from past experiences with the components may be useless for estimating project costs and schedules. For example, it is not hard to connect browsers through a network to a server and then display what is on the server, but the result does not begin to be a medical records system, with its varied and often subtle trustworthiness requirements concerning patient privacy and data integrity. The basic services are even farther from a complete telemedicine system, which must be trusted to correctly convey patient data to experts and their diagnoses back to paramedical personnel. All in all, confidence in budget and schedule estimates for an NIS, as for any engineering artifact, can be high only when the new system is similar to systems that already have been built. Such similarity is rare in the software world and is likely to be even rarer in the nascent field of NIS development.

The difficulties of cost estimation and scheduling explain why some projects are initiated with unrealistic schedules and assignments of staff and equipment. The problem is compounded in commercial product development (as opposed to specialized, one-of-a-kind system development) by marketing concerns. For software-intensive products, early arrival in the marketplace is often critical to success in that marketplace. This means that software development practice becomes distorted to maximize functionality and minimize development time, with little attention paid to other qualities. Thus, functionality takes precedence over trustworthiness.

A major difficulty in project management is coping with ambiguous and changing requirements. It is unrealistic to expect correct and complete knowledge of requirements at the start of a project. Requirements change as system development proceeds and the system, and its environment, become better understood. Moreover, software frequently is regarded (incorrectly) as something that can be changed easily at any point during development, and software change requests then become routine. The effect of the changes, however, can be traumatic and lead to design compromises that affect trustworthiness.

Another difficulty in project management is selecting, tailoring, and implementing the development process that will be used. The Waterfall development process (Pressman, 1986), in which each phase of the life cycle is completed before the next begins, oversimplifies. So, when the Waterfall process is used, engineers must deviate from it in ad hoc ways. Nevertheless, organizations ignore better processes, such as the Spiral model (Boehm, 1988; Boehm and DeMarco, 1997), which incorporates control and feedback mechanisms to deal with interaction of the life-cycle phases.

Also contributing to difficulties in project management and planning is the high variance in capabilities and productivity that has been documented for different software engineers (Curtis, 1981). An order-of-magnitude variation in productivity is not uncommon between the most and the least productive programmers. Estimating schedules, assigning manpower, and managing a project under such circumstances are obviously difficult tasks.

Finally, the schedule and cost for a project can be affected by unanticipated defects or limitations in the software tools being employed. For example, a flawed compiler might not implement certain language features correctly or might not implement certain combinations of language features correctly. Configuration management tools (e.g., Rochkind, 1975) provide other opportunities for unanticipated schedule and cost perturbation. For use in an NIS, a configuration management tool not only must track changes in locally developed software components but also must keep track of vendor updates to COTS components.

None of the difficulties are new revelations. Brooks, in his classic work *The Mythical Man Month* (Brooks, 1975), noted similar problems more than two decades ago. It is both significant and a cause for concern that this book remains relevant today as evidenced by the recent publication of a special 20th anniversary edition. The difficulties, however, become even more problematic within the context of large and complex NISs.

Requirements at the Systems Level

Background

There is ample evidence that the careful use of established techniques in the development of large software systems can improve their quality. Yet many development organizations do not employ techniques that have been known for years to contribute to success. Nowhere is this refusal to learn the lessons of history more pronounced than with respect to requirements documents.

Whether an NIS or a simple computer game is being implemented, a requirements document is useful. In special-purpose systems, it forms a contract between the customer and the developer by stating what the customer wants and thereby what the developer must build. In projects aimed at producing commercial products, it converts marketing and business objectives into technical terms. In the development of large systems, it serves as a vehicle for communication among the various engineering disciplines involved. And it also serves as a vehicle for communication between different software engineers responsible for developing software, as well as between the software engineers and those responsible for presenting the software to the outside world, such as a marketing team.

It is all too common, however, to proceed with system development without first analyzing and documenting requirements. In fact, requirements analysis and documentation are sometimes viewed as unnecessary or misdirected activities, since they do not involve creating executable code and are thought to increase time to market. Can system requirements not be learned by inspecting the system itself? Requirements derived by such a posteriori inspections, however, run the risk of being incomplete and inaccurate. It is not always possible to determine a posteriori which elements of an interface are integral and which are incidental to a particular implementation. In the absence of a requirements document, project staff must maintain a mental picture of the requirements in order to respond to questions about what should or could be implemented. Each putative requirements change must still be analyzed and negotiated, only now the debate occurs out of context and risks overlooking relevant information. Such an approach might be adequate for small systems, but it breaks down for systems having the size and complexity of an NIS.

The System Requirements Document

The system requirements document states in as much detail as possible what the system should (and should not) do. To be useful for designers and implementers, a requirements document should be organized as a reference work. That is, it should be arranged so that one can quickly find the answer to a detailed question (e.g., What should go into an admissions form?). Such a structure, more like a dictionary than a textbook, makes it difficult for persons unfamiliar with the project to grasp how the NIS is supposed to work. As a consequence, requirements documents are supplemented (and often supplanted) with a concept of operations

(Conops) that describes, usually in the form of scenarios (so-called "use cases"), the operation of the NIS. A Conops for the example HMO system might, for example, trace the computer operations that support a patient from visiting a doctor at a neighborhood clinic, through diagnosis of a condition requiring hospitalization, admission and treatment at the hospital, discharge, and follow-up visits to the original clinic. Other scenarios in the Conops might include home monitoring of chronic conditions, emergency room visits, and so forth. The existence of two documents covering the same ground raises the possibility of inconsistencies. When they occur, it is usually the Conops that governs, because the Conops is the document typically read (and understood) by the sponsors of the project.

Review and approval of system requirements documents may involve substantial organizational interaction and compromise when once-independent systems are networked and required to support overall organizational (as opposed to specific departmental) objectives. The compromises can be driven more by organizational dynamics than by technical factors, a situation that may lead to a failure to meet basic objectives later on. That risk is heightened in the case of the trustworthiness requirements, owing (as is discussed below) to the difficulty of expressing such requirements and compounded by the difficulty of predicting the consequences of requiring certain features. In the case of the HMO system, for example, advocates for consumer telemedicine might insist on home computer access to the network in ways that are incompatible with maintaining even minimal medical records secrecy in the face of typical hackers. Anticipating and dealing with such a problem require predicting what sorts of attacks could be mounted, what defenses might be available in COTS products, and how attacks will propagate through an NIS whose detailed design might not be known for several years. Making the worst-case assumption (i.e., all COTS products are completely vulnerable and all defenses must be mounted through the locally developed software of the NIS) will likely lead to unacceptable development costs. Similar situations arise for other dimensions of trustworthiness, such as data integrity or availability.

Notation and Style

Requirements documents are written first in ordinary English, which is notorious for imprecision and ambiguity. Most industrial developers do not use even semiformal specification notations, such as the SCR/A7 tabular technique (Heninger, 1980). The principal reason for using natural language (in addition to the cynical observation that without ambiguity there can be no consensus) is that, despite significant R&D investment in the 1970s (Ross, 1977), no notation for system-level requirements has shown sufficiently commanding advantages to achieve dominant acceptance.

Finally, many— if not most—software developers are forced to lead "unexamined lives." The demand for their services is so great that they must move from one project to the next without an opportunity for reflection or consideration of alternatives to the approaches they used before. The paradoxical result of this situation is that the process of developing software, which has had revolutionary impact on many aspects of society and technology, is itself quite slow to change.

One common strategy for coping with the problems inherent in natural language is to divide the requirements into two classes: criteria for success (often called "objectives" or "goals") and criteria for failure (sometimes called "absolute requirements"). The criteria for success can be a matter of degree: situations where "more is better" without clear cutoff points. The criteria for failure are absolute—conditions, such as causing a fatality, that render success in other areas irrelevant. In the HMO example, a criterion for success might be the time needed to transfer a medical record from the hospital to an outpatient facility—quicker is better, but unless some very unlikely delays are experienced, the system is acceptable. A criterion for failure might be inaccessibility of information about a patient's drug allergies. If the patient dies from an allergic reaction that could have been prevented by the timely delivery of drug allergy data, then nothing else the system has done right (such as the smoothness of admission, proper assignment of diagnostic codes, or the correct interfacing with the insurance carrier) really matters.

It is often posited that requirements should state what a particular criterion is but not how that criterion should be achieved. In real-world systems development, this dictum can lead to unnecessarily convoluted and indirect formulations of requirements. The issue is illustrated by turning to building codes, which are a kind of requirements document. Building codes distinguish between performance specifications and design specifications. A performance specification states, "Interior walls should resist heat of x degrees for y minutes." A design specification states, "Interior walls should use 5/8-inch Type X sheetrock." Performance specifications leave more room for innovation, but determining whether they have been satisfied is more difficult. Design specifications tend to freeze the development of technology by closing the market to innovations, but it is a simple matter to determine whether any given design specification has been fulfilled. More realistic guidance for what belongs in a requirements document is the following: If it defines either failure or success, it belongs in the requirements document, no matter how specific or detailed it is.

A distinction is sometimes made between functional requirements and nonfunctional requirements. When this distinction is made, functional requirements are concerned with services that the system should provide and are usually stated in terms of the system's interfaces; nonfunctional requirements define constraints on the development process, the structure of the system, or resources used during execution (Sommerville, 1996). For example, a description of expected system outputs in response to various inputs would be considered a functional requirement. Stipulations that structured design be employed during system development, that average system response time be bounded by some value, or that the system be safe or secure exemplify nonfunctional requirements.

Nonfunctional requirements concerning execution theoretically can be translated into functional requirements. Doing that translation requires knowledge of system structure and internals. The resulting inferred functional requirements may concern internal system interfaces that not only are unmentioned in the original functional requirements but also may not yet be known. Moreover, performing the translation invariably will involve transforming informal notions, such as "secure," "reliable," or "safe," into precise requirements that can be imposed on the internals and interfaces of individual modules. Formalizing informal properties at all and decomposing systemwide global properties into properties that must be satisfied by individual components are technically very challenging tasks—tasks often beyond the state of the art (Abadi and Lamport, 1993; McLean, 1994).

Where to Focus Effort in Requirements Analysis and Documentation

The process of requirements analysis is complicated by the fact that any NIS is part of some larger system with which it interacts. An understanding of the application domain itself and mastery of a variety of engineering disciplines other than software engineering may be necessary to perform requirements analysis for an NIS. Identification of system vulnerabilities is one process for which a broad understanding of the larger system context (including users, operators, and the physical environment) is particularly important. Techniques have been developed to deal with some of these issues. Modeling techniques, such as structured analysis (Constantine and Yourdon, 1979), have been developed for constructing system descriptions that can be analyzed and reviewed by customers. Rapid prototyping tools (Tanik et al., 1989) offer a means to answer specific questions about the requirements for a new system, and prototyping is today a popular way to determine user interface requirements. Systematic techniques have been developed for determining application requirements by either interviewing application experts or observing the actions of potential users of the system (Potts et al., 1994).

Interviews conducted in the 1970s with experienced project managers revealed their skepticism about making significant investments in system-level requirements documents (Honeywell Corporation, 1975). Those veterans of large-scale aerospace and defense projects believed that any significant efforts regarding requirements should be directed to the level of subsystems or components. They argued that system-level requirements documents were seldom consulted after detailed component-level requirements were written. Change—sometimes significant change—in system-level requirements was quite common and rendered obsolete a system-level requirements document.

Changes in requirements originate from a variety of sources:

• The outside environment may change—the example HMO could merge, restructure, or be affected by new statutory or regulatory forces.
• The advent of new technology could generate a desire for the enhanced capability that the technology provides. This factor would be amplified for the HMO's NIS by the current rapid development pace of Internet-related technology (so-called Internet time) and the false perception that components and features can be added to an NIS with relative ease.

Requirements errors are the most expensive to fix, because they typically are not found until significant resources have been invested in system design, implementation, and, in some cases, testing and deployment. The high cost of repairing such errors would then justify expending additional resources on systems requirements analysis and documentation. But that argument is incomplete, for it presumes that the additional expenditures could prevent such errors. Published (Glass, 1981[3]) and unpublished (Honeywell Corporation, 1975) studies of requirements errors indicate that errors of omission are the most common. Experienced program managers, who have internalized the experience of unpleasant surprises resulting from combinations of inputs and internal states (or other phenomena that were thought to be impossible), understand that no amount of effort is likely to produce a complete requirements document.

Resources expended in requirements analysis and documentation are, nevertheless, usually well spent. The activity helps a system's developers to better understand the problem they are attacking. Design and coding

---

[3]This reference contains the classic "Reason for Error" entry in a trouble report: "Insufficient brain power applied during design."

decisions are thus delayed until a clearer picture of needs and constraints has emerged. It is not the documentation but the insight that is the important work product. Conceivably, other techniques could be developed for acquiring this insight. However, systems requirements documents serve also for communication within a project team as well as with customers and suppliers; any alternative technique would have to address this need as well.

Doing a bad job at requirements analysis actually can have harmful long-term repercussions for a development effort. Requirements analysis invariably goes astray when analysts are insufficiently familiar with the anticipated uses of the system being contemplated or with the intended implementation technology. It also can go astray when analysts become grandiose and formulate requirements far in excess of what is actually needed. Finally, inevitable changes in context and technology mean that requirements analysis and documentation should be an ongoing activity. To the extent possible, requirements should be determined at the outset of development and updated as changes occur during development. In practice, requirements analysis and documentation mostly occur early in the process.

Top-level Design

The trustworthiness of a system depends critically on its design. Once the system's requirements and (optionally) the Conops are approved, the next step is development of a top-level design. This document is often called an "architecture" to emphasize just how much detail is being omitted. During development of the top-level design, basic types of technology are selected, the system is divided into components and subsystems, and requirements for each component are defined. This process has been called "programming in the large," to distinguish it from writing code, or "programming in the small" (DeRemer and Kron, 1976).

Components are building blocks for integration, and subsystems are clusters of components that are integrated first as a group and then the assemblage integrated into the whole. For software that is being developed (as opposed to purchased), the size of a component or subsystem is determined by the number of lines of code, the programming language used, and the complexity of the algorithms involved. A rough rule of thumb is that a component (or "module") is a body of software that can be fully grasped[4] by one or two programmers. Using the same principle, a

---

[4]That is, some member of the team can answer any question about the subsystem; it is not necessary (or even desirable) that every member of the team be able to answer every question.

subsystem is a body of code that can be fully grasped by a team of three to five programmers, which happens also to be the maximum size group that can be supervised effectively by a team leader.

There exist no generally accepted notations for top-level design. Most designs are described using diagrams. Such diagrams rarely have precisely defined semantics, so they are not always helpful for determining whether a top-level design includes all the necessary functions or satisfies all of its requirements.

A dependency analysis (Parnas, 1974) should be performed on the top-level design, where a dependency is defined to exist between components A and B if the correct operation of A depends on the correct operation of B. The results of a dependency analysis are captured in a dependency diagram.[5] Experienced designers attempt to move functions among components to eliminate cycles in the dependency diagram. In a cycle, the correctness of one component depends directly or indirectly on the correctness of another, and the correctness of the second depends directly or indirectly on the correctness of the first, thereby forming a circular relationship. Where a cycle exists, all components in the cycle must be integrated and tested as a unit. In the extreme case—so-called "big bang" integration—all components are integrated at one time; that process seldom has a positive outcome. At present there is no scientific foundation for determining, analyzing, or changing dependency relationships among components in large-scale systems.

Many would argue that interface determination and design are the essence of system design (Lampson, 1983). Therefore, an important output of the top-level design activity is precise specifications for the system's interfaces. These specifications define the formats and protocols for interactions between components and subsystems. A rigorous interface description is particularly important when the interface being defined is between subsystems implemented by different teams.[6] The definition of interfaces and the determination of which interfaces are sufficiently important to warrant control by project management are, like the rest of top-level design, more an art than a science.

---

[5]As with the top-level design itself, there exist no generally accepted notations for such diagrams, nor do there exist widely used tools to support the development of dependency diagrams.

[6]There is an element of program management lore called Conways's Law whose essence is that the human organization of a software project and the technical organization of the software being produced will be congruent. The law was originally stated as, "If you have four teams working on a compiler, you get a four-pass compiler." A more general formulation is that "a system's structure resembles the organization that produces it" (Raymond and Steele, 1991).

Despite the innovative design concepts that have appeared in the literature in areas such as object-oriented design (Meyer, 1988) and architectural description languages (Garland and Shaw, 1996), still no comprehensive approach to the design and analysis of NISs exists. Important challenges remain in design visualization, design verification, design techniques (that accommodate long-term evolution), COTS, and legacy components, as well as tool support for the creation and analysis of designs. Among the most critical issues are design verification and design evolution, since assuring that a design will continue to implement the necessary trustworthiness properties—even as the system evolves—is central to building an NIS. Moreover, because top-level design occurs relatively early in the life cycle, detection of defects during the top-level design stage has great leverage.

Perhaps the greatest design challenges concern techniques to compose subsystems in ways that contribute directly to trustworthiness. NISs are typically large and, therefore, they must be developed and deployed incrementally. Significant features are added even after an NIS is first deployed. Thus, there is a need for methods to identify feature interactions, performance bottlenecks, omitted functionality, and critical components in an NIS that is being developed by composition or by accretion.

There exists a widening gap between the needs of software practitioners and the ability to evaluate software technologies for developing moderate- to large-scale systems. The expense of building such systems renders infeasible the traditional form of controlled scientific experiment, where the same system is built repeatedly under controlled conditions but using differing approaches. Benefits and costs must be documented, risks enumerated and assessed, and necessary enhancements or modifications identified and carried out. One might, instead, attempt to generalize from the experiences gained in different projects. But to do so and reach a sound conclusion requires understanding what aspects of a system interact with the technology under investigation. Some advantages would probably accrue if only software developers documented their practices and experiences. This activity, however, is one that few programmers find appealing and few managers have the resources to support.

Critical Components

A critical component is one whose failure would result in an undetected and irrecoverable failure to satisfy a trustworthiness requirement. Experienced designers attempt to produce top-level designs for which the number of components that depend on critical components is not constrained but the critical components themselves depend on as few other components as possible. This strategy achieves two things: it enables developers to use freestanding tests and analyses to build trust in the critical components, and it permits an orderly integration process in which trusted components become available early. Unless the critical components come from vendors with impeccable credentials, development teams generally prefer, wherever feasible, to implement the critical components themselves. That way, all aspects of the design, implementation, and verification of critical components can be strictly controlled. There are two risks in pursuing this approach. One is that the criticality of a component has been overlooked—a danger that is increased by the lack of a scientific basis to assess the criticality of components. A second is that it may not be feasible to implement a critical component in-house or, for a vendor-provided critical component, it may not be possible to obtain sufficient information to be convinced of that component's trustworthiness.[7]

The Integration Plan

Once the basic structure of the system has been established, the integration plan is produced. Ideally, the plan involves two activities:

1. Integration of components into subsystems that reside on single network nodes; and

2. Connection of network nodes into subsystems that perform definable functions and whose behavior can be observed and evaluated, followed by the connection of the subsystems into the final NIS.

The essence of the integration process is progress toward a completely operational system on a step-by-step basis. Observed defects can be localized to the last increment that was integrated—if one build passes its tests and the next build fails its tests, then the most likely sources of difficulty are those components that turned the first build into the second. Working in this manner, the integration team should not have to revisit previously integrated components or subsystems during the integration process. And this process avoids a cycle of "fix and test and fix again" that could continue until time, money, or management patience runs out. Note that for the integration process to be successful, the top-level design must exhibit proper dependency relationships between components. An inte-

---

[7]In the case of a browser, which might well be a critical component in an NIS, this situation is ameliorated by Netscape's recent decision to release the Netscape Navigator source code. A development team now can examine the code and possibly eliminate unwanted functionality.

gration plan thus can serve another purpose: to force the detailed analysis of a top-level design. Top-level designs lacking straightforward integration plans are likely to be ambiguous, incomplete, or just plain wrong.

Integration skills today are developed only through experience. There is essentially no theoretical basis for deciding what should constitute a build, nor has the problem received serious scientific examination. System integration continues to be practiced as a craft that is passed along through apprenticeship. The drift of university computer science research from emphasizing large experimental systems projects (such as Multics, c.mmp, and Berkeley UNIX) toward undertaking smaller engineering efforts is of particular concern. Looking back at the master's and Ph.D. thesis topics at the Massachusetts Institute of Technology (as an example) during the Multics era, it is striking how many concern software that had to be integrated into the larger system in a planned and disciplined manner. The shrinking of this skills base in orderly integration is further exacerbated by the reward system of the personal computer market. Financial benefits flow principally to authors of the freestanding application or component (the so-called "killer app") that attracts large numbers of consumers or is selected for use in information systems assembled from COTS components. This latter case involves a different set of skills from those required to design, implement, and integrate a large system from scratch.

Project Structure, Standards, and Process

Other branches of engineering rely heavily on controlling the development process to ensure the quality of engineering artifacts. The Software Engineering Institute's Capability Maturity Model (CMM) is a step in that direction for software design and development (see Box 3.1). As with requirements definition and analysis, there is considerable anecdotal evidence and some experimental evidence that having a systematic process in place contributes to the quality of software systems that an organization develops. There is, however, little evidence that any one process can be distinguished from another, nor is there evidence that different characteristics of development processes are correlated with product quality.

Rigorous, repeatable processes are sometimes thought to result when software development standards are imposed on organizations. Such standards typically prescribe overall process structure, documents to be produced, the order of events, techniques to be used, and so on. A recent study found 250 different standards that apply to the engineering of software, yet the authors of the study found that the standards were largely ineffective and concluded that software technology is too immature to standardize (Pfleeger et al., 1994).

BOX 3.1
The SEI Capability Maturity Model for Software

The Software Engineering Institute's (SEI) Capability Maturity Model (CMM) for software was first introduced in the late 1980s. The current version, version 1.1, was introduced in 1993.[1]   According to the SEI: "The Capability Maturity Model for Software (SW-CMM or CMM) is a model for judging the maturity of the software processes of an organization and for identifying the key practices that are required to increase the maturity of the processes. The SW-CMM is developed by the software community with stewardship by the SEI" (Paulk et al., 1993).

The CMM defines a maturity framework that has five levels: (1) initial, (2) repeatable, (3) defined, (4) managed, and (5) optimized. The five levels are carefully defined and based on key process areas (KPAs). The KPAs are, as the name suggests, the most important aspects of software processes. At CMM level 2, for example, requirements management is a KPA.

It is important to understand that the CMM is intended only to measure maturity. It is not a software development process standard or a mechanism for assessing specific software development techniques. It also is not a means of achieving high levels of either productivity or software quality (although some users report that both tend to improve after higher CMM levels have been achieved). Rather, the CMM aims to assess the ability of an organization to develop software in a repeatable and predictable way. Thus, an organization possessing a high CMM level will not necessarily develop software more quickly or of better quality than an organization having a lower level. The higher-ranked organization will, however, develop software in a more predictable way and will be able to do so repeatedly.

After a careful analysis, an assessed organization is rated at one of the five levels of the CMM framework. Attainment of some specified minimum CMM level is sometimes required to bid on certain government contracts. (The practice seems to be becoming more common within the Department of Defense.) Whether having such a minimum CMM level ensures higher-quality work is not clear, but it has succeeded in making corporate management aware of the importance of software development processes.

A second benefit of the CMM has been reported by organizations seeking to improve their ratings. The staff of such organizations become more conscious of the software technology they are using and how it can be improved. Esprit de corps tends to be generated when the entire staff is involved in a single process-improvement goal.

Although there is no specific intention that higher CMM rankings will be associated with higher quality or productivity, there is some evidence that more mature processes do yield those advantages. Watts and his colleagues document a variety of benefits and important lessons they observed at Hughes Aircraft after moving from CMM level 2 to level 3 (Watts et al., 1991). Dion reports increased productivity and

continues on next page

BOX 3.1 continued

large cost savings at Raytheon after it moved from level 2 to level 3 (Dion, 1993). And Motorola, which observed the development performance of 34 different projects with roughly equal numbers of projects rated at each CMM level (Diaz and Sligo, 1997), has reported reduced cycle time, reduced defect rates, and improved productivity as CMM level increased.

However, a recent paper by McGarry, Burke, and Decker (1997) is less favorable in discussing the correlation between CMM level and software development metrics based on data from more than 90 projects within one organization (a part of Computer Sciences Corporation). The results of the study were mixed, and in most cases improvements were not correlated with CMM level.

Impacts of process improvement have also been surveyed. Brodman and Johnson (1996) report survey data in the form of return on investment to industry. Their results document a wide variety of benefits associated with achieving higher CMM levels. Lawlis, Flowe, and Thordahl (1995) investigated the effect of CMM level on software development cost and schedule. They found a positive correlation between CMM level and cost and schedule performance. Another survey reporting positive results of using the CMM has been published by Herbsleb and Goldenson (1996).

The actual CMM assessment process has also been studied. Kitson and Masters (1993) identify which KPAs are major factors affecting CMM ratings, thereby suggesting areas of weakness in industrial software practice.

Although many successes of the CMM have been reported, the CMM itself has also been criticized. Bollinger and McGowan (1991) raised a number of important questions about the practical benefits of an initial version of the CMM in the context of government contracting. Their concerns were mainly with the relative simplicity of the assessment process and the fact that CMM levels would be used for rating government contractors. The criticisms of Bollinger and McGowan were addressed by the developers of the CMM in Watts and Curtis (1991). More recently, Fayad and Laitinen (1997) criticized aspects of the CMM ranging from the cost of assessment to the fact that a single assessment scheme is used for organizations of all sizes. Although these criticisms have merit, they do not appear to be fundamental flaws in the CMM concept.

---

[1]The CMM of the Software Engineering Institute is available online at <http://www.sei.cmu.edu/technology/cmm.html>.

Barriers to Acceptance of New Software Technologies

The high costs associated with adopting new software technologies make managers less likely to do so. The concern is that, despite claimed benefits, problems might arise in using the new technology and these problems might lead to missed deadlines or budget overruns. Sticking with technology that has been used before—the conservative course—reduces the risks.

Managers' fears are well founded in many cases, as many new software technologies do not work when tried on industrial-scale problems. Things that work well in the laboratory are not guaranteed to work well in practice. All too often, laboratory assessments of software technology are based on experiences with a few small examples. The need to investigate the scaling of a new technology is common to all branches of engineering but, as already discussed, the expense of performing large-scale software experiments makes such experiments infrequent. To assess a new software technology, the technology should be observed in full-scale development efforts. Any research program that aspires to relevance should include plans for compelling demonstrations that the resultant technology is applicable to industrial-scale problems and that its benefits justify the costs of learning and applying it.

Many new software technologies are also tool-intensive. They try to improve software development practices by replacing or supplementing human effort. Testing an interactive application that employs a graphic user interface, for example, requires the manipulation of complex software structures, the management of extensive detail, and the application of sophisticated algorithms. It all could be undertaken by hand, but having computers perform as much of the work as possible is preferable. Yet, software tools are notoriously expensive to develop because, although the essence of a new idea might be relatively simple to implement, providing all the basic services that are needed for practical use is neither simple nor inexpensive. In addition, learning to use new software tools takes time. The result is one more barrier to the success of any new software technology.

Findings

1. Although achieving connectivity and providing basic services are relatively easy, providing specialized services—especially trustworthy ones—is much more difficult and is complicated by the decentralized and asynchronous nature of NISs.

2. Project management, a long-standing challenge in software development, becomes even more problematic in the context of NISs because of

their large and complex nature and the continual software changes that can erode trustworthiness.

3. Whereas a large software system cannot be developed defect free, it is possible to improve the trustworthiness of such a system by anticipating and targeting vulnerabilities. But to determine, analyze, and, most importantly, prioritize these vulnerabilities requires a good understanding of how the software interacts with the other elements of the larger system.

4. It seems clear from anecdotal evidence that using any methodical and tested technique for the capture and documentation of requirements— no matter what its shortcomings—is better than launching directly into design and implementation.

5. No notation for system-level requirements has shown sufficiently commanding advantages to become dominant.

6. System-level trustworthiness requirements typically are first characterized informally. The transformation of the informal notions into precise requirements that can be imposed on system components is difficult and often beyond the current state of the art.

7. NISs generally are developed and deployed incrementally. Thus, techniques are needed to compose subsystems in ways that contribute directly to trustworthiness.

8. There exists a widening gap between the needs of software practitioners and the problems that are being attacked by the academic research community. In most academic computer science research today, researchers are not confronting problems related to large-scale integration and students do not develop the skills and intuition necessary to develop software that not only works but also works in the context of software written by others.

9. Although systematic processes may contribute to the quality of software systems, specific processes or standards that accomplish this goal have not been demonstrated.

10. Since the investment of resources needed for a large software development project is substantial, managers are reluctant to embrace new software technologies because they entail greater risks.

BUILDING AND ACQUIRING COMPONENTS

Component-level Requirements

It is useful to distinguish between two kinds of component-level requirements: allocated or traceable requirements, which devolve directly from system requirements, and derived requirements, which are consequences of the system architecture. In the HMO system, for example, there might be an overall trustworthiness requirement that medical records must be available 24 hours a day, 7 days a week. One way to meet that need would be to replicate records on two different servers; the data management software then has the derived requirement of ensuring the consistency of the data on the two servers. The requirement is "derived" because it results not so much from an interpretation or clarification of the original trustworthiness requirement but rather from the architectural strategy—replication—being used to satisfy the trustworthiness requirement.

A common practice is to insist that all requirements at the component level be testable. That is, each requirement must be accompanied by some experiment for assessing whether that requirement is satisfied. These tests must be chosen with care because, in actual practice, cost and schedule pressures drive a development team toward making sure their component passes the tests as a first priority. If a test is not chosen carefully and described unambiguously, then a component that does not satisfy the spirit or even the letter of the actual requirements statement might be deemed acceptable.

The relationship between the requirements, which capture intent, and a test, which determines acceptance, is especially problematic for nonfunctional requirements in support of trustworthiness concerns. Continuing with the HMO medical record example, the test may check that the two copies of the medical record are synchronized within so many seconds of a change having been made, that the failure of the primary server is detected by the switchover logic within so many seconds, that switchover is accomplished in so many seconds, and so on. The problem is that the list of tests is not equivalent to the requirement being tested (i.e., availability 24 hours a day, 7 days a week). For example, the tests do not take into account simultaneous or cascading failures (e.g., primary fails while secondary is running backup, secondary fails immediately after switchover, synchronization request comes in at just the wrong time as switchover is being initiated, and so on). There are thus circumstances in which the component or subsystem will pass its tests but fail to satisfy the intent of the requirement.

Detailed, component-level requirements for user interfaces are difficult to write. So-called storyboards, which show display configurations for various inputs, outputs, and states of the system, can be hard to follow. However, the popularity of graphical user interfaces has led to the development of tools that enable designers to rapidly prototype user interfaces. Generally speaking, prototyping is sensible in requirements analysis and can even serve as an executable requirements document. But the cost of building prototypes can be high, thereby preempting other higher-payoff forms of requirements analysis. For example, devoting too much effort to prototyping a user interface can lead to software in which an elaborate user interface surrounds a poorly thought-out core.

Component Design and Implementation

To project managers, component design and implementation are the least visible of the phases. A large number of activities are proceeding in parallel, the staff are focused on their individual tasks (perhaps ignoring the global view), and the tasks themselves are highly technical. All conspire to make measuring progress or even anecdotal observations of status extremely difficult. While there is an extensive literature on the problem of demonstrating that a component satisfies its specification, there is considerably less literature devoted to determining whether a component-level specification properly reflects or contributes toward satisfying system requirements.

For code written in traditional languages (such as C) running on a single node, and interacting in limited and controlled ways with users and other software, the craft of programming has evolved into a generally accepted process. As practiced within the aerospace, defense, and other large-scale computing system development communities (but not necessarily in commercial practice) over the last two decades, that process consists of roughly the following steps:

- Review the component requirements document for sanity.
- Prepare a component design in some notation, often called "pseudocode." (Pseudocode is usually a mixture of programming language statements and some less detailed notation, not excluding natural language.)
- Conduct an organized inspection of the component design ("structured walkthrough") with an emphasis on the logic flow.
- Write component test scripts or test drivers to exercise the component after it has been written.
- Write the component in some appropriate higher-level language ("source code").[8]
- Conduct a structured walkthrough of the source code.
- Compile the component into executable form.

---

[8]This and the preceding step are often reversed, and the test drivers are not written until after the component is. The order given in the text is preferable because the detailed design and coding of a test driver force implementers to rigorously analyze and understand component-level requirements.

- Exercise the component ("unit test" or "level 1 testing") using the test scripts or drivers.
- Release the component to the integration process.

This process, and ones like it, have been synthesized from the wreckage of expensive failures, and a significant percentage, if not a majority, of experienced practitioners would caution that any of these steps are omitted at one's peril. One variation is to repeat the cycle frequently, making very small changes at each iteration. This approach was used successfully in the Multics project (Clingen and van Vleck, 1978) and has long been part of the program management lore in high-consequence real-time systems.

Today's turnover rate among software personnel somewhat reduces the effectiveness of the component-development process just described. Software development is still typically learned through apprenticeship. Yet personnel shortages, the potential financial rewards and short life cycles of start-up companies, and the deterioration of corporate loyalty as a result of downsizing and restructuring make it less likely that a junior practitioner will witness a complete project life cycle, much less several projects conducted in the same organization. Ultimately, this will impede the development of an adequate skill base in critical areas, like synthesis and analysis of design, integration, or structuring of development organizations.

The above component development process is predicated on starting with a modular design. Achieving modularity is intellectually challenging and costly; it requires management and design discipline. In addition, modular systems often are larger and slower. So there is a tension between system modularity and cost (along a variety of cost dimensions); it can be hard to know when system modularity is needed and when it is not worth the cost. Moreover, certain NIS building blocks—mobile code and Web browsers with helper applications, for example—compromise the advantages of modular design by permitting unrestricted interactions between different software components.

Programming Languages

Modern programming languages, such as C++, Java, and Ada, include compile-time checks to detect a wide range of possible errors. The checks are based on declaring or inferring a type for each object (i.e., variables and procedures) and analyzing the program to establish that objects are used in ways consistent with their types. This kind of automated support is especially helpful for detecting the kinds of errors (such as passing arguments that overflow a corresponding parameter) so successfully used by attackers of operating system and network software. Ever more expressive type systems are a continuing theme in programming language research, with considerable attention being directed recently at the representation of security properties using types (Digital Equipment Corporation, 1997). Success would mean that compile-time checks could play an even bigger role in supporting trustworthiness properties.

Modern programming languages also contain features to support modularity and component integration. Ada, for example, provides type checking across separate compilations; Ada also integrates component linking with compilation, so that statements whose validity depends on the order in which compilation occurs can be checked. Other modern languages provide equivalent features. At the other end of the spectrum, scripting languages (Ousterhout, 1998) (such as Visual Basic and TCL) are today attracting ever-larger user communities. These languages are typically typeless and designed to facilitate gluing together software components. The preponderance of COTS and legacy components in a typical networked information system assures the relevance of scripting languages to the enterprise.

Also of interest to NIS developers are very-high-level languages and domain-specific languages, which provide far-higher-level programming abstractions than traditional programming languages do. The presence of the higher-level abstractions enables rapid development of smaller, albeit often less efficient, programs. Moreover, programming with abstractions that have rich semantics and powerful operations reduces the opportunity for programming errors and permits more sophisticated compile-time checking.

There is much anecdotal and little hard, experimental evidence concerning whether the choice of programming language can enhance trustworthiness. One report (CSTB, 1997) looked for hard evidence but found essentially none. Further study is needed and, if undertaken, could be used to inform research directions in the programming language community.

Systematic Reuse

Systematic reuse refers to the design and implementation of components specifically intended for instantiation in differing systems. It is one of the most sought-after goals in software research, because it offers the potential for substantial software productivity improvements.[9] More-

---

[9]It is worth noting that the infamous year 2000 problem would be far easier to address if a small number of date packages had been reused in date-sensitive applications. There would still be the problem of database conversion, though, once the date format is changed.

over, components intended for reuse can be more intensely scrutinized, since the higher cost of analysis can be amortized over multiple uses. The current economic emphasis on short-term results, however, serves to inhibit the acceptance of any method of systematic reuse that requires (as appears inevitable) up-front investment.

Certain commercial vendors, such as SAP, whose R/3 enterprise-applications software (Hernandez, 1997) has captured one-third of the worldwide client-server market for business systems, claim to have solved the systematic reuse problem in a cost-effective manner for large classes of applications. R/3 is an integrated software package that includes interwoven reusable components for all the major functions of a commercial enterprise, from order entry and accounting through manufacturing and human resources. In addition, R/3 is built to use a COTS operating system along with COTS database management systems, browsers, and user-interface software. Other commercially driven attempts at providing components or infrastructure for systematic reuse include the C++ standard template library (STL) (Musser and Saini, 1996), common object request broker architecture (CORBA),[10] common object model (COM) (Microsoft Corporation and Digital Equipment Corporation, 1995), distributed common object model (DCOM) (Brown and Kindel, 1998), and JavaBeans (Hamilton, 1997).

There is always a tension between the pressure to innovate and the stability associated with components intended for reuse. That tension is particularly acute for COTS components, for which the addition of new features and time to market are such strong forces. New features are usually accompanied by new bugs; careful analysis of components enhances stability but delays product release. Moreover, when bugs in COTS components do get fixed, the fixes are often bundled in a release that also introduces new features. The COTS component user must then choose between living with a bug and migrating to a release that may be less stable due to new bugs.

Commercial Off-the-Shelf Software

The Changing Role of COTS Software

Success for a COTS software component often leads to deployment in settings never intended. A component might start as an interesting piece of software at the periphery of trustworthiness concerns and ultimately

---

[10]COBRA 3.0 was introduced by the Object Management Group (OMG) in December, 1994. Additional information is available online at <http://www.omg.org>.

become a critical component in some NIS. In 1994, it would have been absurd to suggest that a bug in a Web browser could kill someone. Yet in the HMO system we are using as an example, a Web-based telemedicine application could allow precisely that outcome. That software can be used for tasks not envisioned by its developers is a double-edged sword, especially if COTS development practices cause developers to compromise trustworthiness for other requirements.

COTS software development practices in the personal computer (PC) era arose in a technical and economic environment that tended to ignore trustworthiness. PC operating systems and applications ran on isolated desktops; the consequences of failure were limited to destruction of perhaps valuable, but certainly not life-critical, data. Failures had no way of propagating to other machines. Therefore, an organizational and programming culture arose that was very accepting of errors and malfunctions, epitomized by the notorious shrink-wrap license whose primary feature is a total disclaimer of responsibility by the developer.

This climate was amplified by economic conditions of the early PC era. Software was purchased separately rather than being bundled with a leased computer, as in the mainframe era. Consequently, there was less financial leverage for dissatisfied customers to affect vendor, and therefore developer, attitudes. A customer's financial leverage was limited to consuming vendor resources in calls to telephone help-lines, which could be ignored by inept or uncaring vendors,[11] and refusing to purchase other software or the next revision of the malfunctioning product from that vendor. The latter option is reduced by the diminishing diversity of the marketplace, the need to exchange data with other users, and the investment the customer may have in data that can be processed only by the product in question.

As the PC market exploded, visionary entrepreneurs realized that market share was the dominant factor in corporate survival and personal financial success. Market share is heavily influenced by market entry time. Specifically, the first product to reach a market has the greatest opportunity both to gain market share and to establish the de facto standard upon which the software industry currently operates. Another influence on market share is the richness of features and user interface, which impresses users and reviewers in the technical press. Something must be sacrificed, and it has been trustworthiness aspects such as robustness and security.

One way to reduce time to market is to reduce the time spent in

---

[11]This situation is changing. A vendor, albeit of hardware, has recently settled a class action suit requiring an increase in warranty and support coverage (Manes, 1998). Similar actions against software vendors are likely to follow from this precedent.

testing. By making early releases (beta test versions) available to interested users and by freely distributing incremental updates to production software, vendors enlist the help of the user community in finding errors. From a societal perspective, the PC software industry's attitude toward errors was relatively unimportant, since the worst consequence of PC software errors was the time lost by individuals trying to reconstruct destroyed work or otherwise get their PCs to do their bidding. But today, COTS software is moving toward being a business of providing components—and possibly critical components—for NISs that can be high consequence, either because they were explicitly designed that way or because people assign to them a level of trust that their designers never intended.

General Problems with COTS Components

The use of COTS components presents special problems for the responsible developer of an NIS. COTS software typically is full of features that vary in quality and are a source of complexity. The complexity, in turn, means that specifications for COTS components are likely to be incomplete, and users of those components will discover features by experimentation. Being conservative in exploiting these discoveries is prudent—semantics not documented in an accompanying written specification may or may not have been intended and consequently may or may not persist across releases. Moreover, wise developers learn to avoid the more complex features of COTS components because these are the most likely to exhibit surprising behavior and their behavior is least likely to remain stable across releases. When these features cannot be avoided, encapsulating components with wrappers, effectively narrowing their interfaces, can protect against undesirable behaviors.

The COTS developer's reliance on customer feedback[12] as a significant, or even primary, quality assurance mechanism can lead to uneven quality levels in different subsystems or functionality in a single COTS product. Press coverage is not guaranteed to be accurate and may not convey the implications of the problem being reported.[13] For example, security vulnerabilities in components such as Web browsers, which are

---

[12]Handling calls to customer-support telephone help-lines is sometimes claimed to be a significant portion of COTS software costs. The committee was unable to explore the veracity of this claim. However, the use of customer feedback in place of other quality control mechanisms does allow a software producer to externalize costs associated with product testing.

[13]See, for example, the February 1997 coverage of the Chaos Computer Club demonstration of a supposed security flaw in Microsoft's Internet Explorer.

used directly by the public, receive widespread coverage, as do ultimately inconsequential (and unsurprising) exploits, such as the use of large numbers of machines on the Internet to "break" cryptographic algorithms by brute-force searches. Feedback from customers and the press, by its very nature, occurs only after a product has been distributed. And experience with distribution of bug fixes clearly indicates that many sites do not, for a variety of reasons, install such upgrades, thereby leaving themselves vulnerable to attack through the now highly publicized methods.[14] Reliance on market forces to select what gets examined and what gets fixed is haphazard at best and is surely not equivalent to performing a methodical search for vulnerabilities prior to distribution.

Finally, using COTS software in an NIS has the advantages and disadvantages that accompany any form of "outsourcing." COTS components can offer rich functionality and may be better engineered and tested than would be cost-effective for components developed from scratch for a relatively smaller user community. But an NIS that uses COTS components becomes dependent on a third party for decisions about a component's evolution and the engineering processes used in its construction (notably regarding assurance). In addition, the NIS developer must track new releases of those COTS components and may be forced to make periodic changes to the NIS in response to those new releases. It all comes down to a trade-off between cost and risk: the price of COTS components can be attractive, especially if the functionality they provide is a good match for what is needed, but the risk of ceding control may or may not be sensible for any given piece of an NIS.

Interfacing Legacy Software

Legacy software refers to existing components or subsystems that must be retained and integrated more or less unchanged into a system. Legacy software is used when developing an NIS because reusing an existing system is cheaper and less risky than completely reimplementing it, especially given the migration costs (training, rebuilding online records) associated with deploying a replacement system. In the HMO example, it would be very likely that the Clinical Laboratory or Pathology departments had been operating for decades with freestanding computerized systems. Incorporating such a freestanding system into an NIS poses special problems:

---

[14]Even when administrators diligently apply security-bug fixes, the fixes can then be lost when a crashed system is restored from backup media. Since such restorations are often done in a crisis atmosphere, the need to perform the additional update step is easily overlooked in the rush to restore service.

- NIS designers must recognize that they might be dealing with an operational subsystem that performs critical functions and cannot be rendered inactive for days or even hours.
- The legacy subsystem might not have been designed with networking in mind, and conversion to one that supports networking might not be feasible.
- The system may be an "orphan" product whose vendor no longer exists or supports this version. Or, if the system was developed locally, documentation and expertise about its internals might have evaporated over time.

The general approach to dealing with these problems is to fool some interface of the legacy system into thinking it is operating in isolation when, in fact, it is connected to a network. Often, an existing interface of the legacy system can be wrapped in a new layer of software (called a wrapper) that hides the network, perhaps by making the network look to the legacy software like an existing user interface (e.g., a keyboard and display). And a legacy system might be adapted to use a new communications protocol in place of an old one by writing software that uses the old protocol to simulate the functionality of the new one; this is called tunneling. The risk with such schemes is that the legacy system's interface, designed to serve one type of client, might not be able to handle the characteristics of the new load. For example, the volume of transactions arriving over the network might overwhelm an interface that was written to serve a single human user typing at a terminal. Inadequate or incomplete documentation for a legacy system's interfaces also can complicate employing the approach.

Findings

1. It is difficult to devise component-level acceptance tests that fully capture the intent of requirements statements. This is particularly true for nonfunctional and user interface requirements.

2. High turnover of programming staff is impeding the development of an adequate skill base in critical areas, such as NIS synthesis and analysis of design, integration, or structuring.

3. There are some accepted processes for component design and implementation. However, the performance needs of NISs can be inconsistent with modular design, and this fact can limit the applicability of an effective design tool to NIS design.

4. Modern programming languages include features, such as compile-time checks and support for modularity and component integration, that promote trustworthiness. The potential may exist for further gains

by developing even more expressive type systems and other compile-time analysis techniques.

5. There is inadequate experimental evidence to justify the utility of any specific programming language or language feature with respect to improving trustworthiness.

6. Despite theoretical concerns,[15] as a practical matter the use of higher-level languages increases trustworthiness to a degree that outweighs the risks.

7. Basing the development of an NIS on libraries of reusable trusted components and using those components in critical areas of the system can provide a cost-effective way to implement component-level dimensions of trustworthiness.

8. New commercial software that includes usable components or infrastructure for systematic reuse is increasingly available, but it is too early to know how successful it will be.

9. COTS software originally evolved in a stand-alone environment in which trustworthiness was not a primary concern. Furthermore, market pressures contribute to reducing time spent on testing before releasing software to users, while emphasizing features that add to complexity but are useful for only a minority of applications.

10. COTS software offers both advantages and disadvantages to an NIS. COTS components may be less expensive, have greater functionality, and be better engineered and tested than is feasible for customized components. Yet the use of COTS makes developers dependent on outside vendors for the design and enhancement of important components; specifications may be incomplete and may compel users to discover features by experimentation.

11. Incorporating legacy software into an NIS poses risks for trustworthiness because problems may arise as a result of including a previously freestanding system into a networked environment for which it was unintended.

INTEGRATING COMPONENTS INTO
A TRUSTWORTHY SYSTEM

System Integration

Subsystem integration is the orderly aggregation of unit-tested components into a subsystem, along with incremental testing to increase confidence in the subsystem's correctness. There are three basic approaches:

---

[15]For example, a theoretically effective attack based on a maliciously modified compiler was described over a decade ago in Thompson (1984).

bottom-up integration, top-down integration, and thread integration. To illustrate, consider the Clinical Laboratory subsystem for our HMO's NIS. Lower-level components in the subsystem would control the keyboard and display, maintain local data files, and control interactions with test instruments; upper-level management components would select which of the lower-level ones are activated and in what order.

In bottom-up integration, a series of programs (called test drivers) is written that simulates the upper-level components of the subsystem. The lower-level components (e.g., the ones that control test instruments in the Clinical Laboratory subsystem) are aggregated first, and only when their correct interactions have been observed are the upper-level components added. The origin of the name "bottom up" should be clear. The approach was popular in the early days of real-time control systems. Computer memory was a scarce resource then, and the integration team obtained an early warning of excessive software size by proceeding from the bottom up. Bottom-up integration carries with it the significant disadvantage that the overall logical operation of the subsystem is observed only relatively late in the process, when limited time and resources are available to deal with incorrect behavior.

The opposite of bottom-up integration is top-down integration. In this approach, upper-level components are integrated first. The components are tested using routines (called stubs) that simulate the behavior of the lower-level components. The stubs are then replaced one by one with the components that they are simulating. With top-down integration, logical correctness of the subsystem is established first, but the actual size of the entire system is not determined until relatively late in the integration process. Thus, if system size is not an issue, top-down integration is superior to bottom-up integration; if size is an issue, then with top-down integration, failure would likely be due to size problems rather than incorrect logical operation of the system.

In both top-down and bottom-up integration, confidence in correct behavior is gained through the use of simulated rather than actual components; stubs are used in top-down integration, and test drivers are used in bottom-up integration. Clearly, the use of the actual components would be preferable, so software developers devised a more sophisticated approach known as thread integration or thread testing.

In thread integration, the components being joined are selected subsets of the overall subsystem, and test cases are carefully defined to activate only the subset of components under test. There are two ways to select a subset of components to integrate. One is to select a subset of the system-level requirements. This works when the requirements map onto the top-level design in a straightforward manner. The second and more common approach is to select subsets of components according to the top-level design and the sequence of component activations (the call tree).[16]

As an example, a single build in a thread integration of our Clinical Laboratory subsystem might combine the keyboard and display component, the management component, and an interface to a single test instrument (say, for blood sugar). A thread test of this build would involve an operator sitting at the console and initiating a blood sugar test; the fact that, say, the hepatitis antibody test components are not yet integrated does not matter, since these components would not be activated by the test.[17] When all the builds are complete, confidence is increased that the components not only work properly in isolation (which is the concern of unit testing) but also work together.

In traditional software development, the word "subsystem" in the preceding discussion could be replaced by the word "system." Once the integration of a single node was complete, the job was done. However, the structure of an NIS adds another level to the integration process. Disparate nodes in a network must interact to perform a single, coordinated task. Relatively little is known about approaches to performing this additional level of integration compared with what is known about subsystem integration. By their very nature, networks pose special problems to an integration team. For one thing, inputs may have to be submitted miles from where corresponding outputs must be observed. For another, system behavior might be load dependent, but operational loads are very hard to simulate (notwithstanding various efforts over many years). In fact, when public networks are being used, various aspects of network behavior become uncontrollable, which means certain tests might not be possible and others might not be repeatable.

System Assurance

Review and Inspection

One commonly used technique for improving software quality is to undertake technical reviews, sometimes known as inspections (Fagan, 1986), in which objective critics examine a design or artifact in detail. A subsequent meeting of the critics allows discussion of specific defects that their examinations have revealed; the meeting also facilitates brainstorming about more systemic flaws that were observed. A great deal of effort

---

[16]The "thread of control"—hence the name of the technique.

[17]In actual use, stubs are incorporated to raise alarms if the decision-making component activates the wrong thing.

has gone into studying various types of technical reviews and various ways of organizing them, and much is known about the benefits of the approaches (Porter et al., 1997), yet their utility in security is not well documented. For example, no evidence could be identified to confirm whether traditional forms of technical reviews could facilitate the detection of security vulnerabilities in an implementation.[18] A simple checklist-based review might be helpful for eliminating well-known vulnerabilities, such as failure to validate arguments, but the overall impact of this activity on trustworthiness properties has not been determined and should be studied. It might also be possible to employ technical reviews in order to identify assumptions being made by designers of a system—assumptions that can become vulnerabilities should an attacker cause them to be violated.

Formal Methods

Formal methods is the name given to a broad class of mathematically based techniques for the description and analysis of hardware, software, and entire computing systems. The descriptions may range, on the one hand, from general statements about desirable system properties, as might be found in a requirements document or high-level specification, to, on the other hand, detailed depictions of intended behavior for specific pieces of software or hardware. The analyses enable developers to derive and check whether specific properties are implied by the formal descriptions.

A system developer, for example, might employ a formal method to check whether a description of requirements is sensible (i.e., not contradictory, unambiguous, and complete) or simply implies some specific property of interest, like (for the HMO system example) "at any time, at most one surgery is scheduled for a given operating theater." Or, for a program text or a more abstract description of an algorithm (viz., any detailed description of behaviors), a formal method could be used to establish that some general condition on execution holds, like "variables and arguments declared with type integer are only assigned values that are integers," or that some specific characterization of behavior is entailed, like "messages sent using the network are delivered uncorrupted and are not reordered."

Formal methods attempt to extend the capabilities of developers by eliminating the need for exhaustive case analyses and/or by facilitating

---

[18]The emphasis of "red teaming," "vulnerability assessment," and "penetration testing" is to focus on selected areas in which intuition, experience, or other evidence indicates that problems may arise (Weissman, 1995). This contrasts with technical reviews as discussed in Fagan (1986), which seek to examine all logical paths in a component.

the construction of long and intricate arguments, so that some property of interest can be certified for a given (formal) description. They are most effective when the property of interest is subtle but can be rigorously defined and when either the description of the object being analyzed is relatively small or the formal method being used supports analyses that can be automated.

Formal methods, however, are useful only when the developer can pose the right questions. For example, establishing that a system implements multilevel security using mandatory access control, whether by formal methods or any other means, does not imply the absence of security vulnerabilities in that system, nor does it imply that the resulting system is capable of performing useful computation. Moreover, some properties (e.g., "the absence of security vulnerabilities") have no system-independent formalization and, therefore, are not amenable to direct analysis using formal methods.[19]

Growth in cost-effective desktop computing power continues to move the field of formal methods toward computer-aided and fully mechanized formal methods from more manual ones. A second significant force has been the need to build confidence when programming ever richer system behaviors (involving time, other physical processes, fault-tolerance, security) as well as when using complex programming constructs (for parallel and distributed systems, object orientation, and so on).

Early work in formal methods emphasized logics and theorem proving. A practitioner constructed proofs largely by hand, with automated assistance limited to proof checking and the synthesis of low-level inferences. The inability to construct a proof could signify a flaw in the implementation being analyzed, but it could equally well reflect insufficient creativity by the person attempting the proof. More recently, with model checking, raw computing cycles have replaced the manual construction of proofs. Model checking always terminates, reporting that the implementation satisfies the given specification or giving a scenario that shows inconsistency of the implementation with the specification. Inherently limited to systems having finite-sized state spaces, today it is possible to apply model checking to systems having upwards of 200 state variables and 10^{120} states (making the approach powerful enough for industrial use in hardware design); ongoing research into abstraction techniques continues to push the limits ever higher.

---

[19]For any given system, there will exist properties that together imply "the absence of security vulnerabilities." But careful thought by a system developer is required to identify these constituents, and there is no formal way to ever establish that the system developer has listed them all.

Formal methods are being used increasingly in commercial and industrial settings.[20] Hardware efforts have provided the most visible successes so far, perhaps because specifications for hardware tend to be relatively stable, the specifications are short relative to the size of implementations, there is agreement on the choice of languages for writing specifications, and the cost of design flaws in chips is very high. Examples of successes include the following:

• Intel has used formal methods in the development of its P5 processor (Pentium processor) and P6 processor (Pentium Pro processor) to prove that the hardware implements the required functionality specified at the register transfer level and to prove that hardware realizations of some of the more complex protocols correctly implement higher-level specifications.[21]

• A tool called Verity has been used widely within IBM for designing processors, including the PowerPC and System/390 (Kuehlmann et al., 1995).

• Model checkers have enabled bugs to be found in the IEEE Futurebus+ standard (Clarke et al., 1993) and the IEEE scalable coherent interface (SCI) standard (Dill et al., 1992).

• The ACL2 theorem prover was used to find bugs in the floating-point square-root microcode for the AMD5K86 processor as well as to find pipeline hazards in the Motorola complex arithmetic processor (CAP), a digital signal processor intended for use in a secure multimode joint-service programmable radio (Brock et al., 1996).

• The microarchitecture and fragments of the microcode for the Collins AAMP5 (Srivas and Miller, 1995) and AAMP-FV avionics processors were analyzed using SRI's PVS theorem prover (Owre et al., 1995).

Commercial and industrial software efforts have also benefited from formal methods. Formal methods applied to requirements analysis has led to some of the more visible of these industrial successes. By formulating requirements in a language having unambiguous semantics, developers can better understand requirements and can use automated tools to discover ambiguity, inconsistency, and incompleteness. The entire set of requirements need not be formalized to enjoy the benefits—often, the most cost-effective course is to treat a carefully chosen subset (with only those elements of concern present). The intricate or novel aspects of the

---

[20]See Clarke and Wing (1996), Dill and Rushby (1996), Rushby (1995), and Craigen et al. (1993) or its summary (Craigen et al., 1995) for the many more examples and details than can be given here.

[21]Based on a telephone interview with Gadi Singer, General Manager of Design Technology, Intel Corporation, on June 8, 1998.

requirements are thereby checked without formalizing an entire set of requirements, which, as observed above in the section on system-level requirements, is likely to be neither complete nor stable. Some of the better-known successful industrial uses of formal methods for analyzing requirements include these:[22]

• With the Software Cost Reduction (SCR) program's tool suite, engineers at Rockwell were able to detect 24 errors—many of them significant—in the requirements specification for a commercial flight guidance system (Miller, 1998). Also using the SCR tool suite, Lockheed engineers formalized the operational flight program for the C-130J Hercules aircraft and found six errors in nondeterminism and numerous type errors.[23]

• An informal English specification for the widely deployed aircraft collision avoidance system TCAS II was abandoned for a formal version written in requirements state machine language (RSML) after the English specification was deemed too complex and unwieldy. That formal specification has since been mechanically checked for completeness and consistency (Heimdahl and Leveson, 1996).

Formal methods were originally developed as an alternative to exhaustive testing for increasing one's confidence that a piece of software satisfies a detailed behavioral specification. To date, this use for formal methods has been applied outside the laboratory only for relatively small safety-critical or high-consequence computing systems, for which development cost is not really a concern but flaws are. Examples include the verification of safety-critical software used in the Hercules Cl30 aircraft (Croxford and Sutton, 1995), parts of the next-generation command-and-control ground system for the ARIANE rocket launcher (Devauchelle et al., 1997), and highly secure operating systems (Saydjari et al., 1989).

Constructing extremely large proofs is infeasible today and for the foreseeable future, so formal methods requiring the construction of proofs for an entire system are not practical when developing an NIS having tens to hundreds of millions of lines of code. Even if size were not an issue, COTS components are rarely accompanied by the formal specifications necessary for doing formal verification of an NIS built from COTS components. It would be wrong, however, to conclude that formal verification cannot contribute to the construction of an NIS.

---

[22]In addition to Clarke and Wing (1996) and Craigen et al. (1993), further examples of this use of formal methods appear in Easterbrok et al. (1998).

[23]As Connie Heitmeyer, U.S. Naval Research Laboratory, described at the NRC's Information Systems Trustworthiness Committee workshop, Irvine, CA, February 5-6, 1997.

For one thing, critical components of an NIS can be subject to formal verification, thereby reducing the number of flaws having system-disabling impact.[24] The aircraft hand-off protocol (Marzullo et al., 1994) in the Advanced Automation Systems air-traffic control system built by IBM Federal Systems Division illustrates such an application of formal methods. Second, entire (large) systems can be subject to formal verification of properties that are checkable mechanically. This is the impetus for recent interest by the software engineering community in so-called lightweight formal methods, like the LCLint tool, which is able to check C programs for a variety of variable type and use errors (Detlefs, 1996), and Eraser, a tool for detecting data races in lock-based multithreaded programs (Savage et al., 1997).

Size problems can be circumvented by subjecting a model of the NIS to analysis instead of analyzing the entire NIS. The model might be smaller than the original in some key dimension, as when confidence is built in a memory cache-controller by analyzing a version that handles only a small number of cache-lines. Alternatively, a model might be smaller than the original by virtue of the details it ignores—checking a high-level description of an algorithm or architecture rather than checking its implementation in a real programming language. Illustrative of this latter approach are the various logics and tools for checking high-level descriptions of cryptographic protocols (Burrows et al., 1990; Lowe and Roscoe, 1997; Meadows, 1992). For instance, with a logic of authentication (Burrows et al., 1990), successive drafts of the CCITT X.509 standard were analyzed and bugs were found, including a vulnerability to replay attacks even when keys have not been compromised.

Observe that a great deal of benefit can be derived from formal methods without committing a project to the use of formal notations either for baseline specifications or throughout. Some argue that formal methods analyses are more effective when performed later, to shake out those last few bugs, rather than earlier, when less costly techniques can still bear fruit.

A well-documented example of industrial use of formal methods in building an NIS was the development by Praxis of the CCF display information system (CDIS) component of the central control function (CCF) air traffic management subsystem in the United Kingdom (Hall, 1996).[25] Here, various formal methods were used at different stages of the development

---

[24]At least for those properties that can be described formally.

[25]This system involved 100 processors linked by using dual local area networks and consisted of approximately 197,000 lines of C code (excluding comments), a specification document of approximately 1,200 pages, and a design document of approximately 3,000 pages.

process: VDM (Jones, 1986) was used during requirements analysis, VVSL (Middleburg, 1989) was used for writing a formal specification for the system, and CSP (Hoare, 1985) was used for describing concurrency in CDIS and its environment. With automated assistance, proofs of correctness were constructed for a few critical protocols. And Hall (1996) reports that productivity for the project was the same or better than has been measured on comparable projects that used only informal methods. Moreover, the defect rate for the delivered software was between two and ten times better than has been reported for comparable software in air traffic control applications that did not use formal methods.

Beyond the successful industrial uses of formal methods discussed above and in the work cited, there are other indications that formal methods have come of age. Today, companies are marketing formal verification tools for use in hardware design and synthesis.[26] And there are anecdotal reports that the number of doctoral graduates in mechanized formal methods is now insufficient to fill the current demands of industry.[27]

Although once there was a belief that the deployment of formal methods required educating the entire development team, most actual deployments have simply augmented a development team with formal methods experts. The job of these experts was beautifully characterized by J S. Moore:[28]

> Like a police SWAT team, members are trained in the use of "special weapons," in particular, mathematical analysis tools. But they are also extremely good at listening, reading between the lines, filling in gaps, generalizing, expressing precisely the ideas of other people, explaining formalisms, etc. Their role is not to bully or take credit, but to formalize a computing system at an appropriate level of abstraction so that certain behaviors can be analyzed.

Here, the absence of shared application assumptions with the development team actually benefits the formal methods expert by facilitating the discovery of unstated assumptions.

Formal methods are gaining acceptance and producing results for industry. What are the impediments to getting broader use and even

---

[26]Examples include Formal Check from Lucent Technologies, RuleBase from IBM Corporation, VFormal from Compass, and Checkoff from View Logic.

[27]As John Rushby described at the NRC's Information Systems Trustworthiness Committee workshop, Irvine, CA, February 5-6, 1997.

[28]Position statement on the state of formal methods technology submitted for the committee's workshop held on February 5-6, 1997, in Irvine, CA. Moore credits Carl Pixley of Motorola with the SWAT-team simile.

further leverage from formal methods? With minor exceptions (Taylor, 1989), the formal methods and testing communities have worked independently of each other, to the advantage of neither. Also, the need for better-integrated tools has been articulated by researchers and formal methods practitioners alike (Craigen et al., 1993), and research efforts are now being directed toward combining, for example, model checkers and proof checkers. Another trend is the development of editors and library support for managing larger proofs and for facilitating development of reusable models and theories.

Over the last decade, formal methods researchers survived only by devoting a significant fraction of their effort to performing realistic demonstration exercises (and these have helped to move formal methods from the research laboratory into industrial settings). More-fundamental research should be a priority. Significant classes of properties remain difficult or impossible to analyze, with fault-tolerance and security high on the list. Methods for decomposing a global property into local ones (which could then be checked more easily) would provide a basis for attacking limitations that bar some uses of formal methods today.

Finally, there is a growing collection of pragmatic questions about the use of formal methods. A key to building usable models of NISs is knowing what dimensions can be safely ignored. Answering that question will require a better understanding about the role of approximation and of simplifying assumptions in formal reasoning. Frictionless planes have served mechanical engineers well—what are the analogous abstractions for computing systems in general and NISs in particular? Idealized models of arithmetic, for example, can give misleading results about real computations, which have access only to finite-precision fixed or floating-point arithmetic. And any assumption that might be invalidated constitutes a system vulnerability, so analysis predicated on assumptions will be blind to certain system vulnerabilities.

There are also questions about the application of formal methods: Where can they give the greatest leverage during system development? When does adding details to a model become an exercise in diminishing returns, given that most errors in requirements and specification are errors of omission (and therefore are likely to be caught only as details are added)? And—a question that is intimately linked to the problem of identifying and characterizing threats—How does one gain confidence that a formal specification is accurate?

Testing

Testing is a highly visible process; it provides confidence that a system will operate correctly, because the system is seen to be operating correctly during testing. And industry today relies heavily on testing. Unfortunately, most real systems have inputs that can take on large numbers of possible values. Testing all combinations of the input values is impossible. (This is especially problematic for systems employing graphical user interfaces, where the number of possible point-and-click combinations is unworkably large.) So, in practice, only a subset of all possible test cases is checked, and testing rarely yields any quantifiable information about the trustworthiness of a program. The characteristics of networked information systems—geographic distribution of inputs and outputs, uncontrollable and unmonitorable subsystems (e.g., networks and legacy systems), and large numbers of inputs—make this class of system especially sensitive to the inadequacy of testing only subsets of the input space.

Much of the research in testing has been directed at dealing with problems of scale. The goal has been to maximize the knowledge gained about a component or subsystem while minimizing the number of test cases required. Approaches based on statistical sampling of the input space have been shown to be infeasible if the goal is to demonstrate ultra-high levels of dependability (Butler and Finelli, 1993), and approaches based on coverage measures do not provide quantification of useful metrics such as mean time to failure. The result is that, in industry, testing is all too often defined to be complete when budget limits are reached, arbitrary milestones are passed, or defect detection rates drop below some threshold. There is clearly room for research—especially to deal with the new complications that NISs bring to the problem: uncontrollable and unobservable subsystems.

System Evolution

Software systems typically are modified after their initial deployment to correct defects, to permit the use of new hardware, and to provide new services. Accommodating such evolution is difficult. Unless great care is taken, the changes can cause the system structure to degenerate. That, in turn, can lead to new defects being introduced with each subsequent change, since a poorly structured system is both difficult to understand and difficult to modify. In addition, coping with system evolution requires managing the operational transition to new versions of that system. System upgrade, as this is called, frequently leads to unexpected difficulties, despite extensive testing of the new version before the upgrade. In some cases, withdrawal of the new system once it has been introduced is a formidable problem, because data formats and file contents have already changed. The popular press is full of incidents in which system failures are attributed to system upgrades gone awry.

New facilities can be added to an NIS, and especially a Web-based NIS, with deceptive ease: a new server that provides the desired service is connected to the network. However, such action can affect performance and reliability. The dispersed nature of an NIS user community can make it difficult to gauge the impact of new features. And the lack of quality-of-service controls can make one NIS a hostage to changes in the load or features in another.

Another potential area of difficulty for NIS evolution is having critical COTS components change or be rendered obsolete. The advent of so-called "push" technology, in which commercial off-the-shelf software is silently and automatically updated when the user visits the vendor's Web site, can cause COTS components to drift away from the configuration that existed during test and acceptance; the situation leads to obscure and difficult-to-locate errors.

Findings

1. Very little is known about the integration of subsystems into an NIS. Yet methods for network integration are critical for building an NIS. NISs pose new challenges for integration because of their distributed nature and the variability of network behavior.

2. Even though technical reviews are generally considered by the practitioner community to be effective, the utility of technical reviews for establishing trustworthiness properties is not well documented.

3. Formal methods are most effective when the property of interest is subtle but can be rigorously defined, and when either the description of the object being analyzed is relatively small or the formal method being used supports analyses that can be automated.

4. Formal methods are moving from more manual methods toward computer-aided and fully mechanized approaches.

5. Formal methods are being used with success in commercial and industrial settings for hardware development and requirements analysis and with some success for software development.

6. Formal methods should be regarded as but one piece of technology for eliminating design errors in hardware and software. Formal methods are particularly well suited for identifying errors that become apparent only in scenarios not likely to be tested or testable.

7. Fundamental research problems in formal methods should not be neglected in favor of demonstration exercises. Research progress in core

areas will provide a basis for making significant advances in the capabilities of the technology.

8. Although the large size of an NIS and the use of COTS limit the use of formal methods for analyzing the entire system, formal verification can still contribute to the development process.

9. Testing subsets of a system does not adequately establish confidence in an NIS given its distributed nature and uncontrollable and unobservable subsystems.

10. Research in testing that addresses issues of scale and concurrency is needed.

11. Postdeployment modification of software can have a significant negative impact on NIS trustworthiness and security.

12. Research directed at better integration of testing and formal methods is likely to have payoffs for increasing assurance in trustworthy NISs.

REFERENCES

Abadi, Martin, and Leslie Lamport. 1993. "Composing Specifications," *ACM Transactions on Programming Languages and Systems*, 15(1):73-132.
Boehm, B. 1981. *Software Engineering Economics*. Englewood Cliffs, NJ: Prentice-Hall International.
Boehm, B. 1988. "A Spiral Model of Software Development and Enhancement," *IEEE Computer*, 21(5):61-72.
Boehm, B., and T. DeMarco. 1997. "Software Risk Management," *IEEE Software*, 14(3):17-19.
Bollinger, Terry, and Clement McGowan. 1991. "A Critical Look at Software Capability Evaluations," *IEEE Software*, 8(4):25-41.
Brock, Bishop, Matt Koffman, and J Strother Moore. 1996. "ACL2 Theorems About Commercial Microprocessors," pp. 275-293 in *Proceedings of Formal Methods in Computer-aided Design*. Berlin: Springer-Verlag.
Brodman, Judith G., and Donna L. Johnson. 1996. "Return on Investment from Software Process Improvement as Measured by U.S. Industry," *Crosstalk: The Journal of Defense Software Engineering*, 9(4). Reprint available online at <http://www.stsc.hill.af.mil/crosstalk/1996/apr/>.
Brooks, Frederick P., Jr. 1975. *The Mythical Man-Month. Essays on Software Engineering*. Reading, MA: Addison-Wesley.
Brown, Nat, and Charlie Kindel. 1998. *Distributed Component Object Model Protocol—DCOM/1.0*. Microsoft Corporation, January. Available online at <http://www.microsoft.com/oledev/olecom/draft-brown-dcom-v1-spec-02.txt>.
Burrows, Michael, Martin Abadi, and Roger Needham. 1990. "A Logic of Authentication," *ACM Transactions on Computer Systems*, 8(1):18-36.
Butler, R., and G. Finelli. 1993. "The Infeasibility of Quantifying the Reliability of Life-critical Real-time Software," *IEEE Transactions on Software Engineering*, 19(1):3-12.
Clarke, Edmund M., O. Grumberg, H.S. Jha, D.E. Long, K.L. McMillan, and L.A. Ness. 1993. "Verification of the Futurebus+ Cache Coherence Protocol," *Transactions A (Computer Science and Technology)*, A32:15-30.
Clarke, Edmund M., and Jeanette M. Wing. 1996. "Formal Methods: State of the Art and Future Directions," *ACM Computing Surveys*, 28(4):626-643.

Clingen, C.T., and T.H. van Vleck. 1978. "The Multics System Programming Process," pp. 278-280 in *Proceedings of the 3rd International Conference on Software Engineering*. New York: IEEE Press.

Computer Science and Telecommunications Board (CSTB), National Research Council. 1997. *ADA and Beyond: Software Policies for the Department of Defense*. Washington, DC: National Academy Press.

Constantine, L.L., and E. Yourdon. 1979. *Structured Design*. Englewood Cliffs, NJ: Prentice-Hall.

Craigen, Dan, Susan Gerhart, and Ted Ralston. 1993. *An International Survey of Industrial Applications of Formal Methods*. Gaithersburg, MD: National Institute of Standards and Technology, Computer Systems Laboratory, March.

Craigen, Dan, Susan Gerhart, and Ted Ralston. 1995. "Formal Methods Reality Check: Industrial Usage," *IEEE Transactions on Software Engineering*, 21(2):90-98.

Croxford, M., and J. Sutton. 1995. "Breaking through the V and V Bottleneck," pp. 334-354 in *Proceedings of Ada in Europe, in Frankfurt/Main, Germany*. New York: Springer.

Curtis, Bill. 1981. "Substantiating Programmer Variability," *Proceedings of the IEEE*, 69(7):846.

DeRemer, F., and H.H. Kron. 1976. "Programming-in-the-Large Versus Programming-in-the-Small," *IEEE Transactions on Software Engineering*, 2(3):80-86.

Detlefs, D. 1996. "An Overview of the Extended Static Checking System," pp. 1-9 in *Proceedings of the First Workshop on Formal Methods in Software Practice*. New York: ACM Press.

Devauchelle, L., P.G. Larsen, and H. Voss. 1997. "PICGAL: Lessons Learnt from a Practical Use of Formal Specification to Develop a High-Reliability Software," *European Space Agency SP 199*, 409:159-164.

Diaz, Michael, and Joseph Sligo. 1997. "How Software Process Improvement Helped Motorola," *IEEE Software*, 14(5):75-81.

Digital Equipment Corporation. 1997. *Workshop on Security and Languages*. Palo Alto, CA: Digital Equipment Corporation, Systems Research Center, October 30-31. Available online at <http://www.research.digital.com/SRC/personal/Martin_Abadi/sal/home.html>.

Dill, David L., A.J. Drexler, A.J. Hu, and C.H. Yang. 1992. "Protocol Verification as a Hardware Design Aid," pp. 522-525 in *Proceedings of the IEEE International Conference on Computer Design: VLSI in Computers and Processors*. Los Alamitos, CA: IEEE Computer Society Press.

Dill, David L., and John Rushby. 1996. "Acceptance of Formal Methods: Lessons from Hardware Design," *IEEE Computer*, 29(4):16-30.

Dion, Raymond. 1993. "Process Improvement and the Corporate Balance Sheet," *IEEE Software*, 10(4):28-35.

Easterbrok, Steve, Robyn Lutz, Richard Covington, John Kelly, and Yoko Ampo. 1998. "Experiences Using Lightweight Formal Methods for Requirements Modeling," *IEEE Transactions on Software Engineering*, 24(7):4-13.

Fagan, M.E. 1986. "Advances in Software Inspections," *IEEE Transactions on Software Engineering*, 12(7):744-751.

Fayad, Mohamed, and Mauri Laitinen. 1997. "Process Assessment Considered Harmful," *Communications of the ACM*, 40(11):125-128.

Garland, David, and Mary Shaw. 1996. *Software Architecture: Perspectives on an Emerging Discipline*. Englewood Cliffs, N.J.: Prentice-Hall.

Glass, R.L. 1981. "Persistent Software Errors," *IEEE Transactions on Software Engineering*, 7(2):162-168.

Hall, Anthony. 1996. "Using Formal Methods to Develop an ATC Information System," *IEEE Software*, 13(6):66-76.

Hamilton, Graham, ed. 1997. *JavaBeans*. Palo Alto, CA: Sun Microsystems.

Heimdahl, M., and Nancy G. Leveson. 1996. "Completeness and Consistency in Hierarchical State-based Requirements," *IEEE Transactions on Software Engineering*, 22(6):363-377.

Heninger, K. 1980. "Specifying Software Requirements for Complex Systems: New Techniques and Their Application," *IEEE Transactions on Software Engineering*, 6(1):2-13.

Herbsleb, James, and Dennis Goldenson. 1996. "A Systematic Survey of CMM Experience and Results," pp. 323-330 in *Proceedings of the 18th International Conference on Software Engineering (ICSE)*. Los Alamitos, CA: IEEE Computer Society Press.

Hernandez, J.A. 1997. *The SAP R/3 Handbook*. New York: McGraw-Hill.

Hoare, C.A.R. 1985. *Communicating Sequential Processes*. Englewood Cliffs, NJ: Prentice-Hall.

Honeywell Corporation. 1975. *Aerospace and Defense Group Software Program, Final Report*. Waltham, MA: Honeywell Corporation, Systems and Research Center.

Jones, C.B. 1986. *Systematic Software Development Using VDM*. Englewood Cliffs, NJ: Prentice-Hall.

Kitson, David, and Stephen Masters. 1993. "An Analysis of SEI Software Process Assessment Results: 1987-1991," pp. 68-77 in *Proceedings of the 15th International Conference on Software Engineering (ICSE-15)*. Los Alamitos, CA: IEEE Computer Society Press.

Kuehlmann, A., A. Srinivasan, and D.P. LaPotin. 1995. "Verity—A Formal Verification Program for Custom CMOS Circuits," *IBM Journal of Research and Development*, 39(1/2):149-165.

Lampson, Butler W. 1983. "Hints for Computer System Design," *Operating Systems Review*, 17(5):33-48.

Lawlis, Patricia K., Robert M. Flowe, and James B. Thordahl. 1995. "A Correlational Study of the CMM and Software Development Performance," *Crosstalk: The Journal of Defense Software Engineering*, 8(9):21-25.

Leveson, Nancy. 1995. *Safeware*. Reading, MA: Addison-Wesley.

Leveson, Nancy G. 1987. *Software Safety*. Pittsburgh, PA: Carnegie Mellon University, Software Engineering Institute, July.

Lowe, Gavin, and Bill Roscoe. 1997. "Using CSP to Detect Errors in the TMN Protocol," *IEEE Transactions on Software Engineering*, 23(10):659-669.

Manes, Stephen. 1998. "Settlement Near in Technical Help-line Suit," *New York Times*, March 3, p. F2.

Marzullo, K., Fred B. Schneider, and J. Dehn. 1994. "Refinement for Fault Tolerance: An Aircraft Hand-off Protocol," pp. 39-54 in *Foundations of Ultradependable Parallel and Distributed Computing, Paradigms for Dependable Applications*. Amsterdam, The Netherlands: Kluwer.

McGarry, Frank, Steve Burke, and Bill Decker. 1997. "Measuring Impacts of Software Process Maturity in a Production Environment," *Proceedings of the 21st Goddard Software Engineering Laboratory Software Engineering Workshop*. Greenbelt, MD: Goddard Space Flight Center.

McLean, John. 1994. "A General Theory of Composition for Trace Sets Closed Under Selective Interleaving Functions," pp. 79-93 in *Proceedings of the IEEE Computer Society Symposium on Research in Security and Privacy*. Los Alamitos, CA: IEEE Computer Society Press.

Meadows, Catherine. 1992. "Applying Formal Methods to the Analysis of a Key Management Protocol," *Journal of Computer Security*, 1(1):5-36.

Meyer, Bertrand. 1988. *Object-oriented Software Construction*. Englewood Cliffs, NJ: Prentice-Hall.

Microsoft Corporation and Digital Equipment Corporation. 1995. *The Component Object Model Specification (COM)*. Microsoft Corporation and Digital Equipment Corporation, October. Available online at <http://www.microsoft.com/oledev/olecom/title.htm>.

Middleburg, C.A. 1989. "VVSL: A Language for Structured VDM Specifications," *Formal Aspects of Computing*, 1(1):115-135.

Miller, Steven P. 1998. "Specifying the Mode Logic of a Flight Guidance System in CoRE and SCR," pp. 44-53 in *Proceedings of the 2nd Workshop on Formal Methods in Software Practice*. New York: ACM Press.

Musser, David R., and Atul Saini. 1996. *STL Tutorial and Reference Guide: C++ Programming with the Standard Template Library*. Reading, MA: Addison-Wesley.

Neumann, Peter G. 1995. *Computer Related Risks*. New York: ACM Press.

Ousterhout, John K. 1998. "Scripting: Higher-level Programming for the 21st Century," *IEEE Computer*, 31(3):23-30.

Owre, Sam, John Rushby, Natarajan Shankar, and Frederich von Henke. 1995. "Formal Verification for Fault-tolerant Architectures: Prolegomena to the Design of PVS," *IEEE Transactions on Software Engineering*, 21(2):107-125.

Parnas, D.L. 1974. "On a 'Buzzword': Hierarchical Structure," pp. 335-342 in *Programming Methodology. A Collection of Articles by Members of the IFIP Congress*, D. Gries, ed. Berlin: Springer-Verlag.

Paulk, Mark C., Bill Curtis, Mary Beth Chrissis, and Charles V. Weber. 1993. "Capability Maturity Model for Software Version 1.1," *IEEE Software*, 10(4):18-27.

Pfleeger, S.L., N. Fenton, and S. Page. 1994. "Evaluating Software Engineering Standards," *IEEE Computer*, 27(9):71-79.

Porter, A.A., H.P. Siy, C.O. Toman, and L.G. Votta. 1997. "An Experiment to Assess the Cost-Benefits of Code Inspections in Large Scale Software Development," *IEEE Transactions on Software Engineering*, 23(6):329-346.

Potts, Colin, Kenji Takahashi, and Annie I. Anton. 1994. "Inquiry-based Requirements Analysis," *IEEE Software*, 11(2):21-32.

Pressman, Roger S. 1986. *Software Engineering: A Practitioner's Approach*. New York: McGraw-Hill.

Raymond, Eric, and Guy L. Steele. 1991. *The New Hacker's Dictionary*. Cambridge, MA: MIT Press.

Rochkind, Marc J. 1975. "The Source Code Control System," *IEEE Transactions on Software Engineering*, 1(4):364-370.

Ross, Douglas T. 1977. "Guest Editorial—Reflections on Requirements," *IEEE Transactions on Software Engineering*, 3(1):2-5.

Rushby, J. 1995. *Formal Methods and Their Role in Certification of Critical Systems*. Menlo Park, CA: SRI International, March.

Savage, Stefan, Michael Burrows, Greg Nelson, Patrick Sobalvarro, and Thomas E. Anderson. 1997. "Eraser: A Dynamic Data Race Detector for Multi-threaded Programs," *Operating Systems Review*, 31(5):27-37.

Saydjari, O. Sami, J.M. Beckman, and J.R. Leaman. 1989. "LOCK Trek: Navigating Uncharted Space," pp. 167-175 in *Proceedings of the IEEE Symposium on Security and Privacy*. Los Alamitos, CA: IEEE Computer Society Press.

Sommerville, Ian. 1996. *Software Engineering*. 5th Ed. Reading, MA: Addison-Wesley.

Srivas, Mandayam K., and Steven P. Miller. 1995. "Formal Verification of the AAMP5 Microprocessor," *Applications of Formal Methods*, Michael G. Hinchey and Jonathan P. Bowden, eds. Englewood Cliffs, NJ: Prentice-Hall.

Tanik, Murat M., Raymond T. Ye, and guest editors. 1989. "Rapid Prototyping in Software Development," *IEEE Computer Magazine*, Vol. 22, Special Issue (5).

Taylor, T. 1989. "FTLS-based Security Testing for LOCK," *Proceedings of the 12th National Computer Security Conference*. Washington, DC: U.S. Government Printing Office.

Thompson, Kenneth. 1984. "Reflections on Trusting Trust," *Communications of the ACM*, 27(8):761-763.

Watts, Humphrey, and Bill Curtis. 1991. "Comment on 'A Critical Look,'" *IEEE Software*, 8(4):42-46.

Watts, Humphrey, Terry Synder, and Ronald Willis. 1991. "Software Process Improvement at Hughes Aircraft," *IEEE Software*, 8(4):11-23.

Weissman, Clark. 1995. "Penetration Testing," *Information Security*, M.D. Abrams, S. Jajodia, and H.J. Podell, eds. Los Alamitos, CA: IEEE Computer Society Press.

4

Reinventing Security

INTRODUCTION

Increasing the immunity of a networked information system (NIS) to hostile attacks is a broad concern, encompassing authentication, access control, integrity, confidentiality, and availability. Any solution will almost certainly be based on a combination of system mechanisms in addition to physical and personnel controls.[1] The focus of this chapter is these system mechanisms—in particular, what exists, what works, and what is needed. In addition, an examination of the largely disappointing results from more than two decades of work based on what might be called the "theory of security" invites a new approach to viewing security for NISs— one based on a "theory of insecurity"—and that, too, is discussed.

---

[1]Personnel security is intrinsic in any NIS, since some set of individuals must be trusted to some extent with regard to their authorized interactions with the system. For example, people manage system operation, configure external system interfaces, and ultimately initiate authentication of (other) users of a system. In a similar vein, some amount of physical security is required for all systems, to thwart theft or destruction of data or equipment. The physical and personnel security controls imposed on a system are usually a function of the environment in which the system operates. Individuals who have access to systems processing classified information typically undergo extensive background investigations and may even require a polygraph examination. In contrast, most employers perform must less stringent screening for their information technology staff. Similarly, the level of physical security afforded to the NISs that support stock markets like the NYSE and AMEX is greater that that of a typical commercial system. Although physical and personnel controls are essential elements of system security, they are largely outside the scope of this study.

The choice of system security mechanisms employed in building an NIS should, in theory, be a function of the environment, taking into account the security requirements and the perceived threat. In practice, NISs are constructed with commercial off-the-shelf (COTS) components. What security mechanisms are available is thus dictated by the builders of these COTS components. Moreover, because most COTS components are intended for constructing a range of systems, their security mechanisms usually are not tailored to specific needs. Instead, they reflect perceptions by a product-marketing organization about the requirements of a fairly broad market segment.[2] The task faced by the NIS security architect, then, is determining (1) how best to make use of the given generic security mechanisms and (2) how to augment those mechanisms to achieve an acceptable level of security. The NIS security architect's task is all the more difficult because COTS products embody vulnerabilities, but few of the products are subjected by their builders to forms of analysis that might reveal these vulnerabilities. Thus, the NIS security architect will generally be unaware of the residual vulnerabilities lurking in a system's components.

This chapter's focus on security technology should not be misconstrued—an overwhelming majority of security vulnerabilities are caused by "buggy" code. At least a third of the Computer Emergency Response Team (CERT) advisories since 1997, for example, concern inadequately checked input leading to character string overflows (a problem peculiar to C programming language handling of character strings). Moreover, less than 15 percent of all CERT advisories described problems that could have been fixed or avoided by proper use of cryptography. Avoiding design and implementation errors in software (the subject of Chapter 3) is an essential part of the security landscape.

Evolution of Security Needs and Mechanisms

In early computing systems, physical controls were an effective means of protecting data and software from unauthorized access, because these systems were physically isolated and single-user. The advent of multiprogramming and time-sharing invited sharing of programs and data among an often closed community of users. It also created a need for mechanisms to control this sharing and to prevent actions by one user

---

[2]Some COTS products do allow a system integrator or site administrator to select from among several options for security facilities, thereby providing some opportunity for customization. For example, one may be able to choose between the use of passwords, challenge-response technology, or Kerberos for authentication. But the fact remains that COTS components limit the mechanisms available to the security architect.

from interfering with those of another or with the operating system itself. As computers were connected to networks, sharing became even more important and access control problems grew more complex. The move to distributed systems (e.g., client-server computing and the advent of wide-spread Internet connectivity) exacerbated these problems while providing ready, remote access not only for users but also for attackers from anywhere in the world. Closed user communities are still relevant in some instances, but more flexible sharing among members of very dynamic groups has become common. See Box 4.1 for a discussion of threats from within and outside user communities.

The evolution of computing and communication capabilities has been accompanied by an evolution in security requirements and increased demands on security mechanisms. Computing and communication features and applications have outpaced the ability to secure them. Requirements for confidentiality, authentication, integrity, and access control have become more nuanced; the ability to meet these requirements and enforce suitable security policies has not kept up. The result: successful attacks against NISs are common, and evidence suggests that many go undetected (U.S. GAO, 1996). The increasing use of extensible systems and foreign or mobile code (e.g., Java "applets" and ActiveX modules delivered via networks) further complicates the task of implementing NIS security.

Of growing concern with regard to controlling critical infrastructures is denial-of-service attacks, which compromise availability. The attack may target large numbers of users, preventing them from using a networked information system, or may target individuals, destroying their ability to access data, or may target a computing system, preventing it from accomplishing an assigned job. Only recently have denial-of-service attacks become a focus of serious countermeasure development. Clearly, these attacks should be of great concern to NIS security architects.

ACCESS CONTROL POLICIES

It is common to describe access controls in terms of the policies that they support and to judge the effectiveness of access control mechanisms relative to their support for those policies. This might leave the impression that access control policies derive from first principles, but that would be only partly true. Access control policies merely model in cyberspace notions of authorization that exist in the physical world. However, in cyberspace, programs—acting on behalf of users or acting autonomously—and not the users themselves are what interact with data and access other system objects. This can be a source of difficulty since actions by users are the concern but action by programs is what is governed by the policy.

BOX 4.1
Insiders Versus Outsiders

A debate has raged for some time over whether the major threat to system security arises from attacks by "insiders" or by "outsiders." Insiders have been blamed for causing 70 to 80 percent of the incidents and most of the damage (Lewis, 1998). But independent of the reliability of this estimate, it is clear that insiders do pose a serious threat. Two questions then arise: What is the definition of insider? How is damage assessed?

There are three plausible definitions for an insider:

1. A person with legitimate physical access to computer equipment. Thus, a janitor is an insider, but a burglar or casual visitor is not.

2. A person with some sort of organizational status that causes members of the organization to view requests or demands as being authorized. In this view, a purchasing agent is an insider, but a vendor is not.

3. A person with some level of privilege or authority with regard to the computer system. This characterization is particularly difficult to assess in today's networked environment. A casual Internet user accessing a vendor's Web site and running a well-known attack would, in the eyes of most observers, constitute an "outsider" attack. And if the administrator of the Web site used authorizations to make mischief, that would generally be viewed as an "insider" attack. But what of the vendor who is granted putatively limited privilege on a corporate network and then attempts to increase that privilege or otherwise gain information about competitors? It is equally unclear whether a traditional spy or saboteur, operating from the inside at the behest of an outside organization, is an "insider," an "outsider," or yet a third class of entity.

Assessing damage from attacks is equally problematic. Overestimation of damage is rife when prosecution or insurance claims are involved. Perhaps the most egregious case of overestimation occurred in connection with the so-called "Knight Lightning" case. A prosecutor claimed that a particular item of intellectual property was worth $70,000, but closer examination showed that copies were sold by its owners for $30.00 and that the information in the document was made available, again by its owners, in other forms for free (Sterling, 1992). On the other hand, damage is (it is rumored) allegedly underreported in the financial community to avoid loss of customer confidence. Only recently have commercial institutions begun to come forward, albeit under the cloak of anonymity (War Room Research LLC, 1996).

Arguably, the nature of the reporting process inflates the relative numbers of insider incidents, as they are often easier to discover and report. Sophisticated outsider attacks leave minimal traces and force those suspecting an attack to go to great lengths to convince authorities that one is under way (Stoll, 1989). Furthermore, insider attacks, when discovered, tend to be prosecuted more energetically and to gain more publicity than other forms of white-collar crime (Schwartz, 1997). Various estimates add to the confusion. The Federal Bureau of Investigation estimated total damages to the U.S. economy from computer crime to be on the order of $300 billion. Yet reported damages totaled "only" $100 million (War Room Research LLC, 1996). If the otherwise unverified estimate of 70 percent insider damage is accurate, then the possible range of damages is $70 million to $210 billion. A more accurate estimate will not be possible until comprehensive reporting mechanisms are in place and are used.

Most would classify as insiders embezzlers and disgruntled employees operating alone or as part of a conspiracy who mount frauds and destroy data. But the insiders who can cause the most damage are the administrators of the network and its attached computers. They typically have both the knowledge and the authority to alter, copy, or destroy data, cover their tracks by modifying audit logs, and then modify audits and other information to direct suspicion at other individuals.

Organizations today tend to array their defenses around the perimeter of their computing network and rely on deterrence mechanisms, such as audits, to discourage insider attacks. Fine-grained access control is absent inside these perimeters because it can get in the way of users, especially during emergencies. Technical controls on the actions or authorities of administrators are minimal. There is, however, a growing concern about the inherent limitations of perimeter security (see the section titled "Firewalls" in this chapter). As a result, some organizations are turning to internal network-access controls as a way of buttressing perimeter security. Ironically, this latter access-control technology is more consistent with the traditional meaning of the term "firewall" as imposing unbreachable partitions in a structure.

Intrusion-detection systems frequently are advocated for combating the insider threat, as well as for detecting outsider attacks that have successfully breached perimeter defenses. These systems collect data on computer and network usage, apply pattern matching or heuristics, and trigger alarms if they detect what appears to be a pattern of improper activity.[1] When directed toward insiders, intrusion-detection systems have proved deficient. The amount of data that must be collected imposes a performance penalty and, in many cases, raises concerns about improper workplace surveillance. Although the assumption underlying most heuristics for recognizing improper activity is that users exhibit fairly constant patterns of behavior, this assumption is generally invalidated, for example, during emergencies, the very time when a deluge of security alarms is least tolerable. Adept users can also subvert a heuristic by making gradual shifts in their behavior, such as slowly increasing the number of files accessed each day so that file accesses that once would trigger an "improper browsing" alarm are now treated as normal.

The insider threat is a classic example of security as a management problem. Technical defenses tend to be expensive, cumbersome, or largely ineffective. The most practical solution is to know the people who have significant authority on the system and to work to maintain their loyalty to the organization.

---

[1]Most of these systems look for specific attack "signatures" rather than attempt to detect deviation from nominal behavior. In this sense, such systems are much like antivirus programs.

The evolution of access control policies and access control mechanisms has attempted, first, to keep pace with the new modes of resource sharing supported in each subsequent generation of systems, and, second, to repel a growing list of attacks to which the systems are subjected. The second driving force is easily overlooked, but crucial. Access controls can enforce the principle of least privilege.[3] In this fashion, they prevent and contain attacks.

Before suggesting directions for the future, it is instructive to examine the two basic types of access control policies that have dominated computer security work for over two and a half decades: discretionary access control and mandatory access control.

Discretionary access control policies allow subjects, which model users or processes, to specify for objects what operations other subjects are permitted to perform. Most of the access control mechanisms implemented and deployed enforce discretionary access control policies. Individual users or groups of users (or computers) are identified with subjects; computers, networks, files or processes, are associated with objects. For example, *read* and *write* permissions might be associated with file system objects (i.e., files); some subjects (i.e., users) might have *read* access to a given file while other subjects do not. Discretionary access control would seem to mimic physical-world policies of authorization, but there are subtleties. For instance, transitive sharing of data involving intermediary users or processes can subvert the intent of discretionary access control policies by allowing a subject to learn the contents of an object (albeit indirectly) even though the policy forbids (direct) access to that object by the subject.

Mandatory access control policies also define permitted accesses to objects for subjects, but now only security administrators, rather than individual users, specify what accesses are permitted.[4] Mandatory access control policies typically are formulated for objects that have been labeled, and the policies typically are intended to regulate information flow from one object to another. The best-known example of mandatory access controls arises in connection with controlling the flow of data according to military classifications. Here, data are assigned classification labels (e.g., "top secret" and "unclassified") and subjects are assigned clearances; simple rules dictate the clearance needed by a subject to access data that have been assigned a given label.

---

[3]The principle of least privilege holds that programs and users should operate using the least set of privileges necessary to complete the job.

[4]In fact, there exist policies that are mandatory access control but user processes do have some control over permissions. One example is a policy in which a user process could irrevocably shed certain permissions.

Mandatory access controls can prevent Trojan horse attacks; discretionary access controls cannot. A Trojan horse is a program that exploits the authorization of the user executing a program for another user's malicious purposes, such as copying information into an area accessible by a user not entitled to access that information. Mandatory controls block such attacks by limiting the access of all programs—including the Trojan horse—in a manner that cannot be circumvented by users. Discretionary access controls are inherently vulnerable to Trojan horse attacks because software executing on behalf of a user inherits that user's privilege without restriction (Boebert and Kain, 1996).

Shortcomings of Formal Policy Models

Despite the lion's share of attention from researchers and actual support in deployed system security mechanisms, many security policies of practical interest cannot be formulated as discretionary and mandatory access control policies. Discretionary and mandatory access control focus on protecting information from unauthorized access. They cannot model the effects of certain malicious or erroneous software, nor do they completely address availability of system resources and services (i.e., protection against denial-of-service attacks). And they are defined in an access control model—defined by the Trusted Computer System Evaluation Criteria (U.S. DOD, 1985)—that has only limited expressive power, rendering the model unsuitable for talking about certain application-dependent access controls.

The access control model defined by the Trusted Computer System Evaluation Criteria, henceforth called the DOD access control model, presupposes that an organization's policies are static and have precise and succinct characterizations. This supposition is questionable. Organizations' security policies usually change with perceived organizational needs and with perceived threat. Even the Department of Defense's policy—the inspiration for the best-known form of mandatory access control (Bell and La Padula, 1973)—has numerous exceptions to handle special circumstances (Commission on Protecting and Reducing Government Secrecy, 1997). For example, senior political or military officials can downgrade classified information for diplomatic or operational reasons. But the common form of mandatory access control does not allow nonsensitive objects to be derived from sensitive sources, because the DOD access control model does not associate content with objects nor does it (or can any model) formalize when declassifying information is safe.[5] Policies

---

[5]This also means that the underlying mathematical model is unable to capture the most basic operation of cryptography, in which sensitive data become nonsensitive when enciphered.

involving application-specific information also cannot be handled, since such information is not part of the DOD access control model.[6]

At least two policy models that have been proposed do take into account the application involved. The Clark/Wilson model (Clark and Wilson, 1987) sets forth rules for maintaining the integrity of data in a commercial environment. It is significant that this model contains elements of the outside world, such as a requirement to check internal data (e.g., inventories) with the physical objects being tabulated. The "Chinese Wall" model (Brewer and Nash, 1989) expresses rules for separating different organizational activities for conformance with legal and regulatory strictures in the financial world.

Still, from the outset, there has been a gap between organizational policy and the 1970s view of computing embodied by the DOD access control model: users remotely accessing a shared, central facility through low-functionality ("dumb") terminal equipment. And, as computing technology advanced, the gap has widened. It is significant that, in a glossary of computer security, Brinkley and Schell (1995) use a passive database (a library) as the example and include the important passage:

> . . . the mapping between our two 'worlds':
>
> 1. The world independent of computers, of people attempting to access information on paper.
> 2. The world of computers, with objects that are repositories for information and subjects that act as surrogates for users in the attempt to access information in objects.

Processes, for example, are complex, ephemeral entities without clear boundaries, especially in the distributed and multithreaded systems of today. A modern computing network comprises independent computers that are loosely linked to each other and to complexes of servers. And modern programs likely have their own access controls, independent of what is provided by the underlying operating system and the DOD access control model. An access control model that does not capture this aspect of computing systems is fatally flawed.

Subsystems more and more resemble operating systems, and they should be treated as such. To be sure, a subsystem cannot exceed permissions granted to it by an underlying operating system. And even though

---

[6]It should be noted that a formal access control model of a complex application has been defined, and the corresponding implementation subjected to extensive assurance activity. The exercise explored many issues in the construction of such models and is worth study. See Landwehr et al. (1984) for details.

the resources that a subsystem protects are the user's own, that protection serves an important function. Moreover, even if the access control model did capture the policies of subsystems, there still remains the problem of composing those policies with all the other policies that are being enforced. Such composition is difficult, especially when policies are in conflict with each other, as all too often is the case.

The object abstraction in the DOD access control model also can be a source of difficulty. Real objects seldom have uniform security levels, despite what is implied by the DOD access control model. Consider a mailbox with multiple messages. Each message may have field-dependent security levels (sensitive or nonsensitive message body, sensitive or nonsensitive address list, and so on), and there may be multiple messages in the mailbox. What is the level of the mailbox as a whole? The alternative is to split messages so that individual fields are in individual objects, but that leads to a formulation that could be expensive to implement with fidelity.

The all-or-nothing nature of the DOD access control model also detracts from its utility. Designers who implement the model are forced to err on the side of being restrictive, in which case the resulting system may be unusable, or to invent escapes, in which case knowing that a system adheres to the model has limited practical significance. In the battle between security and usability, usability loses. Moreover, since the DOD access control model does not account for contemporary defensive measures, such as virus scans, approaches to executable content control, or firewalls, the system architect who is bound by the model has no incentive to use these technologies. Deploying them makes no progress toward establishing that the system is consistent with the model and, in addition, transforms the model into an incomplete characterization of the system's defensive measures (thereby again limiting the model's practical utility).

Evidence that DOD has recognized some of the problems inherent in building systems that enforce the DOD access control model appears in the new DOD Goal Security Architecture (DGSA; see Box 4.2). DGSA does not legislate that only the DOD access control model be used; instead it supports a broad set of security policies that go far beyond the traditional information-flow policies. DGSA also does not discourage DOD end users from employing the latest in object-based, distributed systems, networks, and so on, while instituting rich access control, integrity, and availability policies. However, DGSA offers no insights about how to achieve an appropriate level of assurance that these policies are correctly implemented (despite upping the stakes significantly regarding what security functionality must be supported). Thus it remains to be seen if the DGSA effort will spur significant progress in system security.

BOX 4.2
DOD Goal Security Architecture

The DOD Goal Security Architecture (DGSA) (DISA, 1996) has evolved over the last decade as a series of architecture documents. Most of the principles have remained constant during this evolution.

DGSA is oriented toward supporting a range of access controls and integrity policies in an object-oriented, distributed-system environment. The range of security policies to be supported goes far beyond the Bell-La Padula information flow security policy that has dominated DOD security for more than 20 years. Multiparty authorization, multilevel objects, originator control of release, role-based authorization, and variable levels of availability are among the security features offered by DGSA.

DGSA embraces commercial off-the-shelf (COTS) products and commercial network resources. Commercial networks can readily be employed through the use of (conventional, high-assurance) network security devices. But there is the matter of achieving availability in excess of what most commercial users seek.[1] If commercial networks are vulnerable to disruption on a global or targeted basis, then DOD communications traversing these networks would be vulnerable to denial-of-service attacks.

Use of COTS operating systems and applications raises questions about how to create multilevel information objects and how to enforce appropriate information flow security, as labeling is generally not supported in such commercial offerings. Perimeter security devices (e.g., firewalls and guards) are limited in the granularity at which they can enforce data separation, especially in the absence of labels.

At present, DGSA must be viewed more as a list of goals than as an architectural specification. Available (COTS) technology and even research and development prototypes lag far behind what DGSA calls for. Most of the goals will require substantial research, and some of the goals may be unattainable relative to credible, national-level threats. Moreover, DGSA still embodies a notion of "absolute protection" despite the practical impossibility of attaining that. An excellent overview of DGSA, including a characterization of some of the research and development challenges it poses, is offered by Feustel and Mayfield (1998).

---

[1]Commercial users with high real-time communication availability concerns do not now depend on the Internet. For example, U.S. stock exchanges employ redundancy at multiple layers to achieve sufficient availability using commercial communications. See Chapter 2 for additional discussions of vulnerabilities in the public telephone network and Internet.

A New Approach

One can view the ultimate goal as the building of systems that resist attack. Attackers exploit subtle flaws and side effects in security mechanisms and, more typically, exploit interactions between mechanisms. Testing can expose such previously hidden aspects of system behavior, but no amount of testing can demonstrate the absence of all exploitable flaws or side effects.

An alternative to finding flaws in a system is to demonstrate directly that the system is secure by showing the correspondence between the system and some model that embodies the security properties of concern. One problem (system security) is thus reduced to another (model security) presumably simpler one. Sound in theory, success in this endeavor requires the following:

1. Models that formalize the security policies of concern.
2. Practical methods for demonstrating a correspondence between a system and a formal model.

But the arguments given earlier suggest that suitable formal models for NIS security policies, which invariably include stipulations about availability and application semantics, do not today exist and would be difficult to develop. Moreover, establishing a correspondence between a system and a formal model has proved impractical, even for systems built specifically with the construction of that correspondence in mind and for which analysts have complete knowledge and access to internals. Establishing the correspondence is thus not a very realistic prospect for COTS components, which are not built with such verification activities in mind and, generally, do not offer the necessary access to internals.

Experience has taught that systems—and, in particular, complex systems like NISs—can be secure, but only up to a point. There will always be residual vulnerabilities, always a degree of insecurity. The question one should ask is not whether a system is secure, but how secure that system is relative to some perceived threat. Yet this question is almost never asked. Instead, notions of absolute security, based on correspondence to formal models, have been the concern. Perhaps it is time to contemplate alternatives to the "absolute security" philosophy.

Consider an alternative view, which might be summarized in three "axioms":

1. Insecurity exists.
2. Insecurity cannot be destroyed.
3. Insecurity can be moved around.

With this view, the object of security engineering would be to identify insecurities and move them to less exposed and less vulnerable parts of a system. Military cryptosystems that employ symmetric-key cryptography illustrate the approach. Radio transmissions are subject to interception, so they are enciphered. This encryption does not destroy the insecurity (disclosure of message contents) but rather moves the insecurity to the cryptographic keys, whose compromise would lead to the disclosure of intercepted transmissions. The keys must be distributed. And they are, subject to elaborate physical controls and auditing that are impractical for radio transmissions.[7] So, the use of encryption moves insecurity from one part of the system to another and does so in a manner that decreases the overall vulnerability of the system relative to some perceived threats. (In a world where monitoring radio transmissions was difficult but kidnapping diplomatic couriers bearing cryptographic keys was easy, the perceived threats would be different and the encryption solution no longer would be appropriate.)

Vulnerability assessments provide a well-known way to identify system insecurities. Here, attack by an adversary is simulated using a team whose technical and other resources are comparable to the actual threat. The team undertakes an unconstrained search for vulnerabilities, examining the system in its context of use and attempting to exploit any aspect of the system, its implementation, or its operational context to cause a security breach. A methodical approach to this process is described in Weissman (1995).

Vulnerability assessment has the advantage that all aspects of the system are stressed in context. But it does have disadvantages. No overt evidence of security is presented. The approach is potentially quite costly, because assessment must be carried out on a per system basis. And finally, systematic methods do not yet exist for predicting how vulnerabilities and attacks can propagate in systems. Were it possible to analyze vulnerability and attack propagation, designers could begin to think about a design philosophy based on relocating insecurities, to move them away from threats. The result would be a methodology especially attractive for securing NISs—an alternative to the "absolute security" philosophy.

Findings

1. Existing formal policy models have only limited utility because they concern only some of the security properties of interest to NIS builders. To the extent that formal models are useful (as descriptive vehicles and for inferring consequences from policies) further development is needed to remove the limits of existing policies, both with regard to the system model and with regard to what types of security are captured.

2. Demonstrating the correspondence between a system and a formal model is not a practical approach for gaining assurance that an NIS is

---

[7]Although even these precautions do not guarantee security, as the celebrated "Walker Case" showed (Kneece, 1986).

resistant to attack. An alternative to this "absolute security" philosophy is to identify insecurities and make design changes to reposition them in light of the nature of the threat. Further research is needed to determine the feasibility of this new approach to the problem.

3. Some practical means for evaluating the security characteristics (both security features and residual vulnerabilities) of COTS system components is essential. Evaluation must not be so costly or time-consuming that vendors will shun it or that evaluated products will be obsolete (relative to their nonevaluated counterparts).

IDENTIFICATION AND AUTHENTICATION MECHANISMS

Identification is an assertion about an entity's identity. In the simplest case, this assertion could be a claim that the entity makes. Authentication refers to the process by which a system establishes that an identification assertion is valid. A number of authentication mechanisms are commonly used in practice; each has advantages and disadvantages. Historically, the mechanisms have been characterized as something you know, something you have, or something you are. The latter refers to innate biological properties of the user and therefore is not applicable for computer-to-computer authentication.[8]

Network-based Authentication

Network-based authentication relies on the underlying network (and possibly the host computer) to authenticate the identity of the source of network traffic. The reliability of the approach is thus closely tied to characteristics of the underlying network. For example, Chapter 2 discusses the ease with which Internet Protocol (IP) addresses in the Internet and caller ID information in the public telephone network (PTN) can be forged, and so using these for authentication would probably be imprudent.

When implemented with a moderate degree of assurance, network-based authentication can be appealing. It relies on a third party—the network provider—rather than burdening end users or servers. The network provider arguably even has a business incentive to provide such a service and may be able to justify larger investments in the development of a high-assurance service than any single client of that service could. But positioning an authentication service at the network provider is not consistent with the principle of least privilege and thus is a questionable design choice.

---

[8]Attempts have been made, though, to use "signatures" of analog radio devices.

Cryptographic Authentication

Secure forms of authentication for an NIS generally rely on cryptography.[9] While many different schemes are used, all involve possession of a secret by the entity being authenticated. If this secret is compromised, then so is the authentication process.

The simplest form of cryptographic authentication is based on an implicit property of encryption: if an entity does not possess the proper key, then encrypted messages sent or received by that entity decrypt into random bits. More-sophisticated forms employ cryptographic protocols—stylized exchanges between two or more parties—to authenticate callers and to distribute short-term cryptographic keys. But the design of such protocols is a subtle business, and flaws have been found in many published protocols (Abadi and Needham, 1994).

A major advantage of cryptographic authentication is that it can provide continuous authentication, whereby each packet sent during a session is authenticated. The alternative is to validate the identity of an entity only at the time the authentication process is invoked (typically at the start of a session), but that alternative is vulnerable to session "hijacking" whereby an attacker impersonates a previously authenticated entity (Joncheray, 1995). As the sophistication of attackers increases, the need for continuous authentication has become more critical.

Cryptographic authentication can be based on symmetric (conventional) or on asymmetric (public-key) cryptosystems. For deployment in large-scale contexts, both types of cryptosystems typically require the use of a trusted third party to act as an intermediary, and the existence of this third party constitutes a potential vulnerability. For symmetric cryptosystems, the third party (e.g., a Kerberos key-distribution center is discussed later in this chapter) is usually accessed in real time as part of the key-distribution process; for asymmetric cryptosystems, interaction with this third party (e.g., a certification authority) can be offline.

Cryptographic authentication mechanisms require the possession, and thus storage, of a secret or private key. For a human user, if no auxiliary storage is available, such as a smart card or other hardware token, the secret/private key is commonly derived from a conventional password. If this is done, the cryptographic communications protected by this key can be attacked using password guessing (Gong et al., 1993). Such attacks have been reported against S/Key (Haller, 1994) and Kerberos (Neuman and Ts'o, 1994). Although techniques to guard against the attacks are known (Bellovin and Merritt, 1992; Gong et al., 1993), they are rarely employed.

---

[9]Cryptographic-based authentication is usually based on authentication and integrity algorithms (e.g., digital signatures and keyed one-way hash functions, not on encryption algorithms).

Token-based Mechanisms

An authentication technique that has gained popularity over the last few years is use of so-called hardware tokens. A number of different types of hardware tokens are available. All contain a cryptographic key in (nominally tamper-resistant) storage. Some use the key to encrypt a local (current) clock value; others use the key to transform a challenge supplied by the server; and still others execute a complete cryptographic protocol.

Some sort of personal identification number (PIN) or password is usually required in order to enable a hardware token. Because an attacker is assumed not to have access to the token itself or to its memory contents, such a PIN is not susceptible to dictionary and other forms of password-guessing attacks unless the token has been stolen. Theft is further discouraged by employing a counter to trigger erasure of the hardware token's key storage after a few incorrect entries. Tokens that can be electrically connected to a user's computer, such as smart cards, Java rings, and PC cards, are often used to support cryptographic authentication protocols. The degree of tamper resistance provided by these tokens varies widely, so their resistance to attacks involving physical theft is uneven. Hardware tokens are evolving into full-fledged, personal cryptographic devices, capable of providing services beyond authentication.

Biometric Techniques

Biometric authentication techniques rely on presumed-unique characteristics of individuals: voice-print systems, fingerprint readers, retinal or iris scanners, and so forth. Apart from questions about the reliability of the methods themselves, principal disadvantages of biometric techniques are the cost and availability of suitable input devices and the unwillingness of people to interact with such input devices. Few computers come equipped with fingerprint-scanning hardware, and few people are willing to subject their eyes to retinal scanning. Consequently, biometric authentication is employed only in high-threat settings. When used across a network environment, cryptography must complement the biometrics, since a recording of a thumbprint transmitted across a network is just as susceptible to interception and replay as a plaintext, reusable password.

As personal computers and workstations have acquired more sophisticated audio-visual interfaces, there is renewed interest in employing biometric authentication technology in the network environment. For example, a growing number of computers now come equipped with microphones, and low-cost video cameras are also becoming more common. However, a limitation is the need for security of the capture medium. For example, biometric authentication data offered by a personal computer could have been generated by the presumed scanning device or it could be a bit string supplied by an attacker. Thus, to the extent that it is possible to generate bit strings that appear to be valid biometric data, these systems are vulnerable. Moreover, possession of the template needed to validate a biometric scan, plus knowledge of the algorithm used to create that template, probably provides enough information to generate such bit strings (for any user whose template is compromised); disclosure of template data stored at *any* biometric authentication server could compromise use of that biometric technique for the affected users, forever!

Findings

1. Network-based authentication technology is not amenable to high-assurance implementations. Cryptographic authentication represents a preferred approach to authentication at the granularity that might otherwise be provided by network authentication.

2. Cryptographic protocols are difficult to get right. Legitimate needs will arise for new cryptographic authentication protocols (e.g., practical multicast communication authentication), but the technology for verifying these protocols is far from mature. Further research into techniques and supporting tools should be encouraged.

3. The use of hardware tokens holds great promise for implementing authentication. Cost will be addressed by the inexorable advance of digital hardware technology. But interface commonality issues will somehow have to be overcome. The use of PINs to enable hardware tokens is a vulnerability that the use of biometrics could remove. When tokens are being used to sign data digitally, then an interface should be provided so that a user can know what is being signed.

4. Biometric authentication technologies have limitations when employed in network contexts. Still, for use in a closed NIS, biometric techniques that employ existing (or envisioned) interfaces in personal computers (e.g., microphones, low-cost cameras) are worth exploring.

CRYPTOGRAPHY AND PUBLIC-KEY INFRASTRUCTURE

It is impractical to provide strong physical, personnel, and procedural security for a geographically distributed, heterogeneously administered computing system like an NIS. Cryptographic mechanisms, however, can provide security for this setting. They have not been widely deployed, especially in large-scale distributed systems. So even where the theory is well understood, there is much to be learned about the practical aspects of deployment and use. The discussion that follows outlines some of the problems that will have to be confronted by NIS developers.

BOX 4.3
Basic Cryptographic Services

Preserving confidentiality of data. This service is implemented by the sender encrypting the data and the receiver decrypting that data. Wiretappers see only encrypted data, which (by definition) reveals nothing about the original data.

Protecting the integrity of data. This service is implemented by using a message integrity code (MIC), a relatively short (fixed-size) value computed by the sender of data and validated by the receiver. The MIC is a complex function of both the data being protected and a cryptographic key.

Authenticating parties in a conversation. This service is frequently implemented using a challenge/response protocol, in which one party picks a random number and challenges the other to encrypt (or decrypt) it. Only parties with knowledge of a secret key are able to satisfy the challenge.

Nonrepudiation of message origins. This service allows the receiver of a message not only to authenticate the sender but also to prove to a third party that the message came from that sender.

The subject of cryptography ranges from foundational mathematics to applied engineering topics, and a great deal of reference material exists (Schneier, 1996; CSTB, 1996; Menezes et al., 1996). For this report, familiarity with some basic cryptographic services, as sketched in Box 4.3, will suffice.

The two fundamental types of cryptographic systems are secret-key (or symmetric key) cryptography and public-key (or asymmetric key) cryptography. Secret-key cryptography has been known for thousands of years. Public-key cryptography is a relatively recent invention, first described in the public literature[10] in 1976.

With secret-key cryptography, the key used to encrypt a message is the same as the key used to decrypt that message, and the key used to compute the message integrity code (MIC) is the same as the key used to verify it. This means that pairs of communicating parties must share a secret, and if that secret becomes known to some third party, then that third party becomes empowered (1) to decrypt and modify messages in transit undetectably and (2) to generate spurious messages that appear to be authentic. Arranging for both parties of a conversation—and nobody else—to know a secret is one of the central challenges in cryptographic system design.

---

[10] A recent disclosure indicates that the best-known public-key techniques were actually invented first in a classified setting several years before their development in the academic community (see <http://www.cesg.gov.uk>).

With public-key cryptography, different keys are used to encrypt and decrypt messages, and the decryption key cannot be derived from the encryption key. Similarly, different keys are used to generate an integrity check and to verify it, and the generation key cannot be derived from the verification key. The keys used for decryption and integrity-check generation are called private keys; they are kept secret and generally known only to a single party. The keys used for encryption and integrity-check verification are called public keys; these can be freely published (hence the name "public-key cryptography"). Having separate public and private keys simplifies the distribution of keys, especially in large systems.

Public-key cryptography can implement cryptographic services that cannot be built with secret-key cryptography.[11] For example, a digital signature is an integrity check that can be verified by any party. (An integrity check generally can be verified only by the intended recipient of a message.) Digital signatures can be implemented using public-key cryptography—a private key is used by the sender to "sign" the message and that sender's public key (which is accessible to all) is used to verify the signature—but not by using secret-key cryptography.[12]

Versatility does have its cost. Public-key cryptography is considerably more (computationally) expensive to use than secret-key cryptography. Therefore, most cryptographic systems that make use of public-key cryptography are, in fact, hybrids. For confidentiality, public-key cryptography is employed to encrypt a secret key that, in turn, is used with secret-key cryptography to encrypt data. And, to compute a digital signature of a message, a digest[13] of the message is computed and only the digest is signed. This hybrid approach minimizes the number of public-key operations required. Even so, it requires cryptographic algorithms that keep pace with communications transmission speeds.

---

[11]Note that not all public-key algorithms can offer both confidentiality protection and integrity protection. For example, the Diffie-Hellman algorithm (Diffie and Hellman, 1976) cannot support signatures, and the Digital Signature algorithm cannot support encryption.

[12]Several signature schemes have been developed based on secret-key cryptography, but they are too cumbersome to be seriously considered for "real" systems.

[13]A message digest function is more comparable to a secret-key cryptographic algorithm in its performance and technology. It computes a collision-proof fixed-length "checksum" of any message. "Collision-proof" means that it is practically impossible to find two messages with the same checksum. Because it is collision-proof, a given message digest has only one corresponding message (that one can find), and signing it is as secure as signing the entire message.

Findings

1. Application programming interfaces (APIs) for cryptographic services will promote greater use of such services in NISs. Cryptographic services are an extremely effective means for solving certain security problems in geographically distributed systems.

2. Faster encryption and authentication/integrity algorithms will be required to keep pace with rapidly increasing communication speeds and to deploy this technology in a wider range of applications, such as authentication, integrity, and confidentiality for multicast groups.

The Key Management Problem

The security of a cryptographic system depends, in large part, on the security of the methods and practices used to generate and distribute keys. For small systems, keys can be distributed by manually installing them. But this solution does not work for larger systems. There are two well-known approaches to the key-distribution problem in medium to large-scale systems: key-distribution centers (for secret-key cryptography) and certification authorities (for public-key cryptography).

Key-Distribution Centers

A key-distribution center (KDC) is an online automated secret-key provider. The KDC shares a secret distribution key with every party it serves, so its storage requirements are linear in the number of its clients. If client A wants to talk with client B, then that fact is communicated to the KDC. The KDC then randomly generates a new secret (session) key for A and B to use, and distributes that session key, encrypted under both the distribution key it shares with A and the distribution key it shares with B. The messages sent by the KDC must be both integrity and confidentiality protected, and they must give the identities of the parties who will be using the session key (so that each party can securely know the identity of the other).

Variations of this protocol satisfy additional requirements, but all variants require that the KDC be online and all involve the KDC having access (at one time or another) to each session key generated. The requirement that the KDC be online means that to serve client systems having stringent availability requirements, the KDC itself and the communications links to it must be highly available. Because the KDC has had access to all session keys, it is an ideal target for an attacker trying to decipher previously intercepted traffic. Some KDC designs are especially vulnerable, because they employ long-term key distribution keys. Undetected KDC penetrations are the most serious, as the attacker is then free to impersonate any client of the KDC and (in some designs) to read old messages.

Certification Authorities

With public-key cryptography, the challenge is distributing the public keys in a secure fashion.[14] Confidentiality is not an issue because public keys are not secret, but integrity protection is. If A wants to send an encrypted message to B and A can be misled by an attacker about B's public key, then A can be tricked into encrypting messages for B using the attacker's public key. The encrypted message would then be accessible only to the attacker. The solution is to employ a trusted third party called a certification authority (CA). The CA uses public-key cryptography to sign certificates; each certificate binds a subscriber identity to a public key. If A knows the public key of the CA and A has a CA-signed certificate binding a public key to subscriber identity B, then A can verify the CA's signature on the certificate to determine whether the certificate is genuine. And provided the CA is careful about authenticating each subscriber's identity before issuing certificates, a CA-signed certificate binding a public key to subscriber identify B becomes a reliable way for A to learn B's public key.

CAs are, in some respects, easier to secure than key-distribution centers. In theory, CAs do not have to be online or highly available. A certification authority need only be available to issue certificates when new parties are being added to the system and, therefore, offline CA operation is feasible. Offline operation is even preferable, because it makes access by attackers more difficult, thereby helping to preserve CA security. But in practice, an increasing number of CAs are being operated online—fast response time for issuing certificates is important to (would-be) subscribers, and online operation is the only way to keep response time low.

Even so, exploiting a compromised CA is considerably more difficult than exploiting a compromised KDC. Once a CA has been compromised, it can sign and issue bogus certificates. But that behavior in no way compromises previously signed or encrypted traffic. Moreover, if certificates are being posted publicly anyway, then a CA that suddenly posts uncharacteristically large numbers of certificates will arouse suspicion. Compromise of a CA does become problematic when certificates are used for authentication by an authorization system. Sometimes access control data are even stored in certificates. Covert compromise of a CA then can be a serious matter because the attacker can then grant access permissions.

---

[14]Distributing the private keys, since each is known to a single party, is not necessary.

A certificate should be revoked whenever the corresponding private key has been compromised or the attributes that the certificate is binding to a public key are no longer accurate. For example, a certificate containing access control data must be revoked whenever access control permissions described in that certificate are changed. Implementing timely revocation of certificates requires some sort of service that is highly available, so that users can check the status of a certificate just before use. This server availability requirement somewhat offsets the arguments in favor of CAs (and public-key cryptography) over KDCs (and secret-key cryptography): the CA may not need to be highly available, but public-key cryptography, like secret-key cryptography with its KDC, does need to have some form of highly available service (for checking about revocations).

Actual Deployments of Large-scale Key-Distribution Centers and Certification Authorities

The U.S. DOD first developed KDC-based key management systems in the early 1970s. The STU-II secure telephone system, which served about 40,000 users, was perhaps the largest system deployed by the U.S. government that was based on KDC technology. STU-II was superseded by the STU-III system in the early 1980s; STU-III uses public-key certificates and serves more than 500,000 users. Instances of the Kerberos system (Neuman and Ts'o, 1994) and OSF/DCE (an industry standard for UNIX-based distributed systems that uses Kerberos) appear to be the largest-scale KDC deployments in the commercial sector.

Pretty good privacy (PGP) (a secure e-mail technology) and Lotus Notes (a popular "groupware" product) probably represent the largest deployed public-key systems. Like OSF/DCE, Lotus Notes is usually employed on an interorganizational basis, so that the estimated 10 million certificates associated with Lotus Notes users are distributed over many organizations. Some PGP use is tied to cliques of users, but PGP also is used more globally to provide secure e-mail among an extremely broad set of users. The absence of a formal CA structure within PGP makes it difficult to determine connectivity among users. Numerous examples of inauthentic PGP keys resident in various public servers raise questions about the actual size of PGP's deployment.

Web browsers employ server certificates, usually issued by public CAs (see below), in using the secure socket layer (SSL) protocol to establish encrypted, one-way, authenticated communication paths.[15] This de-

---

[15]SSL also permits two-way authentication, through the use of client certificates, but this option is not often invoked.

ployment of public-key cryptography has been crucial for providing the secure paths necessary to send credit card numbers and other sensitive data in support of e-commerce on the Internet. But the biggest demand for certificates promises to come from secure e-mail (e.g., S/MIME)[16] available in version 4 of both the Netscape and Microsoft browsers and from client certificates used to authenticate users to servers. Deployment of the Secure Electronic Transaction (SET) protocol for credit card transactions over the Internet has been slower than expected, but ultimately it, too, could cause millions of certificates to be issued to the existing users of Visa, MasterCard, American Express, and Discover cards.

Public-Key Infrastructure

The term "public-key infrastructure" (PKI) is used in the literature, and especially in trade publications, for a collection of topics related to public-key management. Here, PKI refers to technical mechanisms, procedures, and policies that together provide a management framework for enabling public-key cryptography deployment in a range of applications:

• The technical mechanisms generally include public-key digital signature and one-way hash algorithms, the syntax of public-key certificates and certificate revocation lists (CRLs), communication protocols for the issuance, reissuance, and distribution of certificates and CRLs, and algorithms for validating sequences of related certificates and associated CRLs.
• The procedures generally concern issuance, reissuance, and requests for revocation of certificates, and the distribution of CRLs.
• The policies encompass the semantics associated with digital signatures, the semantics of certificate issuance and revocation, the operation of certification authorities, legal liability concerns, and so on.

Most of this management framework is concerned with certificates and, therefore, it is instructive to retrace their origin. When public-key cryptography was first described in the open literature, no mention was made of certificates—the public keys associated with identities were simply presumed to be available whenever needed. An MIT bachelor's thesis (Kornfelder, 1978) suggested the idea of a public-key certificate. But certificates only transform the problem of acquiring some subject's public key into the problem of acquiring some certificate issuer's public key (so that the certificate containing a subject's public key can be verified). The effort expended to acquire a certificate issuer's public key to verify a

---

[16]See S/MIME Resources, available online at <http://www.rsa.com/smime/html/resources.html>.

certificate becomes leveraged if there are relatively few issuers and they sign certificates for many subjects. And most PKIs adopt this strategy. A commercial or governmental organization issues certificates to its employees, its customers, or the public in general. The organization also revokes certificates when appropriate. Notice, though, that the CA has now ascended to a somewhat more formal role in the management of certificates, concerned with preserving meaning or accuracy of the bindings in its certificates as well as with the mechanics of disseminating those bindings.

Although PKIs based on CAs are the most common, they are not the only model for certificate issuance. Any user with a public key can issue a certificate whose subject is any other user. PGP works in this fashion; its certification model is called a web of trust. This user-centric model for certification has advantages. Initial deployment is especially easy, for example. But a web of trust also does not scale well to large numbers of subjects. In addition, with a diverse set of certificate issuers, certificates no longer will have a standard meaning—one user's standard of proof for issuing a certificate might not be the same as another's. Without agreement on certification policies, applications are unable to interpret certificates, and the goal of enabling deployment of public-key cryptography is undermined.

Several models of PKI have started to emerge. First, companies such as VeriSign, CyberTrust, and CertCo offer PKI services to all comers. These same companies also offer so-called private-label CA services for other companies, acting as processing agents and issuing certificates on behalf of the other companies. Second, some organizations have started to issue their own certificates in support of Internet business models that call for identifying clients by certificates. Finally, there are companies issuing certificates for internal intranet use, irrespective of external customer requirements. The U.S. Postal Service has announced ambitions to become a CA on a grand scale. It has not yet realized these ambitions, but if it does, then a new category of certificate issuers will be born—one closer to government and for which new legal issues may arise and new customer benefits may be possible. Despite the competition among these models, there are good arguments (Kent, 1997) that users will require multiple certificates, issued by a variety of CAs. This suggests a world in which many CAs co-exist, both domestically and in the international environment.

Given the minimal experience to date with PKIs, many aspects of PKI technology merit further research. This research should focus not only on the issuer (CA) aspects of PKI, but also on the client or consumer side. Most applications that make use of certificates, for example, have poor certificate-management interfaces for users and system administrators;

the result is an unnecessary operational vulnerability. Toolkits for certificate processing are not much better. The development of Intel's common data security architecture (CDSA) as an application program interface (API) for a variety of cryptographic services does not alleviate the problem, as the complex issues associated with certificate validation are below the level of this specification.

The CA models described all focus on binding a public key to an identity, and that identity is presumed to have some real-world semantics. Another approach to certificate use is embodied by what are called "key-centric" systems, such as the Secure Distributed Security Infrastructure (SDSI), in which all names bound to public keys are viewed as having only local significance, for the syntactic convenience of users. The Simple Public-Key Infrastructure (SPKI) working group of the Internet Engineering Task Force (IETF) is attempting to codify these notions into an Internet standard. However, no products that make use of certificates have adopted SPKI or SDSI notions.

Findings

1. Obstacles exist to more widespread deployment of key management technology. Some of the obstacles are understood; others will become apparent only as large-scale deployments are attempted.

2. Although PKI technology is intended to serve very large populations with diverse administrative structures, issues related to timely notification of revocation, recovery from compromise of CA private keys, and name space management all require further attention.

NETWORK ACCESS CONTROL MECHANISMS

Operating system access control mechanisms manage the use and sharing of resources implemented and managed by that operating system. Analogous mechanisms have been developed for network resources —subnetworks, physical and logical channels, network services, and the like. Interest in such network access control mechanisms is relatively new, probably because the need for them became apparent only after networks started playing a central role. This section examines several mechanisms commonly used today to effect access control in networks and makes recommendations regarding additional research.

Closed User Groups

Virtual circuit data networks, such as X.25, frame relay, and asynchronous transfer mode (ATM) networks, often include a mechanism for controlling whether network subscribers should be permitted to communicate. In closed user groups (CUGs), subscriber communication is controlled based on network authentication (i.e., identities represented by network layer addresses), although in some instances other information may come into play as well. For example, inbound versus outbound call initiation (and reverse charging) may be parameters to an access control list check. However, CUGs usually are limited to entities on a single network that are implemented in a single networking technology, managed by a single administration. In an Internet environment, which increasingly characterizes the networked world, the single-network restriction means that CUGs will become increasingly irrelevant.[17]

Virtual Private Networks

Virtual private networks (VPNs) have been implemented both for data and for voice. The idea is to use a public network and to create the illusion of a network comprising transmission and switching resources that are devoted exclusively to subscribers of the VPN. The Centrex service offered by local telephone companies is one example; it is usually implemented through administrative controls in central office switches. In data networks, a VPN can be supported in a similar manner. However, VPNs implemented in this way are vulnerable to wiretapping attacks conducted on the underlying real network and to administrative configuration errors.

To prevent wiretapping, cryptographic protocols can be employed at either the network or Internet layer. Many such schemes have been developed and deployed over the last 20 years, supported by government-funded programs. The first packet network VPN technology was the private line interface (PLI) developed by Bolt, Beranek, and Newman in the mid-1970s (BBN, 1978). The PLI was approved to protect classified data for transmission over the ARPANET, creating a VPN for a set of DOD Secret-level subscribers. Later examples of such technology (developed with government funding or for government use) include the BCR and Blacker (KDC-based VPN systems), the Xerox XEU and the Wang TIU (manually keyed LAN VPN systems), and the Motorola NES and Caneware (certificate-based, Internet VPN systems).

In the commercial arena, various systems have also been developed and deployed, including systems for use with X.25 and ATM networks, as well as those for Internet devices. Although VPN-enabled products have been available from vendors, they typically employ proprietary proto-

---

[17]However, by relying on cryptography, a virtual private network can circumvent this single-network limitation.

cols, making interoperability across vendor product lines difficult. More-over, many VPN-enabled products employ manual key-management, and that prevents their deployment in larger-scale settings. The adoption of the Internet Protocol Security (IPsec) protocol standards (see Chapter 2) is expected not only to increase the number of products incorporating cryptographic VPN capabilities but also to ensure interoperability and promote the use of automated (certificate-based) key management protocols. Widespread use of VPN technology in the Internet will almost surely follow.

IPsec cryptographically protects traffic between subscribers. Because IPsec operates at the Internet layer, it can protect traffic across any local area network or wide area network technology, and it can be terminated at end systems (e.g., personal computers, workstations, or servers) as well as at security gateways (e.g., firewalls). Access control in IPsec is based on cryptographic authentication, effected initially through key distribution and on a continuing basis through the use of a keyed message authentication function. The granularity of access control is determined by local policy and can range from subnet-level protection to per-user and per-application controls.

IPsec is also noteworthy because it includes an optional anti-replay facility, which prevents certain forms of denial-of-service attacks. This not only has intrinsic value but also constitutes important recognition that network security is more than just an extension of access control. However, other degradation or denial-of-service attacks—namely those directed at the switching and transmission media that implement a VPN—are not prevented by IPsec, nor can they be by any VPN implementation. A VPN cannot defend against attacks directed at the resources used to build the VPN.

Firewalls

Firewalls (Cheswick and Bellovin, 1994; Chapman and Zwicky, 1995) are a defensive mechanism typically deployed at the boundary of a trusted and an untrusted computer network (Appendix H briefly describes the four basic kinds of firewalls). Safe—or presumed safe—messages transit the firewall; others are blocked. Thus, computers inside the boundary are protected from (some) attacks originating at computers located outside the boundary. In theory, firewalls should not be necessary. If a single computer can be hardened against attacks, then, in principle, all computers can be. And if all computers on a network are hardened, then there is no need for an additional perimeter defense. In practice, firewalls do offer benefits.

First, hardening computers against attack is not simple. And systems often must run commercial off-the-shelf protocols for which a perimeter defense is the only protection available. As an example, even when cryptographic authentication can be provided in a product, vendors often choose to use more vulnerable network-based authentication. For such products, users have no choice but to rely on add-on protective measures such as firewalls.

A second, more subtle, benefit of firewalls concerns vulnerabilities resulting from software that contains bugs. The best cryptography in the world cannot protect a service if at one end of the connection is an attacker and at the other end is software whose bugs make compromise possible. Since today's software invariably does have bugs, with no solution in sight (see Chapter 3), prudence suggests blocking system access by outsiders. Firewalls allow access by insiders while denying access to outsiders.

Third, it is easier to administer software on one or a small number of firewalls than to do so for the entire collection of workstations, personal computers, and servers composing an organization's computing network. Physical access to a computer's console might be necessary for setting or checking its configuration, for example. Moreover, a firewall can provide a network security administrator with a single point of policy control for an entire network. Thus, while configuration and policy errors on individual computers are not eliminated by deploying a firewall, its presence does reduce outside exposure and thereby prevents those errors from being exploited.

Finally, firewalls often are deployed to present a defense in depth. Even if a system is believed to be secure, with proper authentication and presumed-reliable software, a firewall can provide a layer of insurance.

Limitations of Firewalls

Firewalls can enforce only policies defined in terms of restrictions on inbound and outbound traffic. For example, a policy stipulating that all outbound e-mail is logged could be enforced using a firewall: an authorized mail gateway (which presumably does the logging) would be the only computer whose e-mail packets are passed to the outside, and all other machines would send their e-mail to that gateway for forwarding to the outside. But there are limits to what can be accomplished using restrictions on inbound and outbound traffic. For example, an insider prevented from communicating directly with a Web server—a policy implemented by restricting outbound traffic to port 80—could set up a Web proxy server that monitors port 8000 (say) on some machine outside the firewall. Traffic to port 8000 would not be blocked by the firewall, so the insider could now surf the Web using the outside proxy. More generally, firewalls cannot protect against inside attacks (see Box 4.1). Also, using firewalls is pointless when paths exist to the outside that bypass those firewalls: an authorized link to some outside organization, an unprotected modem pool, or even a careless employee dialing out to an Internet Service Provider.

The decision regarding what protocols are allowed to pass through the firewall is critical for success. An air gap is a more secure and cheaper solution if no protocols are being allowed to send packets through the firewall. Some protocols will be allowed through but as the number of such protocols increases, so do the chances that an attack could be waged by exploiting a flaw in one of them. The transmission of executable content provides a further challenge for firewalls. For example, macros in Microsoft Word or Excel attachments to messages can be dangerous as well as difficult to filter. Similarly, mailers (from a wide variety of vendors) are susceptible to buffer overflow attacks when overly long file names appear in attachments (CERT Advisory CA-98.10, August 1998[18]). A single filter, at the firewall, can protect a whole network of machines.

Other limitations of firewalls come from the protocol layer at which the firewall operates. There are four basic types of firewalls: packet filters, circuit relays, application gateways, and dynamic (or stateful) packet filters. The first three correspond to layers of the protocol stack; the fourth tends to incorporate features of both network and application layer systems. Attacks conveyed using protocol layers higher than the one at which the firewall operates cannot be blocked by the firewall, because the firewall cannot filter those messages. For example, a packet-filter firewall operating at the Internet layer is unable to defend against weaknesses in an application layer protocol such as the Simple Mail Transfer Protocol (SMTP). Similarly, an application-layer firewall that did monitor SMTP packets could not protect against attacks conveyed by e-mail attachments, since such attachments only have interpretations above the layer at which SMTP operates—an e-mail application cognizant of attachment types would have to be involved in that defense.

The utility of a firewall is also limited by the use of end-to-end cryptography. It is obviously impossible for a firewall to inspect the contents of an encrypted packet, so encrypted packets cannot be blocked. Similarly, address translation and other forms of packet modification that some firewalls use are not possible if a packet is going to be cryptographically authenticated. The usual solution is to terminate cryptographic associations at the firewall. In some cases, multiple levels of cryptographic protection are used, with an outer layer permitting passage through the firewall and the inner layer being end to end.

---

[18]CERT advisories are available online at <http://www.cert.org>.

In addition to the intrinsic limitations of firewalls by virtue of what they do, there are pragmatic limitations by virtue of how they are built. Most firewalls are implemented as applications on top of standard operating systems and, consequently, are vulnerable to attacks directed at the underlying operating system. A firewall developer may strip out those portions of an operating system that are considered sources of vulnerabilities, but given the size and complexity of a modern operating system, only limited forms hardening will be achieved in this way. The alternative, building the firewall on a custom operating system, introduces the possibility of new vulnerabilities that have not been detected and remedied through the examination and experience of a large community of users. Perhaps for this reason and the cost, only a small number of the firewalls that have been developed employ custom operating systems.

Many firewalls operate application "proxies," and all of the concerns cited later in this chapter regarding application security apply to them. Moreover, it is common for an application proxy to be developed using existing application code as a base. In such cases, vulnerabilities in the base application may be preserved in the proxy. Also, modifications to application code needed to convert it into a proxy, or an incomplete understanding of the application protocol, can be a source of vulnerabilities.

Guards

Guards have been used in military computing systems for two decades to control the flow of classified electronic information. Most often they are used to permit the flow of information from a lower-sensitivity environment to a higher-sensitivity enclave in support of mandatory access control policies, blocking possible reverse information flow that might accompany protocol acknowledgment and flow-control traffic. Automated filters within guards have been designed to ensure that all traffic conforms to specified criteria, including field-by-field restrictions on types or values. Traffic that does not conform to these criteria is rejected and not permitted to pass the guard. But as traffic formats become more flexible and field values have greater range, it becomes less likely that an automated filter can correctly detect all prohibited traffic. Some designs send all questionable traffic to a human for visual review. Traffic review tends to be monotonous work, and humans may be only slightly better suited to do the filtering than the machine processes.

Despite the limitations of guards, they are one of the most prevalent access control mechanisms for electronic information systems in use today by the military. The security architecture of the MISSI program (see Box 4.4) relies on the use of guards to support electronic mail, directory services, and file transfer across enclave boundaries. For example, the Defense Mes-

---

BOX 4.4
Multilevel Information System Security Initiative

The Multilevel Information System Security Initiative (MISSI) is a program initiated by the National Security Agency (NSA) in the early 1990s. The original goal was to provide a set of products and an architectural framework that would facilitate the development of multilevel secure NISs. The primary components of the architecture originally included the following:

1. Fortezza—a PCMCIA crypto card suitable for use with unclassified data,
2. Caneware—an inline encryption system,
3. Secure Network System (SNS)—a guard,
4. Applique—a multilevel secure operating system (based on T-Mach) and corresponding crypto card for use with classified data, and
5. Network Management System (NMS)—a collection of software for managing the security of the other components.

MISSI evolved over time, and its focus changed. The Applique component was never developed. The NMS component was reduced in scope to encompass only certificate management. Fortezza was redefined to be suitable for protecting Secret data, at least in some contexts. The SNS component was reduced somewhat in scope, but still functions as a high-assurance guard, primarily for separating Top Secret enclaves from less sensitive network environments. Only the Caneware component emerged largely intact, but it is the end product of a series of NSA-funded network security efforts at Motorola dating back to the late 1970s.

A comprehensive multilevel network security architecture has not emerged from MISSI and, instead, the hallmark "managed risk" has become among its most visible contributions. In principle, the message in "managed risk" is consistent with recommendations made elsewhere in this report: the security of a system should rely on an appropriate combination of components organized to counter a perceived threat—highly trusted components need not be used throughout. In practice, however, "managed risk" has been used to justify use of low- or medium-assurance components to secure classified data (especially at the Secret level) without much analysis of the threat or evaluation of the adequacy of the offered countermeasures. That approach is not consistent with the recommendations of this study.

---

saging System (DMS) relies on the use of the Secure Network System (SNS) guard to permit electronic mail to flow in and out of highly sensitive enclaves and to facilitate communication with less-sensitive DMS subscribers.

Findings

1. Closed user groups have some utility in individual, circuit switched networks, but they will become increasingly irrelevant as networking migrates to the Internet proper or to Internet technology.

2. VPN technology is quite promising. Proprietary protocols and simplistic key-management schemes in most products have prevented

VPN adoption in larger-scale settings. The deployment of IPsec can eliminate these impediments, thus facilitating VPN deployment throughout the Internet.

3. Much work remains to further facilitate wholesale and flexible VPN deployments. Support for dynamic location of security gateways, accommodation of complex network topologies, negotiation of traffic security policies across administratively independent domains, and support for multicast communication are all topics requiring additional work. Also, better interfaces for VPN management will be critical for avoiding vulnerabilities introduced by management errors.

4. Firewalls, despite their limitations, will persist as a key defense mechanism into the foreseeable future. As support for VPNs is added, enhancements will have to be developed for supporting sophisticated security management protocols, negotiation of traffic security policies across administratively independent domains, and management tools.

5. The development of increasingly sophisticated network-wide applications will create a need for application-layer firewalls and a better understanding of how to define and enforce useful traffic policies at this level.

6. Guards can be thought of as special cases of firewalls, typically focused at the application layer. Thus, all the issues cited for firewalls are applicable here, but with increased emphasis on assurance and mandatory access control policies.

FOREIGN CODE AND APPLICATION-LEVEL SECURITY

Most users today execute software written by others. The software is either purchased from commercial vendors (e.g., Microsoft, Lotus, Netscape, Intuit, and others) or obtained at no cost from other users as so-called freeware or shareware.[19] Purchased software has traditionally been delivered in some sort of shrink-wrap package that is difficult to counterfeit or tamper with, so it is easy to trust that the package contains what the producer intended. Presumably, the reputation of the producer engenders trust that the software does what it should (to the extent that any software does) and that it does nothing that it should not.[20]

---

[19]Scripting languages and other very-high-level programming vehicles (see Appendix E) make it relatively easy for a nonprogrammer to cobble together software that might be both useful to and usable by others. And there is an ethic that encourages the development, distribution, and constant improvement of freeware.

[20]A 1998 release of Microsoft's spreadsheet program Excel 97 apparently contained a flight simulator that could be accessed by the right combination of keystrokes, starting from a blank work sheet. The existence of gratuitous functionality in commercial software is apparently not rare, and the term "easter egg" has been coined to describe such surprising features.

But a second delivery mechanism has been made possible by the Internet and World Wide Web. Clicking on a Web page enables software to be downloaded to a user's machine and automatically installed. Employed at first for freeware, this electronic avenue for distribution is being used increasingly by commercial vendors because it is both convenient and cheap. But no longer is there the shrink-wrap and, in the case of freeware, producers have no financial stake in preserving their reputations. Embedding an attack inside this software is not difficult. Cautious users do have the option, though, of being selective about what software they download and from where.

With the functionality in place to associate executables with Web pages, the next step was not large. Programs downloaded and executed by a user's computer could be used to enhance a provider's Web pages with animation and other locally generated special effects. Java "applets" and ActiveX modules are the best-known examples of this technology. Here, delivery and execution of the so-called foreign code can occur without a user's knowledge.[21] The number of potential software providers for a given computer is now significantly increased; the control that users exert about what providers to trust and what code to run is significantly decreased. Weak operating system security facilities in personal computers exacerbate the problem, since any software executing under such operating systems has virtually unconstrained access to resources on the PC.

Not only can executables be associated with Web pages, but foreign code is also increasingly being associated with other forms of documents. PostScript is a portable representation language for printing, but it is possible to write PostScript programs that do more than control document printing.[22] Microsoft Word documents can contain macros that access a user's files, destroying or exfiltrating data as shown by the widely disseminated Word "concept virus." Moreover, Word macros are largely platform independent and are excellent vehicles for writing viruses. Industry trends are toward even greater use of "active document" technology (e.g., Apple OpenDoc and Microsoft OLE), which means that more blurring of documents and executable content is likely to occur.

The increased use of foreign code may enable enhanced functionality, but it also will create a problem: system trustworthiness will erode unless security mechanisms are developed and deployed for confining the ef-

---

[21]For example, the default configuration for the Netscape and Microsoft browsers enables JavaScript and Java. Thus a user may have no warning that foreign code has been introduced into her or his environment.

[22]If one views (rather than prints) a PostScript document using an application such as GhostScript, the document can contain a Trojan horse that can access and exfiltrate (or destroy) data on the user's computer.

fects of foreign code. These security mechanisms might exploit unique characteristics of the delivery mechanism or source of the foreign code, or they might be tied to the environment in which the foreign code is executed. If the problem is clear, the solution is not. The remainder of this section, therefore, surveys the problem in more detail and outlines some approaches to a solution.

The ActiveX Approach

The ActiveX security mechanisms allow modules to be digitally signed pieces of code. Users check this signature and, based on that, decide whether a module should be permitted to execute. The signature, analogous to a brand name or the corporate logo on shrink-wrapped software, is thus intended to engender trust that the ActiveX module will behave as intended. The signature also identifies a responsible party should the ActiveX module misbehave.

Underlying this ActiveX Authenticode approach is the presumption that users can decide whether to run a module based on knowing the identity or seeing some credential of a vendor or distributor. This presumption has questionable validity, as the successful deployment in February 1997 of a malicious ActiveX module by the Chaos Computer Club of Hamburg confirmed (Van Eng, 1997). Users either do not bother to look at a signature or cannot make an informed decision upon seeing a signature.[23] The intended analogy between signatures and shrink-wrap packaging is likely flawed. Physical distribution channels impose numerous impediments to the distribution of malicious shrink-wrap software that the Authenticode approach does not. These impediments serve an (unintended) security function by raising the barrier for market entry and by facilitating the tracing of malicious software (due to accounting and shipping trails).

A second difficulty with Authenticode signatures concerns revocation. Compromised signing keys could be used by malicious individuals to sign hostile ActiveX modules. Even if the existence of these compromised keys were discovered, recovery would require revocation across the entire Internet, whose population is, by and large, technically unsophisticated users.[24] Moreover, it is likely that enough prospective vendors of ActiveX modules will be certified that some inadvertently provide

---

[23]The difficulty of attaching semantics to a signature is not unique to ActiveX Authenticode. It is a difficulty that exists today for all uses of signatures in the Internet.

[24]In fact, VeriSign has maintained a revocation list for ActiveX signatories since early 1997. It is checked by the Microsoft mobile code platform, but it has seldom been used by users and administrators.

opportunities to introduce malicious code. Poor physical, personnel, procedural, or computer security practices at any one, for example, could lead to the unintentional signing of malicious code.

The Java Approach

With Java, security is enforced by executing code in a confining environment known as the Java virtual machine (JVM). Early versions forced code to be run with either very tight restrictions or almost none, depending on whether or not the code came from a trusted source. The system has since evolved, and increasingly flexible and expressive permission-based access controls have been added (Gong et al., 1997).

The JVM interprets Java byte code, a stack-based intermediate language that is designed to be platform independent. Java programs, in byte code format, carry type information about their variables, the configuration of the run-time stack throughout execution, and the signatures of routines that are defined and invoked. When a byte code program is loaded, an initial check is performed to verify that the program conforms to certain rules, including type-safety rules. The JVM continues carrying out type-safety and other security checks throughout the execution of the Java program.

Java programs were designed to be compiled to Java byte code and the result interpreted by a JVM. For a variety of reasons, but notably achieving performance improvements, some Java compilers directly generate machine code native to the platform that will execute the program. Running such native code can weaken system security because the Java security model is not designed for controlling execution of non-Java programs.

Early deployments of Java were flawed by implementation and design bugs in the JVM, and the resulting vulnerabilities attracted considerable press attention. The absence of careful and complete definitions for the Java programming language and the JVM doubtless contributed to the problem. The all-or-nothing access control model in the earliest versions of Java was too simple to be very useful—it was impossible to build systems consistent with the principle of least privilege. The security model implemented by the new JDK 1.2 is richer but also more complex. JDK 1.2 programmers must now master this complexity. Also, users and programmers must now correctly assess and configure suitable sets of access rights for executing foreign code.

Findings

1. Foreign code is a growing threat to the security of most desktop systems as well as other systems that employ COTS software.

2. Authenticating the author or provider of foreign code has not and likely will not prove effective for enforcing security. Users are unwilling and/or unable to use the source of a piece of foreign code as a basis for denying or allowing execution. Revocation of certificates is necessary should a provider be compromised, but is currently not supported by the Internet, which limits the scale over which the approach can be deployed.

3. Confining foreign code according to an interpreter that provides a rich access control model has potential, provided programmers and users have a means to correctly assess and configure suitable sets of access rights.

Fine-grained Access Control and Application Security

Enforcing access control in accordance with the principle of least privilege is an extremely effective defense against a large variety of attacks, including many that could be conveyed using foreign code or application programs. Support for fine-grained access control (FGAC) facilitates this defense by allowing a user or system administrator to confine accesses made by each individual software module. Each module is granted access to precisely the set of resources it needs to get the job done. Thus, a module that is advertised as offering a mortgage calculator function (with keyboard input of loan amount, interest, and duration) could be prevented from accessing the file system or network, and a spelling checker module could be granted read access to a dictionary and to the text files the user explicitly asks to have checked but not to other files.

Operating systems usually do provide some sort of access control mechanism, but invariably the controls are too coarse and concern only certain resources.[25] FGAC is not supported. For example, access to large segments of memory is what is controlled, but it is access to small regions that is needed. And virtually no facilities are provided for controlling access to abstractions implemented above the level of the operating system, including accesses that might be sensitive to the state of the resource being controlled and/or the state of the module requesting the access.[26]

---

[25]The notable exception is domain and type enforcement (DTE)-based operating systems (Boebert and Kain, 1996) that are employed in certain limited contexts. In these systems, processes are grouped into domains and are labeled accordingly. All system objects are also given labels, which define their types. A central table then specifies the kinds of accesses each domain can have to each type and to each other domain. The approach, although flexible, is tedious to specify and use. To address this difficulty, extensions are proposed in Badger et al. (1996).

[26]A limited form of FGAC is available for Java programs running under the JDK 1.2 security architecture, but state-sensitive access decisions are not (easily) supported there and the technology is limited to programs written in the single programming language.

Mechanisms for managing FGAC solve only part of the problem, though. Once FGAC support is in place, users and system managers must configure access controls for all the resources and all the modules. Being too liberal in setting permissions could allow an attack to succeed; being too conservative could cause legitimate computations to incur security violations. Experience with users confronting the range of security configuration controls available for compartmented mode workstations, which deal with both discretionary (identity-based, user-directed) and mandatory (rule-based, administratively directed) access policies, suggests that setting all the permissions for FGAC could be daunting. The problem is only exacerbated by the all-too-frequent mismatch between application-level security policies, which involve application-level abstractions, and the low-level objects and permissions constituting an FGAC configuration.

FGAC is important, but there is more to application security than access control. The lack of sound protected execution environments for processes limits what applications can do to protect themselves against users and against other applications. The fundamental insecurity of most deployed operating systems further undermines efforts to develop trustworthy applications: even when users are offered applications with apparent security functionality, they must question any claimed security. For example, Web browsers now incorporate cryptographic mechanisms to protect against wiretapping attacks. However, the keys used are (optionally) protected by being encrypted with a user-selected password and stored in a file system managed by an (insecure) operating system. Thus, an attacker who can gain unauthorized access to the computer (as a result of an operating system flaw) has two obvious options for undermining the cryptographic security employed by the browser:

- Steal the file with the keys and attack it using password searching, or
- Plant a Trojan horse to steal the key file when it is decrypted by the user and then e-mail the plaintext keys back to the attacker.

For some applications, security properties best enforced using cryptographic means are important.[27] For example, security for e-mail entails preventing unauthorized release of message contents, sender authentication, message integrity, and maybe nonrepudiation with proof of submission and/or receipt. And because implementing cryptographic protocols is subtle, a number of efforts are under way to free application developers from this task. The IETF has developed a series of specifications for

---

[27]Note, however, that neither cryptography nor any other application level mechanism will provide protection in the face of operating system vulnerabilities.

making simplified, cryptographically protected (stream or message) communications available using the generic security services application programming interface (GSSAPI). Intel's multilayered CDSA API aims to provide an integrated framework for cryptography, key and certificate management, and related services. CDSA has been submitted to the Open Software Foundation for adoption as a standard, and it has the backing of several major operating system vendors.

More generally, the applications programmer must either build suitable mechanisms or harness existing mechanisms when enforcing any particular application's security policy. There will always be many more applications than operating systems, applications will arise and evolve much faster, and applications will be developed by a much wider range of vendors. These facts of life were understood by the early advocates of secure operating system technology and are even truer today, due to the increasing homogeneity of the operating system marketplace and the advent of mobile code. Thus, it is easy to see why government research and development on computer security in the past focused on securing operating systems.

Yet these efforts have been largely unsuccessful in the marketplace. Moreover, modern applications tend to involve security policies defined in terms of application-level abstractions rather than operating system ones. Thus, while there remains a need for security mechanisms in an operating system, it seems clear that enforcing security increasingly will be a responsibility shared between the operating system and the application. Research is needed to understand how the responsibilities might best be partitioned, what operating system mechanisms are suitable for assisting in application-level security implementation, and how best to specify and implement security policies within applications.

Findings

1. Operating system implementations of FGAC would help support the construction of systems that obey the principle of least privilege. That, in turn, could be an effective defense against a variety of attacks that might be delivered using foreign code or application programs.

2. Access control features in commercially successful operating systems are not adequate for supporting FGAC. Thus, new mechanisms with minimum performance impact are required.

3 Unless the management of FGAC is shown to be feasible and attractive for individual users and system administrators, mechanisms to support FGAC will not be usable in practice.

4. Enforcing application-level security is likely to be a shared responsibility between the application and security mechanisms that are pro-

vided by lower levels of a system. Little is known about how to partition this responsibility or about what mechanisms are best implemented at the various levels of a system.

5. The assurance limitations associated with providing application-layer security while employing a COTS operating system that offers minimum assurance need to be better understood.

Language-based Security:
Software Fault Isolation and Proof-carrying Code

Virtually all operating system and hardware-implemented enforcement of security policies has, until recently, involved monitoring system execution (Box 4.5). Actions whose execution would violate the security policy being enforced are intercepted and aborted; all other actions are executed normally. But another approach to security policy enforcement is also plausible—execute only those programs that cannot violate the security policies of interest:

- By modifying a program before execution commences, it may be possible to add checks and prevent program behavior that will violate the security policy being enforced.
- By analyzing a program before execution commences, it may be possible to prove that no program behavior will violate the security policy being enforced.

Both schemes depend on analysis techniques developed by programming language researchers. And both require incorporating program analysis or some other form of automated deduction into the trusted computing base.

The idea of program rewriting to enforce security was first proposed in connection with memory safety, a security policy stipulating that memory accesses (reads, writes, and jumps) are confined to specified regions of memory. The naive approach—add a test and conditional jump before each machine language instruction that reads, writes, or jumps to memory—can slow execution significantly enough to be impractical. Software fault isolation (SFI) (Wahbe et al., 1993) does not add tests. Instead, instructions and addresses are modified (by "and-ing" and "or-ing" masks) so that they do not reference memory outside the specified regions. The behavior of programs that never attempt illegal memory accesses is unaffected by the modifications; programs that would have violated memory safety end up accessing legal addresses instead. Note that the use of program modification to enforce security policies is not limited to memory safety, and any security policy that can be enforced by moni-

BOX 4.5
Operating System Access Control

Conceptually, access control mechanisms divide into two subsystems, a decision subsystem and an enforcement subsystem. The decision subsystem examines the security attributes of objects and processes according to a security policy and decides whether each particular access (e.g., read, write, execute) should be allowed; the enforcement subsystem then ensures that the decision cannot be circumvented by user or software action. See Appendix G for a summary of the security attributes in some commercial operating systems.

The Decision Subsystem

Decision subsystems for discretionary access control usually employ access control lists (ACLs). An ACL is associated with each data object and consists of a list of users, enumerating what accesses to the object each user is permitted to exercise.

ACLs can be difficult to administer. Expressing authorization for a large number of users becomes awkward when it entails managing lists comprising large numbers of entries. UNIX systems therefore employ a modified scheme: for each object, the owner only specifies object access permissions for the user, for a small number of specified groups of users, and for all other users. Windows NT also addresses this administration problem by supporting access permissions for groups.

The decision subsystem for an ACL-based discretionary policy simply obtains the name of the user on whose behalf a particular process is executing, checks the ACL for an entry containing that user name, and grants accesses according to the ACL entry that is found. This has been called a list-oriented approach.

An alternative to ACLs is to associate with each process a list of capabilities, each of which names an object along with the kinds of access to that object that the capability-holder is permitted (Kain and Landwehr, 1986). The decision subsystem for a capability-based access control mechanism checks the list of capabilities associated with the process making the access to see if a capability is present for the desired data object and access mode. This has been called a ticket-oriented approach.

The Enforcement Subsystem

Enforcement subsystems commonly operate in one of two ways. The first, often called file mapping, employs a processor's memory-management hardware. The decision subsystem initializes this hardware upon the transfer of a file to active memory, and no further software actions occur. The memory-management hardware then enforces accesses. The second method (for which there is no generally accepted name), distributes enforcement throughout the elements of the operating system that are responsible for transferring data from passive (e.g., disk) storage to active memory and those that are responsible for performing other security-sensitive operations. Many operating systems use both kinds of enforcement subsystems.

toring execution can be enforced using a generalization of SFI (Schneider, 1998).

With proof-carrying code (PCC) (Necula, 1997), a program is executed only if an accompanying formal, machine-checkable proof establishes that the security policies of interest will not be violated. The approach works especially well for programs written in strongly typed programming languages because proof generation can then be a side effect of compilation. Of course, the feasibility of automatic proof generation depends on exactly what security policy is being enforced. (Proof checking, which is done before executing a program, is, by definition, automatable. But it can be computationally intensive.[28]) Initial versions of PCC focused on ensuring that programs do not violate memory safety or attempt operations that violate type declarations. However, in reality, the approach is limited only by the availability of proof-generation and proof-checking methods, and richer security policies can certainly be handled.

SFI and PCC are in their infancy. So far, each has been tried only on relatively small examples and only on a few kinds of security policies. Each presumes that an entire system will be subject to analysis, whereas, in reality, COTS products may not be available in a form that enables such processing. And, finally, each is limited by available technology for program analysis, a field that is still moving ahead. In short, there is a great deal of research to be done before the practicality and limits of these approaches can be assessed. Some of that research involves questions about programming language semantics and automated deduction; other research involves trying the approaches in realistic settings so that any impediments to deployment can be identified.

SFI and PCC might well represent the vanguard of a new approach to the enforcement of some security policies—an approach in which programming language technology is leveraged to obtain mechanisms that are more efficient and that are better suited to the higher-level abstractions that characterize applications-level security. Most programming today is done in high-level typed languages, and good use might be made of the structural and type information that high-level languages provide. Moreover, certain security policies, like information-flow restrictions, cannot be enforced by monitoring execution but can be enforced by analyzing entire program texts prior to execution. Any security policies that can be enforced by a secure operating system or by the use of hardware memory protection can be effected by SFI or PCC (Schneider, 1998).

---

[28]Specifically, proof checking for existing versions of proof-carrying code can be polynomial in the size of the input. Proofs, in practice, are linear in the size of the program but in theory can be exponential in the size of the program.

Findings

1. Software fault isolation (SFI) and proof-carrying code (PCC) are promising new approaches to enforcing security policies.

2. A variety of opportunities may exist to leverage programming language research in implementing system security.

DENIAL OF SERVICE

Access control has traditionally been the focus of security mechanisms designed to prevent or contain attacks. But for computing systems that control infrastructures, defending against denial-of-service attacks—attacks that deny or degrade services a system offers to its clients—is also quite important. Probably of greatest concern are attacks against system-wide services (network switching resources and servers supporting many users), as disruption here can have the widest impact.

Whenever finite-capacity resources or servers are being shared, the potential exists for some clients to monopolize use so that progress by others is degraded or denied. In early time-sharing systems, the operating system had to prevent a user's runaway program from entirely consuming one or another resource (usually processor cycles), thereby denying service to other users. The solutions invariably involved are these:

- Mechanisms that allowed executing programs to be preempted, with control returned to the operating system; and
- Scheduling algorithms to arbitrate fairly among competing service and resource requests.

Such solutions work if requests can be issued only by agents that are under the control of the operating system. The control allows the operating system to limit load by blocking the agents making unreasonable demands. Also implicit in such solutions is the assumption that, in the long run, demand will not outstrip supply.[29]

Defending against denial-of-service attacks in an NIS is not as simple. First, in such systems, there is no single trusted entity that can control the agents making requests. Individual servers might ignore specific client requests that seem unreasonable or that would degrade/deny service to others, but servers cannot slow or terminate the clients making those requests. Because the cost of checking whether a request is reasonable consumes resources (e.g., buffer space to store the request, processing

---

[29]For example, in early time-sharing systems, a user was not permitted to log on if there was insufficient memory or processing capacity to accommodate the increased load.

time to analyze the request), a denial-of-service attack can succeed even if servers are able to detect and discard attacker requests. Such an attack, based on the lack of source address verification and the connectionless nature of the User Datagram Protocol (UDP), is the basis of CERT Advisory CA-96.01.

There is also a second difficulty with adopting the time-sharing solution suggested for preventing denial-of-service attacks in an NIS. The difficulty derives from the implicit assumptions that accompany any statistical approach to sharing fixed-capacity resources. In a large, highly interconnected system, like an NIS, no client accesses many services, although most clients are able to access most of the services. Server capacity is chosen accordingly, and scheduling algorithms are used to allocate service among contending clients. But scheduling algorithms are conditioned on assumptions about offered workload, and that means that an attacker, by violating those assumptions and altering the character of the offered workload, can subvert the scheduling algorithm. For example, an attacker might wage a denial-of-service attack simply by causing a large number of clients to make seemingly reasonable requests. On the Internet, such a coordinated attack is not difficult to launch because PCs and many other Internet hosts run operating systems that are easy to subvert and because the Web and foreign code provide a vehicle for causing attack code to be downloaded onto the hosts.

Not all denial-of-service attacks involve saturating servers or resources, though. It suffices simply to inactivate a subsystem on which the operation of the system depends. Causing such a critical subsystem to crash is one obvious means. But there are also more subtle means of preventing a subsystem from responding to service requests. As discussed in Chapter 2, by contaminating the Internet's Domain Name Service (DNS) caches, an attacker can inactivate packet routing and divert traffic from its intended destination. And, in storage systems where updates can be "rolled back" in response to error conditions, it may be possible for an attacker's request to create an error condition that causes a predecessor's updates to be rolled back (without that predecessor's knowledge of the lost update), effectively denying service (Gligor, 1984).

Findings

1. No mechanisms or systematic design methods exist for defending against denial-of-service attacks, yet defending against such attacks is important for ensuring availability in an NIS.

2. The ad hoc countermeasures that have been successful in securing time-sharing systems from denial-of-service attacks seem to be intrinsically unsuitable for use in an NIS.

REFERENCES

Abadi, Martin, and Roger Needham. 1994. *Prudent Engineering Practice for Cryptographic Protocols*. Palo Alto, CA: Digital Equipment Corporation, Systems Research Center, June.

Badger, L., Daniel F. Sterne, David L. Sherman, and Kenneth M. Walker. 1996. *A Domain and Type Enforcement UNIX Prototype*. Vol. 9, *UNIX Computing Systems*. Glenwood, MD: Trusted Information Systems Inc.

Bell, D.E., and Leonard J. La Padula. 1973. *Secure Computer Systems: Mathematical Foundations and Model*. MTR 2547, Vol. 2. Bedford, MA: MITRE, November.

Bellovin, Steven M., and M. Merritt. 1992. "Encrypted Key Exchange: Password-based Protocols Secure Against Dictionary Attacks," pp. 72-84 in *Proceedings of the IEEE Symposium on Security and Privacy*. Los Alamitos, CA: IEEE Compter Society Press.

Boebert, W. Earl, and Richard Y. Kain. 1996. "A Further Note on the Confinement Problem," pp. 198-203 in *Proceedings of the IEEE 1996 International Carnahan Conference on Security Technology*. New York: IEEE Computer Society.

Bolt, Beranek, and Newman (BBN). 1978. "Appendix H: Interfacing a Host to a Private Line Interface," *Specification for the Interconnection of a Host and an IMP*. BBN Report 1822. Cambridge, MA: BBN, May.

Brewer, D., and M. Nash. 1989. "The Chinese Wall Security Policy," pp. 206-214 in *Proceedings of the IEEE Symposium on Security and Privacy*. Los Alamitos, CA: IEEE Computer Society Press.

Brinkley, D.L., and R.R. Schell. 1995. "Concepts and Terminology for Computer Security," *Information Security*, M.D. Abrams, S. Jajodia, and H.J. Podell, eds. Los Alamitos, CA: IEEE Computer Society Press.

Chapman, D. Brent, and Elizabeth D. Zwicky. 1995. *Internet Security: Building Internet Firewalls*. Newton, MA: O'Reilly and Associates.

Cheswick, William R., and Steven M. Bellovin. 1994. *Firewalls and Internet Security*. Reading, MA: Addison-Wesley.

Clark, D.D., and D.R. Wilson. 1987. "A Comparison of Commercial and Military Computer Security Policies," pp. 184-194 in *Proceedings of the IEEE Symposium on Security and Privacy*. Los Alamitos, CA: IEEE Computer Society Press.

Commission on Protecting and Reducing Government Secrecy, Daniel Patrick Moynihan, chairman. 1997. *Secrecy: Report of the Commission on Protecting and Reducing Government Secrecy*. 103rd Congress (pursuant to Public Law 236), Washington, DC, March 3.

Computer Science and Telecommunications Board (CSTB), National Research Council. 1996. *Cryptography's Role in Securing the Information Society*, Kenneth W. Dam and Herbert S. Lin, eds. Washington, DC: National Academy Press.

Defense Information Systems Agency (DISA). 1996. *The Department of Defense Goal Security Architecture (DGSA)*. Version 3.0. 8 vols. Vol. 6, *Technical Architecture Framework for Information Management*. Arlington, VA: DISA.

Diffie, Whitfield, and Martin E. Hellman. 1976. "New Directions in Cryptography," *IEEE Transactions on Information Theory*, 22(6):644-654.

Feustel, E., and T. Mayfield. 1998. "The DGSA: Unmet Information Security Challenges for Operating Systems Designers," *Operating Systems Review*, 32(1):3-22.

Gligor, Virgil D. 1984. "A Note on Denial-of-Service in Operating Systems," *IEEE Transactions on Software Engineering*, 10(3):320-324.

Gong, Li, M.A. Lomas, R.M. Needham, and J.H. Saltzer. 1993. "Protecting Poorly Chosen Secrets from Guessing Attacks," *IEEE Journal on Selected Areas in Communications*, 11(5):648-656.

Gong, Li, Marianne Mueller, Hemma Prafullchandra, and Roland Schemers. 1997. "Going Beyond the Sandbox: An Overview of the New Security Architecture in the Java Development Kit 1.2," pp. 103-112 in *Proceedings of the USENIX Symposium on Internet Technologies and Systems, Monterey, California*. Berkeley, CA: USENIX Association.

Haller, Neil M. 1994. *The S/Key One-time Password System*. Morristown, NJ: Bellcore.

Joncheray, Laurent. 1995. "A Simple Active Attack Against TCP," *Proceedings of the 5th USENIX UNIX Security Symposium, Salt Lake City, Utah*. Berkeley, CA: USENIX Association.

Kain, Richard Y., and Landwehr, Carl W. 1986. "On Access Checking in Capability-based Systems," pp. 95-101 in *Proceedings of the IEEE Symposium on Security and Privacy*. Los Alamitos, CA: IEEE Computer Society Press.

Kent, Stephen T. 1997. "How Many Certification Authorities Are Enough?," Computing-related Security Research Requirements Workshop III, U.S. Department of Energy, March.

Kneece, Jack. 1986. *Family Treason*. New York: Stein and Day.

Kornfelder, Loren M. 1978. "Toward a Practical Public-Key Cryptosystem," B.S. thesis, Department of Electrical Engineering, Massachusetts Institute of Technology, Cambridge, MA.

Landwehr, Carl E., Constance L. Heitmeyer, and John McLean. 1984. "A Security Model for Military Message Systems," *ACM Transactions on Computer Systems*, 9(3):198-222.

Lewis, Peter H. 1998. "Threat to Corporate Computers Often the Enemy Within," *New York Times*, March 2, p. 1.

Menenzes, Alfred J., Paul C. Van Oorschot, and Scott A. Vanstone. 1996. *Handbook of Applied Cryptography*. CRC Press Series on Discrete Mathematics and Its Applications. Boca Raton, FL: CRC Press, October.

Necula, George C. 1997. "Proof-Carrying Code," pp. 106-119 in *Proceedings of the 24th Symposium on Principles of Programming Languages*. New York: ACM Press.

Neuman, B. Clifford, and Theodore Ts'o. 1994. "Kerberos: An Authentication Service for Computer Networks," *IEEE Communications Magazine*, 32 (9):33-38. Available online at <http://gost.isi.edu/publications/kerberos-neuman-tso.html>.

Schneider, Fred B. 1998. *Enforceable Security Policies*, Technical Report TR98-1664, Computer Science Department, Cornell University, Ithaca, NY. Available online at <http://cs-tr.cs.cornell.edu:80/Dienst/UI/1.0/Display/ncstrl.cornell/TR98-1664>.

Schneier, Bruce. 1996. *Applied Cryptography*. 2nd Ed. New York: John Wiley & Sons.

Schwartz, John. 1997. "Case of the Intel 'Hacker,' Victim of His Own Access," *Washington Post*, September 15, p. F17.

Sterling, Bruce. 1992. *The Hacker Crackdown: Law and Disorder on the Electronic Frontier*. New York: Bantam Books.

Stoll, Clifford. 1989. *The Cuckoo's Egg*. New York: Doubleday.

U.S. Department of Defense (DOD). 1985. *Trusted Computer System Evaluation Criteria*, Department of Defense 5200.28-STD, the "Orange Book." Ft. Meade, MD: National Computer Security Center, December.

U.S. General Accounting Office (GAO). 1996. *Information Security—Computer Attacks at Department of Defense Pose Increasing Risks: A Report to Congressional Requesters*. Washington, DC: U.S. GAO, May.

Van Eng, Ray. 1997. "ActiveX Used to Steal Money Online," *World Internet News Digest* (W.I.N.D.), February 14. Available online at <http://www.cosmo21.com/wind/news97/w0297_06.htm>.

Wahbe, Robert, Steven Lucco, Thomas E. Anderson, and Susan L. Graham. 1993. "Efficient Software-based Fault Isolation," pp. 203-216 in *Proceedings of the 14th ACM Symposium on Operating Systems Principles*. New York: ACM Press.

War Room Research LLC. 1996. *1996 Information Systems Security Survey*. Baltimore, MD: War Room Research LLC, November 21.

Weissman, Clark. 1995. "Penetration Testing," *Information Security*, M.D. Abrams, S. Jajodia, and H.J. Podell, eds. Los Alamitos, CA: IEEE Computer Society Press.

5

Trustworthy Systems from Untrustworthy Components

It is easy to build a system that is less trustworthy than its least trust-worthy component. The challenge is to do better: to build systems that are more trustworthy than even their most trustworthy components. Such designs can be seen as "trustworthiness amplifiers." The prospect that a system could be more trustworthy than any of its components might seem implausible. But classical engineering is full of designs that accomplish analogous feats. In building construction, for example, one might find two beams that are each capable of supporting a 200-pound load being laminated together to obtain an element that will support in excess of 400 pounds. Can this sort of thing be done for trustworthiness of computing components, services, and systems? For some dimensions of trustworthiness it already has. Today, many computing services are implemented using replication, and multiple processors must fail before the service becomes unavailable—the service is more reliable than any single component processor. Secrecy, another dimension of trustworthiness, provides a second example: encrypting an already encrypted text, but with a different key, can (although not always; see Menenzes et al., 1997) increase the effective key length, hence the work factor for conducting a successful attack. Again, note how design (multiple encryption, in this case) amplifies a trustworthiness property (secrecy).

Replication and multiple encryption amplify specific dimensions of trustworthiness. But the existence of these techniques and others like them also suggests a new approach for implementing networked information system (NIS) trustworthiness: A system's structure, rather than its individual components, should be the major source of trustworthiness. This chapter explores that theme. By pointing out connections between what is known for specific trustworthiness dimensions and what is needed, the intent is to inspire investigations that would support a vision of trustworthiness by design. Detailed descriptions of specific research problems would be premature at this point—too little is known. Accordingly, this chapter is more abstract than the other technical chapters in this volume. Getting to the point where specific technical problems have been identified will itself constitute a significant step forward.

REPLICATION AND DIVERSITY

Diversity can play a central role in implementing trustworthiness. The underlying principle is simple: some members of a sufficiently diverse population will survive any given attack, although different members might be immune to different attacks. Long understood in connection with the biological world, this principle can also be applied for implementing fault tolerance and certain security properties, two key dimensions of trustworthiness.

Amplifying Reliability

A server can be viewed abstractly as a component that receives requests from clients, processes them, and produces responses. A reliable service can be constructed using a collection of such servers. Each client request is forwarded to a sufficient number of servers so that a correct response can be determined, even if some of the servers are faulty. The forwarding may be performed concurrently, as in active replication (Schneider, 1990), or, when failures are restricted to more benign sorts, serially (forwarding to the next server only if the previous one has failed), as in the primary backup approach (Alsberg and Day, 1976).

This use of replication amplifies the reliability of the components. Observe that the amplification occurs whether or not the servers employed are especially reliable, provided the servers fail independently. The failure-independence requirement is actually an assumption about diversity. Specifically, in this context, "attacks" correspond to server failures, and failure-independence of servers is equivalent to positing a server population with sufficient diversity so that each attack fells only a single server. Processors that are physically separated, powered from different sources, and communicate over narrow-bandwidth links approximate such a population, at least with respect to the random hardware failures. So, this replication-based design effectively amplifies server fault tolerance against random hardware failures. Error correcting codes, used to tolerate transient noise bursts during message transmissions, and alternative-path routing, used to tolerate router and link outages, can also be viewed in these terms—reliability is achieved by using replicas that fail independently.

Notice, however, that replication can diminish another aspect of trustworthiness—privacy—because replicating a service or database increases the number of locations where the data can be compromised (Randell and Dobson, 1986). Use of selective combinations of secret sharing and cryptographic techniques (so-called threshold cryptography) may, in some cases, reduce the exposure (DeSantis et al., 1994). And replication is not the only example in which techniques for enhancing one aspect of trustworthiness can adversely affect another.

Design and implementation errors in hardware or software components are not so easily tolerated by replication. The problem is that replicas of a single component define a population that lacks the necessary diversity. This is because attacks are now the stimuli that cause components to encounter errors and, since all replicas share design and implementation errors, a single attack will affect all replicas. However, if differently designed and implemented components were used, the necessary diversity would be present in the population. This approach was first articulated in connection with computer programming by Elmendorf,[1] who called it "fault-tolerant programming" (Elmendorf, 1972), and subsequently it has been refined by researchers and employed in a variety of control applications, including railway and avionics (Voges, 1988). However, the approach is expensive—each program is developed and tested independently N times and by separate development teams. More troubling than cost, though, are the experimental results that raise questions about whether separate development teams do indeed create populations with sufficient diversity when these teams start with the identical specifications (Knight and Leveson, 1986). See Ammann and Knight (1991) for an overall assessment of the practical issues concerning design diversity.

There are circumstances, however, in which replication can amplify resilience to software design and implementation errors. Program execution typically is determined not only by input data but also by other aspects of the system state. And, as a result of other system activity, the system state may differ from one execution of a given program to the next, causing different logic to be exercised in that program. Thus, an error that

---

[1]Dionysius Lardner in 1834 also pointed out the virtues of this approach to computing. See Voges (1988), page 4, for the Lardner quote: "The most certain and effectual check upon errors which arise in the process of computation is to cause the same computations to be made by separate and independent computers; and this check is rendered still more deci sive if they make their computations by different methods."

causes one execution of the program to fail might not be triggered in a subsequent execution, even for the same input data. Experiences along these lines have been reported by programmers of Tandem systems in which system support for transactions makes it particularly easy to build software that reruns programs after apparent software failures (Gray and Reuter, 1997). Further supporting experiences are reported in Huang et al. (1995), who show that periodic server restarts decrease the likelihood of server crashes. Interestingly, it is this same phenomenon that gives rise to so-called Heisenbugs (Gray and Reuter, 1997)—transient failures that are difficult to reproduce because they are triggered by circumstances beyond the control of a tester. Particularly troubling are Heisenbugs that surface only after a tester adds instrumentation to facilitate debugging a system.

Amplifying Security

Diversity not only can amplify reliability, but it can also be used to amplify immunity to more coordinated and hostile forms of attack. For such attacks, simple replication of components provides no benefit. These attacks are not random or independent; after successfully attacking one replica, an attacker can be expected to target other replicas and repeat that attack. A vulnerability in one replica constitutes a vulnerability for all replicas, and a population of identical replicas will lack the necessary diversity to survive. But a more diverse population—even though its members might each support the same functionality—can provide a measure of immunity from attacks.

The diversity necessary for deflecting hostile attacks can be viewed in terms of protocols, interfaces, and their implementations. Any attack will necessarily involve accessing interfaces because attacks exploiting vulnerabilities in standard protocols can be viewed as attacks against an interface. The attack will succeed owing to vulnerabilities associated with the semantics of those interfaces or because of flaws in the implementation of those interfaces. Different components or systems that provide the same functionality might do so by supporting dissimilar interfaces, by supporting similar interfaces having different implementations, or by supporting similar interfaces having similar implementations. With greater similarity comes increased likelihood of common vulnerabilities. For example, in UNIX implementations from different vendors, there will be some identical interfaces (because that is what defines UNIX) with identical implementations, some identical interfaces in which the implementations differ, and some internal interfaces that are entirely dissimilar. A Windows NT implementation is less similar to a UNIX system than another UNIX system would be. Thus, a successful attack against one UNIX implementation is more likely to succeed against the other UNIX implementations than against Windows NT. Unfortunately, realities of the marketplace and the added complexities when diverse components are used in building a system reduce the practicality of aggressively employing diversity in designing systems.

Findings

1. Replication and diversity can be employed to build systems that amplify the trustworthiness of their components. Research is needed to understand the limits and potential of this approach. How can diversity be added to a collection of replicas? How can responses from a diverse set of replicas be combined so that responses from corrupted components are ignored?

2. Research is also needed to understand how to measure similarities between distinct implementations of the same functionality and to determine the extent to which distinct implementations share vulnerabilities.

MONITOR, DETECT, RESPOND

Monitoring and detection constitute a second higher-level design approach that can play a role in implementing trustworthiness: attacks or failures are allowed to occur, but they are detected and a suitable and timely response is initiated. This approach has been applied both with respect to security and to fault tolerance. Its use for fault tolerance is broadly accepted, but its role in providing security is somewhat controversial.

Physical plant security typically is enforced by using such a combined approach—locks keep intruders out, and alarms, video surveillance cameras, and the threat of police response not only serve as deterrents but also enable the effects of an intrusion to be redressed. This combined approach is especially attractive when shortcomings in prevention technology are suspected. For example, in addition to antiforgery credit card technology and authorization codes for each transaction, credit card companies monitor and compare each transaction with profiles of past cardholder activity. A combined approach may be even more cost-effective than solely deploying prevention technology of sufficient strength.

Limitations in Detection

Whatever the benefits, the monitor-detect-respond approach is limited by the available detection technology—response is not possible without detection. For example, when this approach is used for security, the detection subsystem must recognize attacks (and report them) or must recognize acceptable behavior (and report exceptions) (Lunt, 1993). To recognize attacks, the detection subsystem must be imbued with some characterization of those attacks. This characterization might be programmed explicitly (perhaps as a set of pattern-matching rules for some aspect of system behavior) or derived by the detection subsystem itself from observing attacks. Notice that whatever means is employed, new attacks might go unrecognized. Systems that recognize acceptable behavior employ in effect some model for that behavior. Again, whether the model is programmed explicitly or generated by observing past acceptable behavior, the detection subsystem can be fooled by new behavior— for example, the worker who stays uncharacteristically late to meet a deadline.

With only approximate models to drive the detection subsystem, some attacks might not be detected and some false alerts might occur. Undetected attacks are successful attacks. And with false alerts, one detection problem is simply transformed into another one, with false alerts being conveyed to human operators for analysis. An operator constantly dealing with false alerts will become less attentive and less likely to notice a bona fide attack. Attackers might even try to exploit human frailty by causing false alerts so that subsequent real attacks are less likely to attract notice.

Any detection subsystem must gather information about the system it is monitoring. Deploying the necessary instrumentation for this surveillance may require modifications to existing systems components. That, however, could be difficult with commercial off-the-shelf components, since their internals are rarely available for view or modification. It also may become increasingly difficult if there is greater use of encryption for preserving confidentiality of communications, since that restricts the places in the system where monitoring can be performed. Data must be collected at the right level, too. Logs of low-level events might be difficult to parse; keeping only logs of events at higher levels of abstraction might enable an attack to be conducted below the level of the surveillance. A final difficulty with using the monitor-detect-respond approach to augment prevention mechanisms is its implicit reliance on prevention technology. The surveillance and detection mechanisms must be protected from attack and subversion.

Response and Reconfiguration

For the monitor-detect-respond paradigm to work, a suitable response must be available to follow up the detection of a failure or attack.

When it is failures that are being detected, system reconfiguration to isolate the faulty components seems like a reasonable response. For systems whose components are physically close, solutions for this system-management problem are understood reasonably well. But for systems spanning a wide area network, like a typical networked information system (NIS), considerably less is known. The problem is that communication delays now can be significant, giving rise to open questions about trade-offs involving the granularity and flexibility of the system-management functions that must be added to implement reconfigurations. And there is also the question of how to integrate partitions once they can be reconnected.

When hostile attacks are being detected, further concerns come into play. Isolating selected subsystems might be the sensible response, but knowing how and when to do so requires additional research into how to design an NIS that can continue functioning, perhaps in a degraded mode, once partitioned. Having security functionality be degraded in response to an attack is unwise though, since the resulting system could then admit a two-phase attack. The first phase causes the system to reconfigure and become more vulnerable to attack; the second phase of the attack exploits one of those new vulnerabilities. Finally, system reconfiguration mechanisms also must be protected from attacks that could compromise system availability. Triggering the reconfiguration mechanism, for example, could be the basis for a denial-of-service attack.

Perfection and Pragmatism

The monitor-detect-respond paradigm is theoretically limited by, among other things, the capabilities of the detection subsystem that it employs. This is more of a problem for attack monitoring than for failure monitoring. Specifically, a failure detector for a given system is unlikely to grow less effective over time, whereas an attack detector will grow less effective because new attacks are constantly being devised. Other common defensive measures, such as virus scanners and firewalls, are similarly flawed in theory but useful nevertheless.

There is nothing wrong with deploying theoretically limited solutions. What is known as "defense in depth" in the security community argues for using a collection of mechanisms so that the burden of perfection is placed on no single mechanism. One mechanism covers the flaws of another. Implicit in defense in depth, however, is a presumption about coverage. An attack that penetrates one mechanism had better not penetrate all of the others. Unfortunately, this coverage presumption is one that is not easily discharged—attack detectors are never accompanied by useful characterizations of their coverage, partly because no good characterizations exist for the space of attacks. Analogous to the error bars and safety factors that structural engineers employ, security engineers need ways to understand the limitations of their materials. What is needed can be seen as another place where the research into a "theory of insecurity" (advocated in Chapter 4) would have value, by providing a method by which vulnerabilities could be identified and their system-wide implications understood.

Findings

1. Monitoring and detection can be employed to build systems that amplify the trustworthiness of their components. But research is needed to understand the limits and potential of this approach.

2. Limitations in system monitoring technology and in technology to recognize events, like attacks and failures, impose fundamental limits on the use of monitoring and detection for implementing trustworthiness. For example, the limits and coverage of the various approaches to intruder and anomaly detection are not well understood.

PLACEMENT OF TRUSTWORTHINESS FUNCTIONALITY

In traditional uniprocessor computing systems, functionality for enforcing security policies and tolerating failures is often handled by the kernel, a small module at the lowest level of the system software. That architecture was attractive for three reasons:

* Correct operation of the kernel—hence, security and fault-tolerance functionality for the entire system—depended on no other software and, therefore, could not be compromised by flaws in other system software.
* Keeping the kernel small facilitated understanding it and gaining assurance in the entire system's security and fault-tolerance functionality.
* By segregating security and fault-tolerance functionality, both of which are subtle to design and implement, fewer programmers with those skills were required, and all programmers could leverage the efforts of the few.

Whether such an architecture is suitable for building an NIS seems less clear. For such a system to be scalable and to tolerate the failure of any single component, the "kernel" would have to span some of the network infrastructure and perhaps multiple processors. And, because NIS components are likely to be distributed geographically, ensuring unimpeded access to a "kernel" might force it, too, to be geographically distributed. A "kernel" that must span multiple, geographically distributed processors is not likely to be small or easily understood, making alternative architectures seem more attractive. For example, an argument might be made for placing security and fault-tolerance functionality at the perimeter of the system, so that processors minimize their dependence on network infrastructure and other parts of the system.

An effort was made, associated with the Trusted Network Interpretation (the so-called Red Book) of the Trusted Computer System Evaluation Criteria (TCSEC), to extend the "kernel" concept, for the security context, from a single computer to an entire network (U.S. DOD, 1987). According to the Red Book, there was a piece of the "kernel" in each processing component, and communication between components was assumed to be secure. This approach was found to be infeasible for large networks or even relatively small nonhomogeneous ones.

Too few NISs have been built, and even fewer have been carefully analyzed, for any sort of consensus to have emerged about what architectures are best or even about what aspects of an NIS and its environment are important in selecting an architecture. The two extant NISs discussed in Chapter 2—the public telephone network (PTN) and the Internet—give some feel for viable architectures and their consequences. A proposed third system under discussion within government circles, the so-called minimum essential information infrastructure (MEII), gives insight into difficulties and characteristics associated with specifying a sort of "kernel" for an NIS. Therefore, the remainder of this section reviews these three systems and architectures. While only a start, this exercise suggests that further research in the area could lead to insights that would be helpful to NIS designers.

Public Telephone Network

The PTN is structured around a relatively small number of highly reliable components. A single modern telephone switch can handle all of the traffic for a town with tens of thousands of residents; long-distance traffic for the entire country is routed through only a few hundred switches. All of these switches are designed to be highly available, with downtime measured in small numbers of minutes per year. Control of the PTN is handled by a few centrally managed computers. The end systems (telephones) do not participate in PTN management and are not expected to have processing capacity.

The use of only a small number of components allows telephone companies to leverage their scarce human resources. PTN technicians are needed to operate, monitor, maintain, test, and upgrade the software in only a relatively small number of machines. Having centralized control simplifies network-wide load management, since the state of the system is both accessible and easily changed. But the lack of diversity and centralization does little to prevent widespread outages. First, shared vulnerabilities and common-mode failures are more than a possibility; they have already occurred. Second, after propagating only a short distance (i.e., through a relatively small number of components), a failure or attack can affect a significant portion of the system.

As discussed in Chapter 2, the PTN maintains state for each call being handled. This, in turn, facilitates resource reservations per call that enable quality of service guarantees per call—a connection, once established, receives 56 kbps (kilobits per second) of dedicated bandwidth. But, establishing a connection in the PTN is not guaranteed. If a telephone switch does not have sufficient bandwidth available, then it will decline to process a call. Consequently, existing connections are in no way affected by increases in offered load.[2]

Internet

The Internet, by and large, exemplifies a more distributed architecture than the PTN. It is built from thousands of routers that are run by many different organizations and (as a class) are somewhat less reliable than telephone switches. Control in the Internet is decentralized, and delivery of packets is not guaranteed. Routers communicate with each other to determine the current network topology and automatically route packets, or discard them for lack of resources. The end systems (i.e., hosts) are responsible for transforming the Internet's "best effort" service into something stronger, and hosts are assumed to have processing capacity for this purpose.

The reliability of the Internet comes from the relatively high degree of redundancy and absence of centralized control. To be sure, any given end system on the Internet experiences lower availability than, for instance, a typical telephone. However, the network as a whole will remain up despite outages. No single make of computer or operating system is run everywhere in the Internet, though many share a common pedigree. Diversity of hardware and software protects the Internet from some common-mode design and implementation failures and contributes to the reliability of the whole. But the Internet's routing infrastructure is built using predominantly Cisco routers, with Bay and a few other companies supplying the rest. In that regard, the Internet is like the PTN, relying

---

[2]If the call is declined by a switch, then the call may be routed via other switches or it may be declined altogether by returning a busy signal to the call initiatior.

largely on switches from Lucent, with Nortel, Siemens, and a few others supplying the rest.

With protocol implementations installed in the tens of millions of end systems, it is relatively difficult to install changes to the Internet's protocols. This, then, is one of the disadvantages of an architecture that depends on end-system processing. Even installing a change in the Internet's routers is difficult because of the large number of organizations involved.

As discussed in Chapter 2, the Internet's routers, by design, do not maintain state for connections—indeed, connections are known only to the end systems. Different packets between a pair of end systems can travel different routes, and that provides a simple and natural way to tolerate link and router outages. The statelessness of the Internet's routers means that router memory capacity does not limit the number of end systems nor the number of concurrently open connections. However, there is a disadvantage to this statelessness: routers are unable to offer hosts true service guarantees, and the service furnished to a host can be affected by increases in load caused by other hosts.

In addition to supporting end-system scaling, the statelessness of the Internet helps avoid a problem often associated with distributed architectures: preserving constraints that link the states of different system components. Preservation of constraints, especially when outages of components must be tolerated, can require complex coordination protocols. Note that consistency constraints do link the routing tables in each of the Internet's routers. But these are relatively weak consistency constraints and are, therefore, easy to maintain. Even so, the Internet experiences routing-state maintenance problems, known as "routing flaps." (Routing response is dampened to help deal with this problem, at the level of the Border Gateway Protocol.) State per connection would be much harder to maintain because of the sheer numbers and the short-lived nature of the connections.

Minimum Essential Information Infrastructure

A minimum essential information infrastructure (MEII) is a highly trustworthy communications subsystem—a network whose services are immune to failures and attacks. The notion of an MEII was originally proposed in connection with providing support for NISs that control critical infrastructures.[3] The MEII essentially was to be a "kernel" for many, if not all, NISs.

---

[3]According to Anderson et al. (1998), the term "MEII" is credited to Rich Mesic, a RAND researcher who was involved in a series of information-warfare exercises run by RAND starting in 1995.

The study committee believes that implementing a single MEII for the nation would be misguided and infeasible. An independent study conducted by RAND (Anderson et al., 1998) also arrives at this conclusion. One problem is the incompatibilities that inevitably would be introduced as nonhardened parts of NISs are upgraded to exploit new technologies. NISs constantly evolve to exploit new technology, and an MEII that did not evolve in concert would rapidly become useless.

A second problem with a single national MEII is that "minimum" and "essential" depend on context and application (see Box 5.1), so one size cannot fit all. For example, water and power are essential services. Losing either in a city for a day is troublesome, but losing it for a week is unacceptable, as is having either out for even a day for an entire state. A hospital has different minimum information needs for normal operation (e.g., patient health records, billing and insurance records) than it does during a civil disaster. Finally, the trustworthiness dimensions that should be preserved by an MEII depend on the customer: local law enforcement agents may not require secrecy in communications when handling a civil disaster but would in day-to-day crime fighting.

Despite the impracticality of having a single national MEII, providing all of the trustworthiness functionality for an NIS through a "kernel" could be a plausible design option. Here are likely requirements:

- The "kernel" should degrade gracefully, shedding less essential functions if necessary to preserve more essential functions. For example, low-speed communications channels might remain available after high-speed ones are gone; recent copies of data might, in some cases, be used in place of the most current data.[4]
- The "kernel" should, to the extent possible, be able to function even if all elements of the infrastructure are not functioning. An example is the PTN, whose essential components have backup battery power enabling them to continue operating for a few hours after a power failure and without telephone company emergency generators (which might not be functioning).
- The "kernel" must be designed with restart and recovery in mind. It should be possible to restore the operation, starting from nothing, if necessary.

Note that neither the PTN nor the Internet exhibits all three of these characteristics, although the PTN probably comes closer than the Inter-

---

[4]Applications that depend on a gracefully degrading MEII must themselves be able to function in the full spectrum of resource availability that such an MEII might provide.

BOX 5.1
Taxonomy of Applications for Support by a Minimum Essential Information Infrastructure

• *Military.* Short-term strategic communications and information management needs of the Armed Forces as required to operate national defense systems, gather intelligence, and conduct operations against hostile powers.
• *Nonmilitary federal government.* Communications and information needs of the federal government to communicate with the military and local governments, to coordinate civil responses to natural disasters, and to direct national law enforcement against internal threats, terrorists, and organized crime.
• *National information and news.* Infrastructure required to communicate national issues rapidly to the U.S. public. Current examples include national radio and television networks (both broadcast and cable) and the national emergency broadcast program and national newspapers.
• *National power and telecommunications services.* Communications required to operate natural gas distribution, fuel distribution, the electric power distribution grids, and the public switched telephone network at a moderate level allowing non-military communication.
• *National economy.* Communications required to operate public and private banking systems, stock exchanges, and other economic institutions; the concept may also extend to social service programs, which include income distribution components.
• *Local government.* Communications and information management needs of state and municipal governments to coordinate civil responses to natural disasters, to communicate with federal authorities, and to direct local law enforcement, fire, and health and safety personnel.
• *Local information and news.* Infrastructure required to communicate local information to a local area rapidly. Current examples include local television, radio, and newspapers.
• *Nongovernment civil.* Communications and information management needs of civil institutions, such as the Red Cross, hospitals, ambulance services, and other critical and safety-related civil institutions.
• *Local power and telecommunications.* Communications required to operate local power grids and telephony networks at a restricted level.
• *Local economic and mercantile.* Communication infrastructure required to operate local banks, markets, stores, and other essential mercantile infrastructure.
• *Transportation.* Communications infrastructure needed to manage air traffic, signaling and control infrastructure for controlling railroads, and infrastructure for automobile traffic signaling and control of traffic congestion in cities.

---

net.[5] The development of a "kernel" exhibiting all three of the characteristics might well require new research, and an attempt to build such a "kernel" could reveal technical problems that are not, on the surface, apparent. Implementing an NIS using such a "kernel" could also be a

---

[5]There is some question as to whether the PTN can be disconnected and then restarted from scratch.

useful research exercise, since it might reveal other important characteristics the "kernel" should possess.

An alternative vision of the specification for a trustworthy "kernel" is as a computer network—hardware, communications lines, and software—that has a broad spectrum of operating modes. At one end of the spectrum, resource utilization is optimized; at the other end—entered in response to an attack—routings are employed that may be suboptimal but more trustworthy because they use diverse and replicated routings. In the more conservative mode, packets might be duplicated or fragmented[6] by using technology that is effective for communicating information even when a significant fraction of the network has been compromised.[7]

Notice that for such a multimode MEII implementation to be viable, it must possess some degree of diversity. Thus, there might well be a point after which hardening by using trustworthy components should defer to design goals driven by diversity. Second, detecting the occurrence of an attack is a prerequisite to making an operating-mode change that constitutes a defense in this MEII vision. Tools for monitoring the global status of the network thus become important, especially since a coordinated attack might be recognized only by observing activity in a significant fraction of the network.

A third plausible architecture for supporting trustworthiness functionality is to use some sort of a service broker that would monitor the status of the communications infrastructure. This service broker would sense problems and provide information to restore service dynamically, interconnecting islands of unaffected parts of the communications infrastructure. For example, it might be used in commandeering for priority uses some unaffected parts that normally operate as private intranets.

Findings

1. Attempting to build a single MEII for the nation would be misguided and a waste of resources because of the differing requirements of NISs.

2. Little is known about the advantages and disadvantages of different NIS system architectures and about where best to allocate in a system the responsibility for trustworthiness functionality. A careful analysis of

---

[6]See, for example, Rabin (1989).

[7]Note that this multimode scheme implements resistance to attacks by using techniques traditionally used for supporting fault tolerance, something that seems especially attractive because a single mechanism is then being used to satisfy multiple requirements for trustworthiness. On the other hand, single mechanisms do present a common failure mode risk.

existing systems would be one way to learn about the trustworthiness consequences of different architectures.

3. The design of systems that exhibit graceful degradation has great potential, but little is known about supporting or exploiting such systems.

NONTRADITIONAL PARADIGMS

Other less architecturally oriented design approaches have been investigated for amplifying trustworthiness properties, most notably amplifying fault tolerance. These approaches are more algorithmic in flavor. Further research is recommended to develop the approaches and to better understand the extent and domain of their applicability.

Self-stabilization, for example, has been used to implement system services that recover from transient failures (Schneider, 1993). Informally, a self-stabilizing algorithm is one that is guaranteed to return to some predefined set of acceptable states after it has been perturbed and to do so without appealing to detectors or centralized controllers of any sort. For example, some communications protocols depend on the existence of a token that is passed among participants and empowers its holder to take certain actions (e.g., send a message). A self-stabilizing token management protocol would always return the system to the state in which there is a single token, even after a transient failure causes loss or duplication of the token. More generally, the design of network management and routing protocols could clearly benefit from a better understanding of control algorithms having similar convergent properties. The goal should be control schemes that are robust by virtue of the algorithm being used rather than the robustness of individual components.

It may also be possible to develop a science base for algorithms that amplify resilience or other dimensions of trustworthiness by relying on group behavior. Metaphors and observations about the nature of our natural world—flocking birds, immunological systems,[8] and crystalline structures in physics—might provide ideas for methods to manage networks of computers and the information they contain. The design approaches outlined above—population diversity and monitor-detect-respond—have clear analogies with biological concepts. Studying the organization of free markets and game theory for algorithmic content might be another source of ideas. Of course, there are significant differences between an NIS and the natural world; these differences might restrict the applicability of natural group behavior algorithms to NISs.

---

[8]With regard to the immunology metaphor, sophisticated attacks are like biological weapons, which have always proven effective in overcoming natural immunity.

For example, the actions and behaviors of natural systems arise not from deterministic programming but from complex, sometimes random, interactions of the individual elements. Instead of exhibiting the desirable robust behaviors, collections of programmed computers might instead become synchronized or converge in unintended ways. Clearly, research is needed to establish what ideas can apply to an NIS and to understand how they can be leveraged. See Anderson et al. (1998) for a discussion of how biological metaphors might be applied to the design of an MEII.

Finding

A variety of research directions involving new types of algorithms—self-stabilization, emergent behavior, biological metaphors—have the potential to be useful in defining systems that are trustworthy. Their strengths and weaknesses are not well understood, and further research is called for.

REFERENCES

Alsberg, P.A., and J.D. Day. 1976. "A Principle for Resilient Sharing of Distributed Resources," pp. 627-644 in *Proceedings of the 2nd International Conference on Software Engineering*. Los Alamitos, CA: IEEE Computer Society Press.

Ammann, P.E., and J.C. Knight. 1991. "Design Fault Tolerance," *Reliability Engineering and System Safety*, 32(1):25-49.

Anderson, Robert H., Phillip M. Feldman, Scott Gerwehr, Brian Houghton, Richard Mesic, John D. Pinder, and Jeff Rothenberg. 1998. *A "Minimum Essential Information Infrastructure" for U.S. Defense Systems. Meaningful? Feasible? Useful?* Santa Monica, CA: RAND National Defense Research Institute, in press.

DeSantis, A., Y. Desmedt, Y. Frankel, and M. Yung. 1994. "How to Share a Function Securely," pp. 522-533 in *Proceedings of the 26th ACM Symposium on the Theory of Computing*. New York: ACM Press.

Elmendorf, W.R. 1972. "Fault-Tolerant Programming," pp. 79-83 in *Proceedings of the 2nd International Symposium on Fault-tolerant Computing (FTCS-2)*. Los Alamitos, CA: IEEE Computer Society Press.

Gray, James, and Andreas Reuter. 1997. *Transaction Processing: Concepts and Techniques*. San Mateo, CA: Morgan Kaufmann Publishers.

Huang, Yennun, Chandra Kintala, Nick Kolettis, and N. Dudley Fulton. 1995. "Software Rejuvenation: Analysis, Module, and Applications," pp. 381-390 in *Proceedings of the 25th Symposium on Fault-tolerant Computing*. Los Alamitos, CA: IEEE Computer Society Press.

Knight, J.C., and Nancy G. Leveson. 1986. "An Experimental Evaluation of the Assumption of Independence in Multi-version Programming," *IEEE Transactions on Software Engineering*, 12(1): 96-109.

Lunt, Teresa F. 1993. "A Survey of Intrusion Detection Techniques," *Computers and Security*, 12(4):405-418.

Menenzes, Alfred J., Paul C. Van Oorschot, and Scott A. Vanstone. 1996. *Handbook of Applied Cryptography*. CRC Press Series on Discrete Mathematics and Its Applications. Boca Raton, FL: CRC Press, October.

Rabin, M.O. 1989. "Dispersal of Information for Security, Load Balancing, and Fault Tolerance," *Communications of the ACM*, 36(2):335-348. Available online at <http://www.ACM.org/pubs/citations/journals/jacm/1989-36-2/p355-rabin>.

Randell, B., and J. Dobson. 1986. "Reliability and Security Issues in Distributed Computing Systems," pp. 113-118 in *Proceedings of the Fifth Symposium on Reliability in Distributed Software and Database Systems*. Los Alamitos, CA: IEEE Computer Society Press.

Schneider, Fred B. 1990. "Implementing Fault-tolerant Services Using the State Machine Approach: A Tutorial," *ACM Computing Surveys*, 22(4):299-319.

Schneider, Marco. 1993. "Self-stabilization," *ACM Computing Surveys*, 25(1): 45-67.

U.S. Department of Defense (DOD). 1987. *Trusted Network Interpretation of the Trusted Computer System Evaluation Criteria*, NCSC-TG-005, Library Number S228,526, Version 1, the "Red Book." Ft. Meade, MD: National Computer Security Center.

Voges, Udo. 1988. *Software Diversity in Computerized Control Systems*. Vol. 2 in the series *Dependable Computing and Fault Tolerance Systems*. Vienna, Austria: Springer-Verlag.

6

The Economic and
Public Policy Context

Factors that cause networked information systems (NISs) to be less trustworthy than they might be—environmental disruption, human user and operator errors, attacks by hostile parties, and design and implementation errors—are examined in this report. In a number of instances, research and development efforts have yielded state-of-the-art technological solutions that could be deployed to enhance NIS trustworthiness. Why are such technological solutions not used more widely in practice?

Some experts posit that the benefits from increased trustworthiness are difficult to estimate or trade off, and consumers therefore direct their expenditures toward other investments that they perceive will have more definitive returns. Similarly, producers tend to be reluctant to invest in products, features, and services that further trustworthiness when their resources can be directed (e.g., toward increasing functionality) where the likelihood of profit appears greater. Thus, there seems to be a market failure for trustworthiness. Other factors, such as aspects of public policy, also tend to inhibit the use of existing solutions.

As this report makes clear, while the deployment of extant technologies can improve the trustworthiness of NISs, in many critical areas answers are not known. Research is needed. Most of the research activity related to trustworthiness involves federal government funding. (Although the private sector conducts "research," most of this effort is development that is directed toward specific products.) Inasmuch as the federal government is the major funder of basic and applied research in computing and communications, this chapter examines its interests and research emphases related to trustworthiness. Certain aspects of trustworthiness (e.g., security) are historically critical areas for federal agencies responsible for national security interests. The National Security Agency (NSA) and Defense Advanced Research Projects Agency (DARPA), both part of the Department of Defense (DOD), have particularly influential roles in shaping research priorities and funding for trustworthiness.

In this chapter, there is a greater emphasis on security than on other dimensions of trustworthiness, because the federal government has placed tremendous emphasis on computer and communications security consistent with the importance of this technology in supporting national security activities. As the broader concept of trustworthiness becomes increasingly important, especially in light of the recent concern for protection of critical infrastructures, increased attention to the nonsecurity dimensions of trustworthiness by the federal government may be warranted. This is not to say that attention to security is or will become unimportant—indeed, security vulnerabilities are expected to increase in both number and severity in the future. Additionally, the success of security in the marketplace is mixed at best, so a discussion of the reasons for this situation merits some attention here.

This chapter begins with a discussion of risk management, which provides the analytical framework to assess rationales for people's investment in trustworthiness or their failure to do so. The risk management discussion leads to an analysis of the costs that consumers encounter in their decisions regarding trustworthiness. These first two sections articulate reasons that there is a disincentive for consumers to invest in trustworthiness. Producers also face disincentives (but different ones) to invest in trustworthiness, as discussed in the third section. Then there is a discussion of standards and criteria and possible roles that they may play to address the market failure problem. The important role of cryptography is explicated in Chapters 2 and 4; here, the focus is on the question of why cryptography is not more widely used. The federal government's many interests in trustworthiness include facilitating the use of technology to improve trustworthiness today and fostering research to support advances in trustworthiness. This chapter concludes with a discussion of the federal agencies involved with conducting and/or sponsoring research in trustworthiness. Two agencies with central roles in this arena—the NSA and DARPA—are examined in some detail.

RISK MANAGEMENT

The motivation to invest in trustworthiness is to manage risks. While it is conceivable to envision positive benefits deriving from trustworthiness,[1] the primary rationale for investment in trustworthiness is to help ensure that an NIS does what people expect it to do—and not something else.[2] The study of risk management involves the assessment of risk and its consequences, a framework for analyzing alternatives to prevent or mitigate risks, and a basis for making decisions and implementing strategies. Although there are a number of analytical tools available to assist in risk management, each step in the process is subject to uncertainty and judgment.

Risk Assessment

Risk assessment differs depending on whether the emphasis is on security or on safety and reliability. Threat, for example, is a concept most commonly associated with security. Threat assessment is both speculative and subjective, as it necessitates an evaluation of attacker intent.[3] Speculation is associated with vulnerability assessment, because the *existence* of a vulnerability can be shown by experiment, but the *absence* of vulnerabilities cannot be shown by experiment or any other definitive means. There always exists the possibility that some aspect of the system can be exploited in some unexpected way. Whereas security-critical information systems have to defend against such malicious attacks, safety-critical systems typically do not.

In the security arena, *risk* is the combination of two probabilities: first, the probability that a threat exists that will attempt to locate and exploit a vulnerability; and second, the probability that the attempt will succeed. Security risk assessment compounds two uncertainties—one human and one technical. The human uncertainty centers on the question, Would anybody attack? The technical uncertainty centers on the question, If they did, would they locate and exploit a residual vulnerability?

A vulnerability, once discovered, may be exploited again and again. In the Internet era, a vulnerability may even be publicized to the world in

---

[1]A hypothetical example could entail the use of trustworthiness as a marketing advantage, akin to the Federal Express creed of "when it absolutely, positively has to be there."

[2]There is also the notion that some forms of business activities require or are facilitated by a particular level of trustworthiness (e.g., security as an enabler). In the electronic commerce area, as an example, the availability of secure socket layer (SSL) encryption for Web traffic has caused consumers to feel more comfortable about sending credit card numbers across the Internet, even though the real risk of credit card theft is on the merchants' servers—and that is not addressed by SSL.

[3]The example of residential burglary may help to clarify this point. One may suspect through a series of observations that one's neighborhood has been targeted by burglars: strange cars driving slowly by, noises in the night, phone callers who hang up immediately when the telephone is answered, and so on. One is only sure that burglars are operating when a burglary happens—too late for any practical preventive steps to be taken.

the convenient form of an "attack script" that enables the vulnerability to be easily exploited, even by those who are unable to understand it.[4] Such behavior means that probabilities are nonindependent in a statistical sense. By contrast, risk assessment in the context of safety or reliability is significantly different. Risk in safety or reliability analysis is a function of the probability that a hazard arises and the consequences (e.g., cost) of the hazard. The most common function is the product of the two numbers, yielding an expected value. Informally, risk can be thought of as the expected damage done per unit of time that results from the operation of a system. Because the probability of failure per unit of time is nonzero, the risk is nonzero, and damage must be expected. If the estimated risk[5] is unacceptably high, then either design or implementation changes must be made to reduce it, or consideration has to be given to withholding deployment. But if a safety incident should occur (e.g., an accident), the probability of a second accident remains unchanged, or may even decrease as a consequence.[6]

A major challenge for risk management with regard to trustworthiness is the growing difficulty of differentiating attacks from incompetence and failure or lack of reliability. It is one of several factors that raise the question of whether comprehensive probability estimation or hazard analysis is possible.

Nature of Consequences

Attitudes and behavior depend on the nature of consequences. Safety-critical information systems often control physical systems, where the

---

[4]A simple example is a one-line command that may allow an individual to steal passwords. Access the URL <http://xxx.xxx.xxx/cgi-bin/phf?Qalias=x%0a/bin/cat%20/etc/passwd>, substituting "xxx.xxx.xxx" with the target site of interest. For some Web sites, the encrypted passwords will be returned to you. If this one-line command works, it is because there is a flawed version of PHF in the /cgi-bin directory. PHF allows users to gain remote access to files (including the /etc/passwd file) over the Web. One can run a password-cracking program on the encrypted passwords obtained.

[5]Risk estimation is a systems engineering issue, and it involves careful, extensive, and thorough analysis of all aspects of a safety-critical system by systems engineers, safety engineers, domain experts, and others. An important initial activity in the process is hazard analysis, an attempt to determine the hazards that would be manifested if the system were to fail. A hazard is a condition with the potential for causing an undesired consequence. A hazard of operating a nuclear plant, for example, would be the release of radiation into the environment. A hazard of using a medical device might be patient injury. Various guidelines, procedures, and standards for carrying out hazard analyses have been developed. The central issue with hazard analysis is completeness—it is very important that all hazards be identified if at all possible.

[6]For example, because of greater operator diligence.

consequences of failure include the possibility that lives will be threatened and/or valuable equipment may be damaged (e.g., an air traffic control system). The consequences of failure of non-safety-related systems include the possibility that data will be corrupted or stolen, or that essential services will be unavailable. While the latter are serious outcomes, these consequences are not perceived to be as serious as those associated with safety-critical systems. Financial consequences, especially within the private sector, have also attracted considerable attention because these consequences can be reasonably quantified and the implications to the financial bottom line are readily understood.[7]

Consequences are not static. Consequences that are currently tolerable may become intolerable in the future. For example, as the speed of communications channels continues to increase and applications are designed to rely on this speed, the availability[8] of a connection may not be sufficient for those applications that depend on high bandwidth and low delay. Moreover, as applications become more dependent on quality of service guarantees from networks, a degradation in service may disrupt future applications more than current ones.

It is the nature of an NIS that outages and disruptions of service in local areas may have very uneven consequences, even within the area of disruption. Failure of a single Internet service provider (ISP) may or may not affect transfer of information outside the area of disruption, depending on how the ISP has configured its communications. For example, caching practices intended to reduce network congestion problems helped to limit the scope of a Domain Name Service (DNS) outage.[9] Corporations that manage their own interconnection (so-called intranets) may be wholly unaffected. Even widespread or catastrophic failures may not harm some users, if they have intentionally or unconsciously provided redundant storage or backup facilities. The inability to accurately predict consequences seriously complicates the process of calculating risk and makes it tempting to assume "best case" behavior in response to failure.

A discussion about consequences must also address the questions of who is affected by the consequences and to what extent. While cata-

---

[7]In contrast to privacy, for example.

[8]Increased dependence on connections promotes attention not only to the number of outages but also to the length of outages. For example, a one-second outage in a voice connection may require redialing to reestablish a connection; in a client/server application over a wide-area network, it could require rebooting computers, restarting applications, and considerable other delays that yield a multiplier as compared to voice.

[9]The master file for ".COM," a major address domain, was corrupted; however, most sites only queried the master file for entries not in their caches. Entries that were cached— and those generally included all the usual peers of any given site—were used, despite their apparent deletion from the master file.

strophic failure garners the most popular attention, there are many dimensions to trustworthiness and consequences may involve various subsets of them with varying degrees of severity. For example, cellular telephony fraud has two principal variants approximately equal in size: credit fraud, whereby the cellular telephone owner transfers the account to a second provider and does not pay the first; and cloning, the transfer to a new device of numbers that identify a radio and customer account. In both cases, the service provider loses revenue. Under some circumstances, a legitimate caller may be denied service if illegitimate users saturate the network.[10] In the case of telephone cloning, if the clone user does not saturate the network, the provider loses revenue but users do not incur an immediate cost.[11] Understanding consequences is essential to forming baseline expectations of private action and what incentives may be effective for changing private action, but that understanding is often hampered by the difficulty of quantifying or otherwise specifying the costs and consequences associated with risks.

Risk Management Strategies

Risk management strategies are approaches to managing trade-offs.[12] These strategies address questions about whether it is better to add, for example, a small degree of security to a large number of products or substantial security to a smaller number of specific products, to use high-security/low-availability solutions or low-security/high-availability ones, or to increase assurance or the ability to identify and quarantine attackers. Trade-offs can be made in system design and engineering; they can also be made in deciding whether to invest in technology, procedure, insurance, or inaction.

---

[10]Note that the cost of denied service to the legitimate caller may far exceed the price of the telephone call itself. For example, a delay in requesting emergency services (e.g., a call to the fire department) may carry catastrophic costs.

[11]However, to the extent that the cellular carrier is responsible for the resulting wireline and long-distance charges from the telephone clone, a rise in the cellular carrier's rates may be forthcoming.

[12]It is essential (1) that the actual system matches the model underlying the analysis as closely as possible, and (2) that the failure rates achieved by system components match the estimates used in the model. The former is a systems/safety engineering issue, whereas the latter involves all the engineering disciplines engaged in preparing the components. The process usually followed to achieve these two goals is in two parts: the first is careful management of the development process; the second is iterative evaluation of the system design as it is developed. If changes are made for any reason, the risk estimation might be repeated. If necessary, elements of the system design can be modified to reduce the risk. For example, if a nuclear plant's cooling system is shown to be unable to meet its dependability requirements because a particular type of pump tends to fail more often than is acceptable, then the design can be modified to include a backup pump.

Risk avoidance is a strategy that seeks to reduce risk to the lowest possible value. Reducing risk takes precedence over cost or effect on the operational characteristics of the system in question. Risk avoidance strategies arose in the context of high-consequence systems, such as nuclear weapon command and control or the protection of nuclear weapon stockpiles. At the time these systems were developed, there was a clear boundary between high-consequence applications and "ordinary" software—whose malfunctions could be expensive and annoying but did not threaten human life or significant assets. With the increasing use of Internet technology, this boundary is becoming blurred.

The underlying assumption of risk avoidance strategies, when security is emphasized, is that there exists a highly capable threat that will expend great effort to achieve its goals. The achievement of those goals will involve such extreme consequences (e.g., uncommanded nuclear weapon release) that all possible effort should be devoted to preventing such consequences from being realized. Risk avoidance strategies, in general, incorporate every protection mechanism and invoke every possible assurance step. Many of these assurance steps, which are discussed in detail in Chapter 3, can handle only certain classes of designs or implementation technologies. When these limitations are imposed in addition to those of the rigid design guidance, the result is very often a system that is expensive, slow to deploy, and cumbersome and inefficient to use. Experience with risk avoidance strategies indicates that residual vulnerabilities will remain irrespective of the number of assurance steps taken. These vulnerabilities will often require quite exotic techniques to exploit; exotic, that is, until they are discovered by a threat or (worse yet) published on the Internet.[13]

However, the costs associated with avoiding all risks are prohibitive. Thus, risk mitigation is more typical and is generally encountered when many factors, including security and reliability, determine the success of a system. Risk mitigation is especially popular in market-driven environments where an attempt is made to provide "good enough" security or reliability or other qualities without severely affecting economic factors such as price and time to market. Risk mitigation should be interpreted not as a license to do a shoddy job in implementing trustworthiness, but instead as a pragmatic recognition that trade-offs between the dimensions of trustworthiness, economic realities, and other constraints will be the norm, not the exception. The risk mitigation strategies that are most

---

[13]Some exotic strategies require specialized hardware or physical access to certain systems, whereas other exotic strategies may require only remote access and appropriate software to be executed. It is this latter class of strategies that is particularly susceptible to dissemination via the Internet.

relevant to trustworthiness can generally be characterized according to two similar models:

- *The insurance model.* In this model, the cost of countermeasures is viewed as an "insurance premium" paid to prevent (or at least mitigate) loss. The value of the information being protected, or the service being provided, is assessed and mechanisms and assurance steps are incorporated up to, but not exceeding, that value.
- *The work factor model.* A definition in cryptology for the term "work factor" is the amount of computation required to break a cipher through a brute-force search of all possible key values.[14]   Recently, the term has been broadened to mean the amount of effort required to locate and exploit a residual vulnerability. That effort may involve more efficient procedures rather than exhaustive searches. In the case of fault tolerance, the assumptions made about the types of failures (benign or arbitrary) that could arise are analogous to the concept of work factor.

The two models are subject to pitfalls distinctive to each and some that are common to both. In the insurance model, it is possible that the value of information (or disruption of service) to an outsider is substantially greater than the value of that information or service to its owners. Thus, a "high value" attack could be mounted, succeed, and the "insurance premium" lost along with the target data or service. Such circumstances often arise in an interconnected or networked world. For example, a local telephone switch might be protected against deliberate interruption of service to the degree that is justified by the revenue that might be lost from such an interruption. But such an analysis ignores the attacker whose aim is to prevent a physical alarm system from notifying the police that an intrusion has been detected into an area containing valuable items. Another example is an instance in which a hacker expends great effort to take over an innocuous machine, not because it contains interesting data but because it provides computing resources and network connectivity that can be used to mount attacks on higher-value targets.[15]   In the case of the work factor model, it is notoriously difficult to assess the capabilities of a potential adversary in a field as unstructured as that of discovering vulnerabilities, which involves seeing aspects of a system that were overlooked by its designers.

---

[14]If the cryptography is easily broken (e.g., because the keys are stored in shared memory), the work factor may be almost irrelevant.

[15]A specific example of this comes from the early days of electromechanical cryptosystems. At that time, governments typically deployed an array of different cryptosystems of different strengths: simple (and easier to break) cryptosystems for less sensitive data, and elaborate

Selecting a Strategy

Risk management seeks to provide an analytical framework for deciding how close to the edge one dares to go. Risk avoidance carries with it the danger of overengineering to the point at which the system is never used. Risk mitigation carries with it the danger of underengineering to the point at which the system is defeated, very possibly over and over again. The compound uncertainties of risk management preclude any rigorous method, but it is possible to articulate a few guidelines:

• Understand how long the system will be used in harm's way. Threats are not static; they become more capable over time, through the release of once-secret information from disgruntled former employees and other sources, access to once-esoteric equipment, and through other means.[16]

• Assess how much work is needed to exploit a known residual vulnerability. Does the attack require specialized equipment? Is this the sort of equipment that will drop drastically in cost over the next few years? Is it the sort of equipment that is freely accessible in open environments such as universities? Does the attack require a level of physical access that can be made hard to achieve?

• Context is extremely important. It is necessary to understand how the system might be used, how it is connected to or interacts with other systems, and how it might be exploited in the course of attacking something else.

• Can the system-support infrastructure react to vulnerabilities? Are system updates possible, and if so, at what cost? How many instances of

---

electromechanical devices to encipher highly sensitive data (called, respectively, "low-grade" and "high-grade" systems). This approach can be looked at as a risk-mitigation strategy, on either the insurance or work factor model, depending on how the decision of which system protected which data was used. Only security that was "good enough" was imposed. What the designers of these systems were slow to realize, however, was that the high-grade systems (e.g., the German Enigma machine) were vulnerable to "known plaintext" attacks where the cryptanalyst was able to match unenciphered and enciphered characters and thereby recover the key that deciphered other, previously unknown, messages. The nature of military and diplomatic communication is such that much text is "cut and pasted" from innocuous messages to more sensitive ones. Breaking the low-grade ciphers then provided the "known plaintext" that facilitated attacks on the high-grade ciphers.

[16]The so-called "cloning" attack, which is responsible for a large percentage of cellular fraud today, was at one time understandable only by a small handful of electronic engineers and required expensive, custom-made equipment. Today that attack is embodied in clandestine consumer products and can be mounted by any individual with the will and a few hundred dollars. The will has increased for many because there are more targets: high-use areas make listening for identification numbers more feasible.

the system will be deployed and how widely are they dispersed? Is there a mechanism for security recalls?[17] Can the infrastructure continue critical operations at a reduced and trusted level if attacked?

The difficulties of anticipating and avoiding most risks can lead to strategies that emphasize compensatory action: detecting problems and responding to minimize damage, recovering, and seeking redress in some circumstances. The difficulty with this approach is the implicit assumption that all attacks can be identified. Anecdotal reports of success by "tiger teams" seeking to compromise systems suggest that detection may continue to be a weak vehicle for the future.[18]

Findings

1. Security risks are more difficult to identify and quantify than those that arise from safety or reliability concerns. Safety and reliability risks do not involve malice; the tangible and often severe consequences may often be easily articulated. These considerations facilitate the assessment of risk and measurement of consequences for safety- and reliability-related risks.

2. Although a risk-avoidance strategy may maximize trustworthiness, the prohibitive cost of that strategy suggests that risk mitigation is the pragmatic strategy for most situations.

3. Consequences may be uneven and unpredictable, especially for security risks, and may affect people with varying levels of severity. Safety-related consequences are generally perceived to be more serious than other consequences.

CONSUMERS AND TRUSTWORTHINESS

The spending decisions made by consumers have a profound impact on the trustworthiness of NISs. The consumers of trustworthiness may be partitioned into two groups: information system professionals, who act on behalf of groups of relatively unsophisticated users, and the general public. Information system professionals often have only a modest understanding of trustworthiness because of the limited attention devoted

---

[17]For example, in GSM cellular phones, the security algorithms are embedded in per-subscriber smart cards and in a small number of authentication stations. This permits the relatively easy phaseout of an algorithm that has been cracked, although it remains to be seen whether providers will indeed replace the COMP128 algorithm. See <http://www.isaac.cs.berkeley.edu/isaac/gsm.html> for details.

[18]For example, consider the success of the "Eligible Receiver" exercise in which a team of "hackers" posing as paid surrogates for North Korea could have disabled the networked information systems that control the U.S. power grid (Gertz, 1998).

to trustworthiness within college curricula and professional seminars. Even information system professionals who concentrate on security issues vary greatly in their understanding of issues associated with trustworthiness.[19] The larger group of consumers is the general public, mostly unsophisticated with respect to trustworthiness despite a growing familiarity with information technology in general. The rise of an information systems mass market during the last two decades, and the concomitant influx of unsophisticated users, exacerbates the asymmetric distribution of understanding of trustworthiness concerns.

Consumer Costs

Consumer costs include all costs associated with trustworthiness that are borne by the user. Some of these costs are associated with the prevention or detection of breaches in trustworthiness; other costs are related to recovery from the effects of inadequate trustworthiness. Consumer costs include expenditures for the acquisition and use of technology, the development and implementation of policies and practices, insurance, legal action, and other activities. Consumer costs may be divided into direct costs, indirect costs, and failure costs.

Direct Costs

Direct costs are those expenditures that can be associated unambiguously with trustworthiness. This category includes the purchases of products such as firewalls or anti-virus software. Sometimes, direct costs may represent the incremental cost for products that offer superior trustworthiness compared with alternatives (e.g., fault-tolerant computers). Services may also be categorized as direct costs, as in the case of maintaining hot sites,[20] consulting and training to improve operational practices, analyzing system audit data, or upgrading hardware to improve reliability.

Direct costs vary widely, depending on the requirements of the consumer. Historically, specialized users have had the most demanding requirements and incurred the most costs; the canonical example is the military, but other institutions such as banking, air traffic control systems, and nuclear power facilities also have exacting requirements for security, safety, and reliability. The direct costs relative to trustworthiness are

---

[19]This conclusion was derived from discussions at several committee meetings.

[20]Hot sites are physical locations where an organization may continue computer operations in the case of a major disruption, such as an earthquake that renders the normal operating site largely unusable. Organizations may maintain their own hot sites or may contract for this service with specialty firms.

often incurred by central information service units rather than charged to individuals or user departments, because the costs involve systemwide characteristics that cannot be apportioned easily among users.

Indirect Costs

The implementation of measures to improve trustworthiness often entails costs beyond those that are obvious and immediate. For example, the implementation of cryptography requires increased central processing unit (CPU) power[21] and probably communications resources. The introduction of trustworthiness improvements also often increases system complexity (e.g., the implementation of security controls), thereby causing users to require additional technical support for problems that they otherwise might have been able to resolve themselves. Changes to complex systems increase the possibilities for bugs and, correspondingly, the costs for system maintenance and troubleshooting. Unintended consequences may also result from changes to complex systems, because it is virtually impossible to understand and anticipate all of the ramifications of changes. While it is attempting to improve aspects of trustworthiness, an intervention may introduce new vulnerabilities.

An important indirect cost is often attributable to the "hassle factor." Efforts to improve trustworthiness seldom simplify the use of a system for a consumer. For example, security controls may compel users to take additional steps and time to log in and access information and remember more elaborate policies and practices.

Another form of indirect cost is incurred when an element of trustworthiness prevents the consumer from performing some important function. In some cases these costs can be substantial, such as when a security mechanism denies a physician remote access to the medical records of an emergency patient injured when traveling, or when a flight control system prevents a pilot from moving controls in a particular way during an airborne emergency not anticipated by the design team. Such examples illustrate the difficult balance between overengineering in an attempt to prevent adverse consequences and underengineering in an attempt to avoid monetary and convenience costs.

---

[21]Most desktop PCs and workstations have ample CPU capacity most of the time for data encryption. This is not true for servers and other multiuser machines. In any case, public-key operations are expensive on all platforms. Servers are, in general, multitasking machines; CPU power spent encrypting one user's traffic is not available to process another user's queries. Furthermore, servers often *need* their high-speed network interfaces to handle the aggregate demand from many users. Ubiquitous use of software-based encryption would indeed cause noticeable degradation in total throughput; thus, many servers are being equipped with cryptographic hardware.

Failure Costs

Failure costs arise when the failure or absence of a trustworthiness mechanism permits some adverse outcome to occur, such as loss of service, fraud, sabotage, or the compromise of sensitive information. For example, billing data provide a relatively good indicator of telecommunications fraud, which seems to show a bimodal distribution: a small number of extremely large thefts of service and a large number of small incidents.[22] Theft of notebook computers and other devices, a rapidly increasing form of corporate security exposure,[23] illustrates a different kind of denial of service.

Another kind of failure cost is associated with recovery. Perceived growth in those costs is motivating growth in the market for insurance against computer-related (and telecommunications-related) mishaps. Although that market remains immature,[24] recent developments have suggested growing interest among insurers.[25] Traditional commercial insurance frameworks intended for physical property, equipment, and liability are being adapted for electronic contexts, although the difficulties in valuing information assets, diagnosing and reporting problems, and lack of historical data have constrained the growth of computer and telecommunications-related insurance. Insurance demand appears to be growing with loss experience, including losses arising from legal actions precipitated by information systems problems, and with increased attention to information systems in auditing and, where applicable, regulatory oversight. Although insurance can provide a negative incentive ("moral hazard") to the extent that its presence discourages greater effort in preventing loss, the terms and conditions of coverage may be designed to limit payment to those circumstances where some preventive action, such as the use of code signing,[26] was taken.

Some consumers prefer to insure themselves. Instead of purchasing an insurance policy, a consumer could make provisions for disaster recovery, either directly or through a third-party contractor. Another alternative is inaction. A consumer could react to incidents after the fact and initiate whatever action is deemed to be necessary. This would be consis-

---

[22]Committee discussion with Michael Diaz and Bruce Fette of Motorola, September 19, 1997.

[23]For example, see Masters (1998).

[24]Personal communication, Vincent "Chip" Boylan, executive vice president of Hilb, Eogal and Hamilton Company, September 1997.

[25]In April 1998, Lloyds of London initiated coverage for firms to protect against hackers, viruses, and computer sabotage. See Lemos (1998).

[26]The need for evidence may help to motivate such approaches as code signing (as discussed in Chapter 4): signing mobile code does not provide security; it provides a basis for a value judgment about potential trustworthiness of code based on reputation.

tent with consumer behavior in analogous areas (e.g., home security). It is often stated that most residential alarm sales occur after a home has been burgled, either the home of the purchaser or a neighbor's home.

The failure costs discussed so far are those costs that affect a specific consumer (e.g., the operator of an NIS that runs an electric utility). A system failure resulting from a breach in trustworthiness has costs for the public at large. An electric outage may interrupt the conduct of business (and result in possible loss of revenue) and inconvenience the public. Such costs are not borne by the service provider, the electric utility in this example, or the suppliers of any part of an NIS (because the conventional practice in the information technology industry is to disclaim all liabilities that may arise for any reason).

Imperfect Information

Consumers operate within an environment in which a great deal is unknown. The benefits deriving from greater reliability, availability, or security are difficult to articulate in detail, much less to quantify. Moreover, the consequences of inadequate trustworthiness are difficult to articulate in detail and quantify as well. There is a reluctance to make data about incidents and consequences publicly available,[27] so whatever data are available are likely to represent a biased sample. Not surprising, then, is the observation that relatively little information on trustworthiness is readily available to consumers. Economists refer to this state of affairs as "imperfect information," which distorts market transactions because under high levels of uncertainty, consumers will tend to purchase less of a given product or service than they otherwise would.

The difficulty of assessing the environment is compounded by the difficulty of assessing a technically complex system. Most buyers are not knowledgeable about the technical aspects of trustworthiness and, therefore, cannot conduct the informed assessment that is needed for sound decision making. Other industries, such as pharmaceuticals, have comparable characteristics, but have resolved the problem by requiring the development and disclosure of information through regulatory mandate. A consumer may not be able to assess accurately whether a particular drug is safe but can be reasonably confident that drugs obtained from approved sources have the endorsement of the Food and Drug Administra-

---

[27]The reluctance to make such data publicly available is intended to minimize the public perception and awareness that systems are vulnerable and have been breached. The lack of data about the likelihood, actual incidence, and consequences of problems is not a new observation; it was emphasized in *Computers at Risk* (CSTB, 1991) and the PCCIP report (PCCIP, 1997).

tion (FDA), which confers important safety information.[28] Computer system trustworthiness has nothing comparable to the FDA. The problem is both the absence of standard metrics and a generally accepted organization that could conduct such assessments. There is no *Consumer Reports* for trustworthiness.[29]

Metrics can be reasonably defined for some dimensions of trustworthiness (e.g., availability), while other dimensions (e.g., security) seemingly defy straightforward characterization. Any metric must be defined with respect to some formal model. The act of defining a model, however, suppresses details that might constitute vulnerabilities. For example, a "work-factor" metric for cryptosystems could be characterized by how much computation an attacker must perform to enumerate and check all possible keys for a given piece of encrypted text. The metric does not consider clever attacks and thereby renders the work-factor metric to be of dubious practical value.[30] Whatever formal model is conceived cannot include all possible modes of attack, because some attacks may not even have been invented. Since the definition of security metrics is problematic, the definition of aggregate trustworthiness metrics must necessarily be problematic as well.

How much risk is assumed knowingly is unclear. Anecdotal evidence suggests that in sectors accustomed to assessing and managing risk such as banking, buyer decision making relating to trustworthiness may be more explicit. Banking representatives suggested to this committee[31] and to federal study groups recently (e.g., the President's Commission on Critical Infrastructure Protection, PCCIP) that at least some choices about using the Internet in their business reflected risk assessment. Other testimony to the committee underscored that even in the military, pursuing the primary mission may result in compromises of trustworthiness: as one representative of the DOD observed,[32] one cannot necessarily shut down communica-

---

[28]The situation might be worse for information systems than for pharmaceuticals. The pharmaceutical interface is defined by a chemical that may be more readily understood than software, and the testing of the interaction between a chemical and the human body may be more straightforward than that for an information system. The issues here fall within a larger class of risk regulation concerns. Roger Noll, an economist at Stanford University, has described the uncertainties that confound citizens and government officials and the benefits of better identifying risks and effective responses to them. See Noll (1996).

[29]The International Computer Security Association does "certify" security-oriented products and services, but so far its testing does not appear to be rigorous.

[30]Consider monoalphabetic ciphers, which are sufficiently simple to solve by hand that they are the basis for daily puzzles in some newspapers. Such a cipher has a key length equivalent to about 80, far above what is currently considered exportable. One does not solve such a cipher by an exhaustive search of the key space. More powerful techniques are used.

[31]During the committee's first workshop, in October 1996.

[32]During the committee's first workshop, in October 1996.

tions in the battlefield simply because security is breached. It is possible that compromised communication is preferred to the absence of all communication in some contexts.

Security experts and others who are knowledgeable about the various dimensions of trustworthiness often argue that consumers spend too little on trustworthiness because of imperfect information.[33] Limited actual experience with loss also tends to discourage investments in trustworthiness.[34] Of course, limited actual experience is not equivalent to an absence of risk. Some losses or problems may not even be visible, and most people have not experienced a catastrophe.

Issues Affecting Risk Management

Consumers are sensitive to the perceived opportunity cost from not indulging in risky behavior. The movement toward low-inventory, just-in-time production in various industries; outsourcing of a variety of inputs to production of goods and services; and direct computer-mediated interaction with actual and potential buyers, suppliers, partners, and competitors is motivated by factors deemed essential to commercial vitality: reduction of costs, rapidity of time to market, and responsiveness to customers. The opportunity cost of not relying more on information systems may be not being in business.[35]

The combination of more open networking environments (e.g., the Internet) and more direct electronic transactions implies greater automated interactions among organizations. This increasing level of automated interactions is expected to result in increasing demand for major business automation systems such as PeopleSoft and SAP. How such interaction can proceed in a trustworthy manner and how differences among policies and preferences across organizations can be negotiated and arbitrated are among the questions now emerging.[36] One technolo-

---

[33]Current tax treatment of software, databases, and other information assets reinforce and contribute to what many feel is a tendency to undervalue information assets relative to physical assets; difficulties in appraising value for associated "property" also contributes to slow and uneven growth of insurance coverage for inadequate trustworthiness.

[34]For example, in 1997, the Council on Competitiveness hosted a workshop for the Presidential Commission on Critical Infrastructure Protection on education and training issues relating to development and use of critical systems. A theme of the discussion was that corporate security officers and academic experts found little interest in or motivation for increasing trustworthiness by good practice. The PCCIP report emphasized shortcomings in awareness in its findings and recommendations.

[35]See Computer Science and Telecommunications Board (1994).

[36]The intelligence community once had a marking (ORCON) that means "Originator Controlled." Essentially, this marking states, "I pass this to you but I don't want you to

gist with diverse industry experience made an analogy to the spread of AIDS, noting new concerns about the trustworthiness of the people who constitute one's social network and the dire consequences that could result from the indiscriminate expansion of one's contacts.[37]

Another important factor for consumer risk management is the continuing growth in computer-based interaction and interdependence among individuals and organizations—the rise of a cyberspace economy and society. Greater communication among dispersed parties and collaboration and support for access for those who are mobile or in unconventional locations are easy extrapolations from current conditions. Increasingly, fewer assumptions can be made about whose information or software is running at a given time on a particular hardware, software, and communications platform. A future of greater decentralization has important implications for the locus of control for information and systems. The concepts of control inherent in traditional approaches to security, reliability, and safety may be less and less applicable during the coming years. In contrast to established NISs, where users are often preselected in some way (e.g., bank automated teller machines or the air traffic control system), new participants increasingly will include anybody who requests access. Furthermore, some of these new users will be involved in short-lived and spontaneous interactions, a situation that will create more concerns for ensuring trustworthiness.

Among the various near-term issues, the year 2000 (Y2K) problem has fostered examination and in a variety of instances changes in information systems. The publicity associated with Y2K may well influence some of the decision making; there is more speculation than data about the nature and number of changes being made, which range from focused fixes to more wholesale change.[38] Another relatively near-term influence is the introduction of the European Currency Unit (ECU),[39] which is prompting large banks and possibly other entities to alter systems to support the new currency and the likely demise of other currencies over time. The time

---

pass it on to anybody else without my permission." Commercial nondisclosure agreements almost uniformly contain similar clauses. This simple and easily understood policy has proved resistant to any kind of technical enforcement in shared computer systems except by mechanisms so draconian that no one will put up with them. However, schemes to protect intellectual property seem to be raising the issues again as people explore controls not only on passing something along but also on the potential number of people involved and under what conditions.

[37]William Flanagan, during the committee's third workshop, in September 1997.

[38]See <http://www.2k-times.com/y2kpaper.htm> for articles, news clips, and other reports about Y2K. See also de Jager (1993) and Clausing (1998).

[39]According to the terms of the European Monetary Union, the ECU will become the Euro on January 1, 1999 (Cummins, 1998).

pressures associated with Y2K and the ECU phenomena illustrate how businesses scramble to solve problems, even though these problems could have been anticipated well beforehand. Moreover, businesses are unlikely to apply relevant extant knowledge to their problems.[40] These pressures also foster shifts from custom solutions to selection of recognized, major third-party software systems, such as SAP, thereby contributing to the increasing popularity of commercial off-the-shelf (COTS) software but inhibiting diversity, which can lead to common-mode failures and shared vulnerabilities.

Some Market Observations

The demand for primary functionality—the main purpose of a computing or communications device or system—continues to grow and is fueling demand for features. When confronted with a choice of where to spend an extra dollar, buyers tend to emphasize primary functionality; this is as evident in requests for proposals (RFPs) and actual procurement from the DOD as in the consumer or general business marketplace. Some level of trustworthiness is deemed to be essential and after that level, trustworthiness becomes a secondary differentiator. Even where the trade-off may not be obvious, perceived needs to contain costs result in development and acquisition of systems that minimize redundancy, diversity, and other features that might otherwise enhance trustworthiness.

Products that address problems experienced by consumers have been well received, as are products (e.g., firewalls) that appear to address specific well-known problems. Consumers buy firewalls because they have associated that mechanism with the ability to connect to the Internet, even though considerable risks may remain despite the use of firewalls. Some consumers who have full knowledge of the limited effectiveness of mechanisms such as firewalls may still use them with the goal of appearing to have trustworthiness, but without undertaking the hard work that achieving true trustworthiness demands; this may be the era of patent medicines for information technology.

The development of the mass market has been accompanied by a shift in systems development and expertise from user organizations to vendors. The proliferation and falling relative prices for commercial technology means that organizations that once would develop systems they wanted themselves are more likely to buy at least components if not entire systems.[41] This trend toward COTS systems and an increasing homoge-

---

[40]William Flanagan, during the committee's third workshop, in September 1997.

[41]At the committee's workshop in September 1997, Iang Jeon of Liberty Financial, for example, observed that up until 3 to 4 years earlier financial institutions had to set up

neity of computing platforms, communications infrastructure, and software is discussed in the next section as a major force in the producer landscape.

Findings

1. The costs associated with improved trustworthiness are often incurred by central units of an organization because such costs reflect systemwide characteristics of an NIS and cannot be easily apportioned.

2. One important cost of greater trustworthiness is related to the "hassle factor." Trustworthy systems tend to be more cumbersome to use. This is one reason that costs for the consumer are not equivalent to price.

3. Decision making about trustworthy systems occurs within the context of imperfect information, which increases the level of uncertainty regarding the benefits of trustworthiness initiatives and therefore serves as a disincentive to invest in trustworthiness, thus distorting the market for trustworthiness. The absence of standard metrics and a recognized organization to conduct assessments of trustworthiness is an important contributing factor to the problem of imperfect information. In some industries, such as pharmaceuticals, regulatory mandate has resolved this problem by requiring the development and disclosure of information.

4. Useful metrics for the security dimension of trustworthiness are unlikely to be developed because the corresponding formal model for any particular metric is necessarily incomplete. Therefore, useful aggregate metrics for trustworthiness are not likely to be developed either.

5. The combination of more open and decentralized networking environments and an increasing use of electronic communications and transactions suggests an increasing demand for major business automation systems. This continuing decentralization may render less and less applicable the concepts of control inherent in traditional approaches to security, reliability, and safety. In particular, there will be an increasing need for more individuals to be able to make trustworthiness judgments on an ad hoc, real-time basis.

6. Other things being equal, consumers prefer to purchase greater functionality rather than improved trustworthiness. Products that address problems that have been experienced by consumers or are perceived to address specific well-known problems have been well received.

---

software and telecom systems themselves to support electronic distribution, whereas now it is easier to rely on people whose business is developing packaged software and delivering telecommunications services.

PRODUCERS AND TRUSTWORTHINESS

The Larger Marketplace and the Trend Toward Homogeneity

Before the producers of trustworthiness products, services, and features are discussed, a brief note is warranted on the important trends concerning COTS components and homogeneity in the general marketplace, and the implications of those trends for trustworthiness. Current computing platforms, as well as communications infrastructure and software, are generally homogeneous. Operating systems and computing platforms are dominated by Microsoft Windows and the Intel x86 compatible processor family.[42] Secondary characteristics—display, network interfaces, disks—are made uniform by the adoption of technological standards (e.g., VGA graphics interface or IDE and SCSI disk interfaces) or are presented to application software as common interfaces by operating systems software in the form of device drivers and hardware adaptation layers.

The communications infrastructure today is also fairly homogeneous. Local area networks are typically Ethernets or Token Rings, although some increased diversity is being introduced by asynchronous transfer mode (ATM) networks and the various high-speed Ethernets. Wide area networks are constructed from routers, most of which are sold by a few manufacturers.[43] The software that controls these networks is also homogeneous at multiple levels. A single stack of protocols manages the Internet, and all the Internet protocol implementations descend from a few. The core Internet Protocol (IP) works well over a diverse set of network technologies, further contributing to homogeneity.

In addition to the existing state of relative homogeneity with respect to computing platforms and communications, the important trends in software suggest a continuing decrease in heterogeneity in the coming years. An important reason for this decrease in heterogeneity is the rising popularity of COTS software that is driven by cost considerations and risk reduction, insofar as COTS products are known entities and readily available. Scripting languages and COTS software provide the context

---

[42]In 1997, a significant majority of computer systems sold (85 percent of personal computers and servers by unit volume) contained some version of Intel's "x86" microprocessor (manufactured by either Intel Corporation or one of a small number of others) to implement an IBM-compatible PC architecture. When deployed as personal computers, a significant majority are running a version of the Microsoft Windows operating system. Less than 10 percent of personal computers are a variant of the architecture designed and sold by Apple Computer; a small percentage are variant architectures made by Sun Microsystems, Silicon Graphics, Digital Equipment Corporation, and others. Many among this last group of systems run versions of the UNIX operating system.

[43]Cisco Systems and Bay Networks, for example, dominate the router market.

for the reuse of components and for their assembly into required configurations, with only limited new programming required for custom components. Consequently, user organizations have less need for systems development expertise. The success of large middleware packages underscores the economic and other benefits that users perceive in COTS software. The continued use of SAP, the Web (e.g., Hypertext Transfer Protocol [HTTP]), and a few other software packages favor particular software components, data formats, work flows, and vocabularies.

Risks of Homogeneity

The similarity intrinsic in the component systems of a homogeneous collection implies that these component systems share vulnerabilities. A successful attack on one system is then likely to succeed on other systems as well—the antithesis of what is desired for implementing trustworthiness. Moreover, today's dominant computing and communications environments are based on hardware and software that were not designed with security in mind; consequently, these systems are not difficult to compromise, as discussed in previous chapters.

There is, therefore, some tension between homogeneity and trustworthiness. Powerful forces make technological homogeneity compelling (see Box 6.1), but some attributes of trustworthiness benefit from diversity (see Chapter 5). On the other hand, a widely used trustworthy operating system might be superior to a variety of nontrustworthy operating systems; diversity, per se, is not equivalent to increased trustworthiness.

BOX 6.1
The Rationale for Homogeneity

The existence of a homogeneous computing and communications environment is not an accident. Strong forces favor homogeneity:

- Homogeneity is advantageous for the sale and use of popular software. A larger market gives providers of hardware and software incentives for entry, and providers can also exploit economies of scale.
- Enormous leverage results when computers can communicate and share data, especially in ways that are not anticipated when the computers are procured or the data are created. Homogeneity simplifies interoperability between systems.
- Homogeneity supports more efficient transfer of skills within organizations, effectively lowering the cost of computerizing additional functions.
- Homogeneity also leads to increased skill-lifetimes, because a skill is likely to remain useful even after computing platforms are upgraded.
- Homogeneity enables aggregations of resources to strengthen design, implementation, and testing.

Technological convergence may also be realized through the market dominance of a few suppliers of key components, with monopoly as the limit case when technological homogeneity is dictated by the monopolist.[44] However, the number of suppliers could grow as a result of the diffusion of computing into embedded, ubiquitous environments; the diversification and interoperability of communications services; and the continued integration of computing and communications into organizations within various market niches.

Producers and Their Costs

Insofar as trustworthiness is integral to the design of information technology products and services, trustworthiness should be pervasive throughout the marketplace for such products and services. However, trustworthiness is often considered only after a system is implemented, so there are firms that develop and market products and services specifically targeted at improving the trustworthiness of operational NISs. The marketplace for trustworthiness—in both of these senses—will be explored in some detail after some of the key issues associated with the costs of producing trustworthiness are discussed.

The costs of trustworthiness are difficult to assess and cannot all be quantified, even using order-of-magnitude estimates. Time is a major "currency" cited by vendors, who worry about time from product concept until commercial release. Data on relevant costs are scarce; those cited may be of questionable quality, and analyses of costs tend to be limited at best.

The costs associated with developing trustworthiness features, products, and services have a major labor component. Some vendors also incur research-related expenditures in their efforts to bring trustworthiness products to market, although most of this "research" is actually development. The costs associated with security mechanisms are emphasized in this section because of the pivotal role that security controls play as enablers of other aspects of trustworthiness and the expectation that, in the future, trustworthiness problems will be associated increasingly with security concerns. The purpose of this section is not to provide an exhaustive articulation of all producer costs; instead, the intent is to highlight those producer cost issues that are particularly germane to trustworthiness.

---

[44]Although both standards and monopolies can provide the benefits of homogeneity, only standards enable the competition necessary to ensure that consumers may affect the trustworthiness of available products. Standards are discussed in detail in the section titled "Standards and Criteria."

Costs of Integration and Testing

NIS trustworthiness is inherently a system-level property, and, therefore, the costs associated with improving trustworthiness inevitably involve the costs of integration and testing. These costs will vary, depending on whether or to what extent a mechanism is integrated into a system. A relatively stand-alone mechanism, such as an initial password screen to enter a system, might be written as a software module independently from the remaining modules of the project and have minimal impact on system integration, testing, documentation, and training activities. The costs are readily identifiable and low. Another example of a relatively stand-alone solution is firewalls.

Security controls that have a moderate effect on software development and cost include those that impose multiple access modes within a system. Some menus, data sets, data items, or other appropriate subsets of the system may have unlimited access, whereas others may limit access to certain individuals, organizations, or time of day, or limited functionality (e.g., read access only). These controls affect functionality throughout the system and, therefore, impose a moderate impact on system integration, testing, documentation, and training activities.

Finally, costs are high and difficult to identify specifically in systems where controls are pervasive: the authentication of each user is rigorous; each transaction is scrutinized for its validity and verified against appropriate databases; external transactions are subject to encryption; audit trails are maintained to facilitate routine and ad hoc audits of transactions; and general access levels may also be employed. If security or other attributes are integral to much of the functionality throughout the system, associated controls greatly affect system integration, testing, documentation, and training activities. The controls contribute to the complexity of the system; the debugging activity is more difficult and may require a longer period.

Identifying the Specific Costs Associated with Trustworthiness

Accurate estimation of the direct costs associated with specific project features requires a complex and time-consuming analysis that seems to be seldom performed.[45] Except in the case of stand-alone products, it is often difficult to separate the costs of "regular" functionality from the costs of "enhanced trustworthiness capability." This allocation can be arbitrary. The same could be said for the further distinction between the costs associated with trustworthiness and general overhead costs. Com-

---

[45]A committee conclusion based on its deliberations.

pounding the difficulty of ascertaining accurate cost data is the fact that advocates or opponents of a particular trustworthiness intervention may attempt to manipulate cost data in marshalling their arguments.

Costing methodologies have been published, and they address variation in costs and trade-offs owing to product requirements, producer practices, and other sensitivity factors. These models tend to cover only the development cycle, and their assumptions about the way effort is expended in a software project may not apply in the contemporary market environment, in which some "development" may be purposely postponed to an upgrade in the effort to reduce the time to market.[46]

Time to Market

Many of the segments within the information technology marketplace are intensely competitive, where market share—not profit margin— is the primary business objective. In such markets, a product (e.g., Web browsers) that is available early has the opportunity to develop a customer base or become established as the de facto standard. Consequently, minimizing the time to market is a critical consideration for producers.

Each feature is examined to determine whether its inclusion in the product is necessary for the product to be competitive in the marketplace. Generally, those features with direct customer appeal win. Subtle, hard-to-demonstrate, and pervasive properties—which tend to characterize trustworthiness attributes—tend to be rejected. Trustworthiness features that require extensive integration throughout a product also tend to be omitted, because of the time required to properly integrate and test such features.

Other Issues

To some extent, costs may occur and be traded off at varying points in the life cycle of a product. The discussion in Chapter 3 suggests that the cost of effecting a software change increases through the development cycle (i.e., the later a change is instituted, the more it will cost). Costs may

---

[46]The constructive cost model (COCOMO), a well-developed cost model for software engineering, is the centerpiece of Barry Boehm's book, *Software Engineering Economics* (Boehm, 1981). Boehm discusses security and privacy issues and the reasons these are excluded in COCOMO (p. 490). Standard COCOMO does not include such effects as added product features (security markings, operational controls), reduced access to documentation, and added documentation control. Since these requirements in their stringent form are relatively rare, and even then generally add only 10 percent to project costs, COCOMO does not include this as an added factor on the grounds of model parsimony.

also be traded off from the development to the support phase of the system life cycle. A poor implementation of trustworthiness characteristics during development can translate into higher costs for technical support operations.[47] Not only may costs be shifted over time, but costs may also be incurred by different organizational units or by consumers.

The difficulty of demonstrating and sustaining success in achieving trustworthiness—one can, at best, test a product or practice against a recognized risk—imply a dynamic process of iteration.[48] In some cases, a lot of care goes into anticipating risks and addressing them preemptively,[49] in other cases the trial and error process seems less systematic, and in all cases actual experience drives improvement. Antivirus software provides an example of the inherent limit of anticipation since virus producers continually introduce new strains against which anti-virus software might not work. Thus, the antivirus product development process involves frequent upgrades in response to new forms of viruses. Netscape's approach of offering a reward for detection of security flaws puts another face on iteration: it implies that the cost of finding problems, and perhaps of developing fixes, could be shared between the producer and the consumer, and it may increase the rate and level at which problems are reported.[50] The reality of iteration makes it difficult to estimate costs fully up front, except to the extent that an iteratively escalating process can be modeled and costed. It also argues for the benefit of retrospective analysis to support such costing.

Research relating to trustworthiness could help to reduce costs, but that outcome depends on better understanding of the nature and incidence of costs. Having ways to think about cost ("cost models"), even in the absence of appropriate data, can help in understanding how trustworthiness is perceived or valued and how potential incentives for increasing it may evolve. The expectation that discontinuities will occur—that inci-

---

[47]Both the fact that later life cycle costs are not borne directly by the developers (i.e., technical support is often a distinct organizational unit from development) and the fact that these costs are deferred could act as inducements to shift costs to later stages in the product life cycle.

[48]The iterative process has been compared to an arms race, an escalation of measures and countermeasures as new problems are discovered, some arising in response to previous fixes. Note that target risks may be poorly understood or unspecified, such as the goal of avoiding system crashes due to bugs or unexpected attacks.

[49]From a research perspective, the staged nature of progress raises questions about the relative payoff to investing in successor (major improvement) technologies relative to incremental improvements to existing technologies.

[50]An attacker might discover vulnerabilities and not report them, hoping to exploit them for more substantial gains later. This is a high consequence, but not necessarily a high-likelihood, prospect.

dents attributable to inadequate trustworthiness will result in corrective action and new efforts at prevention or recovery—suggests that how costs are identified and calculated may be relatively fluid.[51]

The Market for Trustworthiness

The supply of trustworthiness technology includes both products and services specifically offered to support one or more aspects of trustworthiness and the trustworthiness of NISs generally. This definition is very broad and could be interpreted to include nearly anything that assists in the design, development, integration, testing, operation, or maintenance of an NIS. This discussion focuses on those products and services that are intended primarily to promote trustworthiness. Because of the special enabling role that security plays with respect to trustworthiness, security products and services are emphasized.

Trustworthiness is a systemwide attribute. The cost required to secure a system is not strictly proportional to the number of people using that system.[52] Consequently, as an NIS is implemented and the number of connections increases, it is plausible to discover that the per-connection cost declines. Some technologies, such as those associated with virtual private networks and higher-quality user authentication, do impose some per-user or per-computer costs. Another important reason that security expenditures, as separately identifiable data, are likely to decline results from the integration of security features into general-purpose information technology products. For example, version 4 of the Netscape browser includes support for SSL and S/MIME, which implement security properties. If this browser were categorized as a "nonsecurity" product, then the market statistics for security would be understated. Another such example is a packet-filtering router—it is a router, but it also implements security. Finally, as in other segments of the information technology marketplace, competitive pressures and technological innovations exert

---

[51]Committee members noted the experience of the market research firm Gartner Group, which found its assessment of the costs of PC ownership reduced to a sound-bite—raising questions about assumptions and about popular capacity to consider more than a single number. The likelihood of change does not diminish the value of studying costs for older technologies and strategies, but it does raise questions about where it is sensible to extrapolate from the past. It also points to the need to understand sensitivity factors and assumptions.

[52]One way of looking at this is the "hard on the outside, soft and chewy on the inside" phenomenon, in which a collection of unprotected nodes (whose individual security cost is essentially zero, so that the aggregate is independent of the number of nodes) are huddled behind a small number of firewall/gateway nodes. Security does not become cheaper as the internal network grows.

downward pressure on prices. These observations also suggest that as security and other aspects of trustworthiness are increasingly incorporated into other products, the task of compiling accurate market data and forecasts for security or trustworthiness will become ever more difficult.

The committee did review a limited number of industry analyses that were compiled by various market research analysis or financial services companies. The data reviewed supported the argument that while the market for security products is growing, this market is declining in relative terms because of the higher growth rate in other sectors of the information technology marketplace. However, the committee was ambivalent about the inclusion of any such data in this report, because such inclusion could be construed as an endorsement of the selected data, methodology, analysis, or firm. The committee was not in a position to make such a determination.

In 1997 and 1998, rapid consolidation was taking place in the computer and network security marketplace, turning small companies into larger and more aggressive firms. The rapid growth of the Internet has driven increased demand, especially by larger and more sophisticated customers who have greater knowledge and demands for security requirements and desire integrated security solutions. Thus, the consolidation in this market is expected to continue. General computer and communications vendors are also increasingly interested in security, thereby further contributing to the turbulent state of the computer and network security marketplace.[53]

Supply and Demand Considerations

Availability is an aspect of trustworthiness that is readily measurable and is highly valued by the public; it certainly contributes to the success of fault-tolerant computer systems (e.g., Tandem and Stratus). Some market successes also exist within the security marketplace, although the demand for security continues to be relatively limited. Niches exist for targeted products, such as firewalls and antivirus software, and for services such as online updates of antivirus software. These two niches are very competitive; satisfying third-party assessment is provided through trade magazines[54] or the International Computer Security's Association certification requirements and constitutes an important competitive advantage.

---

[53]For example, note the significant security content in NT Version 5, and Cisco's recent acquisition of a proxy firewall supplier.

[54]Jimmy Kuo, McAffee Associates, during the committee's third workshop, in September 1997.

Of course, vendors are very keen to provide what potential customers desire with respect to the nature, quantity, pricing, and efficacy of trustworthiness features, products, and services. However, vendors have found that, although people claim that trustworthiness is important in the abstract, when it comes time to spend money, nontrustworthiness expenditures often take precedence. An illustrative case is the effort by Digital Equipment Corporation (DEC) to develop a system that would satisfy DOD's most stringent criteria for so-called trusted systems. After making a considerable investment, DEC canceled the project when it became clear that sufficient demand for the system would not materialize. Experiments with trusted operating systems were also terminated by other major system vendors when they, too, were discouraged by a lack of commercial interest.

Findings

1. Current computing platforms, communications infrastructure, and software are relatively homogeneous, and the degree of homogeneity is expected to increase in the future. Homogeneity tends to cause NISs to be more vulnerable.

2. The increasing use of COTS software is causing user organizations to decrease their level of expertise in system development.

3. Production costs associated with trustworthiness are difficult to assess. An improved understanding and better models are needed. There is a paucity of data. The data that are available are questionable, in part because of the difficulties in distinguishing trustworthiness costs from other direct product costs and overhead costs.

4. Production costs associated with integration and testing represent a substantial proportion of a producer's total costs for improving trustworthiness.

5. Time-to-market considerations discourage the inclusion of trustworthiness features and encourage the postponement of trustworthiness to later stages of the product life cycle.

6. The average expenditure for security per Internet/intranet-capable connection has been declining. This trend is expected to continue because security (and trustworthiness generally) expenditures are relatively independent of the number of connections or users, although the use of virtual private networks and higher-quality user authentication technologies does impose some per-user or per-computer costs. Additional influences include competitive pressures that are driving prices down and the potential to understate security expenditures as they become more difficult to identify specifically from general expenditures for information technology products and services.

STANDARDS AND CRITERIA

The development and adoption of standards constitute one response to the challenge of appraising trustworthiness and mitigating difficulties that arise from imperfect information. Standards can simplify the decision-making process for the purchasers of trustworthiness. They can also simplify the design and production decisions for the producers of trustworthiness by narrowing the field of choices (e.g., adherence to interoperability standards facilitates interconnection among subsystems). Compliance with standards or guidelines supplied by the federal government or an authoritative independent standards-setting organization—such as the federal information processing standards (FIPS) of the National Institute of Standards and Technology (NIST), standards of the American National Standards Institute (ANSI), or standards that may result from the Information Infrastructure Standards Panel (IISP)—provides both third-party validation of a selection of technology and potential relief from liability.[55] There is also the broader notion of criteria (e.g., the U.S. Trusted Computer System Evaluation Criteria [TCSEC]), which includes the consideration of processes and attributes that cannot be assessed by direct examination of the artifact in question. For example, criteria may involve explicit or implicit comparisons with other products or systems. Criteria may also take the form of authoritative statements of how a system should or should not be designed and operated, complemented by some means of demonstrating compliance.[56]

The Character and Context of Standards

The Data Encryption Standard (DES) FIPS is an example of an interoperability standard; it defines the mathematical function that a compliant device must implement to ensure that data encrypted by manufacturer A's DES box can be decrypted using a box made by manufacturer B, and there are a set of tests used to determine if the function has been

---

[55]Technology transfer and avoidance of at least some known problems lie behind past government efforts to promulgate guidelines and criteria for trusted systems—TCSEC and more recent international harmonized criteria that build on the U.S. TCSEC and comparable efforts overseas. Lack of widespread adoption of such guidelines and criteria appears to relate at least as much, and probably more, to nontechnological aspects (e.g., distrust of or limited communication with government sponsors of these programs, delays associated with compliance testing, little market demand) as to issues of technical compliance (e.g., difficulty in satisfying the standard).

[56]Such criteria have increased trustworthiness for transportation equipment, devices that transmit radio frequency, and other complex systems that operate in networked environments.

implemented.[57] By contrast, FIPS 140-1 (Security Requirements for Cryptographic Modules) is largely a performance standard encompassing security functionality and assurance. It is definitely not an interoperability standard. Standards arising in the Internet context are expected to promote the implementation of encryption (e.g., IPsec, S/MIME, SSL), while fostering interoperability. Apart from some consideration of key length and algorithm choice, these standards do not treat cryptographic strength or resistance to attack by other means.

In the Internet environment, the Internet Engineering Task Force (IETF; see Box 6.2) has focused on the security aspects of Internet standards, addressing both specific security standards and the larger problem of reviewing other standards to ensure that they either are secure or can have security added when needed.[58] In other venues, such as trade associations, standards setting for computing and communications is intended to foster interoperability and/or proactively forestall government intervention. Computing and communications trade associations and related groups are directing increasing attention to standards related to trustworthiness. For example, the Information Technology Industry Council has addressed a range of standards and security concerns, and security and privacy are emphases of the Smart Card Forum. A number of these industry-based efforts emphasize security to protect company assets, and they are often undertaken to deter regulation.

There is more history of standards setting in the areas of safety and reliability. In an effort to ensure that the best available techniques are used in certain classes of safety-critical systems, a variety of standards have been developed by government agencies, industry groups, and individual companies (see Box 6.3 for examples). The use of specific techniques and procedures in development is in many cases influenced heavily by these standards, and in some cases their use is required for systems to be supplied to a government or for systems that may affect public safety. Domain-specific standards facilitate the needs of the particular domain, but they deter common solutions across market segments.

---

[57]This FIPS consists of an algorithm description, a set of test vectors, and a very subsidiary set of implementation cautions. It is in no sense a security standard, except implicitly in that its "FIPSness" implies that somebody in the government said it was good enough for certain use. In particular, one cannot exceed the standard and be more secure than DES, since that would take a different algorithm and fail the interoperability test. If someone goes off and puts DES in some stupid box that, for example, coughs up the key on demand, then someone built a stupid box, but it would not be in violation of the FIPS. This FIPS does not specify how one must implement the DES internally; it specifies only the interface.

[58]Placing emphasis on the "larger problem" is a recent phenomenon.

BOX 6.2
Internet Standards and the Internet Engineering Task Force

Most Internet standards are developed by a group called the Internet Engineering Task Force (IETF). Although this is by no means a requirement—any protocol can be run on top of the basic Internet protocols, and there are other bodies that develop standards for specific areas, such as the World Wide Web Consortium (W3C)—most of what we use today on the Internet was codified by the IETF. Although the IETF was initially funded by the National Science Foundation, the IETF has no formal endorsement from the federal government. The IETF's estimated 1998 operating budget is $1.7 million (Wilson, 1998).

The IETF is unusual in a number of respects. There is no formal membership; as a consequence, there is no voting. Instead, standards are accepted by "rough consensus and running code." Standards are developed, and RFCs (nominally "requests for comments") are written by assorted working groups. The working groups are organized into a handful of areas; the directors of these areas collectively form the Internet Engineering Steering Group (IESG). Overall architectural development is nominally directed by the Internet Architecture Board (IAB). The membership of the IESG and IAB is chosen by a nominating committee that is randomly selected from a group of volunteers who are IETF attendees. Final approval is vested in the board of trustees of the Internet Society (ISOC).

Given this procedural context, the process of adopting an Internet standard is complex. Apart from prescribed milestones, the IESG occasionally promulgates a new policy that will apply to all standards-track RFCs. In the spring of 1997, just such a policy was adopted with respect to security: security is important. Specifically, it was decided that the hoary phrase "security considerations are not addressed in this memo" will no longer be permitted in RFCs. Instead, a real security analysis must be done. Protocol designers must consider what vulnerabilities are present and what the consequences would be if each were exploited. Furthermore, the designers must analyze existing security mechanisms to see if some other standard would solve the problems. Only if none is suitable should custom mechanisms be designed. One choice has been ruled out: cleartext conventional passwords are not permitted. When passwords are to be used, some cryptographic mechanism must be employed for authentication purposes.

Further, the IAB and IESG jointly adopted a statement endorsing strong cryptography (Carpenter and Baker, 1996). Limited key lengths, mandatory key recovery, and export controls were specifically rejected. Although this statement does conflict with various national policies, including those of the United States, the belief was that an international technical organization should use only technically sound mechanisms, regardless of limitations imposed by particular governments.

Standards and Trustworthiness

The notion of specification is at the core of all characterizations of trustworthiness attributes. Unless a precise, testable definition for an attribute such as reliability exists, it will not be possible to determine whether the requirements of the definition have been fulfilled. The defi-

---

BOX 6.3
Examples of Safety Standards

The RTCA[1] standard DO-178B, entitled "Software Considerations in Airborne Systems and Equipment Certification," is a standard developed by the commercial air transport industry for software used in commercial aircraft and is adhered to by virtually all developers of aircraft systems as a part of the aircraft certification process. DO-178B defines criticality levels for aircraft software, and different development techniques are required for each level. The standard prescribes development practices, documentation, and recording requirements for all phases of the software life cycle. In addition to defining many aspects of software development, the standard specifies assurance requirements through which the developer demonstrates compliance with the standard to regulatory agencies.

The British Ministry of Defense Standard 00-55, "Requirements for Safety-Related Software in Defense Equipment," is a controversial standard because it mandates the use of mechanical analysis techniques. Section 36.5 of the standard states, for example, the following about the source code for a safety-related system:

- "Static analysis[2] in accordance with 26.2 shall be performed on the whole of the source code to verify that the source code is well formed and free of anomalies that would affect the safety of the system."
- "Proof obligations[3] shall be: (a) constructed to verify that the code is a correct refinement of the software design and does nothing that is not specified; (b) discharged by means of formal argument."

---

[1]RTCA used to be an acronym for Radio Technical Commission for Aeronautics, but the organization's name was formally changed to just RTCA in 1991.
[2]This is the analysis of a computer program by any means other than executing it. A grammar checker is an example of a simple static analyzer.
[3]A proof obligation is a proposition that must be true in order for some larger aspect of a system to hold. It is something that has to be shown to be true independently of the larger aspect, usually to allow a proof to be developed for a theorem. A theorem-proving system might be able to establish that a program satisfies its specification, but only if it is able to make certain "assumptions." For the theorem to be proven, the assumptions must be shown to hold separately.

---

nitions in use by the community permit availability and reliability to be measured and compared, thereby allowing a system to be regarded as "sufficiently reliable," for example, if the measured or predicted reliability of the system meets or exceeds some prescribed threshold. An analogous situation does not exist for security, where there does not seem to be a testable definition and where a specification cannot anticipate all of the problems that may arise.

There are exceptions, as is illustrated by the DES, whose presence and widespread adoption clearly benefited all concerned. Yet security experts

BOX 6.4
Cryptographic Challenges

The design and implementation of secure cryptographic algorithms, as well as protocols that make use of such algorithms, have proven to be difficult. Over the last 20 years (the interval during which public interest in cryptography has grown substantially), there have been many examples of missteps:

• Symmetric and public-key cryptographic algorithms and one-way hash functions developed by respected members of the academic and commercial cryptographic community all too often have succumbed to cryptanalysis within a few years after being introduced. Examples include the Merkle-Hellman trapdoor knapsack public-key algorithm, some versions of the FEAL cipher, the Snefru one-way hash function, and the MD4 hash algorithm.

• Authentication and key-management protocols have suffered a similar fate, as they have been shown to be vulnerable to various sorts of attacks that undermine the security presumed provided by them. Examples include the original Needham-Schroeder key-management protocol and the various protocols that were intended to repair its flaws (Needham and Schroeder, 1978, 1987; Denning and Sacco, 1981).

These experiences emphasize the need for cryptographic algorithm standards and security protocol standards that have been carefully developed and vetted. Because implementations of security technology represent a major source of vulnerabilities, there is also a need for high-assurance implementations of this technology. This latter need has sometimes been met through the use of government or third-party evaluation programs for hardware or software components supporting cryptography or cryptographic protocols (e.g., in connection with FIPS 140-1 and ANSI X9.17 standards).

As an example, consider the Data Encryption Standard (DES). The DES was developed initially by IBM and submitted as a FIPS in the mid-1970s. Even though the design of DES was public, the algorithm met with considerable skepticism from some members of the largely academic cryptographic community because the design principles were not disclosed and because of concerns over the key size. Over time, as this community developed improved cryptanalytic methods, DES actually came to be viewed as a well-designed algorithm. DES became widely used, promoting interoperability among a number of security products and applications. DES hardware (and, later, software) was evaluated and certified by NIST, providing independent assurance of an implementation.

However, the key size is now too short for today's technology, as demonstrated in July 1998, when a team under the auspices of the Electronic Frontier Foundation (1998) designed and built a key search engine for less than $250,000 (the cost of the parts). Although DES has exceeded its originally projected lifetime, it is an open question at what time in the past brute-force cracking became economically feasible, especially for nation-states (Wiener, 1994; Meissner, 1976; Hellman, 1979).

consider DES to be an unusual case, given other experiences with standards, which illustrate the risk of treating standards as indicators of assurance (see Box 6.4).

Technical standards imply extensive discussion, review, and analysis by experts and stakeholders, which minimizes the number of remaining flaws.[59] However, the existence of standards also introduces risks. Technical standards may provide an adversary with detailed technical information that facilitates the discovery of flaws. Interoperability facilitates legitimate use, but it also allows a vulnerability to be exploited in multiple contexts. Finally, it is easier to mount attacks against multiple representatives of a single standard than against differing implementations of several standards.

Security-based Criteria and Evaluation

European and North American governments[60] are moving to establish a unified security criteria, called the Common Criteria for Information Technology Security Evaluation. The Common Criteria (CCv2)[61] attempts to reconcile the requirements of the Canadian Trusted Computer Product Evaluation Criteria (CTCPEC) (Canadian System Security Centre, 1993), the European Information Technology Security Evaluation Criteria (ITSEC) (Senior Officials Group, 1991), and the United States Trusted Computer System Evaluation Criteria (TCSEC) (U.S. DOD, 1985).

All these criteria share two underlying dimensions: the extent of the security mechanisms being rated, often called the functionality axis, and the degree to which the mechanisms can be trusted to perform their functions correctly, often called the assurance axis (Figure 6.1). Examples of security functionality include authentication mechanisms, access control lists, and cryptographic features. Examples of assurance steps are testing, examination by independent teams, use of formal methods, and the degree of rigor in the development process.

The rating received by a given product or system is a combination of both components (see Box 6.5). For illustrative purposes and to avoid the semantic baggage of using a particular criterion's terminology, the discussion that follows uses a hypothetical rating system of 1 to 5 on each axis, where [f1,a1] is a system with minimal security functions and minimal trustworthiness, and [f5,a5] is one that exhibits state of the art in each. The reader should assume that a "reasonable" definition may be articulated for each, which is a nontrivial assumption. The discussion that

---

[59]This is especially true for standards that are a result of consortia or other cooperative efforts among the stakeholders. For de facto standards that derive from a dominant vendor, one might also expect reduced design flaws, or at least a general awareness of the problems and work-arounds identified.

[60]United States, Canada, France, Germany, the United Kingdom, and the Netherlands.

[61]Information available online at <http://csrc.nist.gov/cc/ccv20/ccv2list.htm>.

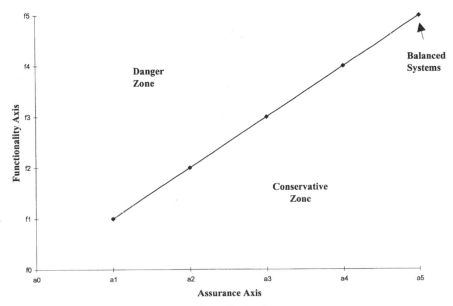

FIGURE 6.1 Hypothetical security-based criteria.

follows is not dependent on any specific definition or process to assign the values.

Laying out the possible ratings on a two-dimensional grid quickly makes clear distinct "zones" in the grid (see Figure 6.1). Along the diagonal ([f1,a1] to [f5,a5]) lie what could be viewed as "balanced" systems, in which the effort placed in assurance matches the security functionality being provided. On one side of the diagonal is the "danger zone" of high functionality relative to assurance, such as [f3,a1]. The danger is, of course, that the product exhibits superficial characteristics of security but cannot be trusted, because no significant effort has been made to show that the features work as promised, especially in the face of hostile analysis and attack. Interestingly, this is the zone in which nearly all commercial security products lie today, because features sell, whereas assurance is the concern of the specialist. On the other side of the diagonal is the "conservative zone," in which mechanisms are placed under a high degree of scrutiny relative to functionality, such as a [f1,a3] system.

How much is a high rating worth? While it is plausible to conclude that a higher rating has a higher market value than a lower one, the rating is only one of many factors that consumers consider in their decision making, and the discussion in the cost section suggests that other considerations, such as functionality, take precedence. Vendors are keenly interested in the value of a rating because all current rating systems compel

---

BOX 6.5
The TCSEC, ITSEC, and Common Criteria: Two Values or One?

The oldest set of criteria is the Trusted Computer System Evaluation Criteria (TCSEC) (U.S. DOD, 1985). During its development there was a substantial debate as to the format of the rating. One school felt that the rating should directly reflect the underlying two-axis structure. A rating would therefore consist of two parts. Education and discretion on the part of the evaluators would prevent "danger zone" products from being deployed. A second school, and the one that prevailed, held that a two-part rating was both excessively complex and risky. The ratings were accordingly devised as a single value that attempted to define "balanced" systems alone.[1] Although the single-value approach precluded the "danger zone," it also precluded the "conservative zone," where many potentially useful products could exist, especially in a networked world.[2]

The Common Criteria Version 2 (CCv2) follows the Information Technology Security Evaluation Criteria (ITSEC) in taking the opposite approach. Ratings have two values: a "protection profile" that seeks to capture the security functionality, and an "evaluation assurance level" that seeks to capture the degree of trust one could place in that functionality. The CCv2 is then conceptually the mirror image of the TCSEC: "danger zone" products are possible and must be discouraged through education and de facto regulatory steps; "conservative zone" products are allowed; and a product's rating is both more complex and more informative. Also, the ability to add new protection profiles allows for the possibility that the criteria can adapt to new technologies and increased threat. The Common Criteria are also more modular, less confidentiality centric, and more current[3] than the TCSEC.

---

[1]As finally devised, the diagonal was not completely followed. An A1 rating adds assurance steps to a B3 rating but maintains the same security functions. Thus, if a B3 rating is seen as [f4,a4], an A1 is [f4,a5].

[2]The choice of balance is indeed a problem. Refer to Neumann (1990) and Ware (1995) for critical analyses of TCSEC and the criteria approach.

[3]For example, the Common Criteria includes provisions for nonrepudiation, a critical concern in electronic commerce systems.

---

the vendor to invest in satisfying the criteria and, in some cases, in paying for the evaluation process itself. The investments can be substantial, particularly in terms of opportunity cost and lost sales because the extended time to market is added to the direct cost of becoming "evaluation ready."

A rating is also useful as a reflection of the ability of a product to resist analysis and manipulation by the threat; in this context, the value of a rating is called the "operational value." As noted before, threats are ever increasing, and therefore, the operational value of a rating correspondingly decreases over time. (One way to retard growth in the sophistication of attackers is to keep some aspects of a design implementation secret. See Appendix I for a discussion.) This depreciation of a rating's value occurs on both axes. On the functional axis, for example, crypto-graphic key lengths that are perfectly adequate at one time may become wholly inadequate several years later, owing to the increased computing power available to the threat. A similar phenomenon occurs on the assur-ance axis. Assurance steps attempt to uncover flaws before a product is exposed to the threat; in some sense they attempt to take a "deeper look" at a mechanism than any element of the threat could afford. Assurance steps that "look deeper" than a single attacker can look may have been adequate before the onset of the Internet, but are made obsolete by an environment that facilitates anonymous and unplanned technical collabo-ration among like-minded individuals. The depreciation of the opera-tional value of a particular rating has not been a concern for individual products, because it has been slower than the rate at which products become obsolete or uncompetitive for other reasons.

Criteria, because they must cover a variety of products and technolo-gies, are inevitably written in general terms. When applied to a specific product they must be interpreted, and anyone who has gone through the process of having a system evaluated against criteria will attest that the interpretation sets the height of the bar that the product must clear. This situation, combined with the background of an ever-escalating threat, leads to tensions in the evaluation process.

On the one hand, there is significant pressure to maintain consistency between evaluations of different products over time. That is, the diffi-culty of achieving, say [f3,a3], in 1995 should be about the same as achiev-ing it in 1998. The motive is fairness. Since it is likely that the market value (as reflected in increased sales of product) of an [f3,a3] rating will be the same in 1998 as it was in 1995, it is arguably unfair for the later vendor to be subjected to a more stringent set of interpretations (and the associ-ated increased cost) than the earlier one.

On the other hand, evaluators are aware of the decreased operational value of a rating (as manifest in a particular set of interpretations) over time. They are, accordingly, under pressure to increase the stringency of the interpretations over time, a process called "criteria creep" in the TCSEC arena.

The dilemma inherent in the process then is as follows: If the interpre-tations are constant over time, then the operational value of a given rating becomes progressively less and products are placed in harm's way with progressively less protection relative to the threat. If the interpretations become more stringent over time, the ratings maintain their operational value but vendors are discouraged from participating because the invest-ment required to achieve a given rating increases over time. This contradic-tion has not been resolved to date in the TCSEC evaluations. The Common Criteria effort hopes to overcome this by adding new protection profiles to respond to the increased threat. Given the inevitable bureaucratic and regulatory pressures to maintain fixed objectives, it is doubtful that the criteria evolution can keep pace with the evolution of the threat.

The history of national and international criteria and evaluation systems also raises questions about institutional roles and responsibilities. The national and international criteria have featured government agencies in prominent roles, attributable to both subject matter expertise and agency missions associated with national security. The latter missions have, in turn, inspired distrust and discomfort in the private sector inasmuch as either criteria or evaluation elements and rationales have been incompletely communicated or understood and have been controlled tightly by the national government.[62]

The evaluation under the TCSEC has been done by government (including government contractor organizations) at government expense; according to anecdotes from vendors who have gone through the experience, evaluators appear to have been junior with little computer system development experience and little motivation to expedite evaluations or promote successful outcomes. Costs incurred by vendors undergoing evaluation processes include delay and obsolescence of products, extra documentation costs, and costs of additional work needed to address concerns uncovered by evaluators. Industry has called for self-rating or a broader system of evaluators to expedite the process. A principal concern voiced by vendors is that of degree: the perception of the TCSEC philosophy as "more is better" is associated with the perception that TCSEC compliance and evaluation is excessively costly.

The ITSEC and Common Criteria assume involvement of commercially licensed evaluation facilities (CLEFs), several of which exist today (e.g., in Germany and the United Kingdom, which have an agreement for mutual recognition of evaluation results), vendor payments to CLEFs, and publicly available evaluation manuals. The CLEF-based evaluations are less expensive and more expeditious than governmentally operated evaluations.[63] The NIST, building on a broad program of commercial evaluation of standards compliance, the National Voluntary Laboratory Accreditation Program, has guided commercial evaluation procedures for FIPS 140-1, and it will also build on that program for evaluation of information security products using the Common Criteria under the new National Information Assurance Partnership.[64]

---

[62]Concerns about completeness revolve around the evaluation process, as opposed to the criteria per se. Note that in criteria or standards, completeness concerns tend to arise in specifications for cryptography.

[63] Based on committee members' personal experiences and committee deliberations.

[64]See NIST, "National Information Assurance Partnership Gets Industry Support," Department of Commerce News (Press Release), October 7, 1997.

Experiences with criteria for "trusted systems" have demonstrated a number of practical problems ranging from how criteria are specified to how systems are evaluated. The central conundrum of criteria (or standards) for trustworthiness is this: if a criterion or standard is written as a performance specification, then evaluation is difficult, but if it is written as a design specification, then the criterion is incomplete because no design specification can cover the range of implementations. The evaluation processes associated with criteria raise questions about openness (what do evaluators say to whom, including the developers) and quality (the implications of what the process emphasizes and what the evaluators seem to know and understand about the development process and the product). The processes also impose costs and raise other issues associated with having a certifier at the site where a system is deployed if the certifier needs to know what a system will be used for. If trustworthiness in the system depends on trust in the administrator, problems arise where the designer, administrator, and certifier disagree on security objectives.[65]

Another difficulty with the concept of criteria is that ratings can relate only to a particular component, not to an entire NIS. In principle, security-evaluated components are used as building blocks and could be combined with rigorous system analysis of assembled systems. However, there is a dwindling set of evaluated components and little or no rigorous methodology for assessing the security of whole systems, as discussed in Chapter 4.

Findings

1. There is an increasing interest in the standards associated with trustworthiness by governments, industry associations, and the Internet Engineering Task Force.

2. A precise and testable definition is required to assess whether a standard has been fulfilled or not. Such definitions may often be articulated for some dimensions of trustworthiness such as reliability, but are often difficult to articulate for security.

3. The development and evolution of a standard attract scrutiny that will work toward reducing the number of remaining design flaws and thereby promote trustworthiness. At the same time, the existence of standards promotes the wide availability of detailed technical information about a particular technology, and therefore serves as a basis for assessing where vulnerabilities remain. Moreover, standards that facilitate interoperability increase the likelihood that successful attacks in a system may prove effec-

---

[65]This issue was discussed at the 1997 IEEE Symposium on Security and Privacy, Oakland, California, May 5-7, 1997, according to an informal e-mail report by Mary Ellen Zurko of the Open Group Research Institute.

tive in other systems. Thus, the relationship between standards and trustworthiness is indeterminate.

4. There is a tension in evaluation processes that yield ratings. If interpretations are constant over time, then the operational value decreases as products provide progressively less protection relative to threats. If interpretations become more stringent over time, vendors are discouraged from participating, because the increased investment required to achieve a given rating increases over time. The Common Criteria effort hopes to mitigate this tension, but within the context of the inevitable bureaucratic and regulatory pressures to maintain fixed objectives, it is doubtful that criteria evolution will keep pace with evolving threats.

5. Commercial licensed evaluation facilities are less costly and more timely than those that are government sponsored or operated.

6. While security-evaluated components might be used as building blocks with rigorous system analysis of the assembled system, there is a dwindling supply of evaluated components and little or no rigorous methodology for assessing the security of networked information systems assembled from evaluated components. This suggests that criteria may have limited usefulness for NISs.

CRYPTOGRAPHY AND TRUSTWORTHINESS

As articulated in Chapters 2 and 4, the committee concluded that greater deployment of cryptography is essential to the protection of the Internet and its end points. But why is cryptography not deployed more widely? The most visible reasons are public policy concerns: export controls and demands for key recovery.

Export Controls

U.S. export controls have undeniably retarded the worldwide availability of products incorporating encryption; indeed, this has been the stated goal of U.S. policy in this area, and U.S. vendors are in broad agreement that U.S. export controls on products incorporating encryption have a negative impact on their ability to make foreign sales of many of their products. To the extent that vendors have been reluctant to produce two versions of a product rather than one (to produce one for domestic sale and one for export, or to hinder interoperability between domestic and export versions), U.S. export controls have also hindered the domestic availability of products incorporating encryption.[66] However, if for-

---

[66]See Computer Science and Telecommunications Board (1991, 1996). Also see Diffie and Landau (1998).

eign vendors begin to step into the void left by U.S. export controls, the availability and use of information security products may be less constrained by the unavailability of U.S. products. [67]

Key Recovery

An encryption product can be designed in such a way that the key required to decrypt an encrypted message can be made available to third parties (i.e., a party that is not either the sender or the receiver) without the explicit action of either the sender or the receiver.[68] Since 1993, law enforcement agencies have been in the forefront of the encryption policy debate, insisting that products be designed to provide key recovery for law enforcement purposes with proper legal authorization. Product vendors have insisted just as firmly that the design and sale of encryption products with key recovery should be driven by the market, rather than by government fiat. Furthermore, key-recovery encryption products are by design less secure than encryption products without key recovery, because they provide access to decryption keys through a channel that can be compromised. As of this writing, the public policy debate over key recovery continues unabated. The CRISIS report (CSTB, 1996) argued that key recovery was an unproven though promising technology, and that aggressive deployment and promotion of key recovery were not appropriate as a matter of public policy; this committee sees no reason to alter that assessment today.

To the extent that public policy is unsettled and does not set clear direction, the resulting uncertainty, fear, and doubt affect the marketplace by making it difficult for users and producers to plan for the future. Vendors are reluctant to bring to market products that support security, and potential users are reluctant to adopt information security products that may become obsolete if and when the legal and regulatory environment changes.

Factors Inhibiting Widespread Deployment of Cryptography

Although export controls and key recovery are important factors, the committee has found that there are other important reasons for the lim-

---

[67]This occurrence would not necessarily be all to the good. Such a development might well reduce U.S. economic strengths by ceding increasingly large market shares to foreign vendors of information technology. U.S. national security interests might also suffer (see the section "The Changing Market-Government Relationship" for further discussion).

[68]For encryption products that manage stored files rather than messages, the sender and receiver are the same party. In this case, a "third party" is someone that the file creator does not explicitly wish to have decryption capability.

ited deployment of cryptography in the United States. For example, cryptographically based security measures often reduce the convenience and usability of the NIS they protect. Indeed, the purpose of a security measure is to make the NIS impossible for an unauthorized party to use, a goal that almost always conflicts with the design goal of making the NIS easily accessible to an authorized user. As noted above, the need to undertake even a modest amount of extra work or to tolerate even a modest inconvenience for protection that is not directly related to the primary function of the device is likely to discourage the use of such protection. Security functions that are not transparent to the user and automatically applied are likely to be perceived by the user as costs that interfere with his or her ability to get work done.

A related point is that applications operating in a networked environment must be interoperable with each other. In some cases, the use of certain security measures such as cryptography can detract from the compatibility of applications that may have interoperated in the absence of those measures. For example, the use of network encryption may render networks inoperative because network address translators may not work anymore. Loss of interoperability may be a very high price to pay for adding security measures.

A good example is e-mail. E-mail systems often communicate with each other via translating gateways, which were necessary because of the lack of homogeneous e-mail systems. These translating gateways send and receive e-mail fairly well. However, the introduction of encryption into e-mail systems would cause the gateways to fail. It is difficult to envision security standards until there are standards for general e-mail communication. Attempts at e-mail security that apply to only some of the major e-mail software systems will not be effective—all major products must be included. The lack of easy-to-use e-mail software that has encryption built into it and the lack of a public-key infrastructure suggest that widespread, routine, and transparent e-mail encryption will be difficult to achieve.

A third point is that cryptographically based information security measures often consume computational resources, such as execution time or memory. For example, routine encryption often slows down a server that provides encryption services. Although it is true that processors increase in speed at a very rapid rate, so, too, do user expectations and desires. As a result, increases in computational capability may well be consumed by increased functionality, leaving little for security.

The mere availability of security products is not necessarily sufficient. To be useful across a broad range of users and applications, users would also need access to a national or international infrastructure for managing and exchanging keys. Without such an infrastructure, encryption may remain a niche feature that is usable only through ad hoc methods replicating some of the functions that an infrastructure would provide and for which demand would thus be limited (CSTB, 1996). For example, even if cryptography had been included in the UNIX rlogin command, a key infrastructure (public-key infrastructure or private/symmetric algorithms) would be necessary for the cryptographic features to be used effectively on a wide scale.

Many of the algorithms that are useful in cryptography are protected by patents. Even though a number of key patents have expired (or will expire soon enough), patents still cover some important ideas, like Micali's[69] and Schnorr's.[70] There are also many patents covering everything from encrypting account numbers to constructing keys from hashes. Today, those writing cryptographic software run substantial risks of infringement. In other cases, vendors are confused by the legal arguments among patent holders about the validity of various patents. And, even when a patent on a particular algorithm is undisputed, the fact that the holder may impose various fees and use restrictions on the patent may well inhibit the implementation of certain forms of cryptography. Such inhibitions also exist within academia, despite "free licenses for noncommercial use" that are available, because the source code that is developed cannot be given away, even if it is restricted to the United States.

The patent situation and export policy have particularly chilling effects on universities, because universities do not have the economic incentive to overcome the additional costs that are a consequence (e.g., recoup the costs of obtaining an export license). The impact on universities is of great concern because much of the software in use on the Internet was developed or inspired at universities.

Finally, for the vast majority of electronically carried or represented information, existing NISs do provide adequate protection simply because the content of that information is not valuable enough for an unauthorized party to go to the bother of obtaining it. For example, most users of NISs have an in-house cable plant or a cable plant that runs through telephone company facilities, which are presumed to be sufficiently secure. In general, a hardwired link is secure enough for most information, although perceptions regarding the adequacy of this security may vary widely. Wireless communications are a different story, and a great deal of attention has been paid in recent years to protecting them.

---

[69]Micali's patents are 5,276,737 (January 1994) and 5,315,658 (May 1994).
[70]Schnorr's patent is 4,995,082 (February 1991).

Cryptography and Confidentiality

Chapters 2 and 4 discuss the value of the authentication aspects of cryptography. The committee emphasized the importance of authentication (over confidentiality) for both technical and policy reasons. The technical reason is that authentication is the first line of defense against the most serious threats to NISs for critical infrastructures—intruders attempting to deny the benefits of using NISs to authorized users. It is still important to recognize, however, that confidentiality is an important capability for protecting privacy in general, for securing access to legacy systems, and in providing "defense in depth" for protecting against improper access (e.g., encrypting a password file or bulk transmissions and thereby obscuring the data traffic so that the analysis of this traffic is more difficult).

The policy reason for the committee's emphasis on authentication is that it does not generally involve conflicts among stakeholders. Since 1990 (and before 1990, informally), liberal rules have governed the export of information security products whose functionality is limited to authentication or integrity,[71] a fact that suggests that on balance, national security interests are not significantly affected by widespread foreign access to such products. Indeed, law enforcement authorities have not demanded access to the cryptographic keys underlying authentication and integrity products.

Findings

1. The public policy controversy surrounding export controls and key recovery inhibits the widespread deployment of cryptography. However, there are other important reasons why cryptography is not more widely deployed. These reasons include reduced convenience and usability, possible loss of interoperability, increased computational and communications requirements, lack of a national or international key infrastructure, restrictions resulting from patents, and the fact that most information is already secure enough relative to its value to an unauthorized party.

2. Insofar as information is not secure enough relative to its value to an unauthorized party, the use of cryptography to promote increased confidentiality in NISs would contribute to improved trustworthiness.

---

[71]"Liberal rules" mean such products were regulated exclusively under the Department of Commerce and governed by the Commodities Control List, rather than the more restrictive International Traffic in Arms Regulations of the State Department.

FEDERAL GOVERNMENT INTERESTS IN NIS TRUSTWORTHINESS

The federal government has multiple interests and roles in enhancing NIS trustworthiness:

- To respond to changing government information technology infrastructures,
- To accomplish agency missions, and
- To promote and protect national interests.

The spread of computer networking and activities such as electronic commerce in procurement and acquisition, electronic dissemination of legislative and agency information, the systems adoption and modernization associated with a wide range of efforts to streamline and enhance government services (e.g., National Partnership for Reinventing Government),[72] and the introduction or revision of legislation and administrative guidelines shaping the use of computer-based systems in government indicate that most if not all agencies of the government have a direct, mission-based interest in NIS trustworthiness. For example, the Information Technology Management Reform Act[73] highlighted the importance of strong high-level management of information technology in federal agencies by requiring the designation of a Chief Information Officer for every agency. The Computer Security Act[74] and the Paperwork Reduction Act[75] resulted in Office of Management and Budget Circular A-130, Appendix III, which provides guidance for all federal agencies on their responsibilities regarding computer security.

In addition to mission-based goals and activities, two important trends are influencing government interest in NIS trustworthiness. The first is that the economics of using COTS products and services, including security and other trustworthy-specific products and services, is irresistible for all consumers, including government, and represents a major shift from the government's historical use of custom-made information technology. The second trend is the relatively recent rise of concerns about "information warfare" and protection of critical infrastructure. Information warfare—at least in a strategic sense—blends traditional national

---

[72]The NPRG (formerly the National Performance Review) is an initiative for reengineering government programs and services. See <http://www.npr.gov>. The NPRG was a springboard for an effort by the Federal Networking Council to outline a framework for federal Internet security.

[73]Public Law 104-106.

[74]Public Law 100-235.

[75]Public Law 104-13.

security interests with less traditional defense concerns over economic security and protection of the civilian economy. Although information warfare (or the issue of information assurance, defined approximately as what is needed to combat the information warfare threat[76]) has been the focus of many recent studies (see Chapter 1 and Appendix F), uncertainty abounds about the actual threat associated with NIS vulnerabilities. Pronouncements and programs have been based on uneven and anecdotal evidence, and acknowledgment of the deficient information base is combined routinely with attempts to forecast the nature, uses, and ramifications of information technology. These two trends are related insofar as COTS products and services are available to all and, therefore, tend to reduce the technological superiority of the United States as compared with other nations.

The awareness of information systems trustworthiness issues has been heightened by recent initiatives aimed at promoting the development and use of information systems generally, such as the High Performance Computing and Communications Initiative, which coordinated research and development and has become the Computing, Information, and Communications R&D program; the National Information Infrastructure initiative and the Information Infrastructure Task Force, which promoted research and economy-wide use of information infrastructure;[77] and the presidential framework for electronic commerce (Office of the President, 1997).

On May 22, 1998, the President signed Presidential Decision Directive 63 (PDD-63) on critical infrastructure protection, which calls for a national effort to ensure the security of the increasingly vulnerable and interconnected infrastructures of the United States. Such infrastructures include telecommunications, banking and finance, energy, transportation, and essential government services. The directive requires immediate federal government action, including risk assessment and planning to reduce exposure to attack, and stresses the critical importance of cooperation between the government and the private sector by linking designated agencies with private-sector representatives.

PDD-63 also established the Critical Infrastructure Assurance Office (CIAO) to support the National Coordinator, charged with integrating the various sector plans into a national infrastructure assurance plan and coordinating analyses of the U.S. government's own dependencies on

---

[76]PCCIP favored the term "information assurance," reintroducing a concept used in earlier years at DARPA that has the benefit of not referring to warfare and, outside the community of security experts, is sufficiently ambiguous to support multiple interpretations.

[77]The IITF included activities by the Security Issues Forum, the Technology Policy Working Group, and activities through DARPA, NSA, NIST, DOE, and other agencies.

critical infrastructures. The President's Commission on Critical Infrastructure Protection (PCCIP), the predecessor of the CIAO and the first national effort to address the vulnerabilities created in the new information age, was established in July 1996 by Executive Order 13010.[78]

Across the federal government, the DOD conducts the largest effort in information systems trustworthiness, through its work on information security as it relates to the nation's security interests. For example, in communications security, the National Communications System group and its parent Defense Information Systems Agency (DISA) coordinate with the service provider-oriented National Security Telecommunications Advisory Committee (NSTAC) to ensure that national security and emergency preparedness needs for telecommunications services are met;[79] these and other DOD agencies depend on a significant NSA effort for high-grade communications security. The primary agencies within DOD that support and facilitate research and development on information security are the NSA and DARPA, whose roles are discussed in detail later in this chapter.

On the civilian side of the federal government, the Federal Bureau of Investigation (FBI) has interests in NIS trustworthiness as a part of its law enforcement mission. During the last several years, the FBI has substantially increased its activity in addressing computer-related crimes. The FBI's most visible involvement with the information security issue has been to warn of the dangers that encryption poses to the law enforcement community and to push for the installation of key-recovery features in all encryption products and provide law enforcement authorities with the technical capability to access decryption keys surreptitiously and nonconsensually under court-approved wiretap orders. In February 1998, the National Infrastructure Protection Center was established within the FBI to serve as the federal government's focal point to detect, deter, assess, warn of, respond to, and investigate computer intrusions and unlawful acts, both physical and "cyber," that threaten or target U.S. critical infrastructure.[80]

---

[78]Details available online at <http://www.pccip.gov>.

[79]The NCS is an interagency group of about 23 federal departments and agencies that "coordinates and plans NS/EP [national security/emergency preparedness] telecommunications to support any crisis or disaster." The NSTAC provides industry perspective, advice, and information to the President and executive branch "regarding policy and enhancements to NS/EP telecommunications." NCS was formed in 1963 on a smaller scale after command, control, and communications (C^3) failures during the Cuban Missile Crisis; NSTAC was formed in 1982 in anticipation of the AT&T divestiture and evolving C^3 capabilities and needs.

[80]Information available online at <http://www.fbi.gov/nipc/index.htm>.

Under the Computer Security Act, the National Institute of Standards and Technology (NIST) has government-wide responsibility for civilian government systems and systems handling sensitive but unclassified information. This act also provided for the provision of technical expertise and advice by the NSA for NIST, where appropriate. Although NIST does carry out its mission within budget constraints, the reality is that NIST's budget is too limited for it to acquire or use significant levels of expertise, with the result of perpetuating NSA's de facto authority and influence in the information security domain.[81] In 1997, advisors to the NSA and PCCIP called for greater involvement of NIST with NSA in areas of mutual interest—which, given the dependence of the defense information infrastructure on the national information infrastructure, could be quite extensive.

Agencies that regulate the safety of goods and services have begun to address information system component trustworthiness in products ranging from medical devices (Food and Drug Administration) to aircraft and the air traffic control system (Federal Aviation Administration). In these instances, information systems trustworthiness refers to safety and reliability as well as to the traditional domain of information security. These agencies focus their activities in the context of specific products and circumstances of use, influencing system design, implementation, and use by requiring impact analysis and testing, and they may declare (e.g., by evaluation relative to a standard and/or regulation and certification) products safe or unsafe for use in a particular context.

The regulation of telecommunications services has been extended to the promotion of reliability and interoperability. For example, the Network Reliability and Interoperability Council, established under the auspices of the Federal Communications Commission and later privatized, has promoted industry monitoring and the minimization of outages. It is worth noting, however, that this regulatory response could be viewed as a corrective response to the erosion of trustworthiness that some attribute to regulatory changes that promote competition.[82] By contrast, in the

---

[81]The principal vehicles for NIST action have included federal information processing standards, research relating to associated measurement issues, focused workshops, hosting of the Computer System Security and Privacy Advisory Board, consultation with and education of federal agency personnel on security practices and issues, and coordination with other agencies; it has not had the resources for and therefore a track record in relevant research. See, for example, Computer Science and Telecommunications Board (1991, 1996).

[82]These changes have been linked to greater sensitivity to cost and time to market among telecommunications providers. Results include decreasing redundancy of facilities, an increase in reliance on software, proliferation of features and services (e.g., call forwarding) that promote complexity in telecommunications systems (and unreliability), and other cost-containing steps that can increase vulnerabilities. See Board on Telecommunications and Computer Applications (1989).

finance sector, regulation has promoted incident reporting, auditing, and other actions that motivate or reinforce plans and procedures to promote trustworthiness, and financial incidents receive special law enforcement assistance via the U.S. Secret Service.

Public-Private Partnerships

A telling sign of the growing importance of the commercial information technology sector relative to government is the rise in rhetoric about public-private partnerships. Experiences with information security suggest that outside certain safety- and reliability-critical contexts, government mandates and controls on technology are decreasingly effective and that some form of cooperation is the logical alternative. At the same time, neither the Computer Security Act nor any other legislation assigns responsibility for assisting nongovernmental entities to protect their information systems and networks.[83]

The PCCIP has called expressly for public-private partnerships to increase information systems trustworthiness, as has the White House Office of Science and Technology Policy (Executive Office of the President, 1997). Complementary work was undertaken earlier and concurrently by the NSTAC and its Information Assurance Task Force, which drew on participants from private firms.

Today, the meaning of "partnership" must be developed and translated into action. What can and will happen will depend on developing increased trust between the private and public sectors, and in particular, the degree of trust in the government. The cryptography policy debates suggest a loss of trust in government by the commercial information technology sector that must be acknowledged in formulating new policies and approaches. Trade and advocacy organizations[84] articulate industry positions to Congress and executive branch agencies, and a wide range of issues relating to trustworthiness are now argued in government circles that previously might have been simply decided with minimal consultation with the private sector or even ignored. Unilateral government insistence on its position or its preferred solutions—even if cloaked in the

---

[83]The absence of an effective structure for addressing civilian and commercial needs was highlighted in two CSTB reports, *Computers at Risk: Safe Computing in the Information Age* (CSTB, 1991) and *Cryptography's Role in Securing the Information Society* (CSTB, 1996).

[84]Such organizations include the Information Technology Information Council (formerly the Computer and Business Equipment Manufacturers Association), the Information Technology Association of America (formerly the Association of Data Processing Systems Organizations), the Software Publishers Association, the Business Software Alliance, the Computer Systems Policy Project, the Electronic Frontier Foundation, and the Electronic Privacy Information Center, among others.

guise of promoting partnerships with or education of nongovernmental entities—is unlikely to result in lasting or stable engagement with the private sector.

If equipped with resources adequate to do the job and to appear independent in its action, NIST could facilitate such partnerships; its moves to facilitate commercial system evaluation (i.e., National Information Assurance Partnership) support this prospect. The PCCIP endorsed a greater role for NIST while calling for more involvement of a number of agencies in the information assurance cause. One ongoing experiment is called the Manhattan Cyber Project, a private-sector group with government inputs aimed at documenting attacks and incidents (Harreld, 1997).

The Changing Market-Government Relationship

In the not-so-distant past, the number of commercial firms capable of providing trustworthiness products or services was relatively small. Thus, the federal government needed to influence only a small number of organizations in order to promote greater trustworthiness. These organizations had incentives to respond positively to federal government concerns because of a formal relationship that existed with the federal government (e.g., AT&T as a regulated monopoly), or because they were motivated to be cautious as a consequence of ongoing antitrust investigations (in the case of IBM), or because they sold products in large quantities to the federal government (in the case of both AT&T and IBM).

Today's vendors of trustworthiness-related products are many and diverse, ranging in size from small start-ups to Fortune 100 companies. Many of today's product vendors and service providers have arisen in a more competitive and libertarian culture, and market responsiveness is the most highly held value for these companies. Despite some degree of concentration in the supply of computing systems (in both hardware platforms and software), it is now harder to find large telecommunications or computer systems providers with both the market penetration and the tradition of responding to public-sector requests for reliability that historically characterized AT&T and IBM. Although the federal government continues to be the largest customer of computing and communications products and services, its market share has decreased dramatically during the past few decades—with a concomitant decline in the federal government's influence in the marketplace.

The emergence of a number of important suppliers from other countries complicates matters further, as foreign governments and firms have even less motivation to be friendly to U.S. government or societal interests. Examples raised by people who note this concern include Siemens, Alcatel, Checkpoint, and SAP, on the basis of ownership rather than any specific evidence. For example, Baan and SAP are non-U.S. companies whose significant number of U.S.-based customers will entrust their operating models and internal manufacturing system knowledge to their products and, by extension, sales forces (Edmondson et al., 1997). Checkpoint, an Israeli-owned company, is one of the leading firewall vendors. Indeed, there arises the possibility that these non-U.S. firms may be responsive to their home governments rather than the U.S. government.

Findings

1. The federal government has a broad and increasing interest in NIS trustworthiness. Trustworthy NISs are important for the government to accomplish agency missions, address changing government information technology infrastructures, protect national interests, and facilitate and support research and development in areas critical to the nation.

2. Federal government mandates and controls on technology are decreasingly effective. Therefore, some form of cooperation with the private sector (e.g., partnerships) is appropriate. Building trust between the private and public sectors is essential to achieving increased cooperation in efforts to improve NIS trustworthiness.

3. The federal government has less influence on vendors than in the past because the number of vendors of trustworthiness products and services has increased considerably and these vendors include small start-ups that, in particular, are focused on marketplace demands. As trustworthiness-related products and services are increasingly provided by non-U.S. companies, the influence of foreign firms and governments on the trustworthiness marketplace is a new concern.

THE ROLES OF THE NSA, DARPA, AND OTHER FEDERAL AGENCIES IN NIS TRUSTWORTHINESS RESEARCH AND DEVELOPMENT

Research relating to NIS trustworthiness is conducted and supported by many federal government organizations. Some agencies conduct research directly (e.g., NSA, Department of Energy national laboratories); others fund research that is conducted externally (e.g., DARPA); and a few agencies support both internal and external research (e.g., NSA). Internal research, some of which is classified, is difficult to assess; time constraints precluded further consideration in this report. As discussed earlier in this chapter, industry also conducts "research," but it emphasizes applied research and development in its activities and rarely achieves depth in any given area of inquiry (Mayfield et al., 1997). This short-term emphasis by the private sector may lead to products, but it also creates an enduring federal role in trustworthiness research. Moreover, some requirements that are unique to the federal government are unlikely to be met by the commercial market.

Through its national laboratories, the Department of Energy (DOE) has supported projects that have developed information security tools for network inspection and workstation protection; these tools are available to the entire DOE community, including its contractors. The Lawrence Livermore National Laboratory is the host for the Computer Security Technology Center, which serves the entire federal government with respect to information security needs. Sandia National Laboratories conducts a variety of research activities that support the development of high-assurance software, more from a reliability and safety rather than a security standpoint. In addition, Sandia National Laboratories has a long history of conducting vulnerability assessments of high-consequence systems, such as those intended to prevent uncommanded release of nuclear weapons.

The National Aeronautics and Space Administration (NASA), through its Assessment Technology Branch (ATB), develops advanced methods for the specification, design, and verification of complex software systems used in critical aerospace applications to minimize the frequency of design errors and to promote fault tolerance in the presence of component failures. ATB's work focuses on formal methods for assuring safety and integrity and develops measures of system quality and tools to apply those measures. Techniques and approaches showing significant potential for improving the quality or safety of aerospace computing systems are transferred to U.S. aerospace interests and to other U.S. customers. In addition to coordinating its work with that of the DOD, ATB works with the Federal Aviation Administration to transfer applicable research results to civil aircraft certification guidelines, specifications, and recommended procedures.[85] NASA also supports the Software Independent Verification and Validation Facility, whose role is to assist customers in the development of high-quality software.

Finally, the National Science Foundation (NSF) supports some research on information systems trustworthiness. For example, the Software Engineering and Languages Program in the Division of Computing and Communications Research supports research on technical issues that underlie the design, validation, and evolution of software-based systems. Research topics include domain-specific languages for specification and

---

[85]Description adapted from material available online at <http://atb-www.larc.nasa.gov/atb-charter.html>.

design; various approaches to software design and evolution; issues of software modularity and composition; techniques to enhance confidence and quality; software security; and software design environments that incorporate semantic knowledge.[86] The NSF has also funded cryptography projects as a part of its efforts in computational and complexity theory.

Incomplete and incompatible statistics complicate an assessment of relevant research support across federal agencies, and the tendency for individual agency programs to change regularly (as projects start and finish and as programs are revised) compounds the problem. Some gross observations can be made to characterize the situation as of this writing. Within the federal government, external research relating to information systems trustworthiness is coordinated by the interagency Computing, Information, and Communications (CIC) R&D Subcommittee. About 12 federal departments and agencies participate in coordinating program planning, budgeting, and review. The CIC R&D Subcommittee is divided into five components, and trustworthiness activity is largely associated with the High Confidence Systems (HCS) component.[87] In terms of research support, NSA and DARPA dominate the CIC agencies involved with HCS, with FY 1997 spending listed as $7.3 millon and $10 million, respectively, out of a $30 million component total. Other components include High End Computing and Computation, Large Scale Networking, Human Centered Systems, and Education, Training, and Human Resources—each of which can contribute to or be affected by trustworthiness.

The federal government has sought to promote coordination among entities on trustworthiness R&D, and it has linked defense and civilian and mission and research agencies through the HCS working group. There is also an evolving information security (infosec) research council that includes DARPA, DISA, NSA, NIST, DOE, the CIA, and the military services. The PCCIP has recommended additional interagency coordination structures, building on the teams it assembled while conducting its work.

---

[86]Description adapted from material available online at <http://www.cise.nsf.gov/ccr/sel_home.html>.

[87]The HCS program was announced as one of six focus areas in the 1995 Strategic Implementation Plan of the Committee on Information and Communications (CIC) R&D, which coordinates computing and communications R&D across the federal government. CIC planning includes R&D activity in the areas of components, communications, computing systems, support software and tools, intelligent systems, information management, and applications.

The focused coordination effort comes from the DARPA-NSA-DISA Joint Technology Office (JTO).[88] Specifically, the role of the Information Systems Security Research-Joint Technology Office (ISSR-JTO) is "to optimize use of the limited research funds available, and strengthen the responsiveness of the programs to DISA, expediting delivery of technologies that meet DISA's requirements to safeguard the confidentiality, integrity, authenticity, and availability of data in Department of Defense information systems, provide a robust first line of defense for defensive information warfare, and permit electronic commerce between the Department of Defense and its contractors."[89]

National Security Agency

The National Security Agency is responsible for (1) providing intelligence through the interception, collection, decryption, translation, and processing of foreign communications signals and (2) developing cryptographic and other information security techniques to protect classified and unclassified (but sensitive) U.S. communications and computer systems associated with national security.[90] In support of its information security mission, the NSA historically has developed very high quality cryptographic equipment and keying material for the Department of Defense and other customers in the U.S. government (e.g., the State Depart-

---

[88]The Joint Technology Office (JTO) was announced in the 1995 "ARPA/DISA/NSA Memorandum of Agreement Concerning the Information Systems Security Research Joint Technology Office." Complementing DARPA's ongoing research program relating to system security as well as NSA's research efforts, the JTO is intended to further coordination of research and technology development relevant to meeting DOD's needs for trustworthy systems. It also aims to make the goals and decision-making processes for such R&D more open and responsive to public needs and concerns. Organized as a "virtual" entity that draws on personnel and resources otherwise housed at the participating agencies, the JTO is expected to harmonize the individual agency programs much as the High Performance Computing and Communications Initiative has harmonized those of its component agencies, while leaving research management (e.g., broad area announcements in the case of DARPA) and ultimate source selection decision making to those agencies.

[89]See "Memorandum of Agreement Between the Advanced Research Projects Agency, the Defense Information Systems Agency, and the National Security Agency Concerning the Information Systems Security Research Joint Technology Office"; MOA effective April 2, 1995. The full text of the MOA is available online at <http://www.ito.darpa.mil/ResearchAreas/Information_Survivability/MOA.html>.

[90]Under the National Security Act of 1947, a restructured intelligence community was created. Subsequent executive orders have revised or reordered the intelligence community (and continue to do so). The National Security Agency (which replaced the Armed Forces Security Agency) was created by presidential directive by President Truman in 1952. A number of documents that describe NSA's mission are classified, but a basic mission statement is now available on an NSA Web site, <http://www.nsa.gov:8080>.

ment). For years, the primary focus of the NSA was on protecting the confidentiality of communications. As the boundary between communications and computing has blurred, the NSA has focused its protection on information security rather than more narrowly on communications security (see Box 6.6).

The growing dependence on COTS technology in the DOD necessitates a strong NSA interest in COTS trustworthiness and the integration of cryptography into COTS products. NSA's special customer market is small enough and the potential for NSA control is sufficient to discourage many producers of COTS products from meeting NSA's special needs directly; because of its low and shrinking influence on the market, NSA needs to understand and work with COTS technology and vendors. The shift to COTS products raises questions about the scope of national security concerns and what they imply for technology strategies to meet the needs of national security entities, the primary client of NSA.

BOX 6.6
The NSA Mission:
From Communications Security to Information Security

The 1995 National Security Agency (NSA) Corporate Plan for Information Systems Security laid out a broad mission:

[NSA's] INFOSEC [information security] mission is to provide leadership, products, and services necessary to enable customers to protect national security and sensitive information in information systems pursuant to federal law and national policies, and to provide technical support to the government's efforts to incorporate information systems security into the national information infrastructure. Our customers include national security community members handling classified and sensitive information, as well as those civil government agencies and, when requested, private sector organizations providing vital national services. We serve our customers by assessing their needs, delivering solutions, and creating advanced INFOSEC technologies. We also promote security for the national information infrastructure through our policy and standards work, our efforts in public advocacy and education, and our role in shaping commercially available security technology. (p. ii)

More recently, the 1996 National Cryptologic Strategy for the 21st Century[1] explicitly related military and commercial vulnerability to interconnectivity, interoperability, and increased reliance on commercial off-the-shelf products and services.

---

[1] Using July 1996 briefing charts, John Davis, NCSC director, described this program to the committee during its October 21, 1996, visit to NSA.

Partnerships with Industry

Increasingly, partnering with industry is seen as an approach for lowering government research costs, ensuring the relevance of solutions, and expediting the transfer of research into products. On the other hand, anecdotal evidence[91] points to concerns about the direct and opportunity costs of engineering efforts that respond to NSA's concerns without generating products that see widespread use (Mayfield et al., 1997). Meanwhile, growing recognition of the need for trustworthiness combined with increased dependence on NISs continues to lead more organizations (e.g., banks) with high levels of concern about information security to approach NSA for consultation and assistance. The National Computer Security Center was formed by NSA in the early 1980s as a communications conduit for information security technology. More recently, the NSA National Cryptologic Strategy[92] described and encouraged a "zone of cooperation" among the law enforcement and national security communities, the public sector generally, and the private sector.

Another example of reaching out is the NSA effort in the early 1990s concerning the Multilevel Information Systems Security Initiative (MISSI), which was originally intended to provide a set of products and an architectural framework that would facilitate the development of multilevel secure NISs. A key aspect of MISSI was to promote broader use of Fortezza technology[93] through partnerships with industry. MISSI embodied the view that secure hardware and software had to be developed together, something that the COTS market eschews. For this and other reasons, it is widely acknowledged that MISSI was both a technical and marketplace failure; nevertheless, the multilevel security concerns embodied in MISSI—that truly secure solutions require integrated approaches—continue to shape NSA management thinking.[94] An alternate way to leverage COTS technology is through the development of standards, such as common application programming interfaces (APIs) that permit the development and use of security products with differing strength. Such standards have promise in satisfying the needs of diverse communities of security customers. The use of APIs seems to the committee to be more appealing to industry than MISSI, although acknowledging that APIs and MISSI are not directly comparable because APIs do not

---

[91]Such evidence includes the experiences of committee members.

[92]John Davis, NCSC director, described this program to the committee during its October 21, 1996, visit to NSA.

[93]Fortezza was originally designed for use with only unclassified data. Other products, never deployed, were to provide analogous cryptographic protection for classified data. However, over time MISSI's focus changed (see Chapter 4, Box 4.4, for additional details).

[94]Committee discussion with R2 managers, October 21, 1996.

address system security or assurance issues. However, APIs are consistent with the notion that successful solutions in industry are likely to be add-ons, rather than integrative solutions. Furthermore, some APIs, notably those for cryptographic functions, can run afoul of export control restrictions.

The U.S. Trusted Computer System Evaluation Criteria (TCSEC) effort represents a further attempt by NSA to partner with the private sector. In this area, NSA insisted on specific conceptual models and corresponding technology, such as the information flow security models for access control at higher levels of the TCSEC. The result was a different and more costly orientation to authentication and access control than evidenced by policy models apparent in industry. No commercially viable products emerged from this effort, and today it is regarded as essentially irrelevant to current COTS information technology.

The effectiveness of such outreach efforts has been limited in the past by such factors as public mistrust of a historically secretive agency; the lack of public awareness, understanding, and support for the TCSEC and Evaluated Product List; and the ambiguity inherent in a public outreach arm in an agency constrained by statute to national security interests (CSTB, 1991). Current efforts may prove more successful, but they must overcome a legacy of suspicion originating in NSA's traditional secrecy as well as its role in controversies surrounding such efforts as the TCSEC, Clipper chip/Fortezza, and its desires for controls on exports of information security devices.[95]

Other factors inhibit cooperation between NSA and the private sector. The environment in which private-sector information security needs are manifested may be different enough from the defense and foreign policy worlds that these technologies may not be particularly relevant in practice to the private sector.[96] Furthermore, the rapid pace of commercial developments in information technology may make it difficult for the private sector to use technologies developed for national security purposes in a less rapidly changing environment (CSTB, 1996).

---

[95]This distrust and suspicion of NSA are enhanced by NSA's history of control-oriented interactions with industry. The technology marketplace is a worldwide marketplace. For many companies at least half of their income is derived from outside the United States. Advanced technology, especially cryptography, is subject to export controls, and NSA has played a significant role in advising the U.S. government on which technologies can be exported as commodities. The recent declassification of SKIPJACK and KEA is a step in the right direction; the declassification was done explicitly to allow industry to implement Fortezza-compatible software, thus enabling very low cost cryptographic "soft tokens."

[96]For example, military users may be willing to tolerate a higher degree of inconvenience to obtain the benefits of security.

R2 Program

To support its mission, NSA funds and conducts research through an organization called R, which has research subunits and staff groups that provide support for technology forecasting and infosec research outreach. R2 is the NSA research subunit responsible for information security research programs; it is organized into three research divisions: cryptography, engineering, and computer science. In 1997, R2 had more than 100 staff members and a contracting budget in the tens of millions of dollars, a portion of which is coordinated with DARPA.

The major foci of R2 research are enumerated in Box 6.7. The dominant areas of R2 research are secure communications technology, assurance technology, and security management infrastructure.[97] Although cryptography has been the centerpiece of NSA's communication security products and is the dominant technique for providing security within NISs, cryptography was not identified as a dominant emphasis. Classified research and research performed by other NSA research elements and other government and government-supported research organizations presumably provide research support to NSA in this area.

The NSA and its R2 organization have developed close working relationships with a group of companies and organizations that have acquired a significant understanding of NSA's goals and the technologies involved in satisfying those goals. A large portion of the research work funded by R2 is conducted by selected contractors, federally funded research and development centers (FFRDCs), and researchers at national laboratories (e.g., work on quantum cryptography, an example of the more fundamental work supported by R2). Although R2 does not, for the most part, use the same open solicitation process used by DARPA, for example, it does review and sometimes funds proposals submitted to DARPA. Such coordination is a goal of the JTO.

R2's small University Research Program (URP) publishes open solicitations for research and provides modest security-related contracts ($50,000 to $100,000) to principal investigators in a number of colleges and universities. The program is intended to encourage professors to work in computer and communications security, although published results have not been noteworthy. For example, R2 has supported operating systems (OS) work that its management recognizes has not affected mainstream OS work and formal methods work that also has had limited impact (e.g., formal verification tools have not been developed as hoped for).

---

[97] As reflected in unclassified briefings and materials on funding and staffing levels provided to the committee.

BOX 6.7
R2's Research Activities

• Secure communications technology—dealing primarily with optical, wireless, digital speech encoding and compatible digital encryption technology in very high speed communications networks.

• Assurance technology—including formal methods, risk management, and fault tolerance.

• Secure management infrastructure—significant effort in key and certificate management, protocols including IPsec and ISAKMP, standardization efforts, and multicast key management.

• Identification and authentication—with significant emphasis on biometrics.

• Policy invocation and enforcement—including architectures, system composition, and distributed computing.

• Damage detection and response—covering defensive information warfare, damage indicators, and recovery responses.

• Information domain definition—including boundary defenses and mapping network boundaries.

• Cryptography—primarily classified research by its own staff (only part of the National Security Agency's cryptography research effort).

SOURCE: Based on program management information supplied by R2 in 1997.

In a recent study (Anderson et al., 1998), 45 NSA-funded projects in the area of information system security and survivability were identified. Although the enumeration may not be comprehensive, it does indicate the nature and scope of the research funded by NSA (see Appendix J).

Of R2's contract funds, a significant portion goes to support nonresearch activities such as participation in standards-setting organizations (e.g., the Internet Engineering Task Force, where R2 contributed the ISAKMP protocol to the IPsec standards effort), consortia membership (e.g., the ATM Forum, where R2 also contributed to security protocol standards), and support for infosec education (e.g., Biometrics consortium, Network Security Management Forum, and support for infosec studies at the Naval Postgraduate School and the University of Maryland). Numerous activities, both external and contract funded, are focused on understanding and assessing various products and technologies (e.g., hacker tools, cryptography for electronic cash). R2 also supports several efforts to modify COTS products to incorporate new or expanded security functionality (e.g., biometrics access controls and intrusion detection for Windows NT).

Issues for the Future

The committee reviewed a draft of R2's "Information System Security Research Program Plan," which was revised multiple times in 1996-1997.[98] This plan calls for greater interaction with the entire infosec community and a more open but focused R2 research program, which would be based on input from an infosec research council (sponsored by NSA and including participants from the relevant agencies and the military services), a national infosec technical baseline (established by NSA, DOE, and DOE's national laboratories), and an infosec science and technology study group (composed of leading experts who would provide an infosec perspective from the private sector). By design, the draft plan would support technology R&D "consistent with the fundamental security principles and concepts articulated in the DOD Goal Security Architecture" (Burnham, 1997). To ensure a supply of knowledgeable experts in the future, the draft plan calls for the establishment of academic centers for infosec studies and research. The plan also emphasizes technology transfer to the infosec side of NSA, to the military services, and to industry.

The committee believes that R2 faces two related challenges. One challenge is its research portfolio. Because NSA both funds external infosec research and performs internal infosec research, questions arise as to the appropriate allocation of effort (internal and external) and its coordination. Decisions about internal effort, like decisions about external effort, should recognize where the parties have comparative advantage. Highly classified cryptographic research is a natural choice for internal research; NSA has widely recognized strength in that area and has better access to mathematical talent in terms of both caliber and number or researchers. Other areas of trustworthiness, less constrained by classification requirements, seem more appropriate for R2 to pursue externally.

The second critical issue is the recruitment, retention, and continuing education of high-quality talent to pursue noncryptographic trustworthiness research areas. In these areas, especially those that depend on computer science, highly skilled researchers available in many academic and commercial organizations can make significant contributions to infosec technology. R2 will have to compete for that talent with other agencies that have established relationships with top researchers. Furthermore, top-tier talent with security expertise is scarce, and nongovernment em-

---

[98] Authored by Blaine Burnham, NSA. This document was provided to the committee by R2 when the committee asked for insight into R2's thinking about future directions. The committee examined this document not as a formal plan for NSA, but as a white paper—as a source of possibilities for the future.

ployers would appear to offer more rewards, from recognition to pay (Lardner, 1998). Skills developed in an infosec research group, especially those relating to network security, cryptography, and COTS software, are easily marketable in the commercial sector—a fact that constrains both hiring and retention in R2. Finally, there is the perception that the "cloak and dagger image" that once attracted some people to NSA is no longer as strong, because of a smaller defense budget and rapidly growing private-sector alternatives (Lardner, 1998).

As previously indicated, senior management at NSA and NSA advisory groups have stated that it is difficult to obtain and retain highly qualified technical research staff with computer-related expertise for the R2 organization.[99] Within R2, staff is spread thinly, and loss of an individual can have a significant impact on organizational coverage. Further, the ability of a technologist to do research is reportedly limited by administrative and other obligations. The adoption of a rotation program, comparable to those at the NSF and DARPA for program managers, could be considered as a complement to hiring regular staff members. To be effective, such a program would have to be carefully designed to attract the desired researchers to the NSA.

R2 may be at a disadvantage within NSA inasmuch as its work is removed from fielded results that constitute NSA successes and its work is not as directly linked to NSA's mission as that of other units. These circumstances can constrain internal communication, and anecdotal evidence suggests that R2 may not always benefit from knowledge of relevant work done by sister units. By contrast, program managers pursuing trustworthiness topics at DARPA and NSF have more visibility, and they and the researchers they fund are free to publish their results.

Although R2 funds and performs unclassified work, it shares the NSA environment and mind-set of tightly controlled information. This environment presents a real conflict with the need for access to open research information. It can encourage a closed community of workers who do not communicate with others in the community either to seek or contribute information. Although R2 has increased its outreach, the conferences in which it seems most active as an organization, the NSA-NIST-sponsored National Information System Security Conference and its own Tech Fest, tend to attract a small community of researchers with long-standing connections to NSA. These audiences have only limited interaction with the larger community of computer science researchers with whom other HCS agency program managers have regular contact.

---

[99]They note that R2 has not recruited from the academic researchers it supports.

Findings

1. Some government customers have particularly high needs for security, and there are a handful of systems (e.g., "The President's Laptop") that face levels of threat and require the strength of a mechanism that is not available in commercial products and that would have insufficient demand to support a product in the marketplace. The NSA is particularly well situated to develop such mechanisms. Classified cryptographic research is also a natural fit for the NSA internal research program.

2. The R2 university research program emphasizes relatively short term and small projects. Such projects do not tend to attract the interest of the best industrial and academic researchers and institutions.

3. Rotation of R2 researchers with researchers in industry and academia could help to broaden and invigorate the R2 program. Such rotation would be most effective with institutions that have large numbers of leading researchers.

4. Inadequate incentives currently exist in R2 to attract and retain highly skilled researchers. Improved incentives might be financial (e.g., different salary scale) and/or nonfinancial (e.g., special recognition, greater public visibility). R2 faces formidable challenges in the recruitment and retention of the very best researchers.

5. R2 has initiated several outreach efforts, but these efforts have not significantly broadened the community of researchers who work with R2. Effective outreach efforts are those that are designed to be compatible with the interests, perspectives, and real needs of potential partners.

Defense Advanced Research Projects Agency

DARPA's charter is to fund research that is likely to advance the mission of the DOD.[100] The DOD has requirements, such as the need for high reliability, accommodation of hostile physical environments, and adaptation to varying contexts of use (e.g., whether and what kind of wireline communications are possible; nature of wireless infrastructure available), that are unique to its mission, as well as requirements that are common to other segments of society.

Trustworthiness is an issue that cuts across DARPA's portfolio to varying degrees.[101] Relevant work is concentrated in the Information Survivability program (with an approximate budget of $40 million per year) within DARPA's Information Technology Office (ITO) (with a budget of $300 million to $350 million per year), which supports research

---

[100]Information about DARPA is available online at <http://www.darpa.mil>.

[101]Based on examination of publicly available project descriptions.

directly applicable to NIS trustworthiness. As noted above, this program is coordinated with NSA's R2 program using the JTO established between the two agencies (and DISA) for that purpose. Universities and industrial research establishments are supported, with a program that in 1997 was divided into four subareas—high-confidence computing, high-confidence networking, survivability of large-scale systems, and wrappers and composition.

A reasonably broad set of topics is covered (see Appendix J), with some emphasis on fault tolerance and intrusion detection, at least as measured by the number of funded projects in these areas. Research in other areas important for NIS trustworthiness, as articulated in previous chapters—containment, denial-of-service attacks, cryptographic infrastructures, for instance—although present, is not treated as prominently as it should be. To support greater use of COTS products, the DARPA Information Survivability program has sponsored research in wrappers and other technologies for retrofitting trustworthiness properties to existing components.

Other programs within ITO also support research that impinges on NIS trustworthiness in areas such as software engineering, programming languages, computer networks, and mobile communications. For example, encryption, reliability, and various aspects of information security are all concerns in the mobile communications (Global-Mobile) program. Other DARPA offices, including the Information Systems Office, support some work in electronics and other areas related to NIS trustworthiness. Finally, DARPA has provided funding to NSF to support smaller-scale and more theoretically oriented research projects in trustworthiness and software assurance.

DARPA funds research based on proposals that it receives from investigators. These proposals are written in response to published broad area announcements (BAAs), which outline general areas of research of interest based on interactions among program managers, operating units of the DOD with specific technology needs, and members of the research community. Proposals are evaluated by DARPA staff as well as others within the federal government, and competition for the funding is keen. Funding levels are high relative to other government sources of research support, reflecting the emphasis on systems that often require research teams and significant periods of time to develop, allowing DARPA-funded projects to undertake nontrivial implementation efforts as well as long-range research.

The ITO's culture and its practice of organizing office- and program-wide principal investigator meetings have fostered contact between DARPA program managers and the researchers that they support. This contact enables the research community to contribute to future DARPA-funded research directions, and it helps program managers to catalyze research communities. DARPA principal investigator meetings also facilitate interchange among those involved in DARPA-funded projects. Longer-term issues and planning are considered annually at a special, retreat-style information science and technology (ISAT) activity organized around specific topics. ISAT enables program managers to interact intensively with small groups of researchers to better understand research areas (potential BAAs) for which research funding potential is timely.

DARPA program managers typically are employed on temporary assignments, although there is a small cadre of longer-term staff. The ranks are populated by academics on leave from their universities, as well as scientists and developers from other branches of the government and from industry. Limited-term appointments mean that DARPA's direction and priorities are not static, with obvious advantages and disadvantages. Most problematic is that longer-term research agendas may suffer from changes in personnel, as newer program managers seek funding for research programs they wish to create, which can be achieved only by reallocating resources at the expense of existing programs. Another concern is the ability to attract top researchers for brief government stints. Those academics with well-developed research programs are reluctant to leave them for 2 to 3 years, while those researchers who have been unable to develop such programs are probably not the candidates that DARPA would like to recruit.[102] On the other hand, top researchers who serve for brief government stints bring state-of-the-art thinking to DARPA and may be more willing than career employees to abandon less promising streams of research. Because the existence of effective research programs in trustworthiness and survivability is essential, whatever challenges exist in attracting topflight academics must be overcome.

The types of research undertaken have varied over the years, depending on priorities within the DOD and DARPA as well as outside influences (e.g., the NSA, Congress). Historically DARPA projects have been high risk, pushing the envelope of technological capabilities to achieve potentially high payoffs.

For example, in the early to mid-1970s, there was strong interest in DARPA security research, sparked in part by a Defense Science Board task force established to address the security problems of multiaccess, resource-sharing computer systems. In an effort to attain the widely shared goal of creating a multilevel secure operating system, the DOD aggressively funded an external research program that yielded many fun-

---

[102]Interview conducted by Jean E. Smith for the Computing Research Association on March 25, 1998. Data is available online at <http://www.cra.org/CRN/>.

damental advances in computer security. As one view of DARPA in the 1970s put it: "The route to a solution—implementing a reference monitor in a security kernel—was widely agreed upon" (Mackenzie and Pottinger, 1997). By reducing some of the research and development risks, the DARPA-funded research stimulated the market to develop enhanced security capabilities (CSTB, 1991) at the same time that, not coincidentally, the United States led the computer security field and agreement emerged about the nature and role of an organization that would certify the security of actual systems.

Not every project was successful. Some were canceled, others exceeded budgets, and yet others outlived their practicality. These experiences illustrate some of the difficulties inherent in research. Some "failures" are a positive sign as indicators that challenging ideas are being pursued (which entails some risk) and that spin-offs and learning take place, which may be applied to future successful projects.

Issues for the Future

A few university computer science departments have several faculty members who emphasize computer security research, but many departments have none who do. In any event, the number of computer security researchers is small compared to the number in other specialties, such as operating systems or networks. Among the consequences are a paucity of educational programs in security and a dearth of security experts. In recent years, DARPA funding for computer security research has been primarily incremental and short term. Longer-range research projects need to be funded, particularly those that address fundamental questions, to develop the basic research that is needed for the long-term vitality of the field.

Even fewer faculty conduct research programs in some other areas of trustworthiness, such as operational vulnerabilities. Increased funding is imperative to enable reasonable progress in the critical research areas needed to improve the trustworthiness of NISs.

Although the DOD-support mission does not seem to restrict what research areas DARPA pursues, pressures to demonstrate the relevance of their research investments have generally led DARPA program managers to encourage their investigators to produce short-term results and make rapid transitions to industry. This approach can discourage investigation of more fundamental questions and experimental efforts, and thus affect which research topics are explored. Some of the research problems outlined in this report require long-term efforts (e.g., achieving trustworthiness from untrustworthy components); expecting short-term payoff may well have the effect of diverting effort from what may be the more critical problems or the most effective solutions.

The need for an increased emphasis in research on improving the trustworthiness of NISs in the long term is not consistent with the stated emphases of current ITO direction. The current director, in a recent interview,[103] articulates three main thrusts for ITO: "Let's get physical" refers to moving beyond the metaphor of a human directly interacting with a computer system to one that places greater attention on the physical world. The second main theme, "Let's get real" suggests an increased focus on real-time applications; the third theme is "Let's get mobile," referring to mobile code research. The committee believes that while some part of this focus is relevant to the research agenda needed to advance the trustworthiness of NISs (e.g., refer to the discussion on mobile code in Chapters 3 and 4), the three themes do not embrace the large majority of the most important topics.

The PCCIP calls for an increase in federal spending on information assurance R&D from an estimated $250 million currently to $500 million in FY 1999 and $1 billion in FY 2004 (PCCIP, 1997). While the study committee certainly endorses the need to increase federal spending on trustworthiness R&D, the study committee has not seen any published rationale for this magnitude of increase. The study committee observes that for the next several years, the population of experts who are qualified to conduct trustworthiness-related research is relatively fixed, because of the lead time needed to recruit and educate new researchers. Thus, increased activity in trustworthiness-related research must be conducted by extant researchers who are already engaged in other work. The study committee believes that a quadrupling of the level of activity in the proposed time frame is therefore unnecessary. Instead, a lower rate of growth that is sustained over a greater number of years would probably be more effective, especially if it is coupled with programs to increase the number of university training programs in trustworthiness.

Findings

1. DARPA funds some research in important areas for NIS trustworthiness. However, other critical topics—including containment, denial-of-service attacks, and cryptographic infrastructures—are not emphasized to the extent that they should be.

2. The use of academics on temporary assignment as program managers has both advantages and disadvantages. This rotation of program managers ensures that state-of-the-art thinking is constantly being in-

---

[103]Interview conducted by Jean E. Smith for the Computing Research Association on March 25, 1998. Data is available online at <http://www.cra.org/CRN/>.

fused into DARPA (assuming that the leading researchers in the field are appointed). On the other hand, such rotation does not promote long-term research agendas because a program manager's tenure typically lasts for only 2 to 3 years.

3. DARPA uses a number of mechanisms to communicate with the research community, which include principal investigator meetings, ISATs, and broad area announcements. These mechanisms seem to be generally effective in facilitating the exchange of ideas between DARPA and the research community.

4. The nature and scope of major DARPA projects funded in the 1970s—in which security work was an integral part of a large, integrated effort—seem to characterize DARPA's greatest successes in the security domain. Not all of these efforts were entirely successful, as is characteristic of high-risk, high-payoff research. Some level of failure is therefore acceptable.

5. The committee believes that increased funding is warranted for both information security research in particular and NIS trustworthiness research in general. The appropriate level of increased funding should be based on a realistic assessment of the size and availability of the current population of researchers in relevant disciplines and on projections of how this population of researchers may be increased in the coming years.

REFERENCES

Anderson, Robert H., Phillip M. Feldman, Scott Gerwehr, Brian Houghton, Richard Mesic, John D. Pinder, and Jeff Rothenberg. 1998. *A "Minimum Essential Information Infrastructure" for U.S. Defense Systems: Meaningful? Feasible? Useful?* Santa Monica, CA: RAND National Defense Research Institute, in press.

Board on Telecommunications and Computer Applications, National Research Council. 1989. *The Growing Vulnerability of the Public Switched Networks.* Washington, DC: National Academy Press.

Boehm, Barry. 1981. *Software Engineering Economics.* Englewood Cliffs, NJ: Prentice-Hall.

Burnham, Blaine W. 1997. *Information System Security Research Program Plan Version 4.0.* Ft. Meade, MD: National Security Agency (R2) INFOSEC Research and Technology Office, January.

Canadian System Security Centre. 1993. *The Canadian Trusted Computer Product Evaluation Criteria Version 3.0e.* Ottawa, Canada: The Communications Security Establishment, Government of Canada, January.

Carpenter, Brian E., and Fred Baker. 1996. *Informational Cryptographic Technology.* RFC 1984. August.

Clausing, Jeri. 1998. "Federal Reserve Official Warns of Year 2000 Bug," *New York Times,* April 29.

Computer Science and Telecommunications Board (CSTB), National Research Council. 1991. *Computers at Risk: Safe Computing in the Information Age.* Washington, DC: National Academy Press.

Computer Science and Telecommunications Board (CSTB), National Research Council. 1994. *Information Technology in the Service Society: A Twenty-First Century Lever.* Washington, DC: National Academy Press.

Computer Science and Telecommunications Board (CSTB), National Research Council. 1996. *Cryptography's Role in Securing the Information Society,* Kenneth W. Dam and Herbert S. Lin, eds. Washington, DC: National Academy Press.

Cummins, Arthur J. 1998. "Investors Are Scratching Their Heads Over Details of Converting to Euros," *Wall Street Journal,* August 14, p. B8.

de Jager, Peter. 1993. "Doomsday 2000," *ComputerWorld,* 27(36):105.

Denning, Dorothy E., and Giovanni M. Sacco. 1981. "Timestamps in Key Distribution Protocols," *Communications of the ACM,* 24(8):533-536.

Diffie, Whitfield, and Susan Landau. 1998. *Privacy on the Line: The Politics of Wiretapping and Encryption.* Cambridge, MA: MIT Press.

Edmondson, Gail, Stephen Baker, and Amy Cortese. 1997. "Silicon Valley on the Rhine," *Business Week,* November 3, p. 162. Available online at <http://www.businessweek.com/1997/>.

Electronic Frontier Foundation. 1998. *Cracking DES: Secrets of Encryption Research, Wiretap Politics & Chip Design.* Sebastopol, CA: O'Reilly and Associates.

Executive Office of the President, Office of Science and Technology Policy. 1997. *Cybernation: The American Infrastructure in the Information Age, A Technical Primer on Risks and Reliability.* Washington, DC: Executive Office of the President.

Gertz, Bill. 1998. "Infowar Game Shut Down U.S. Power Grid, Disabled Pacific Command," *Washington Times,* April 17, p. A1.

Harreld, Heather. 1997. "Group Says Few Fed Sites Protect Privacy: Lack of Policies and Mechanisms Puts Web Visitors at Risk," *Federal Computer Week,* September 1, p. 10.

Hellman, Martin E. 1979. "DES Will Be Totally Insecure Within Ten Years," *IEEE Spectrum,* 32(7).

Lardner, Richard. 1998. "The Secret's Out," *Government Executive,* August. Available online at <http://www.governmentexecutive.com/features/0898s2.htm>.

Lemos, Robert. 1998. "Lloyds to Offer Firms Insurance Against Hackers," *ZDNN,* April 23. Available online at <http://www.zdnet.com/zdnn/content/zdnn/0423/309664.htm>.

Mackenzie, Donald, and Garrel Pottinger. 1997. "Mathematics, Technology, and Trust: Formal Verification, Computer Security, and the U.S. Military," *IEEE Annals of the History of Computing,* 19(3):41-59.

Masters, Brooke A. 1998. "Laptop Thefts Growing: Businesses Losing Computers, Secrets," *Washington Post,* March 30, p. B1.

Mayfield, William T., Ron S. Ross, Stephen R. Welke, and Bill R. Brykczynski. 1997. *Commercial Perspectives on Information Assurance Research.* Alexandria, VA: Institute for Defense Analyses, October.

Meissner, P. 1976. *Report of the Workshop on Estimation of Significant Advances in Computer Technology.* Washington, DC: National Bureau of Standards, December.

Needham, R.M., and Michael D. Schroeder. 1978. "Using Encryption for Authentication in Large Networks of Computers," *Communications of the ACM,* 21(12):993-999.

Needham, R.M., and Michael D. Schroeder. 1987. "Authentication Revisited," *Operating Systems Review,* 21(1):1.

Neumann, Peter, G. 1990. "Rainbows and Arrows: How the Security Criteria Address Computer Misuse." pp. 414-422 in *Proceedings of the Thirteenth National Computer Security Conference.* Washington, DC: NIST/NCSC.

Noll, Roger G. 1996. *Reforming Risk Regulation.* Washington, DC: Brookings Institution, April.

Office of the President. 1997. *A Framework for Global Electronic Commerce.* Washington, DC: The White House, July 1.

President's Commission on Critical Infrastructure Protection (PCCIP). 1997. *Critical Foundations: Protecting America's Infrastructures.* Washington, DC: PCCIP, October.

Senior Officials Group. 1991. *Information Technology Security Evaluation Criteria.* London: European Community Information Systems Security, Department of Trade and Industry.

U.S. Department of Defense (DOD). 1985. *Trusted Computer System Evaluation Criteria,* Department of Defense 5200.28-STD, the "Orange Book." Ft. Meade, MD: National Computer Security Center, December.

Ware, Willis, H. 1995. "A Retrospective of the Criteria Movement," pp. 582-588 in *Proceedings of the Eighteenth National Information Systems Security Conference.* Baltimore, MD: National Institute of Standards and Technology/National Computer Security Center.

Wiener, Michael J. 1994. "Efficient DES Key Search," paper presented at the Rump Session of Crypto '93, School of Computer Science, Carleton University, Ottawa, Ontario, Canada, May.

Wilson, Janet. 1998. "The IETF: Laying the Net's Asphalt," *Computer,* 31(8):116-117.

7

Conclusions and Research Recommendations

The vulnerability of our nation's critical infrastructures is attracting considerable attention. Presidential Decision Directive 63, issued in May 1998, called for a national effort to ensure the security of the nation's critical infrastructures for communication, finance, energy distribution, and transportation. These infrastructures all exhibit a growing dependence on networked information systems (NISs) that are not sufficiently trustworthy, and that dependence is a source of vulnerability to the infrastructures and the nation. Today's NISs are too often unable to tolerate environmental disturbances, human user and operator errors, and attacks by hostile parties. Design and implementation errors mean that satisfactory operation would not be guaranteed even under ideal circumstances.

There is a gap between the state of the art and the state of the practice. More-trustworthy NISs could be built and deployed today. Why are these solutions not being implemented? The answer lies in the workings of the market, in existing federal policies regarding cryptography, in ignorance about the real costs of trustworthiness (and of not having trustworthiness) to consumers and producers, and in the difficulty of measuring trustworthiness.

There is also a gap between the needs and expectations of the public (along with parts of government) and the extant science and technology base for building trustworthy NISs. Trustworthiness is a multidimensional property of an entire system, and going beyond what is known today will require research breakthroughs. Methods to strengthen one dimension can compromise another; building trustworthy components does not suffice, for the interconnections and interactions of components play a significant role in NIS trustworthiness.

Security is certainly important (with some data indicating that the number of attacks is growing exponentially and anecdotal evidence suggesting that attackers are becoming more sophisticated every day), but it is not all that is important. The substantial commercial off-the-shelf (COTS) makeup of an NIS, the use of extensible components, the expectation of growth by accretion, and the likely absence of centralized control, trust, or authority demand a new approach to security: risk mitigation rather than risk avoidance, technologies to hinder attacks rather than prevent them outright, add-on technologies and defense in depth, and relocation of vulnerabilities rather than their elimination. But other aspects of trustworthiness also demand progress and also will require new thinking, because the networked environment and the scale of an NIS impose novel constraints, enable new types of solutions, and change engineering tradeoffs.

Other studies related to critical infrastructures have successfully raised public awareness and advocated action. This study focuses on describing and analyzing the technical problems and how they might be solved through research, thereby providing some direction for that action. The detailed research agenda presented in the body of this report was derived by surveying the state of the art, current practice, and technological trends with respect to computer networking and software. A summary of the committee's findings, conclusions, and recommendations follows.

PROTECTING THE EVOLVING PUBLIC TELEPHONE NETWORK AND THE INTERNET

The public telephone network is increasingly dependent on software and databases that constitute new points of vulnerability. Business decisions are also creating new points of vulnerability. Protective measures need to be developed and implemented.

The public telephone network (PTN) is evolving. Value-added services (e.g., call forwarding) rely on call-translation databases and adjunct processors, which introduce new points of vulnerability. Some of the new services are themselves vulnerable. For example, caller ID is increasingly used by PTN customers to provide authenticated information, but the underlying telephone network is unable to provide this information with a high assurance of authenticity.

Management of the PTN is evolving as well. Technical and market forces have led to reductions in reserve capacity and the number of geographically diverse redundant routings. Failure of a single link can now have serious repercussions. Cross-connects and multiplexors, which are used to route calls, are becoming dependent on complex software running in operations support systems (OSSs). In addition to the intrinsic vulnerabilities associated with any complex software, information about OSSs is becoming less proprietary owing to deregulation. Information about controlling the OSSs will thus become more widespread, and the vulnerabilities of the OSSs will become known to larger numbers of attackers. Similarly, the Signaling System 7 (SS7) network used to manage central office switches was designed for a small, closed community of telephone companies; with deregulation will come increased opportunities for insider attacks. Telephone companies are also increasingly sharing facilities and technology with each other and the Internet, thereby creating yet another point of new vulnerability. Internet telephony is likely to cause the PTN to become more vulnerable, because Internet-based networks use the same channels for both user data transmission and network management and because the end points on the Internet are much more subject to failure than those of the PTN.

Attacks on the telephone network have, for the most part, been directed at perpetrating billing fraud. The frequency of those attacks is increasing, and the potential for more disruptive attacks, with harassment and eavesdropping as goals, is growing. Thus, protective measures are needed. Better protection is needed for the many number-translation and other databases used in the PTN. Telephone companies need to enhance the firewalls that connect their OSSs to the Internet and to enhance the physical security of their facilities.

In some respects, the Internet is becoming more secure as its protocols are improved and as security measures are more widely deployed at higher levels of the protocol stack. However, the increasing complexity of the Internet's infrastructure contributes to its increasing vulnerability. The end points (hosts) of the Internet continue to be vulnerable. As a consequence, the Internet is ready for some business use, but abandoning the PTN for the Internet would not be prudent for most.

The Internet is too susceptible to attacks and outages to be a viable basis for controlling critical infrastructures. Existing technologies could be deployed to improve the trustworthiness of the Internet, although many questions about what measures would suffice do not currently have answers because good basic data (e.g., on Internet outages) is scant.

The operation of the Internet today depends on routing and name-to-address translation services. The list of critical services will likely expand to include directory services and public-key certificate servers. Analogous to the PTN, these services, because they depend on databases, constitute points of vulnerability. New countermeasures for name-server attacks are thus needed. They must work well in large-scale, heterogeneous environments. Cryptographic mechanisms to secure the name service do exist; however, deployment to date has been limited.

Cryptography, while not in itself sufficient, is essential to the protection of both the Internet and its end points. Wider deployment of cryptography is needed. Authentication-only algorithms are largely free from export and usage restrictions, and they could go a long way toward helping.

There is a tension between the capabilities and vulnerabilities of routing protocols. The sharing of routing information facilitates route optimization, but such cooperation also increases the risk that malicious or malfunctioning routers can compromise routing. In any event, current Internet routing algorithms are inadequate because they do not scale well, they require central processing unit (CPU)-intensive calculations, and they cannot implement diverse or flexible policies. Furthermore, no effective means exist to secure routing protocols, especially on backbone routers. Research in these areas is urgently needed.

Networks formed by interconnecting extant independent subnetworks present unique challenges for controlling congestion (because local provider optimizations may not lead to good overall behavior) and for implementing security (because trust relationships between network components are not homogeneous). A better understanding is needed of the Internet's current traffic profile and how it will evolve. In addition, fundamental research is needed into mechanisms for managing congestion in the Internet, especially in a way that does not conflict with network security mechanisms like encryption. Attacks that result in denial of service are increasingly common, and little is known about defending against them.

Operational errors represent a major source of outages for the PTN and the Internet. Some of these errors could be prevented by implementing known techniques, whereas others require research to develop preventative measures.

Some errors could be prevented through improved operator training and contingency planning. However, the scale and complexity of both the PTN and the Internet (and NISs in general) create the need for tools and systems to improve an operator's understanding of a system's state and the means by which the system can be controlled. For example, research is needed into ways to meaningfully portray and display the state of a large, complex network to a human operator. Research and development are needed to develop conceptual models that will allow human operators to grasp the state of a network and to understand the consequences of actions that the operator can take. Improved routing-management tools are needed for the Internet, because they will free human operators from an activity that is error prone.

MEETING THE URGENT NEED FOR SOFTWARE THAT IMPROVES TRUSTWORTHINESS

The design of trustworthy networked information systems presents profound challenges for system architecture and project planning. Little is understood, and this lack of understanding ultimately compromises trustworthiness.

System-level trustworthiness requirements are typically first characterized informally. The transformation of these informal notions into precise requirements that can be imposed on individual system components is difficult and often beyond the current state of the art. Whereas a large software system such as an NIS cannot be developed defect free, it is possible to improve the trustworthiness of such a system by anticipating and targeting vulnerabilities. But to determine, analyze, and, most importantly, prioritize these vulnerabilities requires a good understanding for how subsystems interact with each other and with the other elements of the larger system—obtaining such an understanding is not possible today. The use of some systematic development processes seems to contribute to the quality of NISs. Project management, a long-standing challenge in software development, is especially problematic when building NISs because of the large and complex nature of such systems and because of the continual software changes. The challenges of software engineering, which have been formidable ones for so many years, are even more urgent in the context of networked information systems.

To develop an NIS, subsystems must be integrated, but little is known about doing this. In recent years, academic researchers have directed their focus away from large-scale integration problems; this trend must be reversed.

NISs pose new challenges for integration because of their distributed nature and the uncontrollability of most large networks. Thus, testing subsets of a system cannot adequately establish confidence in an entire NIS, especially when some of the subsystems are uncontrollable or unobservable as is likely in an NIS that has evolved to encompass legacy software. In addition, NISs are generally developed and deployed incrementally. Techniques to compose subsystems in ways that contribute directly to trustworthiness are therefore needed.

There exists a widening gap between the needs of software practitioners and the problems that are being attacked by the academic research community. In most academic computer science research today, researchers are not confronting problems related to large-scale integration and students do not develop the skills or intuition necessary for developing software that not only works but also works in the context of software written by others. A renewed emphasis on large-scale development efforts is called for.

It is clear that networked information systems will include COTS components into the foreseeable future. However, the relationship between the use of COTS components and NIS trustworthiness is unclear. Greater attention must be directed toward improving our understanding of this relationship.

COTS software offers both advantages and disadvantages to an NIS developer. COTS components can be less expensive, have greater functionality, and be better engineered and tested than is feasible for customized components. Yet, the use of COTS products could make developers dependent on outside vendors for the design and enhancement of important components. Also, specifications of COTS components tend to be incomplete and to compel user discovery of features by experimentation. COTS software originally evolved in a stand-alone environment where trustworthiness was not a primary concern. That heritage remains visible. Moreover, market pressures limit the time that can be spent on testing before releasing a piece of COTS software. The market also tends to emphasize features that add complexity but are useful only for a minority of applications.

Although there are accepted processes for component design and implementation, the novel characteristics of NISs raise questions about the utility of these processes. Modern programming languages include features that promote trustworthiness, and the potential may exist for further gains from research.

The performance needs of NISs can be inconsistent with modular design, and this limits the applicability of various processes and tools. It is difficult to devise component-level acceptance tests that fully capture the intent of systems-level requirements statements. This is particularly true for nonfunctional and user-interface requirements. Basing the development of an NIS on libraries of reusable, trusted components and using those components in critical areas of the system can provide a cost-effective way for implementing component-level dimensions of trustworthiness. Commercial software that includes reusable components or infrastructure is now available, but it is too early to know how successful it will be.

As a practical matter, the use of higher-level languages increases trustworthiness to a degree that outweighs any risks, although there is inadequate experimental evidence to justify the utility of any specific programming language or language feature with respect to improving trustworthiness. Modern programming languages include features, such as compile-time checks and support for modularity and component integration, that promote trustworthiness. The potential may exist for further gains by developing even more-expressive type systems and other compile-time analysis techniques.

> **Formal methods are being used with success in commercial and industrial settings for hardware development and requirements analysis and with some success for software development. Increased support for both fundamental research and demonstration exercises is warranted.**

Formal methods should be regarded as an important piece of technology for eliminating design errors in hardware and software; as such, they deserve increased attention. Formal methods are particularly well suited for identifying errors that only become apparent in scenarios not likely to be tested or testable. Therefore, formal methods could be viewed as a technology complementary to testing. Research directed at the improved integration of testing and formal methods is likely to have payoffs for increasing assurance in trustworthy NISs.

REINVENTING SECURITY FOR COMPUTERS
AND COMMUNICATIONS

Security research during the past few decades has been based on formal policy models that focus on protecting information from unauthorized access by specifying which users should have access to data or other system objects. It is time to challenge this paradigm of "absolute security" and move toward a model built on three axioms of insecurity: insecurity exists; insecurity cannot be destroyed; and insecurity can be moved around.

Formal policy models of the past few decades presuppose that security policies are static and have precise and succinct descriptions. These formal policy models cannot represent the effects of some malicious or erroneous software, nor can they completely address denial-of-service attacks. Finally, these formal policy models cannot account for defensive measures, such as virus scan software or firewalls—mechanisms that should not work or be needed in theory but, in practice, hinder attacks.

The complex and distributed nature of NISs, with their numerous subsystems that typically have their own access controls, raises the question of whether a complete formal security model could ever be specified. Even if such a model could be specified, demonstrating the correspondence between an NIS and that formal model is not likely to be feasible. An alternative to this "absolute security" philosophy is to identify the vulnerabilities in an NIS and make design changes to reposition the vulnerabilities in light of the threats being anticipated. Further research is needed to determine the feasibility of this new approach to the problem.

Cryptographic authentication and the use of hardware tokens are promising avenues for implementing authentication.

Network-based authentication technology is not amenable to high-assurance implementations. Cryptographic authentication represents a preferred approach to authentication at the granularity that might otherwise be provided by network authentication. Needs will arise for new cryptographic authentication protocols (e.g., for practical multicast communication authentication). Faster encryption and authentication/integrity algorithms will be required to keep pace with rapidly increasing communication speeds. Further research into techniques and tools should be encouraged.

The use of hardware tokens holds great promise for implementing authentication. Cost will be addressed by the inexorable advance of digital hardware technology. But interface commonality issues will somehow have to be overcome. The use of personal identification numbers (PINs) to enable hardware tokens is a source of vulnerability that the use of biometrics might address. When tokens are being used to digitally sign data, then an interface should be provided so that a user can know what is being signed. Biometric authentication technologies have limitations when employed in network contexts, because the compromise of the digital version of someone's biometric data could allow an attacker to impersonate a legitimate user over the network.

> **Obstacles exist to more widespread deployment of key-management technology and there has been little experience with public-key infrastructures, especially large-scale ones.**

There are many aspects of public-key infrastructure (PKI) technology that merit further research. Issues related to the timely notification of revocation, recovery from compromise of certificate authority private keys, and name-space management require attention. Most applications that make use of certificates have poor certificate-management interfaces for users and system administrators. Toolkits for certificate processing could be developed. There has been little experience with large-scale deployment of key management technologies. Thus, the scale and nature of the difficulties associated with deploying this important technology is an unknown at this time.

> **Because NISs are distributed systems, network access control mechanisms play a central role in the security of NISs. Virtual private networks and firewalls have proven to be promising technologies and deserve greater attention in the future.**

Virtual private network (VPN) technology is quite promising, although proprietary protocols and simplistic key-management schemes in most products have, to date, prevented adoption of VPNs in larger-scale settings. The deployment of IPsec can eliminate these impediments, facilitating VPN deployment throughout the Internet. Much work remains to further facilitate wholesale and flexible VPN deployments. Support for dynamic location of security gateways, accommodation of complex network topologies, negotiation of traffic security policies across administratively independent domains, and support for multicast communication are other topics deserving additional work. Also, better interfaces for VPN management will be critical for avoiding vulnerabilities introduced by operational errors.

Firewalls, despite their limitations, will persist into the foreseeable future as a key defense mechanism. As support for VPNs is added, firewall enhancements will have to be developed for the support of sophisticated security management protocols, negotiation of traffic security policies across administratively independent domains, and management tools. The development of increasingly sophisticated network-wide applications will create a need for application-layer firewalls and a better understanding of how to define and enforce useful traffic policies at this level. Guards can be thought of as special cases of firewalls, typically focused at the application layer.

Foreign code is increasingly being used in NISs. However, NIS trustworthiness will deteriorate unless effective security mechanisms are developed and implemented to defend against attacks by foreign code.

Authenticating the author or provider of foreign code has not and likely will not prove effective for protecting against hostile foreign code. Users are unwilling and/or unable to use the source of a piece of foreign code as a basis for denying or allowing execution. Revocation of certificates is necessary should a provider be compromised, but revocation is currently not supported by the Internet, a fact that limits the scale over which the approach can be deployed.

Access control features in commercially successful operating systems are not adequate for supporting fine-grained access control (FGAC). FGAC mechanisms are needed that do not significantly affect performance. Operating system implementations of FGAC would help support the construction of systems that obey the principle of least privilege, which holds that users be accorded the minimum access that is needed to accomplish a task.

FGAC also has the potential to provide a means for supporting foreign code—an interpreter that implements FGAC is used to provide a rich access control model within which the foreign code is confined. That, in turn, could be an effective defense against a variety of attacks that might be delivered using foreign code or application programs. However, it is essential that users and administrators can correctly configure systems with FGAC structures, and that has not yet been demonstrated. (Considerably simpler access control models today are often misunderstood and misused.) Enforcing application security is increasingly likely to be a shared responsibility between the application and the lower levels of a system. Research is needed to determine how to partition this responsibility and which mechanisms are best implemented at what level. In addition, more needs to be known about the assurance limitations associated with providing application-layer security when employing a COTS operating system that offers minimum assurance.

A variety of opportunities seem to exist to leverage programming language research in implementing system security. Software fault isolation and proof-carrying code illustrate the application of programming-language analysis techniques to security policy enforcement. But these techniques are new, and their ultimate efficacy is not yet understood.

Defending against denial-of-service attacks is often critical for the security of an NIS, because availability is often an important system property. Research in this area is urgently needed to identify general schemes for defending against such attacks.

No general mechanisms or systematic design methods exist for defending against denial-of-service attacks. For example, each request for service may appear legitimate in itself, but the aggregate number of requests in a short time period that are focused on a specific subsystem can overwhelm that subsystem because the act of checking a request for legitimacy consumes resources.

BUILDING TRUSTWORTHY SYSTEMS FROM UNTRUSTWORTHY COMPONENTS

Improved trustworthiness may be achieved by the careful organization of untrustworthy components. There are a number of promising ideas, but few have been vigorously pursued. "Trustworthiness from untrustworthy components" is a research area that deserves greater attention.

Replication and diversity can be employed to build systems that amplify the trustworthiness of their components, and indeed, there are successful commercial products (e.g., fault-tolerant computers) in the marketplace that do exactly this. However, the potential and limits of this approach are not understood. For example, research is needed to determine the ways in which diversity can be added to a set of replicas, thereby improving trustworthiness.

Trustworthiness functionality could reside in varying parts of an NIS. Little is known about the advantages and disadvantages of the different architectural possibilities, so an analysis of existing NISs would prove instructive. One architecture that has been suggested is based on the idea of a core minimum functionality—the minimum essential information infrastructure (MEII). But building an MEII for the nation would be a misguided initiative, because it presumes that the important "core minimum functionality" could be specifically defined, and that is unlikely to be the case.

Monitoring and detection can be employed to build systems that enhance the trustworthiness of their components. But limitations in system-monitoring technology and in technology to recognize events, like attacks and failures, impose fundamental limits on the use of monitoring and detection for implementing trustworthiness. For example, the limits and coverage of the various approaches to intruder and anomaly detection are not well understood.

A number of other promising research areas merit investigation. For example, systems could be designed to respond to an attack or failure by reducing their functionality in a controlled, graceful manner. And a variety of research directions involving new types of algorithms—self-stabilization, emergent behavior, biological metaphors—may be useful in defining systems that are trustworthy. These new research directions are highly speculative. Thus, they are plausible topics for longer-range research.

SOCIAL AND ECONOMIC FACTORS THAT INHIBIT THE DEPLOYMENT OF TRUSTWORTHY TECHNOLOGY

Imperfect information creates a disincentive to invest in trustworthiness for both consumers and producers, leading to a market failure. Initiatives to mitigate this problem are needed.

Decision making today about trustworthy systems occurs within the context of imperfect information. That increases the level of uncertainty regarding the benefits of trustworthiness initiatives, thereby serving as a disincentive to invest in trustworthiness and distorting the market for trustworthiness. As a result, consumers prefer to purchase greater functionality rather than to invest in improved trustworthiness. Products addressing problems that have been experienced by consumers or that are perceived to address well-known or highly visible problems have been best received.

The absence of standard metrics or a recognized organization to conduct assessments for trustworthiness is an important contributing factor to the imperfect information problem. Useful metrics for the security dimension of trustworthiness are unlikely to be developed because the corresponding formal model for any particular metric would necessarily be incomplete. Therefore, useful aggregate metrics for trustworthiness are unlikely to be developed.

Standards may mitigate some of the difficulties that arise from imperfect information because standards can simplify the decision-making process for the purchasers and producers of trustworthiness by narrowing the field of choices. The development and evolution of a standard attract scrutiny that will work toward reducing the number of remaining design flaws and thereby promote trustworthiness. At the same time, the exist-ence of standards promotes the wide availability of detailed technical information about a particular technology, and therefore serves as a basis for assessing where vulnerabilities remain. Standards that facilitate interoperability increase the likelihood that successful attacks in one sys-tem might prove effective in others. The net relationship between stan-dards and trustworthiness is therefore indeterminate. Heterogeneity tends to cause NISs to be more vulnerable because the scrutiny of experts may not take place, but the negative effects that pertain to standards are also applicable for homogeneity.

Security criteria may also improve the level of information available to both consumers and producers of components. The Common Criteria may or may not prove useful for this purpose. In any case, it is doubtful that any criteria can keep pace with the evolving threats. However, even if there are a sufficient number of security-evaluated components, there is, at present, little or no rigorous methodology for assessing the security of NISs assembled from such evaluated components.

Consumer and producer costs for trustworthiness are difficult to assess. An improved understanding, better models, and more and accurate data are needed.

Trustworthiness typically reflects systemwide characteristics of an NIS, so trustworthiness costs are often difficult to allocate to specific users or uses. Such costs are therefore often allocated to central units. Trust-worthiness also involves costs that are difficult to quantify; one example is the "hassle factor," which captures the fact that trustworthy systems tend to be more cumbersome to use.

It is difficult to distinguish trustworthiness costs from other direct product costs and overhead costs. Not surprisingly, there is a paucity of data, and what little data does exist has questionable accuracy. The pro-duction costs associated with integration and testing represent a substan-tial proportion of total producer costs for improving trustworthiness, and it is often difficult to separate "trustworthiness" costs from other costs. Time-to-market considerations discourage the inclusion of trustworthi-ness features and encourage the postponement of trustworthiness to later stages of the product life cycle.

As a truly multidimensional concept, trustworthiness is depen-dent on all of its dimensions. However, in some sense, the problems of security are more challenging and therefore deserve special attention.

Security risks are more difficult to specify and manage than those that arise from safety or reliability concerns. There is usually an absence of malice with respect to safety and reliability risks as well as tangible and often severe consequences that can be easily articulated; these considerations facilitate the assessment of risk and measurement of consequences for safety- and reliability-related risks, in contrast to security. A precise and testable definition is required to assess whether a standard has been fulfilled or not. Such definitions may often be articulated for some trustworthiness dimensions (such as reliability) but are often difficult to articulate for security.

Export control and key-escrow policy concerns inhibit the widespread deployment of cryptography, but there are other important inhibitory factors that deserve increased attention and action.

The public policy controversy surrounding export controls and key recovery does indeed inhibit the widespread deployment of cryptography. However, cryptography is not more widely deployed for other reasons, which include reduced convenience and usability, possible sacrifice of interoperability, increased computational and communications requirements, lack of a national or international key infrastructure, restrictions resulting from patents, and the fact that most information is already secure enough relative to its value to an unauthorized party.

IMPLEMENTING TRUSTWORTHINESS
RESEARCH AND DEVELOPMENT

In its necessary efforts to pursue partnerships, the federal government also needs to work to develop trust in its relationships with the private sector, with some emphasis on U.S.-based firms.

The federal government has less influence on vendors than in the past, so cooperative arrangements are increasingly necessary. The rise of the marketplace for computing and communications products includes new and/or start-up firms that tend to be focused on marketplace demands generally, and not on the needs of the federal government. Although the federal government is the largest single customer of computing and communications products and services, its relative market share, and therefore its market power, have declined. Building trust between the private and public sectors is essential to achieving increased cooperation in efforts to improve NIS trustworthiness, because the cryptography policy debates concerning export controls and key escrow have created suspicion within the private sector about government intent and plans. As trustworthiness-related products are increasingly provided by non-U.S. companies, the influence of foreign firms and governments on the trustworthiness marketplace is a new concern and suggests that some priority should be placed on partnerships with U.S. firms.

The NSA R2 organization must increase its efforts devoted to outreach and recruitment and retention issues.

The National Security Agency's R2 organization has initiated several outreach efforts, but these have not significantly broadened the community of researchers that work with R2. Effective outreach efforts are those that are designed to be compatible with the interests, perspectives, and realities of potential partners (e.g., acknowledgment of the dominance of COTS technology).

Inadequate incentives currently exist within R2 to attract and retain highly skilled researchers. Improved incentives might be financial (e.g., different salary scale) and/or nonfinancial (e.g., special recognition, greater public visibility) in nature. R2 faces formidable challenges in the recruitment and retention of the very best researchers. The rotation of R2 researchers with researchers in industry and academia would help to broaden and invigorate the R2 program. Such rotation would be most effective if it involved institutions that have large numbers of top researchers. As currently constituted, the R2 university research program emphasizes relatively short-term and small projects, and it does not attract the interest of the best industrial and academic researchers and institutions.

DARPA is generally effective in its interactions with the research community, but DARPA needs to increase its focus on information security and NIS trustworthiness research, especially with regard to long-term research efforts.

The nature and scope of major Defense Advanced Research Projects Agency (DARPA) projects that were funded in the 1970s—where security work was an integral part of a large, integrated effort—seem to characterize DARPA's greatest successes in the security domain. Not all of these efforts were so successful, as is characteristic of high-risk, high-payoff research. DARPA does fund some research today in important areas for NIS trustworthiness. However, other critical topics—as articulated in this study—are not emphasized to the extent that they should be. These topics include containment, denial-of-service attacks, and cryptographic infra-structures.

DARPA uses a number of mechanisms to communicate with the research community, which include principal investigator meetings, information science and technology activities (ISATs), and board area announcements (BAAs). These mechanisms seem to be generally effective in facilitating the exchange of ideas between DARPA and the research community.

The use of academics on temporary assignment as program managers has advantages and disadvantages. This rotation of program managers ensures that state-of-the-art thinking is constantly being infused into DARPA (assuming that the leading researchers in the field are appointed). On the other hand, such rotation does not promote long-term research agendas, because the tenure of a program manager typically is only 2 to 3 years.

An increase in expenditures for research in information security and NIS trustworthiness is warranted.

The committee believes that increased funding is warranted for both information security research in particular and NIS trustworthiness research in general. The appropriate level of increased funding should be based on a realistic assessment of the size and availability of the current population of researchers in relevant disciplines and projections of how this population of researchers may be increased in the coming years.

APPENDIXES

A

Study Committee Biographies

Fred B. Schneider, *Chair*

Fred B. Schneider has been on the faculty of Cornell University's Computer Science Department since 1978. His research concerns concurrent systems, particularly distributed and fault-tolerant ones intended for mission-critical applications. He has worked on formal methods as well as protocols and system architectures for this setting. Most recently, his research has been directed at implementing fault-tolerance and security for mobile processes (so-called agents) that might roam a network.

Dr. Schneider is managing editor of *Distributed Computing*, co-managing editor of the Springer-Verlag texts and monographs in computer science, and a member of the editorial boards for *ACM Computing Surveys, IEEE Transactions on Software Engineering, High Integrity Systems, Information Processing Letters*, and *Annals of Software Engineering*. He is co-author (with D. Gries) of the introductory text, *A Logical Approach to Discrete Math*, and he is author of the monograph, *On Concurrent Programming*. A Fellow of the Association for Computing Machinery and the American Association for the Advancement of Science, Dr. Schneider is also a professor-at-large at the University of Tromso (Norway). He was a member of the 1995 ARPA/ISAT study on defensive information warfare and is a member of Sun Microsystem's Java Security Advisory Council.

Steven M. Bellovin

Steven M. Bellovin received a B.A. degree from Columbia University and an M.S. and Ph.D. in computer science from the University of North Carolina at Chapel Hill. While a graduate student, he helped create netnews; for this, he and the other collaborators were awarded the 1995 USENIX Lifetime Achievement Award. He is a Fellow at AT&T Laboratories, where he does research in networks and security, and why the two do not get along. He is currently focusing on cryptographic protocols and network management. Bellovin is the co-author of the recent book *Firewalls and Internet Security: Repelling the Wily Hacker*, and he is a member of the Internet Architecture Board.

Martha Branstad

Martha Branstad is a computer security researcher and entrepreneur. She was chief operating officer of Trusted Information Systems Inc. (TIS) and president of its Advanced Research and Engineering Division, directing a research program that encompassed security in networked and distributed systems, applications of cryptography, access control and confinement within operating systems, and formulation of security policy and enforcement within dynamically changing systems. Before joining TIS, Dr. Branstad managed the Software Engineering program at the National Science Foundation (NSF), the Software Engineering program at the National Institute of Standards and Technology (NIST), whose program in performance measurement for parallel processing she established, and research groups at the National Security Agency (NSA). She holds a Ph.D. in computer science from Iowa State University.

J. Randall Catoe

J. Randall Catoe is senior vice-president of the Internet Engineering, Solutions, Operations, and Suport Group at Cable and Wireless. Previously, as executive director of engineering, Catoe led the engineering portion of Vinton Cerf's Internet Architecture and Engineering Group for MCI Telecommunications Inc. His responsibilities included design and development of the internetMCI backbone, including applications, security infrastructure, and the operation of Web-hosting services. Before joining MCI in 1994, Mr. Catoe served as the team leader and architect for design of data handling and control systems for NASA's X-Ray Timing Explorer spacecraft. In previous positions, Mr. Catoe has served as a vice-president of engineering for The Wollongong Group, for which he oversaw the development of security features in the company's TCP/IP products.

Earlier in his career, Mr. Catoe led a team of systems and network engineers in the design and development of MCImail while he was employed at Digital Equipment Corporation.

Stephen D. Crocker

Stephen D. Crocker is an Internet researcher and entrepreneur. He was a founder of CyberCash Inc. and served as its chief technology officer. He was previously a vice-president for Trusted Information Systems, a senior researcher at the University of Southern California Information Sciences Institute, and a program manager in the Advanced Research Projects Agency (ARPA). Dr. Crocker was part of the team that developed the original protocols for the ARPANET, which paved the way for today's Internet. He served as the area director for security on the Internet Engineering Task Force for 4 years and was a member of the Internet Architecture Board for 2 years. Dr. Crocker holds a Ph.D. in computer science from the University of California at Los Angeles.

Charlie Kaufman

Charlie Kaufman works for Iris Associates Inc. (a wholly owned subsidiary of Lotus Development, which is in turn a wholly owned subsidiary of IBM) as security architect for Lotus Notes. Previously, he was network security architect for Digital Equipment Corporation, and before that he worked for Computer Corporation of America on a research project designing highly survivable distributed databases. He is a co-author of *Network Security: Private Communication in a Public World*, published by Prentice-Hall. He chairs the Internet Engineering Task Force (IETF) Web Transaction Security Working Group, and he wrote Internet RFC 1507: "DASS—Distributed Authentication Security Service." He holds more than 20 patents in the fields of computer networking and computer security.

Stephen T. Kent

Stephen T. Kent is chief scientist for information security at BBN Corporation and chief technical officer for CyberTrust Solutions, both part of GTE Internetworking. Dr. Kent has been engaged in network security research and development activities at BBN for 20 years. His work includes the design and development of user authentication and access control systems, network and transport layer and electronic messaging security protocols, and a multilevel secure directory system. His most recent projects include public-key certification systems, mobile IP security, and securing routing systems against denial-of-service attacks. Dr. Kent served on the Internet Architecture Board, the oversight body for the Internet standards process, from 1983 to 1994, and chaired the Privacy and Security Research Group of the Internet Research Task Force from 1985 to 1998. In the IETF, he chaired the PEM working group and is currently co-chair of the Public Key Infrastructure working group. He served on several computer and network security study committees for the National Research Council, the Office of Technology Assessment, and other government agencies. He was a charter member of the board of directors of the International Association for Cryptologic Research, served on the presidential SKIPJACK review panel for the Escrowed Encryption System, and chaired the ACM Special Panel on Cryptography and Public Policy and the Technical Advisory Committee to develop a FIPS for key recovery.

Dr. Kent is the author of two book chapters and numerous technical papers on network security and has served as a referee, panelist, and session chair for a number of conferences. He has lectured on the topic of network security on behalf of government agencies, universities, and private companies worldwide. Dr. Kent received the B.S. degree in mathematics from Loyola University of New Orleans, and the S.M., E.E., and Ph.D. degrees in computer science from the Massachusetts Institute of Technology. He is a member of the Internet Society, a Fellow of the ACM, and a member of Sigma Xi.

John C. Knight

John C. Knight received a B.Sc. (mathematics) from the Imperial College of Science and Technology, London, England. He also received a Ph.D. (computer science) from the University of Newcastle upon Tyne, Newcastle upon Tyne, England. From 1974 to 1981 he was employed with NASA's Langley Research Center. He has been a member of the Computer Science Department at the University of Virginia since 1981. From 1987 to 1989 Dr. Knight was on leave from the University of Virginia at the Software Productivity Consortium. Dr. Knight's research interests lie in software engineering for high-dependability applications. The specific topic areas include formal specification, specification-capture processes, software architectures—especially involving protection shells, verification including rigorous inspections and testing, and the exploitation of reuse for dependability.

Steven McGeady

Steven McGeady is vice-president of Intel Corporation's Content Group and director of Intel's Health Technology Initiative. Upon joining Intel in 1985, Mr. McGeady led the software development efforts for Intel's i960 32-bit embedded microprocessor. In 1991, he joined Intel's Senior Vice-President Ron Whittier in forming the Intel Architecture Labs. As vice-president and director of Multimedia Software, Mr. McGeady led the development of Intel's Indeo video compression technology, key components of the ProShare videoconferencing products, Intel's and Turner Broadcasting's CNN@Work networked video delivery system, the Intercast technology for broadcast Web pages, Intel's Common Data Security Architecture, and numerous other advanced technology products.

As vice-president and director of Internet technology, Mr. McGeady led Intel's research into the Internet, the World Wide Web, and Java, intelligent information filtering and autonomous agents, and new classes of human-computer interface. He spent the 1996-1997 academic year as a visiting scientist at the Massachusetts Institute of Technology's Media Lab, researching aspects of emergent behavior in networks of personal computers. During that time his article, titled "The Digital Reformation," was published in the fall 1996 *Harvard Journal of Law and Technology*. Mr. McGeady chairs Intel's Research Council committees for Applications, Interface and Media, charged with funding and oversight of long-range academic research. Mr. McGeady studied physics and philosophy at Reed College in Portland, Oregon, where he became an early developer of the UNIX operating system, compilers, and graphics and networking software.

Ruth R. Nelson

Ruth R. Nelson has been involved in network and computer security research since 1975. Most of her career has been at GTE Government Systems, with shorter stays at BBN and Digital. In 1993, she left GTE and started Information System Security, a research and consulting company. She was an undergraduate and graduate student in pure mathematics at the Massachusetts Institute of Technology.

In 1989, and again in 1992, Ms. Nelson was an invited participant in NSA's Network Security Working Group, which was formed to examine the agency's INFOSEC approach and recommend technical and organizational improvements. She was one of the invited attendees at the conference on Network Evaluation Criteria in 1984 and contributed her comments on several drafts of the Trusted Network Interpretation. She has given several colloquia on computer and network security at the University of Massachusetts in Boston and has assisted on a project to develop a graduate-level course in network security. She has developed and refined the concept of Mutual Suspicion, which includes firewalls, local resource control, and the importance of considering security as risk management.

Allan M. Schiffman

Allan M. Schiffman is chief technologist of SPYRUS and was founder of its Terisa Systems subsidiary, which merged with SPYRUS in mid-1997. Mr. Schiffman has more than 25 years of diverse experience in computing, heading major projects in transportation system modeling, messaging systems, software development tools, programming language environments, and network protocols. He is a regular speaker at industry and academic conferences, frequently gives lectures and tutorials on security, and holds several patents. He has been a member of the World Wide Web Consortium's Security Advisory Board and Netscape's Security Advisory Board and frequently consults on the design of communications security systems for electronic commerce. In 1996, he was part of the team that designed the SET payment card protocol commissioned by MasterCard and Visa.

Before the formation of Terisa Systems, Mr. Schiffman held the position of chief technical officer at Enterprise Integration Technologies (EIT), where he was co-designer of the well-known Secure Hypertext Transfer Protocol (S-HTTP). Also at EIT, Mr. Schiffman served as principal architect of CommerceNet, an industry consortium dedicated to promoting Internet commerce. Before joining EIT, Mr. Schiffman was the vice-president of technical strategy at ParcPlace Systems, where he led the development of the company's well-known Objectworks/Smalltalk product family. He has held other senior positions at Schlumberger Research and the Fairchild Laboratory for AI Research. He received his M.S. in computer science from Stanford University.

George A. Spix

As chief architect in the Consumer Products Division, George A. Spix is responsible for Microsoft Corporation's end-to-end solutions for consumer appliances and public networks. He also serves on the board of the Digital Audio Video Council (DAVIC), the Information Infrastructure Standards Panel (IISP), and the Commerce Department's Computer Systems' Security and Privacy Advisory Board (CSSPAB). Mr. Spix joined Microsoft in 1993 as the director of multimedia document architecture. He was responsible for the Advanced Consumer Technology Division's multimedia tools efforts and early third-party tools acquisitions. Later, as director of infrastructure and services, he headed the team that created the services and networks required for early interactive television trials.

Before joining Microsoft, Spix spent five years as director of systems and software development at Supercomputer Systems Inc. in Eau Claire, Wisconsin. He was responsible for the delivery of systems and software products for a next-generation supercomputer. Before that, he worked for Cray Research Inc. in Chippewa Falls, Wisconsin, as a chief engineer, responsible for systems and software development for the XMP and YMP line of supercomputers. A Purdue University electrical engineering graduate, Mr. Spix was drawn to supercomputers, their systems, and their applications while at Los Alamos National Laboratory.

Doug Tygar

Doug Tygar is a professor at the University of California at Berkeley, with a joint appointment in the Department of Electrical Engineering and Computer Science and the School of Information Management and Systems. Before joining Berkeley, he served on the faculty of the Computer Science Department of Carnegie Mellon University.

Dr. Tygar's interests are in electronic commerce and computer security. He is actively working on several systems projects touching on subjects including electronic auction technology, special electronic commerce protocols for cryptographic postal indicia to prevent forgery, secure remote execution, and user interfaces for computer security. His previous systems work includes NetBill (a system for low-cost online microtransactions), CAE tools (developed for Valid Logic Systems, now part of Cadence), Dyad (a system for using secure coprocessors), ITOSS (Integrated Toolkit for Operating System Security), Miro (a visual language for file system security specification), and Strongbox (a system for self-securing programs).

Dr. Tygar was an NSF Presidential Young Investigator and serves on the INFOSEC Science and Technology Study Group. He is active in the electronic commerce and computer security communities. He consults widely for both industry and government, has taught a number of professional seminars on these topics, and has served as program chair for several conferences in these areas. Dr. Tygar received his bachelor's degree from the University of California, Berkeley, and his Ph.D. from Harvard University.

W. Earl Boebert, *Special Advisor*

W. Earl Boebert is a senior scientist at Sandia National Laboratories. Before joining Sandia he was the founder and chief scientist of Secure Computing Technology Corporation (SCTC), predecessor to today's Secure Computing Corporation (SCC). At SCTC/SCC he led development of the LOCK, Secure Network Server, and Sidewinder systems. He has 40 years of experience in the computer industry, with more than 25 of them in computer security and cryptography. He is the holder of three and co-holder of five patents in the field, the author and co-author of a book and numerous papers, and a frequent lecturer. He has been a member of numerous government and industry working groups and panels in the United States and Canada, including the committees of the National Research Council that produced the reports *Computers at Risk* and *For the Record.*

B

Briefers to the Committee

JUNE 10-11, 1996

John C. Davis, Director, National Computer Security Center, National Security Agency

Robert V. Meushaw, Technical Director, INFOSEC, Research and Technology Organization, National Security Agency

Richard C. Schaeffer, Chief, INFOSEC, Research and Technology Organization, National Security Agency

Howard Shrobe, Assistant Director, Intelligent Systems and Software Technology, Defense Advanced Research Projects Agency

JULY 1, 1996

Jeffrey I. Schiller, Director, Network Services, Massachusetts Institute of Technology

OCTOBER 21, 1996

John C. Davis, Director, National Computer Security Center, National Security Agency

Phil Gollucci, Manager, INFOSEC Research and Technology, National Security Agency

Robert V. Meushaw, Technical Director, INFOSEC, Research and Technology Organization, National Security Agency

Chris McBride, Technology Forecasting, National Security Agency

Dave Muzzy, Manager, INFOSEC Research and Technology, National Security Agency

Rick Proto, Chief, Research and Technology, National Security Agency

Richard C. Schaeffer, Chief, INFOSEC, Research and Technology Organization, National Security Agency

Bill Semancik, Technical Director, National Security Agency

Brian Snow, Technical Director for ISSO, National Security Agency

Carol Taylor, INFOSEC, Research and Technology Organization, National Security Agency

Lee Taylor, Manager, INFOSEC Research and Technology, National Security Agency

Grant Wagner, Technical Director, National Security Agency

Tom Zlurko, INFOSEC, Research and Technology Organization, National Security Agency

FEBRUARY 7, 1997

Mark Schertler, Senior Applications Engineer, Terisa Systems

NOVEMBER 12, 1997

John C. Davis, Commissioner, President's Commission on Critical Infrastructure Protection

C

Workshop Participants and Agendas

WORKSHOP 1: NETWORKED INFRASTRUCTURE

Workshop 1 Participants

Wendell Bailey, National Cable Television Association
Michael Baum, VeriSign Inc.
Steven M. Bellovin, AT&T Labs Research
Barbara Blaustein, National Science Foundation
Earl Boebert, Sandia National Laboratories
Martha Branstad, Computer Security Researcher and Entrepreneur
Blaine Burnham, National Security Agency
William E. Burr, National Institute of Standards and Technology
David Carrel, Cisco Systems Inc.
J. Randall Catoe, Cable and Wireless
Stephen N. Cohn, BBN Corporation
Stephen D. Crocker, Steve Crocker Associates
Dale Drew, MCI Telecommunications Inc.
Mary Dunham, Directorate of Science and Technology, Central
    Intelligence Agency
Roch Guerin, IBM T.J. Watson Research Center
Michael W. Harvey, Bell Atlantic
Chrisan Herrod, Defense Information Systems Agency
G. Mack Hicks, Bank of America
Stephen R. Katz, Citibank, N.A.

Charlie Kaufman, Iris Associates Inc.
Stephen T. Kent, BBN Corporation
Alan J. Kirby, Raptor Systems Inc.
John Klensin, MCI Communications Corporation
John C. Knight, University of Virginia
Gary M. Koob, Defense Advanced Research Projects Agency
Steven McGeady, Intel Corporation
Douglas J. McGowan, Hewlett-Packard Company
Robert V. Meushaw, National Security Agency
Ruth R. Nelson, Information System Security
Michael D. O'Dell, UUNET Technologies Inc.
Hilarie Orman, Defense Advanced Research Projects Agency
Radia Perlman, Novell Corporation
Frank Perry, Defense Information Systems Agency
Elaine Reed, MCI Telecommunications Inc.
Robert Rosenthal, Defense Advanced Research Projects Agency
Margaret Scarborough, National Automated Clearing House Association
Richard C. Schaeffer, National Security Agency
Richard M. Schell, Netscape Communications Corporation
Allan M. Schiffman, SPYRUS
Fred B. Schneider, Cornell University
Henning Schulzrinne, Columbia University
Basil Scott, Directorate of Science and Technology, Central Intelligence
    Agency
Mark E. Segal, Bell Communications Research
George A. Spix, Microsoft Corporation
Doug Tygar, University of California at Berkeley
Abel Weinrib, Intel Corporation
Rick Wilder, MCI Telecommunications Inc.
John T. Wroclawski, Massachusetts Institute of Technology

Workshop 1 Agenda

Monday, October 28, 1996

7:30 a.m.   Continental breakfast

8:00   Welcome and Overview (Stephen Crocker) What is trust?
                • What is complexity?
                • What are your problems composing networked
                infrastructure?

8:15   Session 1 (George Spix and Steven McGeady)

How are we doing? Is the NII trustworthy . . . and how do we know it?
- Tell us a story: What failed and how was it fixed?
- What do you believe is today's most critical problem? What is your outlook for its resolution?
- What is tomorrow's most critical problem? What are you doing to prepare for it?
- What is your highest priority for 5 to 10 years out?
- Is complexity a problem and why?
- Is interdependence a problem and why?

Overview

Panelists
    Earl Boebert, Sandia National Laboratories
    Dale Drew, MCI Telecommunications Inc.

8:45   Panel 1—Suppliers and Toolmakers (George Spix and Steven McGeady)
    Panelists
        David Carrel, Cisco Systems Inc.
        Alan Kirby, Raptor Systems Inc.
        Douglas McGowan, Hewlett-Packard Company
        Radia Perlman, Novell Corporation

9:45   Break

10:00   Panel 2—Delivery Vehicles (George Spix and Steven McGeady)
    Panelists
        Wendell Bailey, National Cable Television Association
        Michael Harvey, Bell Atlantic
        Michael O'Dell, UUNET Technologies Inc.

11:00   Panel 3—Customers (George Spix and Steven McGeady)
    Panelists
        Chrisan Herrod, Defense Information Systems Agency
        Mack Hicks, Bank of America
        Stephen Katz, Citibank
        Margaret Scarborough, National Automated Clearing House Association

12:30 p.m.   Lunch

1:30 p.m.   Session 2 (Steven Bellovin)
Given increasing complexity, why should we expect these interconnected (telco, cableco, wireless, satellite, other) networks and supporting systems to work?

- How do these systems interoperate today in different businesses and organizations?
- How will they interoperate tomorrow—how is the technology changing, relative to context?
- Do they have to interoperate or can they exist as separate domains up to and into the customer premise?

Panelists (plus Session 1 participants)
    Elaine Reed, MCI Telecommunications Inc.
    Frank Perry, Defense Information Systems Agency

2:30   Break

2:45   Session 3 (Allan Schiffman)
- What indications do we have that quality of service differentiated by cost is a workable solution?
- What is the intersection of QOS and trustworthiness? What are the key technical elements?
- How are QOS targets met today across networks and technologies? What are the trustworthiness trade-offs of multitier, multiprice QOS compared to best-effort?

Panelists
    Roch Guerin, IBM T.J. Watson Research Center
    Henning Schulzrinne, Columbia University
    Abel Weinrib, Intel Corporation
    Rick Wilder, MCI Telecommunications Inc.
    John Wroclawski, Massachusetts Institute of Technology

4:00   Break

4:15   Session 4 (Stephen Kent)
The role of public-key infrastructures in establishing trust: tackling the technical elements.
- How is "success" defined in the physical world?
- What are your current challenges (technical, business, social)?
- How can national-scale PKIs be achieved? What technology is needed to service efficiently users who may number from several hundred thousand to tens of millions?
- What is your outlook? What are the hard problems? What topics should go on federal or industrial research agendas?
- If multiple, domain-specific PKIs emerge, will integration or other issues call for new technology?

Panelists
   Michael Baum, VeriSign Inc.
   William Burr, National Institute of Standards and
      Technology
   Stephen Cohn, BBN Corporation

5:30   Reception and dinner

Tuesday, October 29, 1996

7:30 a.m.   Continental breakfast

8:00   Recap of Day One (George Spix)

8:45   Session 5 (Steven McGeady)
              What is the current status of software trustworthiness and
              how does the increasing complexity of software affect this
              issue?
              • Tell us a story: What failed and how was it fixed?
              • What do you believe is today's most critical problem?
              How will it be resolved?
              • What is tomorrow's most critical problem? What are you
              doing to prepare for it?
              • What happens when prophylaxis fails? How do you com-
              pare problem detection, response, and recovery alternatives?
              • How can we implement safety and reliability as compo-
              nents of trust, along with security and survivability?
              • Is distribution of system elements and control an oppor-
              tunity or a curse? What are the key technical challenges for
              making distributed software systems more trustworthy?
              • When will all human-to-human communication be medi-
              ated by an (end-user programmable or programmable-in-ef-
              fect) computer? Do we care, from the perspective of promot-
              ing trustworthy software? Should this influence research
              investments?

              Panelists
                 John Klensin, MCI Telecommunications Inc.
                 Richard Schell, Netscape Communications Corporation
                 Mark Segal, Bell Communications Research

10:00   Break

10:30   Continue discussion, Session 5
11:30   • Hard problems in terms of time frame, cost, and cer-
              tainty of result

• Summary of definitions—trustworthiness, complexity, compositional problems
• What are our grand challenges?
• Discussion, revision; feedback from federal government observers

12:00   Adjourn

WORKSHOP 2: END-SYSTEMS INFRASTRUCTURE

Workshop 2 Participants

Martin Abadi, Systems Research Center, Digital Equipment Corporation
Steven M. Bellovin, AT&T Labs Research
Matt Blaze, AT&T Research
W. Earl Boebert, Sandia National Laboratories
Martha Branstad, Computer Security Researcher and Entrepreneur
Ricky W. Butler, NASA Langley Research Center
Shiu-Kai Chin, Syracuse University
Dan Craigen, Odyssey Research Associates (Canada)
Stephen D. Crocker, Steve Crocker Associates
Kevin R. Driscoll, Honeywell Technology Center
Cynthia Dwork, IBM Almaden Research Center
Edward W. Felten, Princeton University
Li Gong, JavaSoft Inc.
Constance Heitmeyer, U.S. Naval Research Laboratory
Charlie Kaufman, Iris Associates Inc.
Stephen T. Kent, BBN Corporation
Rohit Khare, World Wide Web Consortium
John C. Knight, University of Virginia
Paul Kocher, Cryptography Consultant
Robert Kurshan, Bell Laboratories Inc.
Peter Lee, Carnegie Mellon University
Karl N. Levitt, University of California at Davis
Steven Lucco, Microsoft Corporation
Teresa Lunt, SRI International
Leo Marcus, Aerospace Corporation
John McHugh, Portland State University
John McLean, U.S. Naval Research Laboratory
Steven McGeady, Intel Corporation
Dejan Milojicic, The Open Group Research Institute
J Strother Moore, University of Texas at Austin
Ruth R. Nelson, Information System Security

Clifford Neuman, Information Sciences Institute, University of Southern California
Elaine Palmer, IBM T.J. Watson Research Center
David L. Presotto, Bell Laboratories Inc.
Joseph Reagle, Jr., World Wide Web Consortium
Robert Rosenthal, Defense Advanced Research Projects Agency
John Rushby, SRI International
Allan M. Schiffman, SPYRUS
Fred B. Schneider, Cornell University
Margo Seltzer, Harvard University
George A. Spix, Microsoft Corporation
Mark Stefik, Xerox Palo Alto Research Center
Vipin Swarup, MITRE Corporation
Doug Tygar, University of California at Berkeley
Bennet S. Yee, University of California at San Diego

Workshop 2 Agenda

Wednesday, February 5, 1997

7:30 a.m.   Continental breakfast available in the Refectory

8:30   Welcome and Overview (Fred Schneider)
8:45   Panel 1 (Douglas Tygar)
             Mobile Code: Java
                 Matt Blaze, AT&T Research
                 Edward W. Felten, Princeton University
                 Li Gong, JavaSoft Inc.
                 David L. Presotto, Bell Laboratories Inc.

10:15   Break

10:30   Panel 2 (Douglas Tygar)
             Mobile Code: Alternative Approaches
                 Peter Lee, Carnegie Mellon University
                 Steven Lucco, Microsoft Corporation
                 Dejan Milojicic, The Open Group Research Institute
                 Margo Seltzer, Harvard University
                 Vipin Swarup, MITRE Corporation

12:00 p.m.   Lunch in refectory

1:00   Panel 3 (Allan Schiffman)
             Rights Management, Copy Detection, Access Control
                 Cynthia Dwork, IBM Almaden Research Center

Rohit Khare (accompanied by Joseph Reagle, Jr.), World
Wide Web Consortium
Clifford Neuman, USC/Information Sciences Institute
Mark Stefik, Xerox Palo Alto Research Center

2:30   Break

2:45   Panel 4 (Stephen Crocker)
Tamper Resistant Devices
Paul Kocher, Cryptography Consultant
Elaine Palmer, IBM T.J. Watson Research Center
Bennet S. Yee, University of California at San Diego

4:15   Break

4:30   Continue discussion

5:30   Reception and Dinner

Thursday, February 6, 1997

7:30 a.m.   Continental breakfast

8:30   Introductory Remarks (Fred B. Schneider)
8:45   Panel 5 (Fred B. Schneider)
Formal Methods: State of the Technology
Constance L. Heitmeyer, U.S. Naval Research Laboratory
Robert Kurshan, Bell Laboratories Inc.
J Strother Moore, Computational Logic Inc. and
University of Texas at Austin
John Rushby, SRI International

10:15   Break
10:30   Panel 6 (John Knight)
Formal Methods: State of the Practice
Ricky W. Butler, NASA Langley Research Center
Dan Craigen, Odyssey Research Associates (Canada)
Kevin R. Driscoll, Honeywell Technology Center
Leo Marcus, Aerospace Corporation

12:00 p.m. Lunch in the Refectory

1:00   Panel 7 (Martha Branstad)
Formal Methods and Security
Martin Abadi, Digital Equipment Corporation, Systems
Research Center
Shiu-Kai Chin, Syracuse University

Karl N. Levitt, University of California at Davis
John McHugh, Portland State University
John McLean, U.S. Naval Research Laboratory

2:30   Concluding discussion

3:00   Adjourn

WORKSHOP 3: OPEN SYSTEMS ISSUES

Workshop 3 Participants

Steven M. Bellovin, AT&T Labs Research
Earl Boebert, Sandia National Laboratories
Dick Brackney, National Security Agency
Martha Branstad, Computer Security Researcher and Entrepreneur
Blaine Burnham, National Security Agency
Thomas Buss, Federal Express Corporation
Stephen D. Crocker, Steve Crocker Associates
Michael Diaz, Motorola
Bruce Fette, Motorola
William Flanagan, Perot Systems Corporation
Stephanie Forrest, University of New Mexico
Brenda S. Garman, Motorola
Iang Jeon, Liberty Financial
Charlie Kaufman, Iris Associates Inc.
Stephen T. Kent, BBN Corporation
John C. Knight, University of Virginia
Jimmy Kuo, McAfee Associates Inc.
Steven B. Lipner, Mitretek Systems
Steven McGeady, Intel Corporation
John Francis Mergen, BBN Corporation
Robert V. Meushaw, National Security Agency
Ruth R. Nelson, Information System Security
Allan M. Schiffman, SPYRUS
Fred B. Schneider, Cornell University
George A. Spix, Microsoft Corporation
Doug Tygar, University of California at Berkeley

Workshop 3 Agenda

Monday, September 29, 1997

7:30 a.m.   Continental breakfast

8:30   Welcome and Overview (Fred Schneider and Stephen Crocker)

8:45   Session 1
            Large-Scale Open Transactional Systems
            Panelists
                 Thomas Buss, Federal Express Corporation
                 Iang Jeon, Liberty Financial

10:45   Break

11:00   Session 2
            Antivirus Technology Trends
            Panelist
                 Jimmy Kuo, McAfee Associates Inc.

12:00   Lunch

1:00   Session 3
            Intrusion Detection: Approaches and Trends
            Panelists
                 John Francis Mergen, BBN Corporation
                 Stephanie Forrest, University of New Mexico

2:00   Break

2:15   Session 4
            Costing Trustworthiness: Process and Practice as Levers
            Panelist
                 Michael Diaz, Motorola
            Plenary Discussion—All participants and committee

4:45   Closing Remarks

5:00   Committee caucus
            Discussion and dinner with Steven Lipner

D

List of Position Papers Prepared for the Workshops

WORKSHOP 1

Earl Boebert	"Information Systems Trustworthiness"
Roch Guerin	"Quality of Service and Trustworthiness"
Chrisan Herrod	"Defense Information Infrastructure (DII): Trustworthiness, Issues and Enhancements"
Alan Kirby	"Is the NII Trustworthy?"
Radia Perlman	"Information Systems Trustworthiness"
Henning Schulzrinne	"The Impact of Resource Reservation for Real-Time Internet Services"
Mark E. Segal	"Trustworthiness in Telecommunications Systems"
Abel Weinrib	"QoS, Multicast and Information System Trustworthiness"

WORKSHOP 2

Martin Abadi	"Formal, Informal, and Null Methods"
Ricky Butler	"Formal Methods: State of the Practice"
Shiu-Kai Chin	"Highly Assured Computer Engineering"
Dan Craigen	"A Perspective on Formal Methods"
Edward W. Felten	"Research Directions for Java Security"
Li Gong	"Mobile Code in Java: Strength and Challenges"
Constance Heitmeyer	"Formal Methods: State of Technology"

Rohit Khare	"Rights Management, Copy Detection, and Access Control"
Paul Kocher	"Position Statement for Panel 4"
Robert Kurshan	"Algorithmic Verification"
Karl N. Levitt	"Intrusion Detection for Large Networks"
Leo Marcus	"Formal Methods: State of the Practice"
John McHugh	"Formal Methods for Survivability"
John McLean	"Formal Methods in Security"
Dejan S. Milojicic	"Alternatives to Mobile Code"
J Strother Moore	"Position Statement on the State of Formal Methods Technology"
Clifford Neuman	"Rights Management, Copy Detection, and Access Control"
Elaine Palmer	"Research on Secure Coprocessors"
John Rushby	"Formal Methods: State of Technology"
Margo Seltzer	"Dealing with Disaster: Surviving Misbehaved Kernal Extensions"
Mark Stefik	"Security Concepts for Digital Publishing on Trusted Systems"
Vipin Swarup	"Mobile Code Security"

WORKSHOP 3

Thomas Buss	"Building Strong Transactional Systems"
Michael Diaz	"Assessing the Cost of Security and Trustworthiness"
Stephanie Forrest	"Immunology and Intrusion Detection"
Chengi Jimmy Kuo	"Free Macro Antivirus Techniques"
John Francis Mergen	"GTE Internetworking"

E

Trends in Software

Software is critical for harnessing processing and communication technology. But producing software is difficult, labor-intensive, and time-consuming. Because of this, the trend in industry—which is expected to continue—has been to develop and embrace technologies that reduce the amount of new programming, hence reduce the costs, involved in developing any software system. NISs, which typically involve large and complex software, are acutely affected by this trend.

Perhaps the most visible example of the trend to avoid programming functionality from scratch is the increased use of commercial off-the-shelf (COTS) software (systems, subsystems, and libraries of components). Through the implementation of higher-level abstractions and services, specialized skills and knowledge of a few expert developers are leveraged across a large number of systems, with the following results:

- The COTS software might encapsulate complicated services that would be difficult, costly, or risky to build, thereby freeing programmers to work on other, perhaps easier, tasks.
- The COTS software might implement a user interface, thereby ensuring a consistent "look and feel" over sets of independently developed applications.
- The COTS software might hide lower-level system details, thereby enabling portability of applications across platforms that differ in configuration, operating system, or hardware.

Further leverage can be achieved by using software tools (sometimes called "Wizards") that allow developers to adapt and customize COTS software without mastering the internals of that software. And scripting languages (Ousterhout, 1998), by being typeless and providing programming features such as high-level abstractions for programming graphical user interfaces (GUIs) and network input-output, assume increasing importance in this world where systems are built by "gluing together" existing software.

Middleware, infrastructure for creating client-server applications, has made significant inroads into the commercial and enterprise software sectors. Leading vendors—such as SAP, Oracle, Baan, and PeopleSoft—are now aggressively directing their efforts toward exploiting the capabilities of global computer networks, like the Internet, while at the same time shielding users of their systems from the complexity of distributed systems. An emphasis on interoperability not only enables the interconnection of computing systems within a company, but also increasingly is fostering the interconnection of computing systems at different companies. Once business partners link their computing systems, messages on networks can replace paper as the means by which business is transacted, and new operating modes, such as just-in-time manufacturing, are facilitated because transactions can be initiated automatically and completed virtually instantaneously.

Another way that software developers can avoid writing code from scratch is to exploit the growing collection of tools for transforming high-level descriptions into actual code. Tools along these lines exist today to implement network communications software for client-server distributed systems, databases, and spreadsheets tailored to the needs of some application at hand, and for window-based or forms-based user interfaces. In some cases, the tools output program skeletons, which are then decorated with programmer-provided application-specific routines. In other cases, the tools output self-contained modules or subsystems, which are then integrated into the application being developed.

Software systems in general, and NISs in particular, once fielded, invariably come under pressure to evolve. Needs change, bringing demands for new functionality, and technology changes, rendering obsolete hardware and software platforms. Until recently, the sole solution had been for software developers to periodically issue new releases of their systems. Evolution of a software system was limited to whatever changes a developer implemented in each new release. The result was far from ideal. Users had little control over whether and when their new needs would be addressed; software developers, having limited resources, had difficulty keeping their systems attractive in an expanding market.

Extensible software system architectures allow program code to be incorporated into a system after it has been deployed and often even after it is executing. With extensible architectures, new functionality that can be coded as extensions need not await a new release. Users clearly benefit from the approach, because extensibility empowers them to evolve a system's functionality in directions they desire. And the system's developers benefit by leveraging others' programming efforts: the market for an extensible system now expands with every extension that anyone implements.

There is thus a strong incentive to design and deploy systems that are broadly extensible. Today, Web browsers support extensibility through their "helper applications," which enable the browser to display new forms of content (e.g., video, audio, graphics); extensible operating systems, like Microsoft's Windows NT, allow new types of objects and handlers for those objects to be installed in a running system. The next logical step, a topic of current research (e.g., Bershad et al., 1995; Ford et al., 1997; Hawblitzel et al., 1998; Kaashoek et al., 1997; Seltzer et al., 1996), is placing support for extensibility at the very lowest levels of the operating system, as this would give the largest scope for extension. Much of that work is concerned with trade-offs between efficiency and protection, revisiting problems studied by the operating systems community in the 1970s.

The ultimate form of software system extensibility is mobile code—programs that move from one processor to another in a network of computers. When mobile code is supported, a program—unbidden—can arrive at a host processor and start executing, thereby extending or altering the functionality of that host's software. Although the idea dates back to the early days of the ARPANET (Rulifson, 1969), only recently has it been attracting serious attention as a general-purpose programming paradigm.[1] The now widely available Java programming notation supports a restricted form of code mobility, as do Microsoft's ActiveX controls.

Two technical reasons are usually offered to argue that mobile code is attractive for programming distributed systems. First, the use of mobile code allows communications bandwidth to be conserved and specialized computing engines to be efficiently exploited: a computation can move to a site where data are stored or where specialized computing hardware exists, process raw data there, and finally move on to another site, carrying only some relevant subset of what has been processed.

Second, with mobile code, efficient and flexible server interfaces become practical. Instead of invoking a high-level server operation across a network, a computation can move to the processor where that server is executing and invoke server operations using (local) procedure calls. Since the overhead of local calls is low, there is less overhead to amortize

---

[1]Viruses and the Postscript document description language are both instances of mobile code developed for more specialized applications.

per server-operation invocation. It therefore becomes feasible for server interfaces to offer shorter, more primitive operations and for sequences of these operations to be invoked to accomplish a task. Thus, the mobile code dynamically defines its own high-level server operations—high-level operations that can be both efficient and well suited for the task at hand.

Besides these technical arguments, mobile code also provides an attractive architecture for the distribution of software and for system configuration management. Today, for example, PC software is often installed and upgraded by customers downloading files over the Internet. The logical next step is an architecture where performing an upgrade does not require an overt action by the customer but instead can be instigated by the producer of that software. Mobile code supports just that architecture. Push replaces pull, freeing users from a system management task. But using mobile code in this manner relinquishes control in a way that affects trustworthiness. The approach also deprives the system administrator of control over the timing of software upgrades and configuration management changes. Cautious administrators have long refrained from making system changes during crucial projects; a system that changes itself might be less stable at such times.

REFERENCES

Bershad, Brian N., Stefan Savage, Przemslaw Pardyak, Emin Sirer, Craig Chambers, Marc E. Fiuczynski, David Becker, and Susan Eggers. 1995. "Extensibility, Safety and Performance in the SPIN Operating System," pp. 267-284 in *Proceeedings of the 15th ACM Symposium on Operating Systems Principles*. New York: ACM Press.

Ford, Bryan, Godmar Back, Greg Benson, Jay Lepreau, Albert Lin, and Olin Shivers. 1997. "The Flux OSKit: A Substrate for Kernel and Language Research," pp. 31-51 in *Proceedings of the 16th ACM Symposium on Operating Systems Principles*. New York: ACM Press.

Hawblitzel, Chris, Chi-Chao Chang, Grzegorz Czajkowski, Deyu Hu, and Thorsten von Eicken. 1998. "Implementing Multiple Protection Domains in Java," pp. 259-290 in *Proceedings of the USENIX 1998 Annual Technical Conference, New Orleans, Louisiana*. Berkeley, CA: USENIX Association.

Kaashoek, M. Frans, Dawson R. Engler, Gregory R. Ganger, Hector M. Briceno, Russell Hunt, David Mazieres, Thomas Pinckney, Robert Grimm, John Jannotti, and Kenneth Mackenzie. 1997. "Application Performance and Flexibility on Exokernel Systems," pp. 52-65 in *Proceedings of the 16th ACM Symposium on Operating Systems Principles*. New York: ACM Press.

Ousterhout, John K. 1998. "Scripting: Higher-level Programming for the 21st Century," *IEEE Computer*, 31(3):23-30.

Rulifson, J. 1969. *Decode-Encode Language (DEL)*. RFC 5. June 2.

Seltzer, Margo I., Yasuhiro Endo, Christopher Small, and Keith A. Smith. 1996. "Dealing with Disaster: Surviving Misbehaved Kernel Extensions," pp. 213-228 in *Proceedings of the Second Symposium on Operating Systems Design and Implementation (OSDI '96), Seattle, Washington*. Berkeley, CA: USENIX Association.

F

Some Related Trustworthiness Studies

COMPUTERS AT RISK: SAFE COMPUTING IN THE INFORMATION AGE

Computers at Risk: Safe Computing in the Information Age (CSTB, 1991) focused on security—getting more and better computer and communications security into use, thereby raising the floor for all, rather than concentrating on special needs related to handling classified government information. The report responded to prevailing conditions of limited awareness by the public, system developers, system operators, and policymakers. To help set and raise expectations about system security, the study recommended the following:

- Development and promulgation of a comprehensive set of generally accepted security system principles (GSSP);
- Creation of a repository of data about incidents;
- Education in practice, ethics, and engineering of secure systems; and
- Establishment of a new institution to implement these recommendations.

The report also analyzed and suggested remedies for the failure of the marketplace to substantially increase the supply of security technology; export control criteria and procedures were named as one of many contributing factors. Observing that university-based research in computer security was at a "dangerously low level," the report mentioned broad areas where research should be pursued.

REPORT OF THE DEFENSE SCIENCE BOARD TASK FORCE ON INFORMATION WARFARE DEFENSE (IW-D)

Produced by a Defense Science Board task force, *Report of the Defense Science Board Task Force on Information Warfare Defense (IW-D)* (Defense Science Board, 1996) focused on defending against cyber-threats and information warfare. The task force documented an increasing military dependence on networked information infrastructures, analyzed vulnerabilities of the current networked information infrastructure, discussed actual attacks on that infrastructure, and formulated a list of threats (Box F.1) that has been discussed broadly within the Department of Defense (DOD) and elsewhere. The task force concluded:

> . . . there is a need for extraordinary action to deal with the present and emerging challenges of defending against possible information warfare attacks on facilities, information, information systems, and networks of the United States which [sic] would seriously affect the ability of the Department of Defense to carry out its assigned missions and functions.

Some of the task force recommendations answered organizational questions: Where might various functions in support of IW-D be placed

---

BOX F.1
Taxonomy of Threats

- Hackers driven by technical challenge
- Disgruntled employees or customers seeking revenge
- Crooks interested in personal financial gain or stealing services
- Organized crime operations interested in financial gain or covering criminal activity
- Organized terrorist groups or nation-states trying to influence U.S. policy by isolated attacks
- Foreign espionage agents seeking to exploit information for economic, political, or military purposes
- Tactical countermeasures intended to disrupt specific U.S. military weapons or command systems
- Multifaceted tactical information warfare applied in a broad, orchestrated manner to disrupt a major U.S. military mission
- Large organized groups or major nation-states intent on overthrowing the United States

---

SOURCE: Defense Science Board (1996).

and how might they be staffed and managed within the DOD? How might senior-level government and industry leaders be made aware of vulnerabilities and their implications? What legislation is needed? How can current infrastructure dependencies and vulnerabilities be determined? How can information about ongoing threats and attacks be characterized and disseminated?

The other recommendations concerned both short- and longer-term technical means for repelling attacks. The task force urged greater use of existing security technology, certain controversial encryption technology,[1] and the construction of a minimum essential information infrastructure (MEII). It also suggested a research program for furthering the development of the following:

- System architectures that degrade gracefully and are resilient to failures or attacks directed at single components;
- Methods for modeling, monitoring, and managing large-scale distributed systems; and
- Tools and techniques for automated detection and analysis of localized or coordinated large-scale attacks, and tools and methods for predicting anticipated performance of survivable distributed systems.

The task force noted the low levels of activity concerning computer security and survivable systems at universities.

CRITICAL FOUNDATIONS: PROTECTING AMERICA'S INFRASTRUCTURES

The President's Commission on Critical Infrastructure Protection, whose members were drawn from the private and public sector, studied infrastructures that are critical to the security, public welfare, and economic strength of the United States: information and communications (e.g., telecommunications), physical distribution (e.g., rail, air, and mass transport), energy (e.g., electric power generation and distribution), banking and finance, and vital human services (e.g., water supply, fire fighting, and rescue). In its report, *Critical Foundations: Protecting America's Infrastructures* (PCCIP, 1997), the commission concluded that all these infrastructures were increasingly vulnerable to physical and cyber-threats. And although the threat of cyber-attacks today appears to be small, the

---

[1]Specifically, the task force recommended the deployment of the Multilevel Information Systems Security Initiative (MISSI) and escrowed encryption. Those topics are discussed in Chapters 4 and 6 of the present report.

prospect for such attacks in the future was found to be significant.[2] Along with the increasing threat, the commission noted an absence of any national focus for infrastructure protection. Formation of a public-private partnership was urged. Private-sector involvement was advocated because infrastructure owners and operators, having the expertise and incentive, are best positioned to protect against and detect infrastructure attacks. Federal government involvement is needed to facilitate collection and dissemination of information about tools, threats, and intent. The federal government also is ideally situated for detection of coordinated attacks, for overseeing defense-in-depth and defenses across infrastructures, and for reducing the possibility that disturbances or attacks could propagate within and across critical infrastructures.

Broad public awareness regarding the nature and extent of cyber-threats is a necessary part of any defense that hinges on private-sector participation. Programs were recommended to elevate public awareness of infrastructure threats, vulnerabilities, and interdependencies. The commission also recommended considering legislation that would enable federal and private-sector responses to infrastructure vulnerabilities and attacks. The government was also counseled by the commission to serve as a role model for the private sector in the use of standards and best practices, taking precautions that are proportionate to the threat and the value of what is being protected. Substantially increased support for research was recommended by the commission; the present level of funding[3] was deemed insufficient for future needs (Davis, 1997). Federal support is crucial—for sound business reasons, the private sector is not likely to invest significant resources in longer-term research that could fuel needed advances. The research and development vision articulated by the commission starts with $500 million for fiscal year 1999 and climbs to $1 billion in 2004 for government-sponsored basic research; and the vision has the private sector using that basic research to create new technology for infrastructure protection.

The commission suggests a range of research topics. Those concerning networked computer systems and cyber-threats include the following:

- *Information assurance:* The effective protection of the communications infrastructure and the information created, stored, processed, and transmitted on it.

---

[2]The report notes that attackers' tools are becoming more advanced and more accessible, so less skill is needed to launch ever more sophisticated attacks. Moreover, the increasing interconnectivity and complexity of critical infrastructures increase their vulnerability.

[3]Government funding was estimated at $150 million per year and industrial funding at $1 billion to $1.5 billion per year.

- *Monitoring and threat detection:* Reliable automated monitoring and detection systems, timely and effective information collection technologies, and efficient data reduction and analysis tools for identifying and characterizing localized or coordinated large-scale attacks against infrastructure.
- *Vulnerability assessment and systems analysis:* Methods and tools to identify critical nodes within infrastructures, to examine infrastructure interdependencies, and to help understand the behavior of complex systems.
- *Risk management and decision support:* Methods and tools to help decision makers prioritize the use of finite resources to reduce risk.
- *Protection and mitigation:* System control and containment and isolation technologies to protect systems against the spectrum of threats.
- *Contingency planning, incident response, and recovery:* Methods and tools for planning for, responding to, and recovering from incidents such as natural disasters and physical and cyber-based attacks that affect local or national infrastructures.

CRYPTOGRAPHY'S ROLE IN SECURING THE INFORMATION SOCIETY

A number of mechanisms for enhancing information system trustworthiness depend on the use of cryptography. Cryptography, however, is a double-edged sword. It can help legitimate businesses and law-abiding citizens keep information confidential, but it can help organized crime and terrorists keep information confidential. Conflict between the protection of confidential information for legitimate businesses and law-abiding citizens and the need for law enforcement and intelligence agencies to obtain information has fueled a U.S. policy debate concerning both import/export restrictions and domestic deployment of cryptography.

The issues are subtle. They were explored during an 18-month study by the National Research Council's Computer Science and Telecommunications Board (CSTB)—the so-called CRISIS report (an acronym of the report's full title) edited by Dam and Lin (CSTB, 1996)—that was completed just as the present NIS trustworthiness study was getting under way. Bringing together a wide range of perspectives on the subject, the CRISIS report concluded that the then-current U.S. cryptography policy[4] was not adequate to support the information security requirements of an information society. Although acknowledging that increased use of cryptography placed an increased burden on law enforcement and intelli-

---

[4]The report was released in May 1996.

gence activities, the CRISIS report asserted that the interests of the nation overall would be best served by a policy that fosters a judicious transition toward broad use of cryptography.

CRISIS does not make recommendations for further research, so it is unlike the other studies just surveyed. What CRISIS does say is directly relevant to the present study in two ways. First, the existence of CRISIS helped delimit the scope of the present study. With CRISIS in hand, the present study was freed to concentrate on other aspects of information systems trustworthiness. Second, CRISIS provides a foundation for the present study's discussions about cryptography policy and its implications regarding widespread deployment of cryptography. As discussed in Chapters 2, 4, and 6 of the present study, the broad availability of cryptography can affect how NIS trustworthiness problems are solved.

REFERENCES

Computer Science and Telecommunications Board (CSTB), National Research Council. 1991. *Computers at Risk: Safe Computing in the Information Age*. Washington, DC: National Academy Press.

Computer Science and Telecommunications Board (CSTB), National Research Council. 1996. *Cryptography's Role in Securing the Information Society*, Kenneth W. Dam and Herbert S. Lin, eds. Washington, DC: National Academy Press.

Davis, John C. 1997. (Draft) *Research and Development Recommendations for Protecting and Assuring Critical National Infrastructures*. Washington, DC: President's Commission on Critical Infrastructure Protection, December 7.

Defense Science Board. 1996. *Report of the Defense Science Board Task Force on Information Warfare Defense (IW-D)*. Washington, DC: Office of the Under Secretary of Defense for Acquisition and Technology, November 21.

President's Commission on Critical Infrastructure Protection (PCCIP). 1997. *Critical Foundations: Protecting America's Infrastructures*. Washington, DC: PCCIP, October.

G

Some Operating System Security Examples

MS-DOS is an operating system designed to operate on single-user personal computers. As a consequence, it provides no identification and authentication mechanisms and neither discretionary nor mandatory access control mechanisms. Any user has access to all resources on the system. Any access control is provided solely by controlling physical access to the computer itself. If the computer is electronically connected to any other computer, no access control is possible.

UNIX is a multi-user operating system originally designed by Ken Thompson and Dennis Ritchie of Bell Laboratories. User identification is supported by password-based authentication. User IDs are associated with processes. UNIX provides a modified version of access control lists for files. For each file, three fields of access permissions are established, one for the file owner, one for the group in which the owner resides, and one for others (or everyone else). In each access field, permission to read, write, and execute the file is granted by the owner. For example, a file with access permissions rw-/rw-/r provides the owner read/write access, the owner's group read/write access, and all others only read access to the file. UNIX provides another feature that affects access controls. Each program can have the "setuid" attribute set; if set, the program runs with the access rights of the owner of the program, rather than those of the program's invoker. Thus, for practical purposes, the program's invoker can establish an effective identity other than his or her own that is to be used when determining access permissions.

Microsoft's Windows NT operating system is designed for workstations and servers. User identity is authenticated using passwords. Every active subject in the system has an associated token that includes a unique identifier, a list of group identifiers, and a set of privileges that allows a subject to override restrictions set by the system. Every named object (e.g., files, directories, drivers, devices, and registry keys) in the system has an associated access control list (ACL). ACLs can ascribe generic rights (e.g., read, write, and delete) and specific rights that have semantics only for a specific class of objects. Mediation decisions are made by the Security Reference Monitor based upon the token of the subject, the ACL of the object, and the requested access right. There is provision in the system for "impersonation," that is, using authorization of another subject.

Finally, various products have been designed to provide access control mechanisms as add-ons for specific operating systems, to augment the basic operating system facilities. For example, RACF, ACF2, and Top Secret are all products designed for use with IBM's MVS (which has almost no intrinsic security).

H

Types of Firewalls

The four basic types of firewalls are packet filters, circuit relays, application gateways, and dynamic packet filters.

Packet filter firewalls operate at the network layer, with occasional peeks at the transport-layer headers. The information used to make a pass/drop decision on a packet is contained in that packet; no state is maintained. Typical decision criteria include source address, destination addresses, and transport protocol port number (i.e., service) requested. Not all protocols are compatible with packet filters. For example, a common security policy allows most outgoing calls but no incoming calls. A packet filter can implement this policy if and only if protocol headers contain fields that differentiate between requests and responses. In Transmission Control Protocol (TCP), a single bit value distinguishes the first packet of a conversation from all others, so it is possible to drop incoming packets that do not have this bit properly set. By contrast, User Datagram Protocol (UDP) lacks such a notion, and it is impossible to enforce the desired security policy. Packet filters normally associate several rules with each legal conversation. Not only must messages flow from the client to the server, but replies and even protocol-level acknowledgment packets also must flow in the other direction. The lack of state makes possible interactions between the different rules and that can allow certain attacks—for example, a legal acknowledgment packet may also be an illegal attempt to set up a new conversation.

Circuit relays operate above the transport layer. They pass or drop entire conversations but have no knowledge of the semantics of what they

293

relay. Circuit relays are generally considered to be more secure than packet filters, primarily because they terminate instantiations of the transport protocol. Interactions between rules is unlikely at the transport layer, and the same mechanisms that normally separate different circuits keep together the inbound and outbound packets for a given connection. Because connections now terminate at an intermediate point (namely, the firewall), circuit relays generally require changes in application programs, user behavior, or both. This lack of transparency makes circuit relays unsuitable for many environments, where transparency and compatibility are important.

Applications gateways are closely tied to the semantics of the traffic they handle. Typically, a separate program (proxy) is required for each application. A mail gateway might rewrite header lines to eliminate references to internal machines, log senders and receivers, and so on. Application gateways can handle traffic whose characteristics render packet filters and circuit relays inappropriate enforcement mechanisms. For example, by default the File Transfer Protocol (FTP) (Postel and Reynolds, 1985) uses an inbound channel for data transfers, which packet filters cannot handle safely. An FTP proxy in an application gateway can keep track of when a given incoming call should be accepted, and thus can allow what would otherwise be a violation of normal security policies.

Application gateways are also well suited for sites that require authentication of outgoing calls. Since few if any protocols are designed to provide authentication at an intermediate point like a firewall, a custom design is necessary for each application. One might require a separate log-in, entirely in-band; another might pop up a window on the user's terminal. Application gateways are generally considered to be the most secure type of firewall because a detailed knowledge of protocol semantics makes spoofing difficult.

Dynamic packet filters, the last of the four firewall types, excel at transparency. They merge the packet filter and application gateway types of firewall. With a dynamic packet filter, most packets are accepted or rejected based solely on information in the packet. However, some packets cause additional processing that modifies the rules that will be applied to subsequent packets. This enables the UDP problem mentioned above to be solved: the fact that an outbound query has been sent then conditions the firewall to accept the reply packet, a message that would otherwise have been rejected. More sophisticated processing can be done as well. For example, dynamic packet filters can be sufficiently aware of FTP to permit the incoming data channel call. Some dynamic packet filters are aware of the remote procedure call (RPC) (Sun Microsystems, 1988) and can mediate access to individual services. Even header address translation can be performed (Egevang and Francis, 1994), further isolating internal machines.

REFERENCES

Egevang, K., and P. Francis. 1994. *The IP Network Address Translator (NAT)*. RFC 1631.
   May.
Postel, J., and J. Reynolds. 1985. *File Transfer Protocol (FTP)*. RFC 959. October.
Sun Microsystems. 1988. *RPC: Remote Procedure Call Protocol Specification Version 2*. RFC
   1057.

I

Secrecy of Design

Secrecy of design is often deprecated with the phrase "security through obscurity," and one often hears arguments that security-critical systems or elements should be developed in an open environment that encourages peer review by the general community. Evidence is readily at hand of systems that were developed in secret only to be reverse engineered and have their details published on the Internet and their flaws pointed out for all to see.

The argument for open development rests on assumptions that generally, but not universally, hold. These assumptions are that the open community will devote adequate effort to locate vulnerabilities, that they will come forth with vulnerabilities that they find, and that vulnerabilities, once discovered, can be closed—even after the system is deployed.

There are environments, such as military and diplomatic settings, in which these assumptions do not necessarily hold. Groups interested in finding vulnerabilities here will mount long-term and well-funded analysis efforts—efforts that are likely to dwarf those that might be launched by individuals or organizations in the open community. Further, these well-funded groups will take great care to ensure that any vulnerabilities they discover are kept secret, so that they may be exploited (in secret) for as long as possible. Finally, military systems in particular often exist in environments where postdeployment upgrades are difficult to achieve.

Special problems arise when partial public knowledge is necessary about the nature of the security mechanisms, such as when a military security module is designed for integration into COTS equipment. Residual vulnerabilities are inevitable, and the discovery and publication of even one such vulnerability may, in certain circumstances, render the system defenseless. It is, in general, not sufficient to protect only the exact nature of a vulnerability. The precursor information from which the vulnerability could be readily discovered must also be protected, and that requires an exactness of judgment not often found in group endeavors. When public knowledge of aspects of a military system is required, the most prudent course is to conduct the entire development process under cover of secrecy. Only after the entire assurance and evaluation process has been completed—and the known residual vulnerabilities identified—should a decision be made about what portions of the system description are safe to release.

Any imposition of secrecy, about either part or all of the design, carries two risks: that a residual vulnerability could have been discovered by a friendly peer reviewer in time to be fixed, and that the secret parts of the system will be reverse engineered and made public, leading to the further discovery, publication, and exploitation of vulnerabilities. The first risk has historically been mitigated by devoting substantial resources to analysis and assurance. (Evaluation efforts that exceed the design effort by an order of magnitude or more are not unheard of in certain environments.) The second risk is addressed with a combination of technology aimed at defeating reverse engineering and strict procedural controls on the storage, transport, and use of the devices in question. These controls are difficult to impose in a military environment and effectively impossible in a commercial or consumer one.

J

Research in Information System Security and Survivability Funded by the NSA and DARPA

In a recent study, Anderson et al. (1998) identified a total of 104 individual research projects that were funded in FY 1998 by DARPA's Information Survivability program, a unit of the Information Technology Office (ITO). In addition, 45 information security projects were identified from the NSA and were included in the Anderson et al. (1998) study. These projects were categorized as depicted below (some projects were counted in two categories).

Heterogeneity
　　Preferential Replication/Lifespan, Architectural/Software Diversity, Path Diversity, Randomized Compilation, Secure Heterogeneous Environments
　　NSA R2 = 0 projects; DARPA ITO = 2 projects
Static Resource Allocation
　　Hardware Technology
　　NSA R2 = 1 project; DARPA ITO = 0 projects
Dynamic Resource Allocation
　　Detect & Respond to Attacks/Malfunctions, Dynamic Quality of Services, Active Packet/Node Networks, Dynamic Security Management
　　NSA R2 = 3 projects; DARPA ITO = 12 projects
Redundancy
　　Replication
　　NSA R2 = 0 projects; DARPA ITO = 3 projects

Resilience and Robustness
Cryptography/Authentication, Modeling and Testing, Fault/Failure-Tolerant Components, Advanced Languages & Systems, Wrappers, Firewalls, Secure Protocols, Advanced/Secure Hardware
NSA R2 = 28 projects; DARPA ITO = 54 projects

Rapid Recovery and Reconstitution
Detect and Recover Activities
NSA R2 = 0 projects; DARPA ITO = 2 projects

Deception
Decoy Infection Routines
NSA R2 = 0 projects; DARPA ITO = 0 projects

Segmentation/Decentralization/Quarantine
Secure Distributed/Mobile Computing, Enclave/Shell Protection, Intruder Detection and Isolation, Specialized "Organs," Autonomous Self Contained Units, Damage Containment
NSA R2 = 2 projects; DARPA ITO = 11 projects

Immunologic Identification
Autonomous Agents, "Lymphocyte" Agents, Detection of Anomalous Events, Mobile Code Verification, Self/Nonself Discrimination, Information Dissemination
NSA R2 = 1 project; DARPA ITO = 12 projects

Self-Organization and Collective Behavior
Adaptive Mechanisms, Formal Structure Modeling, Emergent Properties & Behaviors, Node/Software Optimization, Market-Based Architecture, Scalable Networks (VLSI)
NSA R2 = 0 projects; DARPA ITO = 10 projects

Other/Miscellaneous
Multiple Approaches to Network Security/Survivability, Technology Forecasting
NSA R2 = 10 projects; DARPA ITO = 3 projects

REFERENCE

Anderson, Robert H., Phillip M. Feldman, Scott Gerwehr, Brian Houghton, Richard Mesic, John D. Pinder, and Jeff Rothenberg. 1998. A "Minimum Essential Information Infrastructure" for U.S. Defense Systems: Meaningful? Feasible? Useful? Santa Monica, CA: RAND National Defense Research Institute, in press.

K

Glossary

Access generally refers to the right to enter or use a system and its resources; to read, write, modify, or delete data; or to use software processes or network bandwidth.

Access control is the granting or denying, usually according to a particular security model, of certain permissions to access a resource.

Access level is either the clearance level associated with a subject or the classification level associated with an object.

ACL (access control list) refers to a list of subjects permitted to access an object, and the access rights of each one.

ACM is the Association for Computing Machinery.

ActiveX is a set of client and server component interfaces that enables developers to build multitier applications that use an HTML renderer and HTTP and other Internet protocols. ActiveX is the technology used to integrate the Internet in Windows.

Ada is a programming language that was developed, and subsequently mandated, for DOD software projects.

Adjunct processors enable the operation of many enhanced telephone services, such as 800 numbers and voice-menu prompts.

ADSL (asymmetric digital subscriber line) allows an upstream data flow (i.e., from user to server) that is a fraction of the downstream data flow, as is appropriate to support Internet services to the home and video on demand.

ANSI is the American National Standards Institute.

API (application programming interface) is an interface provided for an application to another program.

ARPA: See DARPA.

ARPANET (Advanced Research Projects Agency network) was a federally funded WAN that became operational in 1968 and was used for early networking research. It evolved into the central backbone of the Internet.

AS (autonomous system) is an Internet routing domain under the control of one organization.

Assurance is confidence that a system design meets its requirements, or that its implementation satisfies specifications, or that some specific property is satisfied.

Asymmetric (or public-key) cryptography is based on algorithms that use one key (typically a public key) to encrypt a message and a different, mathematically related key (typically private) to decrypt a message.

ATB (Assessment Technology Branch) is part of NASA.

ATM (asynchronous transfer mode) enables voice, data, and video to be handled with a uniform transmission protocol. It breaks up the information to be transmitted into short packets of data and intersperses them with data from other sources delivered over trunk networks.

Authentication is the process of confirming an asserted identity with a specified, or understood, level of confidence. The mechanism can be based on something the user knows, such as a password, something the user possesses, such as a "smart card," something intrinsic to the person, such as a fingerprint, or a combination of two or more of these.

Availability is the property asserting that a resource is usable or operational during a given time period, despite attacks or failures.

BAA (broad area announcement) is a form of research solicitation used by DARPA and other federal agencies.

BCR (black/crypto/red) was a federally funded project that achieved full end-to-end packet encryption, with full header bypass, in working prototype form in the mid to late 1970s.

Bell and La Padula policy is a security policy prohibiting information flow from one object to another with a lesser or incomparable classification.

BGP (Border Gateway Protocol) is the protocol used by Internet routers to communicate with other routers across administrative boundaries.

Biometric authentication relies on the use of unique characteristics of individuals, such as a voiceprint or fingerprint, for authentication.

Blacker is an integrated set of network layer cryptographic devices designed to secure military data networks.

Blue box refers to a device used to defraud the telephone company in the 1960s and 1970s. It sent network control tones over the voice path.

bps (bits per second) refers to the rate at which data are generated by a source or transmitted over a communications channel. Measurements are often stated in units of 10^3 bits per second (kilobits or kbps) or 10^6 bits per second (megabits or Mbps).

C++ is a programming language.

CA (certification authority) is a trusted party that creates certificates in a secure manner.

Caneware is a certificate-based, military network encryption system for the Internet.

CAP (complex arithmetic processor) is a digital signal processor intended for use in a secure, multimode, programmable radio.

CCITT is the Consultative Committee on International Telephony and Telegraphy.

CCF (central control function) is an air traffic management subsystem.

CCv2 refers to Common Criteria, version 2.

CDIS (central control function display information system) is a component of the CCF.

CDSA (common data security architecture) is an integrated software framework consisting of APIs designed to make computer platforms more secure for applications such as electronic commerce.

CERT/CC (Computer Emergency Response Team/Coordination Center) is an element of the Networked Systems Survivability Program of the Software Engineering Institute at Carnegie Mellon University. It keeps track of attacks on the Internet and issues advisories. CERT advisories are available online at <http://www.cert.org>.

Certificate management is the overall process of issuing, storing, verifying, and generally accepting responsibility for the accuracy of public-key certificates and their secure delivery to appropriate consumers.

Certification is the administrative act of approving a computer system or component for use in a particular application.

CGI (common gateway interface) is a script run by a World Wide Web server in response to a client request.

Checksum consists of digits or bits calculated according to an algorithm and used to verify the integrity of accompanying data.

Chinese Wall (or Brewer-Nash) model is a security policy concerned with separating different organizational activities to conform with legal and regulatory strictures in the financial world.

CIA is the Central Intelligence Agency.

CIAO (Critical Infrastructure Assurance Office) is a unit of the U.S. government established by PDD 63.

CIC R&D (Computing, Information, and Communications Research and Development) refers to a committee of the National Science and Technology Council that involves about 12 federal departments and agencies that coordinate computing and communications programs, budgets, and review.

Ciphertext is the output of any encryption process, regardless of whether the original digitized input was text, computer files or programs, or graphical images.

Cleartext (or plaintext) is the input into an encryption process or output of a decryption process.

CLEF refers to a commercially licensed evaluation facility.

Clipper chip is an escrowed encryption chip that implements the Skip-jack algorithm to encrypt communications conducted over the public switched network (e.g., between telephones, modems, or fax equipment).

CMM (Capability Maturity Model) is used in judging the maturity of the software processes of an organization. It was developed under the stewardship of the Software Engineering Institute.

CMW (compartmented mode workstation) is a computer workstation (rated at least B1 under the TCSEC) that implements both discretionary (i.e., identity-based, user-directed) and mandatory (i.e., rule-based, administratively directed) access policies.

CNN is the Cable News Network.

COCOMO (constructive cost model) is a method for estimating the cost of the development of a software system.

COM (common object model) is an open software architecture.

Confidentiality refers to the protection of communications traffic or stored data against interception or receipt by unauthorized third parties.

Conops (concept of operations) describes the operations of a computing system, typically in the form of scenarios.

COPS (computer oracle password security) is software that checks for cracks, configuration errors, and other security flaws in a computer employing the UNIX operating system.

CORBA (common object request broker architecture) is an OMG specification that provides the standard interface definition between OMG-compliant objects.

Correctness is the property of being consistent with a specification. The specification may stipulate, for example, that proper outputs are produced by a system for each input.

COTS (commercial off-the-shelf) refers to readily available commercial technologies and systems.

Countermeasure is a mechanism that reduces or eliminates a vulnerability.

CPU is a central processing unit.

CRISIS refers to *Cryptography's Role in Securing the Information Society*, a 1996 report by the CSTB.

CRL (certificate revocation list) identifies unexpired certificates that are no longer valid; that is, the binding expressed by the certificates is not considered to be accurate.

Cross-connect is a component of the telephone system that shunts circuits from one wire or fiber to another.

Cryptanalysis is the study and practice of various methods to penetrate ciphertext and deduce the contents of the original cleartext message.

Cryptographic algorithm is a mathematical procedure, often used in conjunction with a key, that transforms input into a form that is unintelligible without knowledge of a key and the algorithm.

Cryptography is the science and technology of establishing or protecting the secrecy, authenticity, or integrity of data that might be accessed by unauthorized parties by using a code or cipher.

CSP (Communicating Sequential Process) is a specification and programming notation for concurrent and distributed systems.

CSTB (Computer Science and Telecommunications Board) is a unit of the National Research Council.

CTCPEC refers to the Canadian Trusted Computer Product Evaluation Criteria.

CUG (closed user group) is an access control concept used in X.25, frame relay, and ATM networks to establish a non-cryptographic VPN. A CUG is limited to a single network and network technology, managed by a single administration.

DARPA is the Defense Advanced Research Projects Agency (known at times in the past as ARPA), which is part of the DOD.

DCE (data communication equipment) refers to the devices and connections of a communications network that connect the circuit between the data source and destination. A modem is the most common type of DCE.

DCOM (distributed common object model) refers to an infrastructure for components that can be systematically reused.

DDN (defense data network) is a global DOD communications network composed of MILNET, other portions of the Internet, and classified networks.

Decryption is the process of transforming ciphertext into the original message, or cleartext.

Denial of service is a form of attack that reduces the availability of a resource.

DES (Data Encryption Standard) is the U.S. government standard (FIPS 46-1) describing a symmetric-key cryptographic algorithm.

DGSA (DOD Goal Security Architecture) is a set of specifications or goals that support a wide range of access controls and integrity policies in an object-oriented, distributed system environment.

Digital signature is a digitized version of a written signature, typically produced by decrypting a digest of the message being signed.

DISA is the Defense Information Systems Agency, a unit of the DOD.

DMS (Defense Messaging System) relies on the SNS guard to permit electronic mail to flow in and out of highly sensitive enclaves and facilitate communication with less-sensitive DMS subscribers.

DNS (Domain Name Service) is a general-purpose, distributed, replicated, data-query service that is used primarily on the Internet for translating host names into Internet addresses.

DOD is the U.S. Department of Defense.

DOE is the U.S. Department of Energy.

DOS is disk operating system, developed by Microsoft Corporation and used widely on IBM-compatible personal computers. It contains no protection against errant programs and no support for partitioning the actions of one user from another.

DSP (digital signal processor) is a specialized integrated circuit used to analyze or alter the characteristics of communications signals.

DSP (downstream service provider) is a local or regional Internet provider.

DTE (domain and type enforcement) is a fine-grained access control mechanism.

DVRP (distance vector routing protocol) enables routers to function without complete knowledge of network topology. Routers broadcast a list of destinations and costs; each recipient adds its cost for traversing its link back toward the sender and rebroadcasts the updated list of destinations and costs (or a lower-cost path to any of those destinations, if available).

Encryption is any procedure used in cryptography to convert plaintext into ciphertext to prevent anyone but the intended recipient from reading the data.

Escrowed Encryption Initiative is a voluntary program intended to improve the security of telephone communications while also meeting the stated needs of law enforcement.

ESP (Encapsulating Security Payload) is a protocol (part of the IETF IPsec series of standards) that provides encryption and/or authentication for IP packets.

Fault tolerance is the capability of a system or component to continue operating despite hardware or software faults. It may be expressed in terms of the number of faults that can be tolerated before normal operation is impaired.

FBI is the Federal Bureau of Investigation.

FCC is the Federal Communications Commission.

FDA is the Food and Drug Administration.

FEAL is a symmetric-key cipher developed in Japan.

FFRDC refers to federally funded research and development centers.

FGAC (fine-grained access control) enables a user or system administrator to control access to small objects, methods, and procedures.

FIPS (federal information processing standards) are technical standards published by NIST. U.S. government agencies are expected either to purchase computer-related products that conform to these standards or to obtain a formal waiver.

Firewall is a defensive mechanism typically deployed at the boundary between a trusted and a mistrusted computer network.

Formal language is language that has precisely defined syntax and semantics. It enables unambiguous descriptions and is often amenable to various degrees of automated analysis.

Formal method is a mathematically based technique for describing and analyzing hardware, software, and computing systems.

Fortezza is a PCMCIA cryptographic token for protecting data. It is a component of the MISSI architecture.

Fortezza Initiative is a U.S. government initiative to promote and support escrowed encryption for data storage and communications.

FTP (File Transfer Protocol) is a client-server protocol that enables a user on one computer to transfer files to and from another computer over a TCP/IP network.

Functionality is the functional behavior of a system. Functionality requirements include confidentiality, integrity, availability, authentication, and safety.

GSM (global system for mobile communications) is a standard for digital cellular communications that is being adopted by more than 60 countries.

GSSAPI (generic security services application programming interface) is an IETF-standard application-level interface to cryptographic services.

GUI is a graphical user interface.

Hardware token refers to a small hardware device that contains a personal cryptographic key as well as processing capability. It is used typically for authentication.

Hash function is a form of checksum.

HCS (High Confidence Systems) is the working group of the Committee on CIC R&D that deals with trustworthiness.

Heisenbug refers to a transient failure that is difficult to reproduce because it is triggered by circumstances beyond the control of a tester.

Hijacking refers, in the computer context, to the impersonation of a previously authenticated entity.

HMO is a health maintenance organization.

HTML (Hypertext Markup Language) is used to represent text and other data for posting and delivery to browsers on the World Wide Web.

HTTP (Hypertext Transfer Protocol) is the client-server TCP/IP protocol used on the World Wide Web for the exchange of HTML documents.

IAB is the Internet Architecture Board.

ICMP (Internet Control Message Protocol) is a feature of IP that allows for the generation of error messages, test packets, and informational messages.

IDE is a disk interface standard.

Identification is an assertion about the identity of someone or something.

IEEE is the Institute of Electrical and Electronics Engineers.

IESG is the Internet Engineering Steering Group.

IETF (Internet Engineering Task Force) is a large, international community of network designers, operators, vendors, and researchers who coordinate the evolution of the Internet and resolve protocol and architectural issues.

IISP is the Information Infrastructure Standards Panel.

IITF is the Information Infrastructure Task Force.

IMP (interface message processor) was a switching node for the ARPANET.

Infosec refers to information security.

Integrity is the property of an object meeting an a priori established set of expectations. In the distributed system or communication security context, integrity is more precisely defined as assurance that data have not been undetectably modified in transit or storage.

Integrity check is a quantity derived by an algorithm from the running digital stream of a message, or the entire contents of a stored data file, and appended to it. Some integrity checks are cryptographically based.

IPsec (IP Security) is a suite of internetwork-layer security protocols developed for the Internet by the IETF working group.

IP (Internet Protocol) is a connectionless, packet-switching protocol that serves as the internetwork layer for the TCP/IP protocol suite. IP provides packet routing, fragmentation, and reassembly.

ISAKMP (Internet Security Association and Key Management Protocol) is a protocol developed by the NSA to negotiate keys for use with data network security protocols.

ISAT (Information Science and Technology) refers to special activities held by DARPA to address long-term issues and plans.

ISDN (integrated services digital network) is a set of communications standards that specify how different types of information (e.g., voice, data, video) can be transmitted in the public switched telephone network.

ISO is the Information Systems Office of DARPA.

ISO is the International Organization for Standardization.

ISOC (Internet Society) is a nonprofit, professional membership organization that facilitates and supports the technical evolution of the Internet; stimulates interest in and educates the scientific and academic communities, industry, and the public about the technology, uses, and applications of the Internet; and promotes the development of new applications.

ISP (Internet service provider) is a company that provides other companies or individuals with access to, or presence on, the Internet. Most ISPs also provide extra services, such as help with the design, creation, and administration of World Wide Web sites.

ISSR-JTO (Information Systems Security Research-Joint Technology Office) involves DARPA, DISA, and NSA.

ITO (Information Technology Office) is a unit of DARPA that supports research in computing and communications.

ITSEC (Information Technology Security Evaluation Criteria) refers to the harmonized criteria of France, Germany, the Netherlands, and the United Kingdom.

IW-D refers to defensive information warfare.

Java is an object-oriented, distributed, architecture-neutral, portable, general-purpose programming language.

JavaBeans is a component architecture for Java that enables the development of reusable software components that can be assembled using visual application-builder tools.

JDK (Java development kit) provides an environment for developing Java programs.

JVM (Java virtual machine) is a specification for software that interprets Java programs compiled into byte codes.

KDC (key-distribution center) is an online, automated provider of secret symmetric keys.

Kernel is a small, trusted portion of a system that provides services on which the other portions of the system depend.

Key is a value used in conjunction with a cryptographic algorithm.

Key-escrow encryption is an encryption system that enables exceptional access to encrypted data through special data-recovery keys held ("in escrow") by a trusted party.

KPA (key process area) refers to the most important aspects of software processes.

LAN (local area network) is a data communications network, such as an Ethernet, that covers a small geographical area (typically no larger than a 1-kilometer radius), allowing easy interconnection of terminals, microprocessors, and computers within adjacent buildings.

Link-State Routing Protocol enables routers to exchange information about the possibility and cost of reaching the other networks. The cost is based on number of hops, link speeds, traffic congestion, and other factors, as determined by the network designer.

MD4 is a hash algorithm.

MEII (minimum essential information infrastructure) is a highly trustworthy communications subsystem originally envisioned for use by NISs that control critical infrastructures.

MIB (management information base) is a database of objects accessed by the Internet management protocols (SNMP).

MIC (message integrity code) is a value that is a complex function of both a set of protected data and a cryptographic key. It is computed by the sender and validated by the receiver.

MILNET is the military network that is part of the DDN and the Internet.

MIME (multipurpose Internet mail extension) is a standard for multipart, multimedia electronic mail messages and World Wide Web hypertext documents on the Internet.

MISSI (Multilevel Information Systems Security Initiative) is an NSA initiative designed to provide a framework for the development of interoperable, complementary security products.

Multics is a multiuser operating system developed in the mid-1960s by MIT, GE, and Bell Laboratories that features elaborate access controls.

Multiplexing is the combining of several signals for transmission on a shared medium.

MVS (multiple virtual storage) is an operating system for system 370 and its successors that supports virtual memory.

NASA is the National Aeronautics and Space Administration.

NCS (National Communications System) is a group of 23 federal departments and agencies that coordinates and plans systems to support responses to crises and disasters.

NCSC (National Computer Security Center) is part of the NSA.

NES (Network Encryption System) is a certificate-based, packet network encryption system certified by the NSA (cf., Caneware).

NIS (networked information system) integrates computing and communications systems, procedures, and users and operators.

NIST (National Institute of Standards and Technology) is a unit of the U.S. Department of Commerce that works with industry to develop and apply technology, measurements, and standards.

NLSP (Netware Link-State Protocol) is a protocol for the exchange of routing information in some networks.

NLSP (Network-Layer Security Protocol) is a protocol (roughly comparable to IPsec) that was developed for OSI networks but is rarely used.

NMS (network management system) is a collection of software for managing the security of the other components in the MISSI architecture.

NOC (network operations center) is a designated site that monitors and controls the elements of a network.

Nonrepudiation is the affirmation, with extremely high confidence, of the identity of the signer of a digital message using a digital signature procedure. It is intended to protect against any subsequent attempt by the signer to deny authenticity.

NPRG (National Partnership for Reinventing Government) is the Administration's ongoing effort to make the U.S. government work better and cost less. It was formerly known as the National Performance Review.

NRC (Network Reliability Council) is the former name of the NRIC.

NRC (National Research Council) is the operating arm of the National Academy of Sciences and the National Academy of Engineering.

NRIC (Network Reliability and Interoperability Council) is the new name of the former Network Reliability Council.

NSA is the National Security Agency, which is part of the DOD.

NSF is the National Science Foundation.

NSTAC (National Security Telecommunications Advisory Committee) provides industry advice to the Executive Branch of the U.S. government.

Object is a hardware or software system or component (e.g., processor, file, database) that can be accessed by a subject.

Object code is the "executable" code of 1s and 0s that instructs a computer on the steps to be performed.

OC-12 (optical carrier 12) is a SONET rate communications channel of 622 megabits per second.

OLE (object linking and embedding) is object-oriented software technology.

OMG (Object Management Group) is a consortium of companies that supports and promotes a set of standards called CORBA.

Orange Book is the common name for the DOD document that provides criteria for the evaluation of different classes of trusted systems. Supplementary documents extend and interpret the criteria.

ORCON (originator controlled) is a term used with very sensitive classified data to denote an access control policy in which the originator of data must approve access.

OS (operating system) is a computer program (e.g., MS-DOS, Windows, UNIX, Mac OS) that provides basic services for applications. Such functions can include screen displays, file handling, and, in the future, encryption.

OSI (open systems interconnection) refers to a seven-layer model of network architecture and a suite of implementing protocols developed in 1978 as a framework for international standards for heterogeneous computer networks.

OSPF (open shortest-path first-interior) is a standard interior gateway routing protocol for the Internet. It is a link-state routing protocol, as distinct from a distance-vector routing protocol.

OSS (operations support system) is a computer system involved in running the telephone network.

P5 is an Intel processor chip known as a Pentium processor.

P6 is an Intel processor chip known as a Pentium Pro processor.

Packet switching is a networking technology that breaks up a message into smaller packets for transmission and switches them to their required destination. Unlike circuit switching, which requires a constant point-to-point circuit to be established, each packet in a packet-switched network contains a destination address. Thus all packets in a single message do not have to travel the same path. They can be dynamically routed over the network as circuits become available or unavailable. The destination computer reassembles the packets back into their proper sequence.

Password is a sequence of characters presented to a system for purposes of authentication of the user's identity or privilege to access the system.

PC is a personal computer.

PCC (proof-carrying code) is a security enforcement approach in which formal, machine-checkable proof is used to establish that a software program will not violate a particular security policy.

PCCIP is the President's Commission on Critical Infrastructure Protection.

PCMCIA is the Personal Computer Memory Card Interface Association, an organization that specifies standards for what are now called PC cards.

PGP (pretty good privacy) is a public-key encryption-based file encryption implementation. PGP enables users to exchange files or e-mail messages with privacy and authentication.

PIN is a personal identification number and is used in much the same manner as a password.

PKI (public-key infrastructure), as used in this report, refers to mechanisms, procedures, and policies that together provide a management framework for the deployment of public-key cryptography.

Plaintext is a synonym for cleartext.

PLI (private line interface) was a network-layer encryptor designed to protect classified data transmitted over the ARPANET, developed and deployed in the mid 1970s.

Privacy ensures freedom from unauthorized intrusion.

Private key is the decryption or signature generation key associated with a given person's public key for a public-key cryptographic system.

Protocols are formal rules describing how different parties cooperate to share or exchange data, especially across a network.

Pseudocode is a program written using a mixture of programming language and informal statements (e.g., plain English).

PTN is the public telephone network.

Public key is the publicly known key associated with a given subject in a public-key cryptographic system.

Public-key certificate is a data structure, typically transmitted electronically over an information network, that establishes the relationship between a named individual or organization and a specified public key.

Public-key cryptography refers to algorithms that use one key to encrypt or digitally sign data and a corresponding second key to decrypt or validate the signature of that data.

QOS (quality of service) refers to performance guarantees offered by a network.

R2 is the NSA unit that is responsible for information security research.

R/3 is a software product from SAP for handling all major functions of a commercial enterprise.

R&D is research and development.

Red Book is the common name for the DOD document containing the trusted network interpretation of the trusted computer system evaluation criteria.

Reliability is the capability of a computer, or information or telecommunications system, to perform consistently and precisely according to its specifications and design requirements, and to do so with high confidence.

RFC (request for comments) refers to a series of numbered informational documents and standards widely followed in the Internet community. All Internet standards are recorded in RFCs, but not all RFCs are standards. RFCs are issued online at <http://www.rfc-editor.org/rfc.html> by the RFC Editor, Information Sciences Institute, University of Southern California, Los Angeles.

RFP is a request for proposals.

Risk is, in the computer context, the likelihood that a vulnerability may be exploited, or that a threat may become harmful.

RPC (Remote Procedure Call) is a protocol that allows a program running on one host to cause code to be executed on another host.

RSML (requirements state machine language) is a specification notation that has a variety of formal methods associated with it.

RSVP (Resource Reservation Protocol) is a protocol designed to provide QOS guarantees on the Internet.

RTCA is now the official name of the former Radio Technical Commission for Aeronautics.

Safety is a characteristic of trustworthiness asserting that a system will not be the cause of physical harm to people or property.

SCC is a strongly connected component.

SCI (scalable coherent interface) is an IEEE standard.

SCR (Software Cost Reduction) is the Naval Research Laboratory program that is developing rigorous techniques for software development. One goal is to reduce the cost of software development.

SCSI (small computer standard interface) is an industry-standard disk interface.

SDNS (Secure Data Network System) was the NSA project that devised a network-layer encryption standard.

SDSI (Secure Distributed Security Infrastructure) is an approach to certificate use in which all names bound to public keys are viewed as having only local significance.

Secrecy is the habit or practice of maintaining privacy. It is an element of security.

Secret key is a key used in conjunction with a secret-key or symmetric cryptosystem.

Secret-key cryptosystem is a symmetric cryptographic process in which both parties use the same secret key to encrypt and decrypt messages.

Security refers to a collection of safeguards that ensure the confidentiality of information, protect the system(s) or network(s) used to process it, and control access to it. Security typically encompasses secrecy, confidentiality, integrity, and availability and is intended to ensure that a system resists potentially correlated attacks.

Security level is either the clearance level associated with a subject or a classification level associated with an object.

SEI is the Software Engineering Institute.

SET (secure electronic transaction) is a protocol for credit card transactions over the Internet.

SFI (software fault isolation) is a security enforcement approach in which instructions and addresses are modified so that they cannot reference memory outside the specified regions.

Shareware is software that is offered publicly, free of charge, rather than sold, but shareware authors usually do *request* payment for the freely distributed software.

SKIPJACK is a symmetric encryption algorithm.

S/MIME (secure/multipurpose Internet mail extension) is a format for secure Internet e-mail.

SMTP (Simple Mail Transfer Protocol) is a protocol used to transfer e-mail over the Internet.

Snefru is a one-way hash function.

SNMP (Simple Network Management Protocol) is the Internet standard protocol that manages nodes on an IP network.

SNS (Secure Network System) is a high-assurance guard (a component of the MISSI architecture) for separating Top Secret enclaves from less-sensitive network environments.

SONET (synchronous optical network) is a broadband networking standard that is generally based on ring topologies to ensure reliability.

Source code is the textual form in which a high-level-language program is entered into a computer.

SP3 (Security Protocol at Level 3) is a network-layer encryption standard developed in the SDNS project.

Specification is a precise description of the desired behavior of a system.

SPKI (Simple Public-Key Infrastructure) is a scheme being developed by an IETF working group attempting to codify SDSI into an Internet standard.

Spoofing is the illicit, deliberate assumption of the characteristics of another computer system or user, for purposes of deception.

SS7 (Signaling System 7) is a protocol suite used for communication with, and control of, telephone central office switches and processors. It uses out-of-band signaling.

SSL (secure socket layer) is a protocol designed to provide secure communications for HTTP traffic on the Internet.

State is retained information from one transaction that is used to determine how to complete a subsequent transaction, often of a related type.

STL (standard template library) is a component designed for systematic reuse.

STU-III (Secure Telephone Unit III) is a standardized voice and data telephone system capable of encryption up to top-secret level for defense and civilian government purposes. STU-III operates over standard dial-up telephone lines and has been extended to cellular applications.

Subject refers, in this report, to an active entity (e.g., a user, or a process or device acting on the user's behalf) that can make a request to perform an operation on an object.

Survivability is the capability to provide a level of service in adverse or hostile conditions.

SWAT is a special weapons and tactics team.

SwIPe is a host-based IP encryptor that led to the IETF working group on IPsec.

TCL is tool command language.

TCP (Transmission Control Protocol) is the most common transport-layer protocol used on the Internet. It provides reliable connection-oriented full-duplex communications, flow control, and multiplexing.

TCSEC (Trusted Computer System Evaluation Criteria) refers to criteria for a graded system of protection contained in the DOD document known as the Orange Book.

Telnet is a protocol that enables a user on one machine to log onto another machine over a network and read the remote files.

Threat is an adversary that is both motivated and capable of exploiting a vulnerability.

Tiger team refers to an organized group of people that tests security measures by attempting to penetrate them, or, more generally, to any official inspection team or special group called in to look at a computer or communications problem.

TIU (trusted interface unit) is an Ethernet LAN data encryption product.

Trojan horse refers to a program that, by exploiting the current user's authorization, provides covert access to information in an object for a user not authorized to access that object.

Trustworthiness is assurance that a system deserves to be trusted—that it will perform as expected despite environmental disruptions, human and operator error, hostile attacks, and design and implementation errors. Trustworthy systems reinforce the belief that they will continue to produce expected behavior and will not be susceptible to subversion.

UDP (User Datagram Protocol) is an Internet transport protocol that provides unreliable datagram services. It adds a checksum and additional process-to-process addressing information on top of the basic IP layer.

UNIX is a multiuser operating system developed by Bell Laboratories in the 1970s that is widely used on the Internet and in the computer science research community. It is much smaller and simpler than Multics and has far fewer access controls and far less structure to support security.

URL (uniform resource locator) specifies an Internet object, such as a file or a newsgroup. URLs are used in HTML documents to specify targets of hyperlinks.

URP (University Research Program) is the program within NSA's R2 that awards contracts to academic investigators for security-related research.

VDM (Vienna definition method) is a formal method.

Verity is a tool used to design processors.

VGA is video graphics adapter.

VLSI (very large scale integration) refers to integrated circuits composed of hundreds of thousands of logic elements, or memory cells.

VPN (virtual private network) is a secure connection through an otherwise insecure network, typically the Internet.

Vulnerability is an error or weakness in the design, implementation, or operation of a system.

VVSL is a formal method.

W3C (World Wide Web Consortium) is an industry consortium standards-setting body for the Web.

WAN (wide area network) is a network extending over an area greater than 1 kilometer in diameter.

Windows NT is Microsoft's multiprogramming, multitasking, and multiuser operating system. It has the ability to control users' access to all system objects. Windows NT is supported on several instruction set architectures.

Work factor is a measure of the difficulty of undertaking a brute-force test of all possible keys against a given ciphertext and known algorithm.

WWW is the World Wide Web.

X.25 is a standard protocol suite for the DTE-DCE interface in a packet-switched network. It was developed to describe how data passes in and out of public data communications networks.

XEU (Xerox encryption unit) is a functionally transparent cipher unit for protecting information on baseband LANs.

Y2K (year 2000) refers to the widespread problem of computers that are not programmed to recognize correctly the years following 1999.

Index

A

Absolute security, philosophy of, 7, 120-121, 247

Access control, 114, 134, 300
  discretionary, 114-115
  granularity of, 134
  mandatory, 96, 114-115
  mechanisms for, as add-ons, 292
  operating system, 147
  violations of, 44

Access level, 44, 300

Access modes, multiple, 193

ACL (access control list), 147, 292, 300

ACL2 theorem prover, 97

ActiveX, 111, 141-142, 283, 300

Ada programming language, 85-86, 300

ADSL (asymmetric digital subscriber lines), 56, 300

Advanced Automation Systems air-traffic control system, 99

Advanced Research Projects Agency network (ARPANET), 29-30, 34, 133, 283, 301
  switching node for, 307

Alcatel, 220

American National Standards Institute (ANSI), 199

Anomaly detection, 9. *See also* Detection

ANSI. *See* American National Standards Institute

APIs. *See* Application programming interfaces

Application-level security, 139-149

Application programming interfaces (APIs), 127, 132, 226-227, 301

Applique, 138

ARPA. *See* Defense Advanced Research Projects Agency

ARPANET. *See* Advanced Research Projects Agency network

Assessment Technology Branch (ATB) of NASA, 222, 301

Assurance, 15, 204-205, 301. *See also* System assurance

Asymmetric cryptography. *See* Cryptography

Asynchronous transfer mode (ATM), 132-133, 301

ATB. *See* Assessment Technology Branch of NASA

ATM. *See* Asynchronous transfer mode

AT&T, 42, 46, 220

Attacks by hostile parties, 13, 22, 47-55
  damage from, 112
  detecting, 160
  measuring, 185
  scripts for, 174

319